Advances in the Spoken Language Development of Deaf and Hard-of-Hearing Children

Perspectives on Deafness

Series Editors
Marc Marschark
Patricia Elizabeth Spencer

The World of Deaf Infants: A Longitudinal Study
Kathryn P. Meadow-Orlans, Patricia Elizabeth Spencer,
and Lynn Sanford Koester

Sign Language Interpreting and Interpreter Education:
Directions for Research and Practice
Edited by Marc Marschark, Rico Peterson, and Elizabeth A. Winston

Advances in the Spoken Language Development of Deaf and Hard-of-Hearing Children
Edited by Patricia Elizabeth Spencer and Marc Marschark

Advances in the Sign Language Development of Deaf Children
Edited by Brenda Schick, Marc Marschark, and Patricia Elizabeth Spencer

ADVANCES IN THE

Spoken Language Development

OF DEAF AND HARD-OF-HEARING CHILDREN

EDITED BY

Patricia Elizabeth Spencer and Marc Marschark

OXFORD
UNIVERSITY PRESS

2006

OXFORD
UNIVERSITY PRESS

Oxford University Press, Inc., publishes works that further
Oxford University's objective of excellence
in research, scholarship, and education.

Oxford   New York
Auckland   Cape Town   Dar es Salaam   Hong Kong   Karachi
Kuala Lumpur   Madrid   Melbourne   Mexico City   Nairobi
New Delhi   Shanghai   Taipei   Toronto

With offices in
Argentina   Austria   Brazil   Chile   Czech Republic   France   Greece
Guatemala   Hungary   Italy   Japan   Poland   Portugal   Singapore
South Korea   Switzerland   Thailand   Turkey   Ukraine   Vietnam

Copyright © 2006 by Patricia Elizabeth Spencer and Marc Marschark

Published by Oxford University Press, Inc.
198 Madison Avenue, New York, New York 10016

www.oup.com

Oxford is a registered trademark of Oxford University Press

Library of Congress Cataloging-in-Publication Data
Advances in the spoken language development of deaf and hard-of-hearing children /
edited by Patricia Elizabeth Spencer and Marc Marschark.
    p. cm.—(Perspectives on deafness)
  Includes bibliographical references and index.
  ISBN-13 978-0-19-517987-3
  ISBN 0-19-517987-0
  1. Deaf children—Language.   2. Hearing impaired children—Language.
3. Language awareness in children.   4. Language acquisition.   5. Oral communication.
I. Spencer, Patricia Elizabeth. II. Marschark, Marc. III. Series.
  HV2391.A38 2005
  401'.93—dc22   2004027122

9 8 7 6 5 4 3 2 1

Printed in the United States of America
on acid-free paper

Preface

Supposedly, every book tells a story. This book tells at least two. The "big" story—about the origins, progress, and future of research concerning spoken language development in deaf and hard-of-hearing children—is told in the various chapters of this volume. That story, beginning with our historical and theoretical introduction, we will allow the various contributors to tell themselves. The other story, only partly reflected in the particular chapters that make up this book, concerns how this volume came to be, who agreed to participate, and who did not.

Part of the story is a function of who we are. One of us (Spencer) is at Gallaudet University, the world's only liberal arts university for deaf students. The other (Marschark) is at the National Technical Institute for the Deaf (NTID), the world's first technical college for deaf students and one of eight colleges within a "mainstream" university (Rochester Institute of Technology). We are both relatively fluent in sign language (although we argue about who is the "better" signer) but learned to sign as adults. We both teach classes to deaf students, although Spencer usually does so using sign language without voice, whereas Marschark usually does so using signed and spoken communication simultaneously, per NTID's policy of allowing its heterogeneous student body of sign-oriented and "oral" students to make the decision about the mode of communication used in the classroom. Importantly, this difference in our day-to-day communication methods should not be seen as either problematic or odd. Rather, it reflects the diversity of the students and the community we serve, composed of

individuals who vary in their histories, skills, and preferences, while
still being clearly representative of both deaf and culturally Deaf communities. Embracing a wide range of communication styles, from "pure"
spoken language to "pure" sign language—and myriad alternatives
between—the deaf people we work with daily demonstrate that members of a community need not be all the same nor use the same language at all times.

We both greatly value our opportunity to work with deaf students
and colleagues who are members of the American Deaf cultural group
and whose language is American Sign Language (ASL); and it is that
language—their language—in which we have sought fluency as a second language. We know from our experiences with Deaf children and
adults that it is possible to live a full life, to participate fully in the
political and social life of the general (mostly hearing) community, and
to achieve academic excellence without ever having acquired the ability
to comfortably produce or receive spoken language. We have also
learned to appreciate, at least to the degree a hearing person can, the
deeply emotional feeling that many Deaf people have for ASL, the language that gives them access to and membership in a close and supportive community. Many Deaf people express feelings about sign
language that are at least the equal of the emotion that hearing people
can experience when listening to a grandly eloquent piece of music or
when listening to their hearing children's first babbles and words. Deaf
people's feelings about spoken language—their appreciation of it, their
frustration in trying to master it, their realization of how much parents
and teachers wanted them to do so—are often also quite strong.

Because we work at institutions in which the Deaf community and
ASL play a large part, we often find ourselves referred to as "supporters" or "proponents" of sign language (and once even "tools of the
manualists"). In fact, both of us seek to understand the roles of language in development and learning by children with significant hearing losses. In our research, we both seek to advance science regarding
language, learning, development, and cognition and to enhance the
quality of life and opportunities for all deaf children. Although we may
have particular orientations regarding our research methodologies and
topics of interest, neither of us believes that either sign language or spoken language represents a panacea for the many challenges facing deaf
children. Rather, we are strong supporters of matching deaf children
with the mode of communication that best meets their needs—and
offering them and their families an array of alternatives in communication and education so as to optimize their everyday experiences and
their future opportunities.

In seeking the middle ground between what have long been polar
opposites in educating deaf children, we have encountered both warm
welcomes and cold shoulders. The latter is not particularly surprising

when they come from some quarters (on both sides of the spectrum), but this does not make them any less disappointing or irritating. On both empirical and emotional grounds, we find it difficult to accept that so many children become caught in the politics of a debate that is likely to determine their developmental trajectories and educational histories. Deaf children are far more heterogeneous than are hearing children, and we do not believe there is a "right" or even "best" method of educating all deaf children—unless one considers eclecticism a method and accepts the notion that both spoken language and sign language might be useful for deaf children in various circumstances. Indeed, it is worth remembering that cued speech, various English-based (or other vernacular) sign systems, and the 200-year-old "combined method" were all founded on the principle that deaf children would use a natural sign language (such as ASL) in social interactions and many aspects of schooling, while the introduction of spoken and written language or bridges to them were deemed essential to the eventual attainment of literacy. Whether or not one feels that these "compromises" have been given fair opportunity or had truly proper implementation, neither has succeeded to any great extent, at least regarding deaf children who will be expected to read and perhaps speak in English (but see Hage and Leybaert, chapter 9 this volume, regarding cued French).

If cold shoulders do not surprise us, the warm welcomes sometimes do. We both make presentations to a variety of audiences, including parents, teachers, and researchers as well as Deaf professionals who may fit into one or more of those categories. Usually, we can "read the crowd" well enough to judge the overall response to our content. But it is the individual parent, teacher, or other person who sees beyond the details of our research to the potential implied by our findings who frequently provides the greatest reward in their comments after our presentations. We understand that parents and teachers of deaf children are looking for answers—preferably simple and easy ones if at all possible, but if not, they will take whatever they can get. It is the willingness to try new things, to be flexible in the face of deaf children's diversity, and to resist bureaucratic answers in favor of child-centered solutions that make some parents and teachers stand above the crowd. It is not surprising to us that one predictor of children's success with a cochlear implant is, literally, the amount of time that their parents spend searching for information on the topic. Armed with diverse perspectives (because one source rarely will be both objective and complete), informed parents are more likely to recognize and pursue all of the support associated with helping a child to succeed with an implant and also be able to assess the likelihood of their child being a good candidate, so that children for whom implants are appropriate get them and those for whom they are not do not. The possibility of contributing to the success of deaf children, one child at a time, or even just to parental peace of mind one parent at a time, makes all of the cold shoulders worthwhile.

That brings us to the story behind this book. Soon after we finished editing the *Oxford Handbook of Deaf Studies, Language, and Education* (New York: Oxford University Press, 2003)—and promising ourselves and each other that we would not edit another book—we realized that the *Handbook* did not go far enough in describing the diverse recent advances regarding research and practice in language development of deaf children. Willfully ignoring history, we started to discuss the possibility of a single book that would describe the current state of the art in the field regardless of whether one was interested in spoken language or sign language. Theoretically, however, we struggled with what such a book would and should include and how one would organize the content in such a volume, particularly because research in these two areas is not parallel. That is, for the most part, investigators interested in deaf children's spoken language tend to conduct research on methods and technologies for improving speech and hearing or, more recently, language development in children who have received cochlear implants. In contrast, investigators who are more interested in deaf children's sign language tend to focus on the acquisition of sign language structures, language used in social interaction, and the development of discourse skills.

Practically, a book that covered all of these topics would be unacceptably (or unaffordably) large, and great care would have to be taken in the organization and focus of contributions in order to avoid giving readers contradictory information and getting unpleasant political fallout. Happily, we had the sense to discuss the project with Dr. McCay Vernon, a pioneer in the field of psychological functioning of deaf individuals and a champion of deaf children. He suggested that trying to combine two historically separate fields of investigation would run the risk of producing a book that many readers would find only "half useful" or, worse, one that was unsatisfactory to everyone. At his suggestion, therefore, this volume is one of a pair being published simultaneously by Oxford University Press, and readers interested in *Advances in the Sign Language Development of Deaf Children* (New York: Oxford University Press, 2005) can find such information there.

The story does not quite end there, however. If the reader spies holes in this volume—topics one would expect to find but does not—we will accept responsibility but not blame. We were surprised that, whether for reasons of practical or theoretical consideration, we were unable to secure contributors willing to write on several important topics. For example, a volume of this sort would benefit from a chapter on current methodology in training speech and auditory skills. Yet some of the experts we approached indicated that they could not provide *research-based* (vs. experiential) chapters on the topics (but see Massaro, chapter 10 this volume), while others said they were simply too busy with practice to do so. Similarly, some of the long-time gaps in the literature pertaining to the acquisition of spoken language, such as characteristics of spoken language in hard-of-hearing children or comparisons of alternative technologies (e.g., analog vs. digital hearing aids) in terms of their effects on spoken language development, were destined to remain gaps. Relatively little data-based research apparently is being done in these important areas, and/or no one we approached seemed particularly interested in synthesizing what information is available. Of course, troublemakers that we are, we also had a few topics in mind that were apparently just too hot to handle—but we will leave those for now. This volume thus may not be as comprehensive as we had originally dreamed, but we believe that it "goes way beyond whatever is in second place." The chapters that follow will indicate areas of unfulfilled current interest, future destinations of research in this field, and some nagging questions for which satisfactory answers have not yet been supplied.

In the chapters that comprise this volume, the reader will find a fascinating panoply of topics that, despite the omissions from our wish list, offers a surprisingly complete mosaic of that current state of the art we were seeking. Our historical/theoretical introduction is followed first by four chapters that address very early development as well as basic processes and supports for spoken language development. In chapter 2, Oller focuses on early vocalizations, how they differ from those in adult language, and how they can best be characterized. Oller's work has provided a foundation for assessment and conceptualization of the effects of lack of auditory stimulation on early vocalizations. He proposes that this approach is of special importance in monitoring the development of infants and toddlers, given early identification and access to current technologies. Masataka provides a cross-cultural and biological look at innate communication processes and their interaction with communicative experiences in chapter 3. He raises questions about the effects on developing communication patterns of deaf infants' usual lack of access to child-directed vocal language and other early auditory experiences. In chapter 4, Ackley and Decker provide an update on current and emerging technologies that identify and specify hearing loss in infants and children, as well as those that provide previously impossible access to sound. Their chapter is indicative of the evolving role of audiology and audiologists as basic supports for spoken language development of children who are deaf and hard of hearing. Blamey, Sarant, and Paatsch in chapter 5 offer examples of continuing difficulties in assessment of children's speech perception abilities, pointing out that many existing tests and procedures assume language skills that have not been attained by young children, a fact that complicates interpretation of test results. They go on to provide an algorithm for identifying contributions to individual children's speech perception performance from hearing versus language skills, a differentiation that can lead to targeted intervention efforts.

Chapters 6–10 present data from studies of intervention methods being used to support deaf children's spoken language development. Beattie in chapter 6 provides a summary and differentiation of various methods often included under the "oral education" umbrella. He points to a scarcity of evaluation research on outcomes of the different methods and notes that, in practice, most of the methods differ only in their emphasis. He includes in the methods discussed several that are based on natural patterns of conversation and communication as opposed to more directive, structured lessons. This more natural approach is emphasized by Brown and Nott in their exposition on early intervention for children in oral education in chapter 7. They discuss how family-centered practice can be conceptualized and organized, providing a model for structuring and implementing such an approach. In chapter 8, L. Spencer and Tomblin survey research on the acquisition of spoken language by children in programs using "total" and "simultaneous" communication approaches, asking what effects the use of signs in addition to spoken language have on children's language and literacy development.

Spoken language development of children using a different kind of visual supplement to spoken language—cued speech—is addressed by Hage and Leybaert in chapter 9. The cued speech system, unlike signs, represents phonetic aspects of spoken language and provides visual-manual information to disambiguate speech sounds that cannot be readily perceived from speechreading and amplified listening. Hage and Leybaert note that current students, many of whom use cochlear implants, show stronger attention to and processing of auditory aspects of the multimodal language cues than did earlier-studied children. In chapter 10, Massaro emphasizes the multimodal nature of perception of spoken languages, as visual information from the speaker's face and lips provides visual help for both hearing and deaf listeners in disambiguating auditory messages. He reports results on vocabulary development of hard-of-hearing children from use of a computer-based program that provides multimodal information along with assistance to teachers and therapists in designing activities for interactive training.

Almost all of the chapters described above refer to cochlear implants in some way and to some degree. The advent and increasingly early use of cochlear implants has had a tremendous impact on deaf children's access to information from spoken language and, consequently, on their developing language skills. The final four chapters of the book address directly the use of cochlear implants and their impact on deaf children's development of spoken language. In chapter 11, Geers presents a comprehensive summary of research findings, concluding that children using cochlear implants attain significantly higher speech and spoken language skills than do children with equal hearing loss who do not use cochlear implants. She presents a detailed critique of complications and confounds in currently available research but concludes that some factors influencing outcomes (e.g., duration of profound hearing loss, updated technologies in the structure and management of the implant device, focus on auditory and speech skills in the educational environment) have been identified. In chapter 12, Nicholas and Geers continue the focus on outcomes of the use of cochlear implants by surveying emerging literature on children who receive their implants during the first 3 years of life. Data presented in this cautiously optimistic chapter, as well as chapter 11, suggest that early implantation results in faster development of auditory and speech skills, with many children who receive them by 2 years of age appearing (at least up to about 3 years postimplant) to function at levels typical for hearing children. The authors suggest that age effects may be represented by a step function, with 2 years of age being one significant break point and about 5 years of age another point marking enhanced potential compared to older ages. They also provide an in-depth discussion of the complications arising from the demands of assessing and working with infants and toddlers and examine ways to avoid potential pitfalls in research tracking their development.

In chapter 13, Yoshinaga-Itano summarizes information from a longitudinal study of children with hearing loss in the Colorado population study, indicating significant spoken language benefits from identification and initial programming during infancy. She then presents three case studies of children with early identification and programming, age-appropriate language levels using signs, and later but highly effective acquisition of spoken language skills after cochlear implantation. Finally, in contrast with the chapters that examine speech and language development in general, Burkholder and Pisoni in chapter 14 focus on specific cognitive processes demonstrated by children using cochlear implants, including memory-related skills of verbal rehearsal, encoding, and serial scanning. The authors provide a provocative, data-based argument that these abilities are supported by the quality and quantity of oral language experiences after cochlear implantation and that the memory abilities, in turn, relate to skills for processing and producing spoken language.

When these chapters are viewed as parts of a larger mosaic, they cannot help but generate a kind of "new century" excitement, a window onto the edge of now, and a peek into the future. With changes in society's views of diversity, at a time of rapidly changing technology, and with a broader view of what research is all about, deaf children today can look forward to opportunities only dreamed of by their deaf parents and grandparents. For those hearing and deaf parents who want their children to acquire spoken language, the contributors to this volume demonstrate that the future is brighter than ever. This is a critical point in the evolution of our field that we want to capture—a snapshot of what will surely be a historically significant moment in science and education pertaining to deaf children. We believe that this volume will be a stepping-off point for parents, educators, linguists, and other professionals who will both ride the wake of the work described and push it forward. Armed with the state of the art in research pertaining to language development and clinical methodologies, parents will be able to make more informed choices, and professionals will be in a better position to support them and their deaf children.

In editing this volume and working with its contributors over the past year, we have been particularly appreciative of the willingness of many of the contributors to go beyond material that they were most comfortable with, in order to give either a more complete picture or a better focus on the shape of things to come. When scholars are willing to describe the shortcomings of their own work in order to spur others to extend it—or to admit that research done at another time or place is not as successful in hindsight as it seemed at the time—you know that you are working with individuals who have the best interests of deaf children at heart. It is thus to our generous (and timely) contributors that we owe our greatest thanks. We also are in debt to our editor at Oxford University Press, Catharine Carlin, for her support, advice, and confidence. Her suggestions at various points in this project, as well as the insightful comments of her anonymous reviewers, helped to hone this volume to a keen edge. We also gratefully acknowledge the patience of our colleagues and especially of our spouses, Ron Outen and Janie Runion, for tolerating us and waiting for us (continually, if not continuously) while we were consumed with various stages of editing.

The hand-off now goes to future investigators, authors, and editors to take the information provided here and do something with it: take our knowledge further, apply it to the benefit of deaf children and their families, and use it to seek out new questions in need of answers. The fact that this volume does not provide all of the simple and easy solutions one might have hoped for is not a weakness but reality and, in our view, a strength. As Confucius noted, "To know that you know what you know, and that you do not know what you do not know, that is true wisdom." We are making progress.

Contents

Contributors

R. Steven Ackley
Department of Hearing, Speech
    and Language Sciences
Gallaudet University
800 Florida Avenue NE
Washington, DC 20002 USA

Rod G. Beattie
Renwick College
Royal Institute for Deaf and
    Blind Children
Parramatta, NSW 2124, Australia

Peter J. Blamey
Department of Otolaryngology
The University of Melbourne
c/o Dynamic Hearing Pty Ltd
2 Chapel Street
Richmond, Victoria 3121,
    Australia

P. Margaret Brown
Deafness, Early Childhood
    Intervention & Special Education

Department of Learning and
    Educational Development
Faculty of Education
The University of Melbourne,
    Parkville
Melbourne, Victoria 3010
    Australia

Rose A. Burkholder
Department of Psychology
Indiana University-Bloomington
1101 E. 10th Street
Bloomington, IN 47405 USA

T. Newell Decker
Department of Special Education
    and Communication
    Disorders
318 Barkley Memorial Center
University of Nebraska-Lincoln
Lincoln, NE 68583-0738 USA

Ann E. Geers
Department of Otolaryngology
Southwestern Medical Center

University of Texas at Dallas
c/o 167 Rocky Knob Road
Clyde, NC 28721 USA

Catherine Hage
Laboratoire de Psychologie
    Expérimentale
Université libre de Bruxelles,
    CP 191
50, avenue F.D. Roosevelt
B-1050 Bruxelles, Belgium
    and Centre Comprendre
    et Parler
101 rue de la Rive
1200 Bruxelles, Belgium

Jacqueline Leybaert
Laboratoire de Psychologie
    Expérimentale
Université libre de Bruxelles,
    CP 191
50, avenue F.D. Roosevelt
B-1050 Bruxelles, Belgium

Marc Marschark
Department of Research
National Technical Institute for
    the Deaf
Rochester Institute of
    Technology
96 Lomb Memorial Drive
Rochester, NY 14623 USA
    and School of
    Psychology
University of Aberdeen
Aberdeen AB24 2UB Scotland

Nobuo Masataka
Department of Behavioral and
    Brain Sciences
Primate Research Institute
Kyoto University
Inuyama, Aichi 484-8506
Japan

Dominic W. Massaro
Perceptual Science Laboratory
Department of Psychology
University of California,
    Santa Cruz
1156 High Street
Santa Cruz, CA 95060 USA

Johanna G. Nicholas
CID Research at WUSM
Department of Otolaryngology
Washington University School of
    Medicine
660 S. Euclid Avenue
St. Louis, MO 63110 USA

Pauline Nott
Cooperative Research Centre for
    Cochlear Implant and Hearing
    Aid Innovation
384-388 Albert Street
East Melbourne, Victoria 3002
    Australia

D. Kimbrough Oller
The University of Memphis
School of Audiology and
    Speech-Language
    Pathology
807 Jefferson Avenue
Memphis, TN 38105 USA and
    Konrad Lorenz Institute for
    Evolution and Cognition
    Research
Adolph Lorenze Gasse 2
A-3422 Altenberg, Austria

Louise E. Paatsch
Deafness Unit
Department of Learning and
    Educational Development
University of Melbourne,
    Parkville
Melbourne, Victoria 3010
    Australia

David B. Pisoni
Speech Research Laboratory
Department of Psychology
Indiana University
1101 E. 10th Street
Bloomington, IN 47401 USA
and DeVault Otologic
Research Laboratory
Department of Otolaryngology,
Head and Neck Surgery
Indiana University School of
Medicine
699 West Drive
Indianapolis, IN 46202 USA

Julia Z. Sarant
Department of Otolaryngology
University of Melbourne
c/o The Bionic Ear Institute
384–388 Albert St.
East Melbourne, Victoria 3002
Australia

Linda J. Spencer
Department of Otolaryngology
Head and Neck Surgery
University of Iowa Hospitals and
Clinics
200 Hawkins Drive
Iowa City, IA 52242 USA

Patricia Elizabeth Spencer
Department of Educational
Administration and Research
Texas A&M University at Corpus
Christi
6300 Ocean Drive
Corpus Christi, TX 78412

J. Bruce Tomblin
Department of Otolaryngology
Head and Neck Surgery
University of Iowa Hospitals and
Clinics
200 Hawkins Drive
Iowa City, IA 52242 USA
and
Department of Speech Pathology
and Audiology
University of Iowa
Wendell Johnson Speech and
Hearing Building
Iowa City, IA 52242 USA

Christine Yoshinaga-Itano
206 Regent Administrative
Center
University of Colorado at
Boulder 18
Boulder, CO 80309-0018 USA

Advances in the Spoken Language Development of Deaf and Hard-of-Hearing Children

1

Spoken Language Development of Deaf and Hard-of-Hearing Children: Historical and Theoretical Perspectives

Marc Marschark & Patricia Elizabeth Spencer

As Blamey, Sarant, and Paatsch (chapter 5 this volume) note, spoken communication has long been seen as central to human society. Yet strong arguments have been made that the first human languages were gestural or signed (Armstrong, 1999; Stokoe, 2001). Today, sign languages are the means of communication and interaction in Deaf communities around the world and have been shown to contain all the linguistic complexities and potentials of spoken languages (Stokoe, 1960/2005). It is clear that both deaf and hearing children can acquire signed languages easily and naturally when they are exposed to fluent models (Schick, Marschark, & Spencer, 2005).

Despite the historically early appearance of signed languages and their functionality in communities with many people who are deaf, spoken languages are used by the great majority of people around the world for interpersonal interaction, commerce, law, politics and cultural expression both within and among communities. Full access to those aspects of the general community is greatly increased for persons who have the ability to perceive and produce spoken languages. Lack of the ability to hear, whether partial, near-total, or total, can limit that access.

Hearing plays important and useful roles in providing environmental and safety information, but the primary disability associated with hearing loss is the challenge it presents for learning and using spoken language. The potential implications of this situation for social and academic domains have been addressed in other places (e.g., Marschark, 1993) and are not at issue here. Nevertheless, it is worth noting that children's spoken language fluency not only affects their development and education directly, but also affects them indirectly in a variety of ways. For example, Most, Weisel, and Lev-Matezky (1996) found that hearing individuals' perceptions of deaf children's cognitive compe- tence and personality traits were closely associated with the intelligi- bility of the children's speech, a finding that clearly speaks to a myriad of short-term and long-term implications. It is only reasonable, there- fore, that much research and intervention effort has been focused on assisting persons who are deaf to attain and to maintain their abilities to comprehend and produce spoken language. For a variety of reasons discussed below, however, we believe it is time for a reconsideration of the history, progress, and future directions of research on spoken language development of deaf children. Such a discussion will help to provide a more a complete understanding of deaf education, the Deaf community, and the development of deaf children in today's context. In this endeavor, a broad perspective is necessary, treading carefully upon both known and unknown shores.

BEYOND LIE DRAGONS

It is said that those who ignore history are doomed to repeat it, and yet that the more things change, the more they stay the same. Both can be true, of course, and to those interested in the language development of deaf children, they often seem to hold simultaneously. Indeed, for those of us involved in educating deaf children—either in language or in academic areas—the conjunction of these two aphorisms serves as a reminder that where we are today in understanding and fostering spo- ken language development in deaf and hard-of-hearing children is a direct result of a self-made history. Decisions (sometimes by omission) that we in the field have made collectively over the past 150 years have influenced not only research, but also the lives of countless deaf chil- dren. Now we find ourselves at another decision point, with an op- portunity to take advantage of recent advances in technology, speech science, and psychological research to fundamentally alter the way we approach language development in deaf children . . . or not.

The conjunction of the above aphorisms also warns us that deaf children and their parents today are unlikely to accept the often unsubstantiated and sometimes contradictory advice they frequently have been given in the past. Parents have long complained about feelings of confusion and aban- donment upon learning of their child's hearing loss, and professionals have long been quite poor at predicting which children would succeed in ac- quiring spoken language skills and in what types of programming those skills would best be achieved. Certainly, there is no shortage of methods advocated for fostering spoken language in deaf children, but even those who favor one particular approach admit that there is often little objective evidence for their positions (e.g., Eriks-Brophy, 2004).

Building and/or remediating spoken language skills can range from unisensory (e.g., acoupedics, auditory-verbal)—in which attention is to be focused almost entirely on developing residual hearing to support listening skills—to bilingual-bicultural programs in which spoken language is most often supported in specific and typically time-limited sessions (Lynas, 1999). Within that continuum are various traditional oral approaches that include an emphasis on the visually-based skill of speechreading and the various forms of "total" or "simultaneous" communication in which signs are modified or created to allow them to accompany spoken language in as time-locked a pattern as possible (see L. J. Spencer & Tomblin, chapter 8 this volume). Considerable resources and energy have been spent in investigations comparing the efficacy of one such method against another, and yet the payoff thus far in terms of theoretical clarity or practical success seems to do little to justify the expenses incurred (Carney & Moeller, 1998).

Recent advances in the technologies for early identification of hearing loss, however, along with technologies for digital and programmable hearing aids and cochlear implants, have increased the access that many children with hearing loss have to the sounds of spoken language in their environment. These advances are so significant that the expectations for deaf and hard-of-hearing children's ability to acquire spoken language skills have changed dramatically. It therefore is both exciting and a bit daunting to be able to declare a new beginning in research and practice concerning language development in deaf children, an interface at which we see great opportunities for progress and synergy in the field, especially in the short- and medium-term. We are at a point at which we should perhaps take our lessons from history and move on, leaving any baggage behind.

UNDERSTANDING LANGUAGE DEVELOPMENT BY DEAF CHILDREN

Theoretical and empirical investigations of language development in deaf children historically have considered hearing children to provide a baseline and comparison group. Research involving the two populations thus has had many parallels, although work involving deaf children usually has lagged behind that involving hearing children, and a number of special-interest tangents have impeded progress in both theory and practice. Most of these historical-theoretical side trips have been related to the linking of instructional methods to support deaf children's spoken language with those concerning deaf education more broadly. Sometimes explicitly and intentionally, and at other times more subtly (at least prior to the establishment of modern funding agencies), the tension between advocates of speech-only versus sign-language–based education—and all points between—has itself influenced the questions asked and methods used in studies of language development. This is not intended as either criticism or compliment, but only recognition of a fact to be considered if we are to be able to interpret progress in the field to date and have any hope of improving it in the future.

Research on methods and outcomes relating to spoken language development by deaf and hard-of-hearing children also has been influenced by the diversity of investigators engaged in the enterprise. Given the complex interaction of environmental, biological, social, educational, and technological factors that bear on the language development of individual deaf children, it is perhaps not surprising that modern research programs concerning spoken language tend to be even more broadly interdisciplinary than those concerning spoken language development in hearing children or sign language development in deaf children. Ideally, this methodological and theoretical mixing should lead to research and practice reflecting a synthesis of the best ideas from diverse perspectives. Unfortunately, it also can lead to whole bodies of research (and researchers) that seem to exist in separate worlds.

This latter description appears apt regarding history of research on the speech—sign language continuum in deaf education, with researchers tending to specialize on one mode of communication or another due largely to the place or orientation in which they were trained, rather than necessarily because of any documented a priori advantage to deaf children. The often-exclusive focus of investigators is also evident in the degree to which emerging knowledge about language development in hearing children is incorporated into studies of language development in deaf children. Investigators who hail from psychology and child development often take a very different approach to deaf children's language than do those who come from speech and language backgrounds or from deaf education. It therefore appears that both our understanding of deaf children's language competence and, ultimately, our efforts to enhance the language abilities so essential for other aspects of learning and development have often been more a product of methodological preference than the outcome of a search for the fundamentals of deaf children's language, independent of its modality. To better understand this situation, let us consider how we got here.

HISTORICAL VIEWS OF LANGUAGE DEVELOPMENT
AND DEAF CHILDREN

Research on the language of hearing children is generally seen as beginning with studies during the mid nineteenth century in Germany, Austria, and Russia with pioneering studies by Löbisch (1851), Sikorsky (1883), and Sigismund (1856). Physiologist Berthold Sigismund's *Kind und Welt* (*The Child and the World*; 1856) was perhaps the first to document in detail the first year of spoken language development, noting the sequential emergence of "crowing" and babbling, followed by the "imitation of musical tones" (in at least two octaves!), and finally spoken sounds and gesture (see Oller, chapter 2 this volume, and Masataka, chapter 3, for updates). August Schleicher (1861) was apparently the first linguist to report observations of children's spoken language, documenting the phonetics of early utterances at a time when phonetics as a field of study was just developing. Like the later studies by Bloch (1913) and Piaget (1928/1951), Schleicher primarily studied his own children. He likened their early productions to phonetic elements of the Indo-European languages he was analyzing and noted idiosyncrasies of pronunciation that stayed with the children into their fourth year, resisting his attempts at regularization through feedback and modeling (see Cazden, 1965).

The roots of theoretical interest in the language of deaf children began at about the same time, in the mid-1800s, with the convergence of two previously distinct domains of study. One of these domains involved the emergence of prescriptive writings concerning the education of deaf children and, more specifically, the roles of spoken and written language. Meanwhile, a growing interest in uniting philosophical views of the nature of the human mind with the new experimental psychology led to scientific interest in deaf children, as psychologists and philosophers struggled to decipher the relations of language, thought, and intelligence. Observations of educational methods for "intelligent mutes" (Fay, 1869) thus brought psychology and education together, offering insights into relations between language and higher mental processes as well as offering insights into the potential for educating young deaf children.

This new area of study is well documented in the first 50 years of the *American Annals of the Deaf and Dumb* (1847–1897). There, a variety of investigators such as Bartlett (1850) argued that thinking skills were intimately tied to spoken language and would be irreparably harmed in its absence. Bartlett's position echoed that of the German Samuel Heinicke, almost 100 years before, who argued that abstract thought depended on speech, and thus deaf children must acquire the ability to articulate vocal language in order to achieve the higher levels of cognitive functioning necessary for educational success. Heinicke, who is often considered the father of the "oral approach" to language instruction for deaf children, had established a school for deaf children in Leipzig in 1778 (around the same time as l'Épée's National Institution for Deaf-Mutes in Paris). Teachers at the school utilized a method of language instruction in which they spoke clearly and slowly, exaggerating some aspects of articulation, such as tongue movements, that might be more difficult to see (see Massaro, chapter 10 this volume). Preyer (1882) took up a similar position in America, arguing along with Bell (1898/2005) for spoken language to be the primary means of communication to and by deaf children.

Although Edward Miner Gallaudet is recognized as a leader in the use of American Sign Language (ASL) in educating deaf children, he also supported providing speech lessons to students who had potential for and interest in spoken language and advocated using reading and writing to teach English (Easterbrooks & Baker, 2002). In Gallaudet's approach, we can see two emerging traditions of language training for deaf children. His use of the "combined method"—using both spoken and sign language—was championed by other eminent educators of the day, such as Westervelt and Peet (1880) and Bell (1898/2005). In Bell's case, there was a clear preference for spoken language, at least for "quasi-deaf" and "quasi-mute" children. Regarding profoundly deaf children, however, Bell expressed some doubts about the effectiveness of spoken language and suggested that "the De L'Épée sign language" might be more effective (p. 28). For those children, Bell (1898/2005) offered a version of the combined method relying primarily on spoken language, augmented by "natural actions and gestures":

> [N]atural actions and gestures are of great utility in the instruction of the Deaf, when used as hearing people employ them, as accompaniments of English words, to emphasize and reinforce their meaning. They are useful to illustrate English expressions, just as pictures illustrate the text of a book. They give life and force to the utterances of thought.... Language unaccompanied by natural actions and expressive gestures, is like a book without pictures, a dry and cold thing to present to little children whether hearing or deaf. (p. 18)

Yet Bell made it clear that gesture was to be used with fingerspelling (p. 21) or spoken words, and not in place of them.

Along with the combined method, Gallaudet's and Bell's focus on reading and writing as a means to acquire spoken language and other English skills was indicative of another popular approach to education and language training for deaf children in the nineteenth century, the "natural method." This method was rather different than what is considered "natural" today, so it will be worth examining the notion a bit further.

SPOKEN LANGUAGE IN DEAF EDUCATION: NATURAL METHODS

By the late 1860s, two prominent "oral" schools for deaf children had been established in the United States, the Lexington School for the Deaf and the Clarke School. Advocates of oral methods in both language and academic instruction of deaf children sought to ensure that they could do more than just acquire basic spoken language vocabulary (or some reasonable approximation to it): Spoken language was seen as a means to the end of offering access to literacy, education, and full participation in society. Brock (1868), for example, argued that because deaf children could not hear people talking, they could not learn to "imitate" the mental operations of parents and other adults the way hearing children do. Brock believed that the learning of signs led to "disconnected" thought processes and suggested connecting sign concepts via writing or spoken language so that relations among concepts will be recognized. With "the sentence as the normal condition of language" (p. 210), he proposed that deaf children would acquire language normally and "energetically," rather than being bored by isolated units out of context. The heart of this natural method of teaching language to deaf children thus involved having them respond to written sentence commands to make them "think in English" (Fay, 1869).

In focusing on the understanding of words and concepts in both textual and behavioral contexts, the natural method came to be contrasted with the "structured method" of drill and practice with individual words and phrases (see Beattie, chapter 6 this volume, and Brown & Nott, chapter 7). The printed word appeared to be a useful way to teach deaf children about the multiple grammatical levels of spoken language (phonological, morphological, and syntactic) as well as its pragmatic and social uses. This emphasis on natural language use in education also would seem to provide a context more conducive to a merging with ongoing research into language development in hearing children, but that convergence was still half a century away. Meanwhile, those individuals most involved in deaf children's language were consumed by the ongoing debate about spoken language versus sign language in education. Although the issue was to have been settled by the 1880 International Congress of Educators of the Deaf, the "war of methods" spilled over into the twentieth century.

LANGUAGE DEVELOPMENT RESEARCH WITH DEAF CHILDREN COMES OF AGE

Through the first two thirds of the twentieth century, most forms of manual communication were frowned on by educators of deaf children—with fingerspelling (including the Rochester method) seen as exceptions, being more akin to spoken than signed language. This focus was consistent not only with the orientation of nineteenth-century thinkers and researchers, but also with the desires of hearing parents of deaf children who wanted them to have access to speech, to be able to function in a variety of school and social settings, and to appear similar to their hearing siblings.

Another historical convergence was to occur in the early 1960s, however, further complicating the issue of the role of language in education. By this time, Stokoe (1960/2005) had introduced the world to the notion that the visual-gestural communication he saw among deaf individuals at Gallaudet College had all of the features of a natural language. Although it took some time to make their way into psychological and developmental research, Stokoe's arguments refreshed the spoken language–sign language debate. At the same time, linguistics in North America was just emerging from the Bloomfieldian tradition of reductionist language description, while psychological study of language was throwing off the bonds of behaviorism and reductionist approaches to language and other forms of human behavior. Skinner's (1957) *Verbal Behavior* had provided an elegant but incomplete explanation of language acquisition as being dependent on incremental, continuous learning via shaping, reinforcement, and conditioning, an approach that fit well with contemporary approaches to teaching spoken language to deaf children. Before Skinner's psychological theory could be applied explicitly to children's language development, however, the theory was trumped by Chomsky's (1957, 1965) linguistic theory of transformational generative grammar and by disconfirming empirical studies. Cazden (1965), for example, showed that correct grammatical expansions of children's utterances were less effective than semantically and contextually appropriate elaborations, presaging cognitive approaches to children's language acquisition in which conversation, social functions, and meaning were seen as the foundations for language development (e.g., Macnamara, 1972; Nelson, 1973).

With the cognitive revolution of the late 1960s, there was much greater concern for the synergistic aspects of language and behavior, first through neobehavioral notions of "mediation" and then greater concern for the mediators themselves (e.g., memory, images, knowledge). Syntax ruled the day, and studies emanating from Chomsky's theory drove both educational and language research involving deaf children just as it did language development more broadly (e.g., Brown, 1973). Syntactic approaches to deaf children's literacy development were most clearly articulated by Quigley and his colleagues (e.g., Quigley, Power, & Steinkamp, 1977; Quigley, Wilbur, Power, Montanelli, & Steinkamp, 1976), but the emphasis on syntax in deaf children's language began with its role in their spoken language. Lenneberg's (1967; Lenneberg, Rebelsky, & Nichols, 1965) work on the biological foundations of language helped to highlight possible differences between early language development of deaf children of deaf versus hearing parents, but even there, the focus was on spoken language, including the onset and role of babbling (see Oller, chapter 2 this volume).

Studies conducted throughout this period generally compared (explicitly or implicitly) deaf children's performance to that of hearing children. From time to time, deaf children were studied in order to test ideas from theory and research on hearing children and thus to add to the general knowledge base concerning language and language development (see, e.g., Siple, 1978). Studies of deaf children were seen as helping to identify aspects of language development and links between language and learning that were robust and could emerge without a child having full access to the sounds of language (e.g., Furth, 1966). In this context, spoken language did not necessarily have a preeminent position among language researchers, but it remained an important goal for many deaf individuals and their families.

SPOKEN LANGUAGE AS PART OF A LANGUAGE COCKTAIL

With increasing interest in the joint functioning of syntax and semantics in the late 1960s and early 1970s, children's understanding of meaning and their integration of information from multiple sources gained greater interest from investigators in language and cognitive development (e.g., Brown, 1973; Halliday, 1975; Macnamara, 1972). With this movement came increasing interest in deaf children's utilization of different sources of language information and renewed interest in natural, combined methods of oral education. Fry (1966), for example, noted that among those deaf children who acquired spoken language, there did not seem to be a strong relation between degree of hearing loss and spoken language receptive or production skills. He suggested that the more important factors are the amount and clarity of the spoken language to which the deaf child is exposed and the efficient use of residual hearing. Integration of visual and auditory cues was seen as an essential component of acquiring spoken language, an assumption made early on by investigators like Wilhelm Wundt (1900), who noticed language delays in blind children, and Brock (1868), who believed that deaf children used exceptionally acute visual memory skills to link signs to objects in the absence of spoken language. Fry argued that at least part of deaf children's difficulties in acquiring spoken language derived from adults not providing clear auditory and visual speech cues in early development.

    In this climate, Orin Cornett (1967) developed "Cued Speech," a system of hand gestures that accompanied oral articulation and represented the sounds of spoken language that are not easily disambiguated with residual hearing and speechreading (see Hage & Leybaert, chapter 9 this volume; Leybaert, Alegria, Hage, & Charlier, 1998), while fingerspelling was used in schools as a greater (in the Rochester method) or lesser (in total communication; Scouten, 1984) supplement to spoken language. Even for those interested in sign language, English played a prominent role, and various systems of English-based signing were developed in the United Kingdom (Anthony, 1971) and United States (Bornstein, 1974; Gustason, Pfetzing, & Zawolkow, 1980). In these systems, signs were produced in the same order as spoken language and accompanied by speech. Many teachers and investigators once again hoped that this combination would support the acquisition of spoken language, and coupled with advances in hearing aids, the concept of "total communication" emerged.

The total communication approach advocates using any and all communication methods and assistive devices with an individual deaf child based on that child's needs and abilities (see L. J. Spencer & Tomblin, chapter 8 this volume). Unfortunately, despite great efforts on the part of parents and educators and advances in the degree of deaf children's self-esteem and their ability to communicate with parents and others, use of this approach did not significantly increase the levels of literacy or spoken language achievements by deaf children (Mayer & Akamatsu, 1999). In part, this failure likely resulted from total communication being implemented by many educators as "simultaneous communication" (i.e., the simultaneous accompaniment of spoken language by one of the English-based signing systems), while the emphasis on audition and speech training got lost in the process. But, as L. J. Spencer and Tomblin (chapter 8 this volume) emphasize, total communication and simultaneous communication are not equivalent.

Use of simultaneous communication has its own challenges. Some opponents argue that the presentation of combined visual and auditory language to children with hearing loss results in their focusing on the visual information instead of the more difficult to process auditory information (e.g., Ling, 2002). This assumption persists despite findings demonstrating that visual information from speechreading supports instead of interferes with children's comprehension of spoken language (e.g., Bergeson, Pisoni, & Davis, 2003; Novelli-Olmstead & Ling, 1984; see Burkholder & Pisoni, chapter 14 this volume). Meanwhile, there have been a variety of reports indicating that that early sign language skills have either no effect or a positive one on children's concurrent or subsequent spoken language skills (e.g., Calderon & Greenberg, 1997; Mayberry & Eichen, 1991; Moores, Weiss, & Goodwin, 1973; Strong, 1988; Yoshinaga-Itano, chapter 13 this volume), although there remains disagreement on this point (see, e.g., Geers, chapter 11 this volume).

PROGRESS THROUGH INNOVATION

Efforts to provide amplified sound input to deaf children (and adults) strengthened in the 1970s with advances in hearing aid technologies and diagnostic techniques. Easterbrooks and Baker (2002) suggested that technological advances during this active period encouraged an increased emphasis on oral approaches to language development simply because they were more likely to be successful: Better hearing led to better speech. However, speech intelligibility remains both a challenge and the touchstone of most approaches to spoken language training for deaf children, and technological efforts to support speech perception and production have their own complex histories of research and practice (see Ackley & Decker, chapter 4 this volume).

by its advocates in North America. Why not? French and English are similar in having considerable variability at the level of phoneme-to-grapheme translation, but in French there are no inconsistencies at the level of grapheme-to-phoneme translation (Alegria & Lechat, 2005). Whether this difference could result in Cued Speech being less effective for learners of English than French remains to be determined (such irregularities do affect performance in some tasks; see Alegria & Lechat, 2005). Nevertheless, the fact that the benefits to deaf children's spoken English have not received empirical support in the decades since the creation of Cued Speech (for English) suggests that such evidence is neither easily produced nor of great generality. How can we expect parents and their deaf children to embrace methods alleged to support the development of spoken language when we are unable to demonstrate their utility?

Observations of this sort are rather different from similar ones made 5 or 10 years ago about cochlear implants. In the case of implants, significant benefits had been demonstrated for hearing soon after implants were developed, and research evaluating implants against hearing aids for children in diverse groups closely tracked technological improvements. For various approaches to spoken language intervention, in contrast, the focus on practice may have given outcome research a lower priority. Or it may be simply that differences among oral interventions are often so minimal that their variations have no discernable effect on their effectiveness, but rather only reflect the orientation of the service provider. In any case, we must agree with Eriks-Brophy (2004) that it is incumbent on the advocates of various approaches to provide evidence of the benefits of their interventions and theoretical justifications for the advice they dispense (see the preface to this volume).

As we noted above, spoken language development of deaf children may be more possible today than ever before. We are poised on a threshold of what often seem like unlimited possibilities. The field is now seeing significant benefits from early identification and early intervention for deaf infants, a better understanding of the need for and processes of early language acquisition, more support for families of young deaf children, and technological advances in devices to assist and improve hearing. All of these raise expectations for deaf children's spoken language development far beyond any we had a right to hold at any point in the past. We are now presented with an opportunity to learn from earlier mistakes and misunderstandings and to synthesize the best ideas from the past with the technological, programming, and social advances of today. If we tread carefully and document our progress, we may finally be able to fulfill the promise of effective support for speech and spoken language for children with hearing loss. Raising and educating a deaf child is about having choices and making decisions. When those decisions are informed, and when the differences between choices are clear, parents and practitioners will be able to optimize developmental and educational opportunities for all deaf children. We cannot ask for anything more.

ACKNOWLEDGMENTS

Preparation of this chapter was supported in part by grants REC-0207394 and REC-0307602 from the National Science Foundation to Marc Marschark. Any opinions, findings and conclusions, or recommendations expressed in this material are those of the authors and do not necessarily reflect the views of the National Science Foundation.

REFERENCES

Alegria, J., & Lechat, J. (2005). Phonological processing in deaf children: When lipreading and cues are incongruent. *Journal of Deaf Studies and Deaf Education 10*, 122–133.

Anthony, D. (1971). *Seeing essential English*. Anaheim, CA: Anaheim School District.

Armstrong, D. F. (1999). *Original signs*. Washington, DC: Gallaudet University Press.

Bartlett, D. E. (1850) The acquisition of language. *American Annals of the Deaf and Dumb, 3*(1), 83–92.

Beebe, H., Pearson, H., & Koch, M. (1984). The Helen Beebe Speech and Hearing Center. In D. Ling (Ed.), *Early intervention for hearing-impaired children: Oral options* (pp. 15–63). San Diego: College-Hill Press.

Bell, A. G. (1898). *The question of sign-language and the utility of signs in the instruction of the deaf*. Washington, DC: Sanders Printing Office. (Reprinted in *Journal of Deaf Studies and Deaf Education, 10*, 111–121, 2005)

Bergeson, T., Pisoni, D., & David, R. (2003). A longitudinal study of audiovisual speech perception by children with hearing loss who have cochlear implants. *Volta Review, 103*(4), 347–371.

Bloch, O. (1913). Notes sur le langage de l'enfant. *Mémoires de la Société de Linguistique de Paris, 18*, 37–59.

Bornstein, H. (1974). Signed English: A manual approach to English language development. *Journal of Speech and Hearing Disorders, 39*, 330–343.

Brock, M. L. (1868). A better method of instructing a class of beginners. *American Annals of the Deaf and Dumb, 13*, 206–217.

Brown, R. (1973). *A first language*. Cambridge, MA: Harvard University Press.

Calderon, R., & Greenberg, M. (1997). The effectiveness of early intervention for deaf children and children with hearing loss. In M. J. Guralnik (Ed.), *The effectiveness of early intervention* (pp. 455–482). Baltimore: Paul H. Brookes.

Carney, A. E., & Moeller, M. P. (1998). Treatment efficacy: Hearing loss in children. *Journal of Speech, Language, and Hearing Research, 41*, 61–85.

Cazden, C. (1965). *Environmental assistance to a child's acquisition of grammar*. Unpublished doctoral dissertation, Harvard University, School of Education.

Chomsky, N. (1957). *Syntactic structures*. The Hague: Mouton.

Chomsky, N. (1965). *Aspects of the theory of syntax*. Cambridge, MA: MIT Press.

Cole, E., & Paterson, M. M. (1984). Assessment and treatment of phonologic disorders in the hearing-impaired. In J. Castello (Ed.), *Speech disorders in children* (pp. 93–127). San Diego: College-Hill Press.

Connor, L. (1986). Oralism in perspective. In D. Luterman (Ed.), *Deafness in perspective* (pp. 117–129). San Diego: College-Hill Press.

Cornett, O. (1967). Cued speech. *American Annals of the Deaf, 112,* 3–13.

Easterbrooks, S., & Baker, S. (2002). *Language learning in children who are deaf and hard of hearing. Multiple pathways.* Boston, MA: Allyn and Bacon.

Erber, N. (1982). *Auditory training.* Washington, DC: Alexander Graham Bell Association for the Deaf.

Eriks-Brophy, A. (2004). Outcomes of auditory-verbal therapy: A review of the evidence and a call to action. *Volta Review, 104,* 21–35.

Fay, E. A. (1869). The acquisition of language by deaf mutes. *American Annals of the Deaf and Dumb, 14*(4), 13.

Fry, D. B. (1966). The development of the phonological system in the normal and the deaf child. In F. Smith & G. A. Miller (Eds.), *The genesis of language.* Cambridge, MA: MIT Press.

Furth, H. G. (1966). *Thinking without language.* New York: Free Press.

Gatty, J. (1992). Teaching speech to hearing-impaired children. *Volta Review, 94*(5), 49–61.

Goldberg, D., & Talbot, P. (1993). The Larry Jarret Houst Program at the Helen Beebe Speech and Hearing Center. *Volta Review, 95,* 91–96.

Gustason, G., Pfetzing, D., & Zawolkow, E. (1972). *Signing exact English.* Rossmore, CA: Modern Signs Press.

Halliday, M. (1975). *Learning how to mean.* London: Edward Arnold.

Houston, D. M., Ying, E., Pisoni, D., & Kirk, K. (2003). Development of pre-word learning skills in infants with cochlear implants. *Volta Review, 103.*

James, W. (1893). Thought before language: A deaf-mute's recollections. *American Annals of the Deaf and Dumb, 18,* 135–145.

Lenneberg, E. (1967). *Biological foundations of language.* New York: John Wiley & Sons.

Lenneberg, E., Rebelsky, F. G., & Nichols, I. A. (1965). The vocalization of infants born to deaf and to hearing parents. *Human Development, 8,* 23–37.

Leybaert, J., Alegria, J., Hage, C., & Charlier, B. (1998). The effect of exposure to phonetically augmented lipspeech in the prelingual deaf. In R. Campbell, B. Dodd, & D. Burham (Eds.), *Hearing by Eye II: Advances in the psychology of speechreading and auditory-visual speech* (pp. 283–301). Hove, UK: Psychology Press.

Ling, D. (2002). *Speech and the hearing-impaired child: Theory and practice* (2nd ed.). Washington, DC: Alexander Graham Bell Association for the Deaf.

Löbisch, J. E. (1851). *Entwickelungsgeschichte der Seele des Kindes.* Wein.

Lynas, W. (1999). Communication options. In J. Stokes (Ed.), *Hearing impaired infants: Support in the first eighteen months* (pp. 98–128). London: Whurr Publishers Ltd.

Macnamara, J. (1972). Cognitive basis of language learning in infants. *Psychological Review, 79,* 1–13.

Marschark, M. (1993). *Psychological development of deaf children.* New York: Oxford University Press.

Marschark, M. (2001). *Language development in children who are deaf: A research synthesis*. Alexandria, VA: National Association of State Directors of Special Education.

Mayberry, R. I., & Eichen, E. B. (1991). The long-lasting advantage of learning sign language in childhood: Another look at the critical period for language acquisition. *Journal of Memory and Language, 30*, 486–512.

Mayer, C., & Akamatsu, C. T. (1999). Bilingual-bicultural models of literacy education for deaf students: Considering the claims. *Journal of Deaf Studies and Deaf Education, 4*, 1–8.

McCartney, B. (1986). An investigation of the factors contributing of the ability of hearing-impaired children to communicate orally as perceived by oral deaf adults and parents and teachers of the hearing impaired. *Volta Review, 88*, 133–143.

Moores, D. F., Weiss, K., & Goodwin, M. (1973). Receptive abilities of deaf children across five modes of communication. *Exceptional Children, 39*, 22–28.

Most, T., Weisel, A., & Lev-Matezky, A. (1996). Speech intelligibility and the evaluation of personal qualities by experienced and inexperienced listeners. *Volta Review, 98*(4), 181–191.

Nelson, K. (1973). Structure and strategy in learning to talk. *Monographs of the Society for Research and Child Development, 38*(149).

Novelli-Olmstead, T., & Ling, D. (1984). Speech production and speech discrimination by hearing-impaired children. *Volta Review, 86*, 72–80.

Paatsch, L. E., Blamey, P. J., & Sarant, J. Z. (2001). Effects of articulation training on the production of trained and untrained phonemes in conversations and formal tests. *Journal of Deaf Studies and Deaf Education, 6*(1), 32–42.

Paul, P. V., & Jackson, D. W. (1993). *Toward a psychology of deafness: Theoretical and empirical perspectives*. Boston: Allyn and Bacon.

Piaget, J. (1928/1951). *The language and thought of the child*. London: Routledge & Kegan Paul, Ltd.

Picheny, M., Durlach, N., & Braida, L. (1986). Speaking clearly for the hard of hearing II: Acoustic characteristics of clear and conversational speech. *Journal of Speech and Hearing Research, 29*, 434–446.

Pollack, D. (1984). An acoupedic program. In D. Ling (Ed.), *Early intervention for hearing-impaired children: Oral options* (pp. 181–253). San Diego: College-Hill Press.

Preyer, W. (1882). *Die Seele des Kindes*. Leipzig.

Quigley, S., Wilbur, R., Power, D., Montanelli, D., & Steinkamp, M. (1976). *Syntactic structure in the language of deaf children*. Urbana: University of Illinois Institute for Child Behavior and Development.

Quigley, S. P., Power, D., & Steinkamp, M. (1977). The language structure of deaf children. *Volta Review, 79*, 73–84.

Schleicher, A. (1861). Some observations made on children. *Beiträge zur Vergleichenden Sprachforschung, 4*, 497–498.

Schick, B., Marschark, M., & Spencer, P. E. (Eds). (2005). *Advances in the sign language development of deaf children*. New York: Oxford University Press.

Scouten, E. (1984). *Turning points in the education of deaf people*. Danville, IL: Interstate Printers and Publishers, Inc.

Serry, T. A., & Blamey, P. J. (1999). A 4-year investigation into phonetic inventory development in children with cochlear implants. *Journal of Speech and Hearing Research, 42,* 141–154.

Sigismund, B. (1856). *Kind und Welt.* Braunschweig.

Sikorsky, I. A. (1883). Du développment du langage chez les enfants. *Archives de Neurologie.*

Siple, P. (1978). *Understanding language through sign language research.* New York: Academic Press.

Skinner, B. F. (1957). *Verbal behavior.* Englewood Cliffs, NJ: Prentice Hall.

Sonneveldt, V., Kelsay, D., Spencer, L., & Barker, B. (n.d.). *Listen! A guide for parents of infants and toddlers with cochlear implants.* Iowa City, IA: University of Iowa Children's Cochlear Implant Program.

Spencer, P. (2003). Parent-child interaction: Implications for intervention and development. In B. Bodner-Johnson & M. Sass-Lehrer (Eds.), *The young deaf or hard of hearing child: A family-centered approach to early education* (pp. 333–368). Baltimore: Paul H. Brookes Publishing.

Spencer, P. (2004). Individual differences in language performance after cochlear implantation at one to three years of age: Child, family, and linguistic factors. *Journal of Deaf Studies and Deaf Education, 9,* 395–412.

Spencer, P. E., & Marschark, M. (2003). Cochlear implants: Issues and implications. In M. Marschark & P. E. Spencer (Eds.), *Oxford handbook of deaf studies, language, and education* (pp. 434–448). New York: Oxford University Press.

Spens, K. E., Huss, C., Dahlqvist, M., & Agelfors, E. (1997). A hand held two-channel vibro-tactile speech communication aid for the deaf: Characteristics and results. 4th International Sensory Aid Conference. *Scandinavian Audiology, 47,* 5–13.

Stokoe, W. C. (1960). *Sign language structure: An outline of the visual communication system of the American deaf.* Studies in Linguistics, Occasional Papers 8. Buffalo, NY: Department of Anthropology and Linguistics, University of Buffalo. (Reprinted in *Journal of Deaf Studies and Deaf Education, 10,* 3–37, 2005)

Stokoe, W. C. (2001). *Language in hand.* Washington, DC: Gallaudet University Press.

Strong, M. (1988). A bilingual approach to the education of young children: ASL and English. In M. Strong (Ed.), *Language learning and deafness* (pp. 113–129). Cambridge: Cambridge University Press.

Tobey, E., Geers, A., & Brenner, C. (1994). Speech production results: Speech feature acquisition. *Volta Review, 96,* 109–130.

Tye-Murray, N., & Kirk, K. I. (1993). Vowel and diphthong production by young users of cochlear implants and the relationship between the phonetic level evaluation and spontaneous speech. *Journal of Speech and Hearing Research, 36,* 488–502.

Westervelt, Z., & Peet, H. P. (1880). The natural method. *American Annals of the Deaf, 25,* 212–217.

Wundt, W. (1900). Exchanges and mutilations of sounds in child language. *Völkerpsychologie, 1,* 314–319.

2

Vocal Language Development in Deaf Infants: New Challenges

D. Kimbrough Oller

In the past 30 years fundamental improvements have been made in the understanding of early vocal development in the deaf infant. But these improvements have required more than merely acquiring new data. They have required a basic readjustment of how we think about the early stages of vocalization. This chapter takes account of both the nature of the new data on early speech in deaf infants and children and the new way of thinking that made the data possible to analyze and interpret. Understanding these theoretical and empirical foundations is critical as a new generation of deaf and hard-of-hearing infants and children using cochlear implants and digital hearing aids are being evaluated regarding speech development. There exists a strong temptation to describe the progress of these children with traditional tools, which, as indicated below, can be extremely misleading at early stages of development. Even when the new perspectives on description are applied, it is tempting to cut corners on the methodological adaptations needed to apply them fully. Such corner cutting can lead to important errors and to misleading data about the progress in vocal development of infants and young children. The goal of this chapter is to examine the shift of perspective that is required in order to elucidate advances in vocalizations that occur as infants, deaf or hearing, begin to show a capacity to produce well-formed speech.

The key events in the growth of information available about the vocalizations of deaf babies are based upon theoretical and methodological adjustments that revise fundamentally how we categorize the sounds babies produce. The new way of looking at infant vocalizations requires

22

abandoning the expectation that there are phonetically transcribable consonants and vowels to be found in the earliest sounds of infancy and recognizing that instead, babies have their own system of categories of sound, categories that are precursors to speech but that do not possess the well-formed qualities of consonants and vowels. This idea applies to vocalizations of both deaf and hearing infants. Instead of transcribing the sounds of babies in the first half year of life as consonants and vowels, it is more reasonable to categorize them in groupings that conform to patterns of apparent repetition and social usage. These categories have been given technical names that draw partly on the common-parlance descriptors of infant sounds, and so some are called "squeals," "growls," and "raspberries." But other sound categories of infants are described with new coinages such as "quasivowels," "marginal babbling," and "canonical babbling" (Oller, 1980, 2000).

In the context of the new way of looking at things, we find that deaf infants are clearly distinguishable from hearing infants by the second half year of life in terms of the *kinds* of sounds they produce; in particular, deaf infants do not enter the "canonical stage" of infant vocal development as early as hearing infants do. In other words, deaf infants do not begin producing consistent canonical babbling (including well-formed syllables or sequences of syllables, e.g., [bababa] or [dadada]) at the age expected in hearing infants, who usually begin the canonical stage by 7 or 8 months and very reliably by 10 months (Oller & Eilers, 1988). Further, deaf infants appear usually to be distinguishable from hearing infants even in the *first* half year of life in terms of their vocalization patterns, an issue considered below. The ability to recognize specific characteristics of vocalizations in deaf babies provides new opportunities to assess the vocal development of infants and new ways to monitor changes in their vocalizations in early phases.

While it is not difficult to differentiate deaf and hearing infants in terms of vocalization characteristics in the latter half of the first year, it is important to issue a few caveats immediately about the extent to which and the methods by which the differentiation can be drawn. First, the differentiation is generally quite easy with profoundly deaf and hearing infants, but the differentiability varies markedly as a function of the degree of hearing loss. Infants with severe hearing loss are not always differentiable from hearing infants in onset of canonical babbling (some appear to show onset of canonical babbling in the normal range; Koopmans-van Beinum, Clement, & van den Dikkenberg-Pot, 2001), and infants with moderate loss appear to be even more likely than those with severe loss to enter the canonical stage within the range of ages seen in hearing infants (Nathani, Neal, Olds, Brill, & Oller, 2001).

But perhaps even a more important caveat for the interpretation of the late onset of canonical babbling in the deaf infant is that the procedures that are needed to make the differentiation between deaf and

hearing infant vocalizations must be applied in a way that takes account thoroughly of the new perspectives in theory and methodology of
description for vocalization. In particular, we have to apply the definition of the notion "canonical syllable" very judiciously. Attempts to
apply the idea casually can lead to misinterpretation and regression
into the errors of reasoning that prevented the recognition of early
stages of vocalization development and special vocal characteristics of
the deaf infant for generations. Late onset of canonical babbling in deaf
infants is a discovery that depends upon the shift of perspective that
this chapter reviews. It is crucial that as the field of assessment of vocal
development in the deaf proceeds we keep our eye on the target: To
recognize canonical babbling and its onset, we must adopt a new way
of looking at the early vocalizations of human infants.

THE HISTORICAL PERSPECTIVE ON OBSTACLES
TO EFFECTIVE RESEARCH ON DEAF INFANT BABBLING

Once our attention is properly focused on the distinction between canonical and precanonical babbling, and once adequate longitudinal samples of
vocalization from deaf and hearing infants are compared, it is not difficult
to recognize that there are stark differences between them. But prior to the
early 1970s, these differences were not known. In fact, it was believed (and
still is by many who have not been exposed to the new research) that deaf
and hearing infants babble very much alike. As we look back, it is possible
to see the obstacles that kept the field from achieving this focus and kept
scientists from acquiring the necessary data to reveal the stark differences
that occur between deaf and hearing infant babbling.

The greatest obstacle to achieving proper focus for description in past
observations on deaf infants' babbling was rooted in the traditional approach to description of infant vocalizations in general. At least as far
back as the eighteenth century with diary research by Dietrich Tiedemann
(Murchison & Langer, 1927/1971), there existed a tradition of describing
infant sounds in terms of phonetic transcriptional elements, that is, transcribing them as if they were well-formed consonants and vowels. In fact,
it is clear that babies do not in the earliest stages of vocal development
systematically produce consonants and vowels. Their sounds are more
primitive, are less well coordinated, and bear only distant similarity to
speech sounds. To treat them as consonants and vowels grossly distorts
their character and encourages a false impression of how the baby sounds
are composed. But, in accord with the long-standing tradition, students of
infant vocalizations have obviously been tempted for many generations
to use phonetic transcription to characterize the sounds of infancy. Even
now, this is a temptation that is not easily controlled. In the past it led to
many false claims about early vocalizations, some of the most important
of which concern babbling in the deaf infant.

The other problem that constituted a major obstacle to advancement of our understanding of vocalization in deaf infants until the 1970s was the simple fact that methods of testing to determine hearing status in infancy were not very reliable until about that time, and claims about vocalizations of deaf babies produced before then may have been based on observations of infants who had a greater degree of hearing than was believed by the observers at the time. Differences between severe and profound hearing loss make a difference in onset of canonical babbling, and such hearing level differences were not reliably determinable in the first half year of life until fairly recently.

MYTHS REGARDING THE BABBLING OF DEAF INFANTS

Even the lay public has been thoroughly exposed to certain myths about deaf infant babbling. The myths have two clear parts: One is that the sound types that occur in deaf and hearing infants are roughly the same, and the other is that volubility (amount of vocalization independent of type) is depressed in deaf infants. The first myth is apparently based on misinterpretation of facts, and the second myth is to this day completely unproven, even though there have been systematic attempts to nail it down. Let us examine the background on the two myths in turn.

While references to babbling in deaf infants can be found in literature dating back to at least early in the twentieth century (see Kaczmarek, 1953/1971; see also references in Lewis, 1936), the recent myth that deaf and hearing infants are not differentiable by the sound types they produce appears to be attributable mostly to an unfortunate history of misinterpretation of the work of Lenneberg, Rebelsky, and Nichols (1965) and to perplexing and apparently misleading phonetic transcription data presented in the doctoral dissertation of Mavilya (1969).

Lenneberg made a distinct attempt to cautiously interpret the research done by himself and his colleagues (Lenneberg, 1967), but he did not actually have much empirical information to work with. Given the meager foundation of data available, the research could not have shown in general that deaf and hearing infants babble with the same set of sounds in the first year of life. First, the studies involved only two presumably deaf infants in the first year of life, along with a sample of hearing infants, and 16 toddlers with hearing loss (in the second year of life or later). Since testing of hearing loss in infancy was not nearly as well developed as it is today, or as it was even a decade later, after foundations for both visually reinforced audiometry and auditory brainstem audiometry had been laid (Jewett, Romano, & Williston, 1970; Moore, Thompson, & Thompson, 1975), it is worth questioning whether the two infants examined in the first year by Lenneberg and colleagues were really profoundly deaf during infancy. But beyond that matter, the system of description of vocalizations that was utilized in the study was extremely gross, including no distinction between canonical and pre-canonical syllables or utterances. Consequently, if the babies were truly profoundly deaf, and if they were producing only precanonical sounds, Lenneberg and colleagues would probably not have been in a position to notice it. So the study provided no reliable basis for the conclusion upon which the first myth about deaf babbling was based.

Mavilya's (1969) dissertation examined three presumably deaf in-fants, where again the question of whether they were actually pro-foundly deaf at the time of the research is not easily answered. Data were gathered longitudinally using phonetic transcription even at very early ages. This approach is now recognized to be untenable because it forces the vocalizations of infants into categories to which they do not in fact pertain. Taken at face value, the data seemed to show that the three deaf babies babbled canonically, early in the first year of life, much as hearing infants do. But even in hearing infants we now know that such a char-acterization is merely the product of the forced categorization. To imply that sounds are well formed by describing them that way does not make them so. When one transcribes all sounds as if they are canonical, one effectively bypasses the empirical question of whether or not infants produce canonical sounds by assuming that all sounds are canonical. Consequently, Mavilya's data are at best difficult to interpret and at worst entirely misleading. They provide no reasonable basis for the claim that deaf and hearing infants babble similarly.

The volubility myth, that deaf infants supposedly produce less vocali-zation (independent of type of vocalization) than hearing infants do, is hard to trace but may also be largely attributable to Lenneberg (1967). The fact is that very little research has directly addressed the question of volubility in infancy. I know of not a single study to cite that provides believable quantitative support for the idea that deaf infants show depressed volu-bility in the first year of life. One of the few investigators directly to compare volubility in deaf and hearing infants using systematic quantitative meth-ods has concluded that there is little if any difference (Koopmans-van Beinum, Clement, & van den Dikkenberg-Pot, 1998; Koopmans-van Bei-num et al., 2001). Similarly Nathani et al. (2001) found no notable depres-sion of volubility in deaf infants in the first year of life. To be clear: I am not arguing that there is no difference between volubility in deaf and hearing infants. I am arguing instead that such a difference has not yet been proven.

THE MODERN PERSPECTIVE ON VOCALIZATIONS IN INFANCY

The common myth of recent times that deaf and hearing infants bab-ble with the very same sounds was overturned during the last three de-cades of the twentieth century. But there were hints in an earlier literature on deaf infants that suggested some may have noticed the late onset of canonical babbling well before that time (Kaczmarek, 1953/1971;

Mykelbust, 1954). But these hints were provided in anecdotal description rather than in formal quantitative analysis of data and so did not have the general impact that has been accorded to the more recent efforts.

In order for a quantitative demonstration of the difference in onset of canonical babbling in deaf and hearing infants to be made, it was necessary first to develop a formal distinction between canonical and precanonical vocalization. This formal distinction was codified and the term "canonical babbling" was coined in the early 1970s (Oller, 1976, 1980; Oller & Eilers, 1975). The basic idea of canonical babbling had emerged from longitudinal description of vocalizations in hearing infants. Three independent laboratories in the United States conducted such work in the 1970s (Oller, 1978; Stark, 1978; Zlatin, 1975), and all of them found it necessary to abandon the primary reliance on phonetic transcription as a method of description that had been traditional to that point. Instead, the researchers in this new wave utilized much more global categories of description, invoking terms such as "squeals," "growls," and "rasp-berries" drawn from common-parlance descriptions of infant sounds. The method of description was similar to that of classical ethology (Lorenz, 1951; Tinbergen, 1951), where scientists simply observe the functional behavior of animals without making preemptive assumptions about what the animals know or what they can do. The categories of observation emerge from the process of observation of functional interactions in nat-ural settings. Since human infants do not produce clear speechlike sounds with well-formed phonetic character in the first months of life, the lon-gitudinal ethological approach resulted in data where such sounds were not attributed to babies in any of the laboratories.

All three laboratories noticed that there were stages of development in the use of certain categories of sounds in human infants, and, notably, all were struck by the occurrence of a stage during which infants, rela-tively abruptly during the middle of the first year, began to produce well-formed syllables. These syllables were recognizable because they appeared to meet the intuitive requirements of syllables in natural languages (unlike prior sounds produced in infancy), and consequently these syllables could have been used to construct words, whereas prior utterances produced by the infants could not have been used to construct words.

I referred to these syllables as "canonical" and provided a formal defi-nition in the mid 1970s that attempted to capture the characteristics that a syllable must possess in order to qualify as a well-formed syllable in a natural language. I mention just a few of the components of the definition (which has been updated in Oller, 2000) here. A canonical syllable must possess

- a full, well-formed vowellike sound (or fully resonant nucleus), which implies that the syllable's nucleus must be produced with the vocal tract postured to produce a vowel (if the vocal tract is at rest, as it is in normal breathing, this requirement is not met);

- at least one articulated margin or consonantlike sound, including a closure or near closure of the supraglottal vocal tract; and
- a well-formed rapid transition between the articulated margin and the nucleus.

The requirements were specified provisionally in acoustic terms that are the subject of further work in our laboratories to the time of this writing. But it seems certain that the basic tenets of the definition will survive the test of time, because they summarize real principles of syllable formation in natural languages. For clarification's sake, let us consider a few examples of utterances that are canonical or noncanonical.

A syllable that sounds like [ba] (as we might pronounce it in saying "bah, humbug") is clearly canonical if it is articulated quickly. However, if one closes the lips for [b], begins to produce voicing, and then gradually opens the lips to the [a] position while continuing to produce voicing, the result is not a canonical but a "marginal" syllable. According to the provisional acoustic criteria of the definition, a canonical syllable requires a transition of 120 ms or less, and anything more than that invalidates the syllable as canonical. Indeed, listeners often take notice of the oddity of a syllable with a transition that seems especially long; they perceive the movement of the vocal tract as being too slow in terms of the pattern of change in the resonances of the vocal tract, which are perceived naturally by the human ear as "formants" of the acoustic signal (see Liberman, Delattre, Cooper, & Gerstman, 1954). Hence, we can say that the rapid transition requirement of articulatory movement in canonical syllables corresponds to a perceived rapid change in formant transitions. The impression given by very slowly articulated transitions is one of discoordination, of formant transitions that are too slow. Such a syllable simply does not sound as speechlike as one that has a rapid transition. Syllables that have full vowels but slow transitions are formally called "marginal babbling," and because their transitions are so long as to be ill-formed, they cannot be portrayed within the International Phonetic Alphabet.

There are other ways for syllables to fail to meet the criteria of canonicity. For example, an isolated vowellike sound does not meet the criterion. One might ask why such sounds should be excluded from the category of canonical babbling since all syllables require a nucleus (which is usually a vowel), since single vowels do constitute syllables, and since languages do sometimes have syllables formed of vowels only. The answer is that the definition of canonical syllables is intended to capture a somewhat more subtle idea than "possible syllable in a natural language." Instead, it is intended to characterize the kinds of syllables that possess all the key properties upon which an extremely efficient system of phonology can be built, a system capable of providing an indefinitely large corpus of word types, and a superefficient production/perception capability. Vowels alone do not offer such an option, but a combination of consonants and vowels in canonical syllables does. If one uses vowels only, the number of one-syllable words that can be created is trivially small (surely not more than a score even in a language with a particularly large vowel system). But as soon as consonants are added to the repertoire, the numbers of possible syllables multiply dramatically. Even languages with relatively streamlined phonologies (where consonant-vowel or CV syllables predominate), such as Spanish, can be shown to have at least a thousand possible single-syllable types, and English, where consonant clusters in both initial and final position are common, clearly has tens of thousands of individual syllables that are possible to draw on.

The advantage of having consonants *and* vowels in syllables also makes possible extremely rapid transmission of information in speech (Liberman, Cooper, Shankweiler, & Studdert-Kennedy, 1967). A remarkable characteristic of the speech code in all natural languages is that it depends so heavily on dynamic information of movement and transition between consonants and vowels. In fact, there is, relative to dynamic information, very little steady-state information in the speech code (Lindblom, 1967, 1983). A reasonable conclusion is that *the rapid formant transition is the critical feature* that makes speech production and speech perception work so well. Any syllable that lacks an auditorily trackable rapid formant transition lacks the capacity to carry the richness of information upon which the code is primarily built. Isolated vowels lack that capacity and so are excluded within the definition of canonicity.

Another category of sounds that are excluded from canonicity are sounds that have glottal consonants only. Again, the reason has to do with the lack of supraglottal articulation during the production of such sounds (consider the sequences [aha] or [aʔa]) and consequent lack of formant transitions that could be easily tracked auditorily. This lack of utilization of the key characteristic that gives phonological systems their power renders syllables with glottal consonants only less valuable than syllables that possess rich formant transitions.

Another category that is excluded from canonicity consists of syllables where the nucleus is not compatible with production of a highly differentiated formant transition because it is produced with the vocal tract at rest or closed, as in the case of syllables possessing a consonant plus a syllabic nasal. The second syllable in the word "button" as pronounced in most dialects of American English, for example, is a syllabic nasal, and because the vocal tract is closed during this nucleus, the transition from the preceding consonant is necessarily restricted in extent of movement, and the formant transitions are similarly more restricted than in the case of syllables with fully resonant, open-mouth nuclei. Babies often produce primitive, precanonical syllables, with nuclei where the vocal tract is closed or where it is in a roughly at-rest position (as in quasivowels). The consonantlike margins that accompany these primitive nuclei do entail formant transitions, but again, the transitions are notably restricted in extent and consequent auditory trackability.

In all these cases of exclusion, the problem with the precanonical syllables is that they do not possess well-formed, rapid transitions that the human ear could easily track and that therefore could participate in the system of phonology upon which both the speed of transmission of speech and the massive vocabulary of speech are built. But perhaps just as important, all these kinds of noncanonical syllables can be shown empirically to occur earlier in development than fully canonical syllables. Marginal babbling, isolated vowellike sounds, syllables with glottal articulations only, and syllables with quasivowels only as nuclei are all observed in infants prior to 6 months of age, so while the definition of canonical babbling is founded on *independent* principles that form the foundation of natural phonological systems, the principles of the definition play out in patterns of development in real infants, a strong indication that the formulation captures the essence of the principles that truly account for the power of speech as a system of communication.

THE AGE OF ONSET OF CANONICAL BABBLING IN HEARING AND DEAF INFANTS

In the context of the definition of canonical babbling, it was easy to see that hearing infants begin a stage where production of canonical syllables becomes routine and repetitive sometime in the middle of the first year of life. The three laboratories pursuing ethologically based description verified this point indisputably during the 1970s. In the context of this outcome, a tacit expectation developed that if an infant were to show very late onset of canonical babbling, there might be something amiss, simply because the onset of canonical babbling seemed to have all the earmarks of other developmental milestones, such as crawling, sitting unsupported, or rolling over. Pediatricians and developmental psychologists had long treated the ability of babies to say "dada" or "mama" as important developmental landmarks (see, e.g., Bayley, 1969; Gesell & Amatruda, 1941). While pediatricians and developmental psychologists of those times did not utilize the sort of systematic distinction between canonical and precanonical syllables that was developed in the 1970s, the germ of the idea seems to have been implied in their approach. Further, it appears that parents have always recognized canonical babbling, at least grossly, for what it is, a major step in development of the speech capacity. It would seem strange if parents did not recognize canonical babbling when it occurs, because otherwise they would have no basis for judging when babies are phonologically ready to start talking. The strange fact is not that parents have always been so capable, but that investigators failed to capture this intuitive capability of parents in scientific frameworks until late into the twentieth century.

My own first opportunity to observe the vocalizations of a deaf infant occurred within a few months of the time that our first longitudinal study had shown typically developing hearing infants consistently beginning canonical babbling about the middle of the first year of life. The definition of canonical babbling had just been formulated in a rough manner, and so the stage was set for a new kind of observation of a deaf infant.

The baby who provided the opportunity had been referred to the clinic at the University of Washington, where I was on the faculty at the time, and after verification of her profound hearing loss, she was entered into our longitudinal study of vocal development. By the time she was near the end of the first year of life, and had not yet begun canonical babbling, our research group had come to be justifiably suspicious that deafness was the cause of the apparent delay. The infant did eventually begin canonical babbling, but not until the second year of life. Data on her vocal development have been reported (although more than a decade after the recordings were made) in publications by our group and subsequent researchers at the University of Washington (Oller & Bull, 1984; Oller & Eilers, 1988; Stoel-Gammon & Otomo, 1986).

This individual child provided the first indication of what would turn into a flood of data showing that profoundly deaf infants develop canonical babbling later than do hearing infants. The first quantitative data published in a scientific journal, to my knowledge, actually came from another deaf infant evaluated at the University of Miami. The infant's recorded vocal samples were compared with those of a group of hearing infants (Oller, Eilers, Bull, & Carney, 1985). The deaf infant showed an onset of canonical babbling later than any of the hearing infants and, as with the prior deaf infant who had been studied, did not begin canonical babbling until the second year of life. Notably, this infant also showed an anomalously large proportion of utterances that included glottal consonantlike sounds only (rendering them, of course, noncanonical according to the formal definition). The syllables consisted of vowellike sounds plus glottal stops. These "glottal sequences" have proven to be notably more common in the early vocal productions of deaf than of hearing infants even during the first half-year of life.

After this report was published, a number of additional publications of longitudinal research data both in North America and in Europe supported the idea that deaf infants show later onset of canonical babbling. The effect has been found to be extremely powerful, with hearing infants nearly always showing onset of canonical babbling by not later than 10 months of age and profoundly deaf infants rarely showing canonical babbling that early and usually not until well into the second year of life (Eilers & Oller, 1994; Koopmans-van Beinum et al., 2001; Oller & Eilers, 1988; Stoel-Gammon & Otomo, 1986; Vinter, 1994a, 1994b).

THE IMPORTANCE OF KEEPING TRACK
OF SEVERITY OF HEARING LOSS

To explain why deaf infants show late-onset canonical babbling, it was posited by many that auditory input must serve as a trigger for the maturation of vocalizations. The logical question posed in the face this hypothesis was, if auditory input is necessary, why should deaf infants ever start canonical babbling? The answer appears to be that, although hearing loss has a retarding effect on the onset of canonical babbling, it is not an absolute effect. Rather, the effect depends on the degree of hearing loss, and perhaps on amount of input from other sensory modalities regarding speech articulation and sound. Even profoundly impaired infants nearly always have some, although very limited, hearing, and so perhaps their onset of canonical babbling is triggered more slowly than in hearing infants by accumulated input through the auditory modality. It has been demonstrated that age at which amplification of impaired hearing is applied is positively correlated with onset of canonical babbling (Eilers & Oller, 1994). A study of an acochlear deaf baby's vocal development showed that even in a child with total lack of auditory information, canonical babbling can eventually begin (Lynch, Oller, & Steffens, 1989). In the case of the acochlear child, it appeared that both visual stimulation in lipreading training and tactile stimulation that was provided through a multichannel vocoder worn by the child during intervention may have played important roles in the onset of canonical babbling. Thus, it seems clear that the delaying effect of hearing loss is relative and should be evaluated in light of degree of hearing loss and possible influences of other sensory modalities.

Koopmans-van Beinum et al. (1998, 2001) have provided evidence that infants even in the near profound range of hearing loss can show an onset of canonical babbling prior to 11 months of age in some instances. By the late 1990s we had observed at least one such case as well, and furthermore, infants in our longitudinal studies who had hearing losses in the severe rather than the profound range tended to have relatively earlier onset of canonical babbling even when that onset was not within the range for hearing infants. Subsequent work has suggested that there may be a retarding effect of hearing loss on onset of canonical babbling even in some moderately impaired infants (Nathani et al., 2001).

The most reasonable conclusion from the existing studies appears to be that deafness does not prevent onset of canonical babbling, but that profound hearing loss dramatically increases the likelihood of a late onset. In general, researchers in the field have been of one voice on the sharp distinction in onset that occurs between hearing infants and infants who show very profound hearing loss, but the data for infants with lesser hearing losses suggest that the differentiability from hearing infants is attenuated.

OTHER SIMILARITIES AND DIFFERENCES
BETWEEN VOCALIZATIONS OF DEAF
AND HEARING INFANTS IN THE FIRST YEAR

It has already been noted that glottal sequences (noncanonical syllable sequences where vocalization is broken up by glottal stops) have
been reported to occur more frequently in deaf than in hearing infants.
A variety of studies have reported this pattern (Koopmans-van Beinum
et al., 2001; Oller, 1991; Oller & Bull, 1984; Oller et al., 1985; Stoel-
Gammon & Otomo, 1986). Glottal sequences are often notably similar
in rhythmic character to the syllables that occur in reduplicated canonical babbling. Glottal sequences have been observed in repetitive
strings in a deaf infant as young as 4 months of age (Oller & Bull, 1984;
Oller, 1991). The significance of this observation is somewhat uncertain,
although glottal sequences do seem to constitute specific precursors to
reduplicated canonical babbling in deaf infants. One of the primary reasons for drawing attention to glottal sequences is that they constitute
the strongest evidence to date that deaf infants may show vocalization
anomalies in comparison with hearing infants during the precanonical
period, even in the first half-year of life.

    In general, observers of the vocalizations of deaf infants agree that,
with only isolated exceptions, such as the occurrence of larger proportions of glottal sequences, vocalizations of deaf infants include many
similarities with vocalizations of hearing infants. Both groups squeal
and growl, yell and whisper; both produce raspberries and many vowellike sounds in vocal play. To say that there are many similarities in
the types of sounds that occur precanonically does not, of course, imply
that other differences will not be found on closer examination. For
example, usage patterns for different vocal types in social interaction of
deaf and hearing infants have scarcely been evaluated to date. Such
research may indeed reveal additional differences between deaf and
hearing infants' babbling.

THE PRACTICAL USES OF THE NEW PERSPECTIVE
IN INFANT VOCALIZATIONS FOR ASSESSMENT
OF VOCAL PROGRESS IN DEAF INFANTS

The sharp differentiation of profoundly deaf and hearing infants in the
onset of canonical babbling has alerted the community of pediatricians,
speech-language pathologists, audiologists, deaf educators, and other
developmental scientists and practitioners to the idea there is a new way
to look at early vocal development. In the absence of a framework of
description that distinguishes clearly between canonical and precanonical
syllables, it would be impossible to notice key early developments. Consequently, researchers evaluating cochlear implants nowadays often take

specific account of the occurrence of canonical and precanonical vocalizations (see, e.g., Ertmer et al., 2002; Gillis, Schauwers, Govaerts, &
Koopmans van Beinum, 2003). The tracking of the onset of canonical
babbling after implantation provides a useful tool to capture the beginning of a key developmental phenomenon. This fact is reflected in substantial predictability in both hearing and deaf infants for onset of real
words within a few months after the onset of canonical babbling in the
vast majority of cases (Oller, Levine, Eilers, & Pearson, 1998).

At a general level, judging the onset of canonical babbling in a hearing
infant is fairly easy. Studies on the ability of parents to designate the
onset of canonical babbling by simply describing their baby's vocalizations show that their judgments match those of independent laboratory
staff trained on the formal definition of canonical babbling along with
systematic exposure to recorded examples of canonical and precanonical
sounds. The degree of parental accuracy is remarkable, with greater than
95% concordance of laboratory and parent judgments (Oller, Eilers, &
Basinger, 2001). Consequently, there is good reason to proceed with
application of the tools of canonical and precanonical babbling evaluation in the case of deaf infants.

THE DANGER OF OVERINTERPRETING THE HIGH RELIABILITY
OF JUDGMENT OF ONSET OF CANONICAL BABBLING

While it is easy to identify a hearing infant as either being in the canonical stage or not based upon a brief sample of not more than a half
an hour, and while it is easy to administer a parent questionnaire, even
on the telephone, to acquire similarly reliable information about an
infant's canonical or precanonical status, it is quite a different matter to
categorize all the syllables in a sample of vocalizations from a baby as
canonical or precanonical. Even the best-trained observers have notable
difficulty in identifying many individual syllables produced by hearing
infants as canonical or precanonical.

This fact produces no major problem if one wishes merely to assign
hearing infants to the canonical or precanonical stage, but it raises very
large issues if one wishes to perform more detailed analyses that are to
be focused, for example, on canonical syllables only (see, e.g., Davis &
MacNeilage, 1995). Phonetic transcription of canonical syllables clearly
has substantial value at some point in development, but it is unclear
whether phonetic transcription reliability is high enough even in the
early canonical stage to warrant the effort of performing it. A critical
issue is that reliability of observation on the phonetic content of canonical syllables cannot be usefully assessed in the absence of a prior
determination of the degree of reliability of the assignment of syllables
to the canonical category. Transcriptions of consonant and vowellike
elements from presumable canonical syllables depend logically upon

the distinction of canonical and noncanonical syllables, and without assessment of reliability on the logically prior canonical assignment, any reliability evaluation on transcription is uninterpretable because it assumes that the error of judgment on canonicity is equal to 0, which we can be sure it is not.

Such methodological problems are particularly notable when we address the vocalizations of the deaf infant, because the onset of canonical babbling in deaf infants is apparently less sharp and less easy to determine than in hearing infants. Our research has taken note of this difficulty for years. Deaf infants appear to be more likely to show fits and starts in the onset of canonical babbling. Further, deaf infants may be particularly likely to continue producing marginal babbling even after some degree of canonical syllable control has entered their repertoire. Consequently, it may be even more difficult with deaf infants than with hearing infants to assign syllables to the canonical or precanonical categories. And the problem of assignment (which attenuates with age as infants gain control of vocalization) of sounds to the canonical category may persist much longer in deaf children than in hearing ones.

RECOMMENDATIONS ABOUT DESCRIPTION OF EARLY VOCALIZATIONS IN DEAF INFANTS

The new perspective on vocalization development suggests that in precanonical stages of vocal development, description of vocalizations of deaf infants should be made with no less caution than in the case of hearing infants (and perhaps more caution is warranted). Since canonical syllables can be expected to occur rarely during precanonical stages, there is no logical justification for using phonetic transcription for infant sounds occurring during those periods. Instead, precanonical sounds should be categorized according to the global groupings to which they or their subunits pertain, for example, quasivowels, full vowellike sounds, squeals, growls, yells, whispers, raspberries, glottal sequences, and marginal babbles.

Of course, occasional canonical syllables will occur even in an infant who is not yet in the canonical stage, but such syllables occur neither frequently nor repetitively in very young infants and so are sensibly deemed to represent *accidental* occurrences of utterances that meet the requirements of canonicity. Infant vocalizations occur with extreme variety, and it should be no surprise that occasionally the exploratory tendency of the infant produces accidental conformity to principles of well-formedness. Only after the infant can produce sounds meeting those principles consistently and under voluntary control can we proceed in the direction of phonetic description with justification.

Even after the canonical stage is reached, however, there are reasons to treat phonetic transcription with great caution, partly because most of the sounds produced by infants early in the canonical stage will still be pre-canonical, and also because phonetic transcription can easily be over-interpreted to imply that infants are fully in control of all the consonant and vowel categories that listeners may perceive in the infants' productions. The fact that an infant produces one syllable that sounds like [ba] and another that sounds like [βa] (with a bilabial fricative) does not necessarily mean that the infant *intends to produce* or *controls the production of* the phonetic contrast implied by the symbols indicated. The baby may in fact produce a wide variety of syllables that include various degrees of voicing at the onsets of the syllables, some of which may sound like [ba] and some like [βa], but until the baby systematically differentiates such elements, as indicated either by repetitive production of each, or by systematic usage of each in different social circumstances, there is no evidence that the baby controls the contrast between the sounds. And until the infant controls the contrast, there is danger of overinterpretation of a transcription that implies the contrast. At most, the infant production of a syllable type within a group of vocalizations that encompasses many variations where some may be perceived by adult listeners as [ba] and some as [βa] suggests that eventually the infant could come to control the contrast (if that contrast occurs in the language the infant is learning). These considerations apply to any speech sound contrast that might be perceived by an adult listener in infant vocalizations. Even if the baby seems to produce very familiar syllables, seemingly demonstrating a contrast between elements of the language the infant is hearing ([ba] and [ma], e.g., for an infant in an English-speaking home), it is not clear that the infant commands the contrast unless the elements can be produced contrastively on some consistent basis. The mere impression that both syllable types have been produced by the baby on some occasion does not prove that the baby intends to produce the contrast or that the baby has control of the contrast.

Further, in the very early canonical stage, production of a well-formed syllable that is transcribed the same way by multiple adult listeners does not prove that the infant possesses command of independent consonants and vowels. For example, infant production of a syllable transcribed as [ba] does not prove that the infant has a consonant [b] and a vowel [a]. It may merely prove that the infant has a syllable with a labial onset and a jaw-lowering movement (MacNeilage, 1998). To provide concrete evidence of the independent function of a consonant and a vowel in the syllable, one must observe that the particular consonant gesture implied by the transcription [ba] can be produced systematically by the baby with other particular vowel sounds and that the particular vowel sound can be produced systematically with other consonants.

There are more than just theoretical reasons for being concerned about the possibility of overinterpreting canonical syllables in infancy when using phonetic transcription. The research of MacNeilage and colleagues on early syllable development has provided empirical evidence that early syllables in infancy are not fully analyzed by infants into consonant and vowel components. Infants tend to use particular consonantlike gestures (as perceived by transcribers) with particular vowellike gestures (as perceived by transcribers). Lack of free recombinability of the apparent consonants and vowels is evidence of lack of independent function of each, and consequently the conservative approach to interpretation must impute to the baby who produces such sounds only syllabic-level units. Ironically, it is through phonetic transcription of baby sounds that MacNeilage and his colleagues have provided the primary evidence of this relative lack of independence of consonant and vowellike elements in the infant. My personal interpretation of this research focuses on its irony: The lack of independence that is seen in the data seems to prove that the method of description that yielded the data is itself inappropriate insofar as it suggests the existence of a level of function in the infant that includes separate categories of consonants and vowels.

So what are we to do in order to quantify early canonical stage vocalizations? Babies who have entered the canonical stage are clearly more advanced than are those who have not, but how do we prove it if we cannot phonetically transcribe the canonical utterances with confidence? We are not totally at a loss here. We can provide a quantitative account by determining the proportion of syllables or utterances in a sample of the infant's vocalizations that meet the canonical requirement. This is called a "canonical babbling ratio" (number of canonical utterances divided by total number of utterances), and we know that this ratio increases with age; consequently, the measure can reasonably be taken as an indicator of the degree to which the infant has gained consolidated control of canonical vocalization (see Lewedag, 1995; Oller, Eilers, Steffens, Lynch, & Urbano, 1994). In fact, the canonical babbling ratio can be used as a justifiable measure of speechlike quality in infant sounds across the entire first year of life.

Of course, it is clear that at some point in development the concerns about using phonetic transcription can be relaxed with confidence. The question is when and how we can tell that the point has been reached. Frankly, we do not yet know where to draw the line. Once a child is using a large number of meaningful words composed of canonical syllables (perhaps 50 or more; see Vihman, 1996) that are clearly differentiable in their contexts of usage by the child, it can be argued reasonably that there must be some true phonetic system that is emerging, including both consonants and vowels. But even a 50-word criterion is at best a heuristic at this point. Science has not yet provided clear criteria for when transcription becomes valid. In fact, it may never be possible to designate a particular point in time when transcription becomes suddenly appropriate. Rather, it may be more sensible to assume that the infant's gradual progress in gaining control of speechlike sounds produces a gradually increasing justification for using a transcriptional method. If we accept this view, we also have to accept the fact that the earlier in development we begin to use phonetic transcription, the more trouble we are likely to have in making sense of the data thus produced.

At the very least, each time one decides to use a phonetic transcriptional method with infants, it is crucial to differentiate between the utterances that are canonical and those that are not. This will not be a trivial problem. While we can determine with high reliability whether a particular hearing infant is in the canonical stage, we cannot assume that every utterance produced by the infant can be judged with similar reliability to be canonical. It appears that we are able to judge reliably at the infant level because *some* utterances of the canonical baby are clearly canonical and because these clear cases occur with sufficient repetitiveness to be noticeable by a variety of listeners. Even in the canonical baby, however, many utterances will be much harder to judge. Marginal babbles and syllables with quasivowels are vexingly difficult to categorize reliably, and many syllables that are deemed canonical by one observer may be judged to be marginal syllables or quasivowel syllables by another. This difficulty of categorization produces a problem that one cannot afford to ignore if one wishes to use phonetic transcription to characterize infant utterances, even if one makes the sensible decision to use phonetic transcription *only* with the canonical sounds. The problem is, as noted above, that the reliability of transcription itself cannot be assessed in the absence of assessing the reliability of the assignment of utterances to the canonical or precanonical categories. One cannot reasonably claim to have, for example, 80% intertranscriber reliability (a value that is typical reported in literature in child phonology) for utterances that are preselected as canonical and then transcribed as such, unless that value of 80% includes the error factor for the selection of canonical syllables as well. Our experience is that transcription of early canonical utterances yields much lower reliability values if one takes the issue of assignment to the canonical category into account. How low the value is may depend on the level of development of the infant, with more advanced infants producing more clearly well-formed utterances and consequently higher reliability for transcription.

Of course, all the problems of methodology are magnified in the case of work with deaf infants whose precanonical stage lasts longer, and whose canonical stage appears to begin less distinctly. Consequently, precanonical sounds persist longer in deaf babies, and whether individual utterances are canonical is harder to determine. And as the difficulty of assigning utterances to the canonical category increases, so the reliability of potential phonetic transcription decreases. Again, all the problems of methodology are magnified in working with deaf infants, all the more reason for us to apply what we have learned about early vocal development in hearing infants with special care when we approach the study of progress in infants and children who are deaf or hard of hearing.

In this new age of cochlear implantation, the press to provide clear evidence of progress in children receiving the intervention needs to be tempered with the awareness that the task of demonstrating progress is dependent upon careful thinking and careful analysis. At the earliest stages of progress, it may be tempting to leap to phonetic transcription, but that leap is interpretively perilous, and there are other, better-founded options for description and tracking of progress. A deaf infant or child who moves from a precanonical condition to the canonical stage has made notable progress. Further, a deaf infant or child whose canonical babbling ratio increases reliably has made notable progress. These are observation types that should stand the test of time. My argument does not, of course, call for the abandonment of phonetic transcription as a tool of description. Instead, I argue for judicious choices in its use and for the recognition that at very early stages of development, phonetic transcription may confuse more than it clarifies.

ACKNOWLEDGMENT

This work has been supported by a grant from NIDCD (R01DC006099 to D. K. Oller, PI) and by the Plough Foundation.

REFERENCES

Bayley, N. (1969). *Bayley scales of infant development: Birth to two years*. New York: Psychological Corporation.

Davis, B. L., & MacNeilage, P. F. (1995). The articulatory basis of babbling. *Journal of Speech and Hearing Research, 38*, 1199–1211.

Eilers, R. E., & Oller, D. K. (1994). Infant vocalizations and the early diagnosis of severe hearing impairment. *Journal of Pediatrics, 124*, 199–203.

Ertmer, D. J., Young, N., Grohne, K., Mellon, J. A., Johnson, C., Corbett, K., et al. (2002). Vocal development in young children with cochlear implants: Profiles and implications for intervention. *Language, Speech, and Hearing Services in Schools, 33*(3), 184–195.

Gesell, A., & Amatruda, C. S. (1941). *Developmental diagnosis*. New York: P. B. Hoeber.

Gillis, S., Schauwers, K., Govaerts, P., & Koopmans van Beinum, F. (2003). *Babbling: A comparison of children with differing degrees of hearing*. International Conference on the Ontogeny and Phylogeny of Syllable Organization. Barcelona: University of Barcelona.

Jewett, D. L., Romano, M. N., & Williston, J. S. (1970). Human auditory evoked potentials: Possible brain stem components detected on the scalp. *Science, 167*, 1517–1518.

Kaczmarek, L. (1971). A general view of the formation of child language. In A. Bar-Adon & W. F. Leopold (Eds.), *Child language: A book of readings* (pp. 133–134). Englewood Cliffs, NJ: Prentice-Hall. (Original work published 1953 as a summary of his book *Ksztaltowanie sie mowy dziecka* [Poznan, 1953]).

Koopmans-van Beinum, F. J., Clement, C. J., & van den Dikkenberg-Pot, I. (1998, July). *Influence of lack of auditory speech perception on sound productions of deaf infants.* Berne, Switzerland: International Society for the Study of Behavioral Development.

Koopmans-van Beinum, F. J., Clement, C. J., & van den Dikkenberg-Pot, I. (2001). Babbling and the lack of auditory speech perception: A matter of coordination? *Developmental Science, 4*(1), 61–70.

Lenneberg, E. (1967). *Biological foundations of language.* New York: John Wiley & Sons.

Lenneberg, E., Rebelsky, F. G., & Nichols, I. A. (1965). The vocalizations of infants born to deaf and hearing parents. *Vita Humana (Human Development), 8,* 23–37.

Lewedag, V. L. (1995). *Patterns of onset of canonical babbling among typically developing infants.* Unpublished doctoral dissertation, University of Miami, Coral Gables, FL.

Lewis, M. M. (1936). *Infant speech.* New York: Harcourt Brace.

Liberman, A. M., Cooper, F. S., Shankweiler, D. P., & Studdert-Kennedy, M. (1967). Perception of the speech code. *Psychological Review, 74,* 431–461.

Liberman, A. M., Delattre, P. C., Cooper, F. S., & Gerstman, L. J. (1954). The role of consonant-vowel transitions in the perception of the stop and nasal consonants. *Psychological Monographs, 68,* 127–137.

Lindblom, B. (1967). Vowel duration and a model of lip mandible coordination. *Speech Transmission Laboratory Quarterly Progress and Status Report, 4,* 1–29.

Lindblom, B. (1983). Economy of speech guestures. In P. F. MacNeilage (Ed.), *The production of speech* (pp. 217–246). New York: Springer-Verlag.

Lorenz, K. (1951). Ausdrucksbewegungen höherer Tiere. *Naturwissenschaften, 38,* 113–116.

Lynch, M. P., Oller, D. K., & Steffens, M. (1989). Development of speech-like vocalizations in a child with congenital absence of cochleas: The case of total deafness. *Applied Psycholinguistics, 10,* 315–333.

MacNeilage, P. F. (1998). The frame/content theory of evolution of speech production. *Behavioral and Brain Sciences, 21*(4), 499–546.

Mavilya, M. (1969). *Spontaneous vocalizations and babbling in hearing impaired infants.* University Microfilms No. 70-12879. Unpublished doctoral dissertation, Columbia University, New York.

Moore, J. M., Thompson, G., & Thompson, M. (1975). Auditory localization of infants as a function of reinforcement conditions. *Journal of Speech and Hearing Disorders, 40,* 29–34.

Murchison, C., & Langer, S. K. (Trans.). (1971). Tiedemann's observations on the development of the mental faculties of children. In A. Bar-Adon & W. F. Leopold (Eds.), *Child language: A book of readings* 13–17. Englewood Cliffs, NJ: Prentice-Hall. (Reprinted from *Pedagogical Seminary and Journal of Genetic Psychology, 34,* 205–230, 1927)

Mykelbust, H. (1954). *Auditory disorders in children.* New York: Grune and Stratton.

Nathani, S., Neal, A. R., Olds, H., Brill, J., & Oller, D. K. (2001, April). *Canonical babbling and volubility in infants with moderate to severe hearing impairment.* Boston, MA: International Child Phonology Conference.

Oller, D. K. (1976, Nov. 18–21). *Analysis of infant vocalizations: A linguistic and speech scientific perspective.* Mini-seminar presented at the Convention of the American Speech and Hearing Association, Houston, TX.

Oller, D. K. (1978). Infant vocalization and the development of speech. *Allied Health and Behavioral Sciences, 1,* 523–549.

Oller, D. K. (1980). The emergence of the sounds of speech in infancy. In G. Yeni-Komshian, J. Kavanagh, & C. Ferguson (Eds.), *Child phonology: Vol. 1. Production* (pp. 93–112). New York: Academic Press.

Oller, D. K. (1991). Similarities and differences in vocalizations of deaf and hearing infants: Future directions for research. In J. Miller (Ed.), *Research on child language disorders: A decade of progress* (pp. 277–284). Austin, TX: Pro-ed.

Oller, D. K. (2000). *The emergence of the speech capacity.* Mahwah, NJ: Lawrence Erlbaum.

Oller, D. K., & Bull, D. (1984, April). *Vocalizations of deaf infants.* Presented as a Poster at the International Conference on Infant Studies, New York, NY.

Oller, D. K., & Eilers, R. E. (1975). Phonetic expectation and transcription validity. *Phonetica, 31,* 288–304.

Oller, D. K., & Eilers, R. E. (1988). The role of audition in infant babbling. *Child Development, 59,* 441–449.

Oller, D. K., Eilers, R. E., & Basinger, D. (2001). Intuitive identification of infant vocal sounds by parents. *Developmental Science, 4*(1), 49–60.

Oller, D. K., Eilers, R. E., Bull, D. H., & Carney, A. E. (1985). Pre-speech vocalizations of a deaf infant: A comparison with normal metaphonological development. *Journal of Speech and Hearing Research, 28,* 47–63.

Oller, D. K., Eilers, R. E., Steffens, M. L., Lynch, M. P., & Urbano, R. (1994). Speech-like vocalizations in infancy: An evaluation of potential risk factors. *Journal of Child Language, 21,* 33–58.

Stark, R. E. (1978). Features of infant sounds: The emergence of cooing. *Journal of Child Language, 5,* 379–390.

Stoel-Gammon, C., & Otomo, K. (1986). Babbling development of hearing impaired and normally hearing subjects. *Journal of Speech and Hearing Disorders, 51,* 33–41.

Tinbergen, N. (1951). *The study of instinct.* Oxford: Oxford University Press.

Vihman, M. M. (1996). *Phonological development: The origins of language in the child.* Cambridge, MA: Blackwell Publishers.

Vinter, S. (1994a). L'analyse du babillage: Une contribution au diagnostic de surdité? *Approche Neuropsychologique des Apprentissages chez l'Enfant, 6*(4), 232–238.

Vinter, S. (1994b). *L'émergence du langage de l'enfant déficient auditif: Des premiers sons aux premiers mots* [The emergence of language in the hearing impaired infant: From the first sounds to the first words]. Paris: Masson.

Zlatin, M. (1975). *Preliminary descriptive model of infant vocalization during the first 24 weeks: Primitive syllabification and phonetic exploratory behavior.* Final Rep., Proj. No. 3-4014, NE-G-00-3-0077. Bethesda, MD, National Institutes of Health.

3

Development of Communicative Behavior as a Precursor of Spoken Language in Hearing Infants, With Implications for Deaf and Hard-of-Hearing Infants

Nobuo Masataka

The purpose of this chapter is twofold. First, it outlines an approach to the development of expressive and communicative behavior of typically developing hearing infants until the onset of single-word utterances. I argued here that expressive and communicative actions are organized as a complex and cooperative system with other elements of the infant's physiology, behavior, and the social environment. Second, implications of the findings for deaf and hard-of-hearing infants will be discussed. By integrating the deafness-related issues, in this chapter I attempt to provide a source of information to chart directions for future research about spoken language development in deaf and hard-of-hearing children.

Although children do not produce linguistically meaningful sounds or signs until they are approximately 1 year old, the ability to produce them begins to develop in early infancy, and important developments in the production of language occur throughout the first year of life. Unless they have a hearing loss, infants acquire phonology during their first year. In spoken language, the acquisition of phonology consists of learning to distinguish and produce the sound patterns of the adult language. At birth, the newborn has the ability to distinguish virtually all sounds used in all languages, at least when the sounds are presented in isolation (Iverson & Kuhl, 1995). The newborn produces no speech sounds, however. During the first year of life, speechlike sounds gradually emerge, beginning with vowellike coos at 6–8 weeks of age, followed by some consonant sounds, then followed by true babbling (Masataka, 2003). By the end of the first year, hearing children are typically babbling sequences of syllables that have the intonation

contour of their target languages. Finally, meaningful words are produced; that is, the onset of speech occurs.

Such an overview of the early process of spoken language acquisition might lead us to question how the presence or absence of any
experience affects the linguistic behavior that infants acquire. In order
to respond to that, a cross-cultural approach is taken in this chapter,
which focuses on the chronological development of infants in Japan but
also includes information about development of infants in other cultures learning different languages. Another variation considered is that
of infants who lack the ability to receive and process auditory input. It
is well known that the speech abilities of children who receive reduced
or no auditory input in infancy are poor or completely absent. Hearing
loss that is bilateral and permanent is estimated to be present in 1.2–5.7
per 1,000 live births (Mauk & Bahrens, 1993). To develop spoken language despite significant hearing loss, therapeutic interventions are required. Nonetheless, as to the question of how the ontogenetic process
for vocal behavior differs between deaf and hearing infants over the
first year of life, little is known to date.

Infants with hearing loss, especially if they are reared by adults who
have acquired any form of sign language, usually develop the ability to
produce meaningful signs by the end of the first year (Takei, 2002). This
strongly indicates that the pattern of early language acquisition in
the manual mode is somehow equivalent to that in the vocal mode.
Nonetheless, the question about the degree to which they are similar to
one another has not yet been adequately answered. This chapter is a
preliminary attempt to address this issue.

THE DEVELOPMENT OF THE ABILITY TO TAKE TURNS

One of the major milestones in early interactional development, before
the onset of true language, is the skill of conversational turn-taking.
The ability to participate cooperatively in shared discourse is fundamental to social development in general. Thus, a considerable amount of
research has been conducted on this issue. Several investigators have
found a marked increase in vocal turn taking between 12 and 18 weeks
of age (Ginsburg & Kilbourne, 1988). Studies suggest that, at this age,
infants begin to forestall vocalization if their mother is speaking and fall
silent if their mother starts to speak (Moran, Krupka, Tutton, & Symons,
1987), a practice that intensifies in subsequent months (Papousek &
Papousek, 1989). Vocal turn taking may be related to maternal attachment. For one thing, infants are more likely to turn off their own voice if
that increases perceptual access to the voice of a person they want to hear
(Barrett-Goldfarb & Whitehurst, 1973). Moreover, Bowlby (1969) suggests that attachment begins in earnest when infants' preference for
their mother's company is satisfied not just facially but either facially or

vocally. Since the phase in which this happens usually begins at about 12 weeks, attachment may commence at about the same time as vocal turn taking. The previous general consensus was that by the time the infant is 8 or 9 months old, the parent and the child achieve remarkably smoothly coordinated sequences in terms of vocalizations and use of gaze. However, it appears that conversational abilities develop in infants much earlier than has been commonly assumed.

In my own experimentation, when a group of 3–4-month-old infants experienced either contingent conversational turn taking or random responsiveness in interaction with their mothers, contingency was found to alter the temporal parameters of the infant's vocal pattern (Masataka, 1993a). Infants tended to produce more bursts or packets of vocalizations when the mother talked to the infant in a random way. When the infants were 3 months old, such bursts of vocalization occurred most often at intervals of 0.5–1.5 s whereas when they were 4 months old they took place most frequently at significantly longer intervals, of 1.0–2.0 s. This difference corresponded to the difference between intervals with which the mother responded contingently to vocalizations of the infant at the age of 3 months and 4 months respectively. While the intervals (between the onset of the infant's vocalization and the onset of the mother's vocalization) rarely exceeded 0.5 s when the infant was 3 months old, they were mostly distributed between 0.5 and 1.0 s when 4 months of age. After vocalizing spontaneously, the infant tended to pause as if to listen for a possible vocal response from the mother. In the absence of a response, he vocalized repeatedly. The intervals between the two consecutive vocalizations were changed flexibly by the infant according to his recent experience of turn taking with the mother. Thus, protoconversational abilities of infants at these ages may already be intentional.

In fact, turn-taking behavior develops even if infants are unable to produce noncry vocalizations. It is known that the newborn human infant sucks in bursts consisting of about 4–10 sucks at rate slightly slower than 1/s. The bursts are separated by pauses of roughly the same order of magnitude, 4–15 s, with the nipple remaining in the infant's mouth. Some 40 mammalian species have had their sucking recorded, and the clustering of sucks into bursts separated by pauses is apparently unique to humans (Brown, 1973; Wolff, 1968). The function of the pauses has long been a mystery (Susswein, 1905). Kaye (1982) found that mothers tend to jiggle their newborn infants at the breast, or jiggle the bottle, during pauses of the newborn's sucking. When mothers engaged in natural and unconstrained feeding of their infants at 2 weeks and 8 weeks old, the cessation of jiggling proved to be a better elicitor of a resumption of sucking than the jiggling itself. My experiment in which bottles were jiggled according to a predetermined, controlled schedule showed that this phenomenon is due to a contingent

response. Which explanation is more plausible could be examined if hearing mother–deaf infant dyads of the same age are observed in the same experimental setting. This is one of the important issues to be investigated in the future, a study that would yield information both about communication development in deaf children and about language development more broadly.

Effects of Adult Responses Upon the Quality of Infant Cooing

The timing and quality of adult vocal responses affect the social vocalizations of 3–4-month-old infants. Moreover, the quality of vocalizations uttered by infants at these ages is found, in turn, to affect the adult. In a study by Bloom and Masataka (1996), adults viewed videotapes of 24 three-month-old infants who were engaged in social vocalizations. Of the 24 infants, three represented each of the six possible dichotomous characteristics: vocal quality (speechlike/nonspeech vocalizations), physiognomic attractiveness (high/low), and gender (female/male). After viewing each infant, the adults were asked to rate the infant on one of two scales of perceived favorableness. The results of this experiment revealed consistent strong preferences by adult for infants who produced speechlike vocalizations, as compared with nonspeech sounds. The experiment was undertaken both in Canada and in Japan, and its results showed robust cross-cultural universality.

As a next step in the analysis, we attempted to determine quantitatively the acoustic properties that distinguished speechlike and nonspeech vocalizations. This was done because the classification of infant sounds that had been reported so far was performed by rather subjective analysis. It had been observed that certain sounds seemed more appealing to adult listeners. Indeed, naive observers make comments such as "this baby sounds as though he is really talking" in reaction to some of the sounds and not to others. By collecting and comparing hundreds of vocalizations, two categories emerged. The categories were actually defined perceptually, that is, in terms of how the vocalizations were perceived by investigators trained to code and count the sounds of 3–4-month-olds. We then conducted spectrographic analysis on Canadian infants' vocalizations that had previously been labeled as either speechlike or nonspeech. Results of the spectrographic analysis revealed that two types of sounds are distinguished from one another by two parameters, their duration and degree of nasality.

We undertook similar analyses on Japanese mother–infant dyads who were interacting with one another under natural circumstances. In this situation, noncry, nonvegetative infant vocalizations were independently categorized as "responded-to" or "not-responded-to" vocalizations. If the mother's utterance occurred within 3 s after the infant's vocalization, the infant's vocalization was categorized as a vocalization that had been responded to. Otherwise, the vocalization was regarded as not responded to. When the same spectrographic analysis was performed, the two types of sounds proved to be acoustically distinguished from one another by exactly the same parameters as those in the previous analysis on Canadian infants, that is, by duration and degree of nasality.

This finding suggests that these acoustic properties actually differentially affect the responses of the mother to infant vocalizations. Furthermore, infant vocalizations that are responded to by mothers under naturalistic circumstances are also preferred by adult listeners on the basis of their acoustic properties alone. Finally, when listening to those vocalizations that vary in degree of nasality but do not differ in duration, Japanese adults perceive less nasal sounds as more favorable. Adults' preference for 3–4-month-old infant vocalizations appears to be determined largely by difference in nasality. Based on this parameter, the more favorable impressions awarded to speechlike vocalization help the adult to maintain "conversations" with nonverbal infants. Because such sounds are more speechlike, they frame the infant as a potential conversational partner, and this phenomenon could be cross-linguistically universal.

As to the question of whether the quality of speechlike vocalizations of deaf infants of the same age is affected or not by the responses of caretakers, no information is available. Concerning nonspeech sounds, however, relations between hearing ability and the acoustic feature of so-called basic cries (Truby & Lind, 1965) were found by Moller and Schonweiler (1999). They found that hard-of-hearing infants' cries had a longer call duration, lower energy in the bands 2–4 kHz and 6.4–9.5 kHz, and a more complex melody contour than did hearing infants' cries, whereas no differences were found between the two groups of infants in fundamental frequency and in tonality. The findings are confirmed by Scheiner, Hammerschmidt, Jurgens, and Zwirner (2002).

The above results were interpreted on the basis of the three-level hierarchical processing model for cry production that was developed by Golub (1980). In the model, physiological input such as pain, blood levels, and respiratory constraints have an influence on the production of cries with respect to the mean and range of fundamental frequency as well as other direct source-related parameters such as tonality. On the other hand, other constituents of the vocalization process such as the control of phonation (melody, intensity) and the spectral shaping (articulation) might be affected by related sensory feedback. Presumably, for example, differences observed between hearing and hard-of-hearing infants likely result from the extra effort on the part of the latter children spent to obtain auditory feedback.

THE DEVELOPMENT OF VOCAL IMITATION

Most previous theories of imitation, whether in the learning theory tradition (Bandura & Walters, 1963; Miller & Dollard, 1941) or in the psychoanalytic tradition (Freud, 1924), assumed that matching (or imitation) behavior by children is primarily a social act that requires perceptual and cognitive skills not likely to be available much before the end of the first year of life. However, there are several alternatives to this common view (e.g., Meltzoff & Moore, 1977). Indeed, it might seem that one achieves linguistic capability and then sets out to use it, but in order to develop the capacity for language the human infant must learn a particular language. An infant learns a language by observing people who are using that language (Kuhl & Meltzoff, 1982; Locke, 1994), regardless of whether the infant learns language in the vocal mode or the manual mode. Nevertheless, virtually all research motivated by such a notion has concerned the spoken language development of hearing infants.

Before they can imitate the spoken language of others, infants must come to separate speech from nonspeech activities and pay preferential attention to the linguistically relevant actions of people who are speaking (because there are many sights and sounds in the infant's environment that are unrelated to talking). Thus, in the first phase in the development of linguistic capacity, hearing infants learn and respond to properties of the human voice. Evidence is converging to suggest that vocal learning begins prenatally, when the fetus learns enough about its mother's voice to recognize it after birth. The 3-day-old neonate's preference for maternal voice (DeCasper & Fifer, 1980) is presumed to occur because the mother's airborne voice resembles her voice as transmitted prenatally through bone conduction and the soft tissues and fluids of her body. At 2–4 days of age, there also is a documented preference for the voice of an adult female that resembles the mother's because it is speaking the same language that the mother spoke prenatally (Mehler et al., 1988; Moon, Cooper, & Fifer, 1993). That human neonates prefer the language heard in utero suggests that, early on, maternal and linguistic preference may be one and the same. It also suggests that a single set of cues permits distinctions among individuals and among spoken languages. Given the filtering effect of soft tissues, these cues would be of the relatively low frequency type that reveal little about specific consonants and vowels but preserve linguistic prosody (DeCasper & Spence, 1986).

After acquiring the phonetic skills to produce speechlike vocalizations, infants come to learn the behavior of vocal matching, again through turn taking with caregivers. Matching occurs with respect to suprasegmental features of vocalizations. That is, pitch contours of maternal utterances are likely to be mimicked by the infants. In order to facilitate the infants' matching, the caregivers make specific efforts when providing contingency with the infants' spontaneous utterances of cooing. When they hear cooing, caregivers are more likely to respond nonverbally; they themselves produce cooings in response to the

infants' cooing. Moreover, cooing produced by the caregivers is matched with respect to pitch contour with the preceding coo of the infant. Even when the caregivers respond verbally, the pitch pattern of
the utterances often imitates that of the preceding infants' cooing. Such
mimicry usually is performed by the caregivers without their awareness. Between 3 and 4 months old, infants seem not to be aware of the
fact that their own vocal production and the following maternal utterance share common acoustic features. However, around the end of the
fourth month of life, they acquire the ability to discriminate similarities
and differences of pitch contour between their own vocal utterance
and the following maternal response. Thereafter, infants rapidly come
to attempt vocal matching by themselves in response to the preceding
utterances of caregivers.

To analyze the developmental processes underlying vocal behavior in infants, Masataka (1992a) used discriminant functional analysis,
which statistically distinguished infants' cooing following five different types of pitch contours of maternal speech. With this procedure,
structural variability in infant vocalizations across variants of maternal
speech was found to be characterized by a set of quantifiable physical
parameters. The parameters were those that actually distinguish the
four different types of maternal speech: rising, falling flat, bell-shaped,
and reversed bell-shaped. Attempts at cross-validation, in which the
discriminant profiles derived from one sample of vocalizations are used
to classify a second set of vocalizations, were successful (overall classification accuracy, 67.6%), indicating that the results obtained are not
an artifact of using the same data set to derive the profiles as used to
test reclassification accuracy. More important, the proportion of cross-
validated vocalizations that were misclassified decreases as infants'
ages increase. Thus, this discriminant analysis is an effective tool to
demonstrate that a statistically significant relation develops between
the acoustic features of maternal speech and those of the following
infant vocalizations as infants grow.

These findings indicate that early vocalizations of hearing infants are
often unstable but acquire stable laryngeal control during the first half
year. A falling pitch contour is the result of a decrease of subglottal air
pressure toward the end of an infant vocalization, with a concomitant
reduction in vocal fold tension and length. However, for a rising pitch
contour to occur, an increase at the end of the vocalization in subglottal
air pressure or vocal fold tension is needed; thus, different, purposeful laryngeal articulations are required. Between the ages of 4 and
6 months, speech-motor control develops dramatically in infants, associated with the tongue, mouth, jaw, and respiratory patterns, to produce
vocalizations with distinctively different types of pitch contour. These
vocalizations were initially the result of the infants' accidental opening
and closing of the mouth while phonating. Six-month-old infants are

found to be able to display an obvious contrastive use of different types of pitch contour. The importance of motor learning for early vocal development thus is greater than has traditionally been assumed. Finally, the problem of which partner is influencing the other is determined experimentally when the controlled prosodic feature of caregiver's vocal behavior is presented to infants. The results showed that 6-month-old infants are able to alter the quality of their responding vocalization according to the quality of preceding maternal speech.

In all, throughout the process of interaction between caregivers and infants, it is the caregivers who first become adept at being influenced by what was emitted by the infants on the last turn. Such a behavioral tendency must, in turn, be learned by the infants. It is on the basis of this learning that the skill of purposeful vocal utterance is considered to be first accomplished by infants (Masataka, 2003). Similarly, one would expect that such processes also occur in the manual mode, because human infants are born as visual animals as well. No data are available concerning this issue at present, simply because of the frequent assumption that *language* is equivalent to *spoken language*. Once again, research of this sort, involving deaf infants and deaf parents as well as hard-of-hearing infants and hearing parents, would be informative regarding both communication development in deaf children and the ontogeny of language more generally.

HOW INFANT-DIRECTED SPEECH INFLUENCES INFANT VOCAL DEVELOPMENT

The purposeful use of one suprasegmental feature of vocalizations, namely, pitch contour, plays an important role as a means of signaling different communicative functions before the onset of single words. Such ability has been considered by many to be one of the earliest linguistic features acquired by the child (Engel, 1973; Lewis, 1951; Weir, 1962). The intonational envelope itself is among the earliest and most basic units of interpersonal signaling in the auditory domain (Stern, Spieker, & MacKain, 1982). Mothers appear to use rising pitch contour in order to gain the infants' attention and engage them in interaction (Ryan, 1978; Sachs, 1977; Stern, Spieker, & Barnett, 1983). From early on, infants are sensitive to variations in pitch contour in the speech of others (Kaplan, 1969; Morse, 1972), and mothers appear to utilize this sensitivity; they use considerably more variation in pitch contour with young infants than with other adults (Stern, Spieker, & Barnett, 1983). Furthermore, infants reportedly produce pitch contours that are similar to those of the adults around them (Menyuk & Bernholtz, 1969; Tonkova-Yampol'skya, 1973), and the variations in vocalizations produced by nonlinguistic infants are systematically related to context (Delack, 1976; D'Odorico, 1984; Furrow, 1984).

Given this evidence of early use of pitch contour by mothers as a means of interacting, early discrimination and production of pitch contour is the child's first association of language form with respects of meaning. This phenomenon has been investigated, so far, in infants exposed to English and Italian. The studies consistently report the association of rising terminal contours with demanding behavior and of falling contours with "narratives." However, it must be noted that English and Italian are both nontonal languages.

In nontonal languages, a change in the pitch contour of a word does not change the meaning of the word; it conveys information about linguistic stress and intonation. In tonal languages, a change in pitch contour alters the meaning of the word. For example, in Japanese, the syllable /ha/ means "leaf" when it is produced with a rising terminal contour, and "tooth" when produced with a falling contour. Notwithstanding this profound difference, when all cooings of 8-month-old infants exposed to Japanese were transcribed and each of them was assigned a communicative function that was an interpretation of how the utterance functioned in the context, a highly significant relation was found (Masataka, 1993b). The finding was that rising contours were more frequently used with utterances that demanded a response such as requests and protests, whereas nonrising contours were more often used with functions that did not demand a response from others. Moreover, intersubject consistency was found in the overall pattern of this association. Given the fact that Japanese is a very different language from English and Italian, this phenomenon appears to be fairly robust: It could not be specific only to certain linguistic environments. Rather, because it occurs in infants whose mothers speak a non-Western, tonal language such as Japanese, the phenomenon should be regarded as being cross-linguistically universal.

However, when cooing data collected from the same group of infants when they were 6 months old were analyzed, no such significant relationship was found and the association between pitch contour of vocalizations and the context in which each of them occurred was random. Thus, it can be concluded that the ability to signal communicative functions develops between 6 and 8 months of life in preverbal infants. Furthermore, for infants to acquire the skill, so-called "motherese" characteristics of parental speech also appear to play an important part. When adults address infants and young children, they tend to modify their speech in distinctive ways. On this modified speech, called motherese, there is a growing literature (Garnica, 1977; Newport, Gleitman, & Gleitman, 1977; Papousek, Papousek, & Bornstein, 1985). These studies report that adult speech to infants is characterized by a higher overall pitch, wider pitch excursions, more distinctive pitch contours, slower tempo, and longer pauses than in normal adult conversations.

Cross-linguistic research has documented common patterns of such exaggerated features in parental speech to infants younger than 8 months across a number of European languages and Japanese (Fernald et al., 1989) and in maternal speech in Mandarin Chinese (Grieser & Kuhl, 1988). These features are thought to serve several functions related to language development. In particular, the use of exaggerated acoustic characteristics in the early preverbal period had been assumed to function primarily to engage the infant's attention and maintain social interaction. Using a conditioned head-turning procedure, Fernald (1985) showed that 4-month-old infants turned their heads more often toward a recording of female infant-directed speech than female adult-directed speech. Werker and McLeod (1989) measured the amount of time infants 4–5 months old and infants 7–9 months old viewed a television monitor that presented either a female or a male actor speaking infant-directed or adult-directed speech. They found that both groups of infants watched the monitor longer when infant-directed speech was being presented. The development of similar behavior in children with hearing loss (of varying degrees and at varying frequencies) would be most enlightening.

MOTHERESE AS A PREVALENT FORM OF LANGUAGE INPUT

In Japanese, too, motherese phenomena have been confirmed. When Japanese-speaking mothers were observed when addressing their own 6-month-old infants, characteristics of higher pitch and wider pitch range appeared in their speech, but there was context specificity. It is well known that for a child to engage in joint interaction with a parent, considerable interactional support by the parent is necessary, especially in the beginning phases of joint action. Parents have to repeat their attempts to elicit vocal responses from infants as long as the infants remain unresponsive (Blount, 1972). In my own observation, in initial moves to draw the infant's attention, when the mother attempted to start interactions with the infant spontaneously, it was hard to find motherese features in her speech (Masataka, 1992b). However, if such attempts were unsuccessful and ignored by the infant, the speech of the mother was likely to become more exaggerated. The mother then made utterances in which pitch shifted upward, and the frequency range was significantly increased.

Interestingly, when comparing the infant's response to maternal speech having motherese features with her speech when without motherese features, the type of pitch contour of the infant's subsequent response was predicted from the mother's preceding utterance only when maternal speech had motherese features. In the latter case, the pitch contour of the infant's response coincided with that of the preceding maternal speech much more frequently than expected by chance.

This indicated that when the infants were responding to maternal speech that had exaggerated pitch patterns, they tended to mimic those patterns, although they tended not to do so in response to maternal speech with nonexaggerated pitch patterns. By presenting exaggerated contours, maternal speech could help infants modify their own vocal responses. From early on, possibly even at birth, the infants are sensitive to such speech. Motherese is an efficient way to provide infants with opportunities for vocal practice: It makes use of the perceptual sensitivity of the infants, and, through this practice, the infants appear to learn to associate their own vocal utterance with different communicative functions. Thus, use of speech with motherese features might be especially helpful when interacting with infants who have hearing loss and are using amplification, even at somewhat older ages.

Moreover, the characteristics associated with motherese may be modality-free properties. In both American Sign Language and Japanese Sign Language (Erting, Prezioso, & O'Grady Hanes, 1990; Masataka, 1992c), it was found that when communicating with their deaf infants, deaf mothers used signs at a significantly slower tempo than when communicating with their deaf adult friends. They tended to repeat the same sign frequently by producing multiple tokens, and the movements associated with each sign were somewhat exaggerated. Sign motherese could parallel spoken motherese in that prosodic patterns of the signal appear to be varied in both registers. Duration, scope, and repetition are all regarded to be dimensions of prosody in signed languages, roughly analogous to duration, pitch, and repetition in spoken languages (Masataka, 2003). Indeed, infants with or without sign input are somehow tuned to these particular properties of sign motherese. When videotapes of such signing were presented, they elicited greater attentional and affective responsiveness of the infants than when videotapes of adult-directed signing were presented. Together, the available data indicate that motherese is a prevalent form of language input to infants in speech or sign and that it serves important social and attentional features in early development.

THE ONSET OF BABBLING

The age of 8 months is a period when speechlike vocalization in infancy culminates in the sense that canonical babbling typically emerges (see Oller, chapter 2 this volume). Unlike the sounds that infants produce before this stage, canonical babbling consists of well-formed consonant–vowel syllables that have adultlike spectral and temporal properties. By evaluating the syllables in terms of the distribution of consonants, vocalization length, and phonotactic structure, Vihman, Macken, Miller, Simmons, and Miller (1985) acoustically demonstrated that there is a significant continuity between the sound system of babbling and that of early speech. Units present in babbling are utilized later in natural spoken languages. Oller and Lynch (1992) proposed that production of babbling of this sort, such as "bababa" and "dadada," termed canonical babbling, marks the entrance of an infant into a developmental stage in which the syllabic foundations of meaningful speech are established. Indeed, there is agreement that the onset of canonical babbling is an important developmental precursor to spoken language and that some predicative relations exist between characteristics of the babbling and later speech and language development (see Stoel-Gammon, 1992, for a review).

A longitudinal investigation by Eilers et al. (1993) reported that hand banging was the only important indicator of a certain kind of readiness to reproduce reduplicated consonant–vowel syllables and that other motor milestones showed neither delay nor acceleration of onset in the same infants. Locke (1993) and Ejiri and Masataka (2001), however, noticed that the onset of repetitive motor action involving the hands is chronologically related to the onset of canonical babbling. We pursued this issue further by conducting meticulous sound spectrographic analyses on all the multisyllabic utterances that were recorded from four infants of Japanese-speaking parents in our longitudinal study. Results of the analyses revealed that the average syllable length of the utterance that did not co-occur with hand banging was significantly longer than that of the utterance that did co-occur with the motor action during the same period. Similarly, the averaged formant transition duration of the utterance that did not co-occur with hand banging was significantly longer than that of the utterance that did co-occur with the motor action. The results indicate that some acoustic modifications in multisyllabic utterances take place only when they are co-occurring with rhythmic manual activity. Given the fact that the parameters that were modified when they co-occurred with motor activity are those that essentially distinguish canonical babbling from earlier speechlike vocalizations, the acquisition of abilities enabling the production of canonical babbling, specifically the ability for complicated articulation, should be guided by such motor practice. For instance, a vocalization that can be transcribed as /ta/ would be deemed canonical if articulated with a rapid transition duration in a relatively short syllable but would be deemed noncanonical if articulated slowly. In the latter case, syllables have been conventionally referred to as marginal babbling (Oller, 1986; see Oller, chapter 2 this volume).

The onset of canonical babbling in the latter half of the first year has been empirically consistent as far as typically developing hearing infants are concerned. Consequently, the onset was previously speculated to be a deeply biological phenomenon, geared predominantly by maturation and virtually invulnerable to the effects of auditory experience or other environmental factors (Lenneberg, 1967).

However, the present general consensus is that the canonical babbling of infants with severe to profound hearing loss differs from that of
hearing infants in a number of ways (Eilers & Oller, 1994). In infants with
hearing loss, the onset of canonical babbling is much later (about 11–
49 months of age), and the variety of phonemes used is reduced. Infants
with hearing loss babble less often (but see Oller, chapter 2 this volume). This is thought to be due to the necessity for auditory feedback in
acquiring articulatory ability, through which the pronunciation of reduplicated consonant–vowel syllables is made possible. Moreover, the
transitions between the consonant and the vowel are significantly longer
in deaf infants than in those of normally hearing infants. Interestingly,
this finding is reminiscent of parallel findings by Moller and Schonweiler (1999), mentioned above, about the acoustic differences of cries
between younger hearing infants and hard-of-hearing infants.

Such a notion led researchers of sign language acquisition to look for
analogues in the manual behaviors of deaf and hearing infants who
have early exposure to signed language. In the course of conducting
research on signing deaf infants' transition from prelinguistic gestures
to their first signs, Pettito and Marentette (1991) closely analyzed the
"articulatory" variables (analogous to "phonetic" variables) of all manual activity produced by deaf infants from 6 months of age and their
deaf parents who were users of American Sign Language. They reported that linguistically relevant units were included in a class of
manual activity that was produced in entirely meaningless ways (i.e.,
manual babbling). Given that this manual activity precedes the onset of
the first recognizable signs in deaf infants, just as vocal babbling precedes the onset of the first meaningful words, Pettito and Marentette
(1991) concluded that the language capacity could manifest itself
equally as sign or speech in human infants. That is, they proposed
that, in hearing infants, the ability for vocal and gestural language can
develop simultaneously and in a similar manner, at least during the
preverbal period. However, as to whether manual babbling is learned
through selective reinforcement by caretakers or not, there is a controversy (Marschark, 2002), which is discussed below.

THE ONSET OF TRUE SPOKEN LANGUAGE

Despite of the acoustical similarity between canonical babbling and early
speech, the onset of babbling around the age of 9 months does not necessarily signal the onset of the true spoken language. It should be noted
that the ability to produce vocalizations with varying suprasegmental features appropriate to different contexts and the volitional ability to
produce vocalizations with varying segmental features develop rather
independently from one another. Infant vocalizations with different pitch
contours tend to occur in association with different communicative

functions, but that is exclusively the case for cooing and not for babbling. Unlike the case of cooing, even when all babbling recorded from 8-month-olds was transcribed in terms of pitch contours, and each example was classified according to its communicative functions, there were no significant relations between pitch contour type and the context in which babbling occurred. Another 3–4 months are required for infants to be able to produce multisyllabic utterances with variable consonant elements that simultaneously, purposefully vary suprasegmental features (Vihman, 1993). Interestingly, in order to combine both of the abilities, the synchronizing tendency of a specific manual action with vocal utterances again appears to play an important role.

The manual action is, in this case, actually index-finger extension, which recently has been suggested to be a precursor of the true "pointing" gesture. Previously the pointing gesture had been considered to first emerge near the end of the first year of life. The general consensus was that pointing differentiates from the movements of reaching and grasping, partly in order to economize the movement as a gesture needed for signaling and partly as a conventionalization of the adult expression learned through imitation and shaping (Bates, Camaioni, & Volterra, 1975; Bruner, 1983; Leung & Rheingold, 1981; Masur, 1983; Murphy, 1978). This assumed that cognitive developments at this age—the ability to carry out, plan, and signal intentions—induce the child to learn the new behavior of pointing. This was a purely cognitive interpretation based on traditional reports of observations of infants beginning to point at the age of 8 months. However, index-finger extensions also have been reported in infants as young as 2 months old, by Fogel and Hannan (1985).

Fogel and Hannan's (1985) investigation found that index-finger extensions are coordinate structures appearing in nonrandom contexts and with ontogenetic significance. Moreover, from the onset these movements frequently synchronize with utterances of speechlike vocalizations. The association between index-finger extension and vocalization is supposedly predispositional, and both are biologically predetermined to temporally co-occur with one another. Consequently, as infants develop, the frequency of speechlike vocalizations tends to increase. At the age of 8 months, manual action is likely to occur, often accompanied by the nonrising pitch contour associated with cooing utterances that do not demand a response from others but just label a person or an object. On the other hand, with the rising pitch contour, pointing occurs significantly less frequently. At 8 months, manual actions do not occur in synchrony with babbling. However, when observations were made on the same subjects 2 months later, at 10 months, the infants came to perform index-finger extension frequently while simultaneously uttering canonical babblings. More important, the occurrence was context specific and most often when labeling a person or an object but rarely in response to others or demanding from others any response.

However, when analyzing the pitch contours of the associated babbling, the attempt to assign each babble with variable communicative functions was totally unsuccessful (Masataka, 2003). In my longitudinal observations, the association between index-finger extension and specific communicative function in babbling tends to be strengthened during the following 2-month period. Then infants begin to produce babbling with a nonrising pitch contour that functions as a comment label and babbling with a rising contour that functions as a request or protest (Flax, Lahey, Harris, & Boothroyd, 1991). Preceding the combination of babbling and index-finger extension, index-finger extension was frequently observed to synchronize with cooing. This could enhance the ability to produce variable pitch contours according to different communicative functions in the transition from cooing to babbling behavior. Furthermore, soon after such purposeful use of babbling, according to different contexts developed, index-finger extension was found to be replaced with the true "pointing" gesture.

Pointing is well known as infants' first clear-cut expression of gestural reference to external objects. Then infants appear to reach the developmental stage proximal to the onset of true spoken language. Although the development of such gestures in deaf children acquiring spoken language is well documented, it remains unclear how finger extension might be affected by children's hearing loss, and in what direction.

SUMMARY AND CONCLUSIONS

The findings reviewed in this chapter have two important implications for future investigation. First, they indicate future directions for research about the linguistic behavior of deaf infants in the vocal mode; for instance, to what extent the absence of the auditory experiences could affect the ontogeny of cooing is still unknown. Virtually no studies have attempted to examine the vocal behavior of prebabbling deaf infants in terms of such questions as the extent to which the timing and the quality of the vocalization of caregivers could affect the vocal behavior of deaf and hard-of-hearing infants, the extent to which the acoustic properties of their vocalizations differentially affect the responses of their mothers to the vocalizations if the mothers are hearing, how skilled use of purposeful vocal utterances develops in the infants as a consequence of their interaction with the caregivers, and so on. Humans are provided with a finite set of specific behavior patterns, each of which is probably phylogenetically inherited as a primate species. The findings described here indicate that the patterns are uniquely organized during ontogeny and a coordinated structure emerges, which eventually leads us to acquire spoken language. The degree to which the process is common in the case of the vocal ontogeny in deaf infants should be investigated.

Second, research discussed in this chapter indicates what is to be investigated to understand the process of the language acquisition of deaf infants acquiring sign language rather than (or as well as) spoken language. A number of elements involved in the onset of language in such infants may occur in a more fluid, task-specific manner than in children acquiring spoken language only, determined equally by the maturational status and experiences of the infant and by the current context the action. Particularly interesting in this regard is the intriguing finding that manual activity performed by hearing babblers, with no exposure to any form of signed languages, is incorporated into the system of acquiring spoken languages while serving social and communicative functions. Apparently, it is hard for many people to regard gestural activity as a manifestation of the hearing child's linguistic competence in the manual mode, even though it appears that hearing and deaf children have similar gestural precursors of language (Marschark, 2002). Nevertheless, in the case of deaf infants, it would not be difficult to assume that the activity is incorporated into the system of producing meaningful signs. Only by comparing the developmental patterns between hearing and deaf infants systematically, can the continuity and the variability of the competence underlying spoken and signed languages be fully elucidated.

REFERENCES

Barrett-Goldfarb, M. S., & Whitehurst, G. J. (1973). Infant vocalizations as a function of parental voice selection. *Developmental Psychology, 8*, 273–276.

Bandura, A., & Walters, R. H. (1963). *Social learning and personality development*. New York: Holt Rinehart & Winston.

Bates, E., Camaioni, L., & Voltera, V. (1975). The acquisition of performatives prior to speech. *Merrill-Palmer Quarterly, 21*, 105–226.

Bateson, M. C. (1975). Mother infant exchanges: The epigenesis of conversational interaction. *Annals of the New York Academy of Sciences, 263*, 101–113.

Bloom, K., & Masataka, N. (1996). Japanese and Canadian impressions of vocalizing infants. *International Journal of Behavioral Development, 19*, 89–99.

Blount, B. C. (1972). Parental speech and language acquisition: Some Luo and Samoan examples. *Anthropological Linguistics, 14*, 119–130.

Brown, J. (1973). Non-nutritive sucking in great ape and human newborns: Some phylogenetic and ontogenetic characteristics. In J. Bosma (Ed.), *Oral sensation and perception: Development in the fetus and infants* (pp. 167–212). Bethesda: U.S. Department of Health, Education, and Welfare.

Bruner, J. S. (1975). From communication to language—a psychological perspective. *Cognition, 3*, 225–278.

Bruner, J. S. (1983). *Child's talk: Learning to use language*. New York: Norton.

Bowlby, J. (1969). *Attachment and loss: Vol. 1. Attachment.* New York: Basic Books.

DeCasper, A., & Fifer, W. P. (1980). On human bonding: Newborns prefer their mothers' voices. *Science, 208,* 1174–1176.

DeCasper, A., & Spence, M. (1986). Prenatal maternal speech influences newborns' perception of speech sounds. *Infant Behavior and Development, 9,* 133–150.

Delack, J. B. (1976). Aspects of infant speech development in the first year of life. *Canadian Journal of Linguistics, 21,* 17–37.

D'Odorico, L. (1984). Non-segmental features in prelinguistic communications: An analysis of some types of infant cry and noncry vocalizations. *Journal of Child Language, 11,* 17–27.

Eilers, R. E., & Oller, D. K. (1994). Infant vocalizations and the early diagnosis of severe hearing impairment. *Journal of Pediatrics, 124,* 199–203.

Eilers, R. E., Oller, D. K., Levine, S., Basinger, D., Lynch, M. P., & Urbano, R. (1993). The role of prematurity and socioeconomic-status in the onset of canonical babbling in infants. *Infant Behavior and Development, 16,* 297–315.

Ejiri, K., & Masataka, N. (2001). Co-occurrence of preverbal vocal behavior and motor action in early infancy. *Developmental Science, 4,* 40–48.

Engel, W. V. R. (1973). The development from sound to phoneme in child language. In C. Ferguson & D. Slobin (Eds.), *Child language development* (pp. 78–124). New York: Holt Rinehart & Winston.

Erting, C. J., Prezioso, C., & O'Grady Hanes, M. (1990). The interactional context of deaf mother-infant communication. In V. Voltera & C. J. Erting (Eds.), *From gesture to language in hearing and deaf infants* (pp. 97–106). Berlin: Springer.

Fernald, A. (1985). Four-month-old infants prefer to listen to motherese. *Infant Behavior and Development, 8,* 181–195.

Fernald, A., Taeschner, T., Dunn, J., Papousek, M., Boysson-Bardies, B., & Fukui, I. (1989). A cross-linguistic study of prosodic modifications in mothers' and fathers' speech to preverbal infants. *Journal of Child Language, 16,* 477–501.

Flax, J., Lahey, M., Harris, K., & Boothroyd, A. (1991). Relations between prosodic variables and communicative functions. *Journal of Child Language, 18,* 3–19.

Fogel, A., & Hannan, T. E. (1985). Manual actions of nine- to fifteen-week-old human infants during face-to-face interaction with their mothers. *Child Development, 56,* 1271–1279.

Freud, S. (1924). The Passing of the Oedipus complex. In A. Strachey & J. Strachey (Trans. and Eds.), *Collected papers* (Vol. 2, pp. 386–496). London: Hogarth.

Furrow, D. (1984). Young children's use of prosody. *Journal of Child Language, 11,* 203–213.

Garnica, O. (1977). Some prosodic and paralinguistic features of speech to young children. In C. E. Snow & C. A. Ferguson (Eds.), *Talking to children: Language input and acquisition* (pp. 189–224). Cambridge: Cambridge University Press.

Ginsburg, G. P., & Kilbourne, B. K. (1988). Emergence of vocal alternation in mother-infant interchanges. *Journal of Child Language, 15,* 221–235.

Golub, H. L. (1980). *A physioacoustic model of the infant cry and its use for medical diagnosis and prognosis.* Unpublished doctoral dissertation, Massachusetts Institute of Technology, Cambridge, MA.

Grieser, D. L., & Kuhl, P. (1988). Maternal speech to infants in a tonal language: Support for universal prosodic features in motherese. *Developmental Psychology, 24,* 14–20.

Iverson, P., & Kuhl, P. (1995). Mapping the perceptual magnetic effect for speech using signal detection theory and multidimensional scaling. *Journal of the Acoustical Society of America, 97,* 553–562.

Kaplan, E. (1969). *The role of intonation in the acquisition of language.* Unpublished doctoral dissertation, Cornell University, Ithaca, NY.

Kaye, K. (1982). *The mental and social life of babies.* Brighton: Harvester Press.

Kent, R. D. (1981). Articulatory-acoustic perspectives on speech development. In R. Stark (Ed.), *Language behavior in infancy and early childhood* (pp. 105–126). Amsterdam: Elsevier.

Kuhl, P. K., & Meltzoff, A. N. (1982). The bimodal perception of speech in infancy. *Science, 218,* 1138–1141.

Lenneberg, E. H. (1967). *Biological foundations of language.* New York: Wiley.

Leung, E., & Rheingold, H. L. (1981). Development of pointing as a social gesture. *Developmental Psychology, 17,* 215–220.

Lewis, M. M. (1951). *Infant speech: A study of the beginning of language.* New York: Humanities Press.

Locke, J. L. (1993). *The child's path to spoken language.* Cambridge, MA: Harvard University Press.

Locke, J. L. (1994). Gradual emergence of developmental language disorders. *Journal of Speech and Hearing Research, 37,* 608–616.

Marschark, M. (2002). Foundations of communication and the emergence of language in deaf children. In G. Morgan & B. Woll (Eds.), *Current developments in child signed language research* (pp. 154–193). Amsterdam: John Benjamins.

Masataka, N. (1992a). Early ontogeny of vocal behavior of Japanese infants in response to maternal speech. *Child Development, 63,* 1177–1185.

Masataka, N. (1992b). Pitch characteristics of Japanese maternal speech to infants. *Journal of Child Language, 19,* 213–223.

Masataka, N. (1992c). Motherese in a signed language. *Infant Behavior and Development, 15,* 453–460.

Masataka, N. (1993a). Effects of contingent and noncontingent maternal stimulation on the vocal behavior of three- and four-month-old Japanese infants. *Journal of Child Language, 20,* 303–312.

Masataka, N. (1993b). Relation between pitch contour of prelinguistic vocalizations and communicative functions in Japanese infants. *Infant Behavior and Development, 16,* 397–401.

Masataka, N. (2003). *The onset of language.* Cambridge: Cambridge University Press.

Masur, E. F. (1983). Gestural development, dual directional signaling, and the transition to words. *Journal of Psycholinguistic Research, 12,* 93–109.

Mauk, G. W., & Bahrens, T. R. (1993). Historical , political, and technological context associated with early identification of hearing loss. *Semin Hearing, 14,* 1–17.

Mehler, J., Jusczyk, P., Lambertz, G., Halsted, N., Bertoncini, J., & Amiel-Tison, C. (1988). A precursor of language acquisition in young infants. *Cognition, 29*, 143–178.

Meltzoff, A. N., & Moore, M. K. (1977). Imitation of facial and manual gestures by human neonates. *Science, 198*, 75–78.

Menyuk, P., & Bernholtz, N. (1969). Prosodic features and children's language production. *MIT Quarterly Progress Report, 93*, 216–219.

Miller, N. E., & Dollard, J. (1941). *Social learning and imitation.* New Haven, CT: Yale University Press.

Moller, S., & Schonweiler, R. (1999). Analysis of infant cries for the early detection of hearing impairment. *Speech Communication, 28*, 175–193.

Morse, P. A. (1972). The discrimination of speech and non-speech stimuli in early infancy. *Journal of Experimental Child Psychology, 14*, 477–492.

Moon, C., Cooper, R. P., & Fifer, W. P. (1993). Two-day olds prefer their native language. *Infant Behavior and Development, 16*, 495–500.

Moran, G., Krupka, A., Tutton, A., & Symons, D. (1987). Patterns of maternal and infant imitation during play. *Infant Behavior and Development, 10*, 477–491.

Murphy, C. M. (1978). Pointing in the context of a shared activity. *Child Development, 49*, 371–380.

Netsell, R. (1981). The acquisition of speech motor control: A perspective with directions for speech. In R. E. Stark (Ed.), *Language behavior in infancy and early childhood* (pp. 165–218). Amsterdam: Elsevier.

Newport, E. L. Gleitman, H., & Gleitman, L. R. (1977). Mother, I'd rather do it myself: Some effects and non-effects of maternal speech style. In C. E. Snow & C. A. Ferguson (Eds.), *Talking to children: Language input and acquisition* (pp. 65–128). Cambridge: Cambridge University Press.

Oller, D. K. (1986). Metaphonology and infant vocalizations. In B. Lindblom & R. Zetterstorm (Eds.), *Precursors of early speech* (pp. 93–112). New York: Stockton Press.

Oller, D. K., & Lynch, M. P. (1992). Infant vocalizations and innovations in infraphonology: Toward a boader theory of development and disorders. In C. A. Ferguson, L. Menn, & C. Stoel-Gammon (Eds.), *Phonological development: Models, research, implications* (pp. 21–36). Timonium, MD: York Press.

Papousek, M., & Papousek, H. (1989). Forms and functions of vocal matching in interactions between mothers and their precanonical infants. *First Language, 9*, 137–158.

Papousek, M., Papousek, H., & Bornstein, M. (1985). The naturalistic vocal environment of young infants: On the significance of homogeneity and variability in parental speech. In T. M. Field & N. A. Fox (Eds.), *Social perception in infants* (pp. 269–297). Norwood, NJ: Ablex.

Pettito, L. A., & Marentette, P. F. (1991). Babbling in the manual mode: Evidence for the ontogeny of language. *Science, 251*, 1493–1496.

Ryan, M. L. (1978). Contour in context. In R. Campbell & P. Smith (Eds.), *Recent advances in the psychology of language* (pp. 372–418). New York: Plenum.

Sachs, J. (1977). The adaptive significance of linguistic input to prelinguistic infants. In C. Snow & C. H. Furgusin (Eds.), *Talking to children* (pp. 285–341). Cambridge: Cambridge University Press.

Scheiner, E., Hammerschmidt, K., Jurgens, U., & Zwirner, P. (2002). Acoustic analyses of developmental changes and emotional expression in the preverbal vocalizations of infants. *Journal of Voice, 16*, 509–529.

Stern, D., Spieker, S., & Barnett, R. K. (1983). The prosody of maternal speech: Infant age and context related changes. *Journal of Child Language, 10*, 1–15.

Stern, D. N. Spieker, S., & MacKain, K. (1982). Intonation contour as signals in maternal speech to prelinguistic infants. *Developmental Psychology, 18*, 727–735.

Stoel-Gammon, C. (1992). Prelinguistic vocal development: Measurement and prediction. In C. A. Ferguson, L. Menn, & C. Stoel-Gammon (Eds.), *Phonological development: Models, research, implications* (pp. 65–111). Parkton, MD: York Press.

Sugiura, H., & Masataka, N. (1995). Temporal and acoustic flexibility in vocal exchange of coo calls in Japanese monkeys (*Macaca fuscata*). In E. Zimmermann, J. D. Newman, & U. Jurgens (Eds.), *Current topics in primate vocal communication* (pp. 121–140). London: Plenum Press.

Susswein, J. (1905). Zur Physiologie des trinkens beim Saugling. *Archiv fur Linderheikunde, 40*, 68–80.

Takei, W. (2002). How do deaf infants attain first signs? *Developmental Science, 4*, 122–135.

Tonkova-Yampol'skya, R. V. (1973). Development of speech intonation in infants during the first two years of life. In C. A. Ferguson & D. I. Slobin (Eds.), *Studies of child language development* (pp. 214–250). New York: Holt Rinehart & Winston.

Truby, H. M., & Lind, J. (1965). Cry sounds of the newborn infant. *Acta Paediatrica Scandinavica, 163*, 8–59.

Vihman, M. M. (1993). Variable paths of early word production. *Journal of Phonetics, 21*, 61–82.

Vihman, M. M., Macken, M. A., Miller, R., Simmons, H., & Miller, J. (1985). From babbling to speech: A reassessment of the continuity issue. *Language, 61*, 395–443.

Weir, R. (1962). *Language in the crib*. The Hague: Mouton.

Werker, J. F., & McLeod, P. J. (1989). Infant preference for both male and female infant-directed talk: A developmental study of attentional and affective responsiveness. *Canadian Journal of Psychology, 43*, 230–246.

Wolff, P. H. (1968). Sucking patterns of infant mammals. *Brain Behavior and Evolution, 1*, 354–367.

4

Audiological Advancement and the Acquisition of Spoken Language in Deaf Children

R. Steven Ackley & T. Newell Decker

A technological impact on the field of audiology has emerged during the past decade that is profoundly influencing speech and language acquisition among deaf children. Notably, improvements in identification of hearing loss and deafness in infancy, as well as a technological renaissance in amplification systems and cochlear implants, have significantly affected speech and language of deaf children. Early identification of hearing loss is now enabling habilitation of speech and language much earlier in life than was possible a decade ago. And, improvements in amplification systems and cochlear implants now enable a clarity of speech signals never achieved in the history of these overlapping industries.

It is obvious to professionals working with deaf children that difficulties in acquiring spoken language stem directly from their limited access to auditory information. The role of audiologists is to identify and characterize the degree to which auditory information is available to a specific child, to assess and provide the results of specialized audiological procedures, and in many cases to provide habilitation or rehabilitation for the consequences of hearing loss.

Since the inception of audiology as a profession during World War II, this field of study has been best defined by its multidisciplinary heritage. Otolaryngologists, speech pathologists, psychologists, and other professionals created this new specialty out of necessity of war casualties who suffered hearing loss and deafness. Initially, determination of the degree and etiology of the condition and appropriate remediation was fundamental to the discipline. Physicians could repair damage to the ear in many cases, but rehabilitation was/is outside their scope of practice. Speech pathologists could help with speech production when the auditory channel was sacrificed but were generally incapable of offering specialized therapy in speechreading (lipreading) and auditory training. Psychologists were skilled at diagnosing unique causes of hearing loss, such as psychogenic deafness, but lacked the expertise, training, and technology to broadly assess the scores of causes of hearing loss. Audiology provided an obvious professional service that was lacking.

During the decades after its early genesis, audiology continued to embrace new disciplines. Notably, biomedical technology has recently catapulted the profession from testing with pure tones and rehabilitating with an auditory trainer to measurement of brain waves and computerized auditory stimulation habilitation following cochlear implantation. It is this professional union that has impacted speech and language acquisition of deaf children the greatest. These recent advances in technology and the availability of technologies and associated procedures have resulted in increased contributions from the field of audiology to the development of spoken language by children who are deaf or hard of hearing. This chapter surveys many of these advances, including (1) the availability of hearing screening in early infancy as well as the assessment procedures used and the protocols or sets of assessment used in these early screenings, (2) newly developed or improved technologies and procedures for specifying the characteristics of an individual's hearing loss and hearing functioning, and (3) increased information about etiologies responsible for increasing access to auditory information and, therefore, to spoken language.

IDENTIFICATION OF HEARING LOSS AND DEAFNESS IN INFANCY

The identification of hearing loss and deafness in infants is a factor that has significantly affected acquisition of language in deaf children in the United States. Clearly, identifying deafness earlier in life facilitates early language development and habilitation. Until recently, the United States had a poor track record among technologically advanced nations in identifying early hearing loss/deafness and providing consistent follow-up. Great Britain and Israel have historically been world leaders in this important health care service. These countries routinely identified hearing loss before 6 months of age. The United States, on the other hand, historically identified hearing loss after 24 months of age. This condition is rapidly changing as the majority of states have implemented statewide hearing screening programs of infants. Comprehensive early hearing detection and intervention (EHDI) programs are presently established between the Centers for Disease Control and Prevention (CDC) and 15 exemplary state programs. Reporting to a central data bank at the CDC, these 15 states provide thorough data regarding hearing loss statistics in infants. Nationwide follow-up is more assured than ever in the history of hearing health care in the United States.

Methods of screening have likewise improved, as has identifying the etiology of hearing loss/deafness of infants. Screening techniques such as automated auditory brainstem response (AABR) and otoacoustic emission (OAE) procedures (described in detail below) have enhanced early hearing screening capability well beyond an old industry hearing screening standard of "crib-o-gram" and various "startle response" techniques. In addition to important advances in infant testing and follow-up when hearing impairment is identified, technology has improved audiological methodology and instrumentation, facilitating better hearing aid fitting, improved determination of cochlear implant candidacy, and earlier and better aural habilitative procedures. To be sure, the beneficiaries of this technology and improved techniques are the children who will develop spoken language earlier in life, leading to better academic performance and sustained higher quality of life.

The impact of many of the processes described in this chapter has yet to be determined because many of the recipients of the services may be just entering school. For example, the national impact of the EHDI program may soon show improvement in language acquisition and school performance. Literature now supports the notion that when hearing loss/deafness is detected before 6 months of age, improvements are seen in early school performance (Yoshinaga-Itano, 1999). The concept is not new. In fact, it was reported 35 years earlier (Downs & Sterritt, 1967). However, definitive data now support earlier suspicions and give impetus to all states adopting comprehensive hearing screening of infants.

Technological advances in biomedical instrumentation and research have resulted in breakthrough methodology of hearing screening. These methods include OAEs, auditory steady-state response (ASSR), and AABR techniques and instruments. In addition, advancements in tympanometry have made this procedure now suitable for testing infants.

Otoacoustic Emissions

OAEs are audio frequencies that are transmitted from the cochlea to the middle ear and into the external ear canal, where they can be recorded (Kemp, 1986). Four types of OAEs have been measured: spontaneous OAEs (SOAEs), transient evoked OAEs (TEOAEs), intermodulation/distortion product OAEs (DPOAEs), and continuous stimulus frequency OAEs (SFOAEs). These various emissions offer a unique window onto the workings of the sensory (cochlea) portion of the auditory system.

The detection and measurement of all types of emissions require that a sensitive, low-noise microphone be placed in the external ear canal. This microphone records the sound present in the external ear canal, which includes the stimulus source and the audio frequencies transmitted from the inner ear. Devices that fit into the ear canal are now available that contain both the sound source and the measurement microphone(s). Depending on the type of emission being recorded, recovery and analysis of the emission require some amount of signal averaging in the time or the frequency domain.

Spontaneous OAEs

SOAEs are low-level acoustic signals measured in the ear without external stimulation (Kemp, 1979). They occur in approximately 50% of healthy ears at frequencies that are peculiar to each ear (Kemp, Ryan, & Bray, 1990) and are typically detected between 1000 and 5000 Hz (Bonfils, 1989).

To record SOAEs a low-noise microphone is inserted into the ear canal. Since no external stimulation is required, there is no associated stimulus delivery apparatus. The microphone output is led to a low-noise amplifier and then routed to a signal spectrum analyzer that can provide real-time Fourier analysis (fast Fourier transform, FFT) of the signal. A specified frequency range (e.g., 20–20,000 Hz) can then be analyzed for SOAEs by analysis of discrete frequency bandwidths. Usually a number of samples of the energy in a given bandwidth are submitted to signal averaging procedures to resolve the emission from the background noise. Spontaneous emissions are defined as discrete peaks that are repeatable and are at some specified level above the noise floor of the instrumentation. Because of their idiosyncratic nature between ears in the same subject and because not everyone has SOAEs, they have not received much clinical attention.

Transient Evoked OAEs

These emissions were described by Kemp (1978) and dubbed Kemp "echoes." They seem to be present to some degree in nearly all healthy ears but are generally not observed in ears where hearing loss as mild as 25–30 dB HL has occurred (Kemp, 1978). They are found most frequently between 500 and 4000 Hz (Elberling, Parbo, Johnsen, & Bagi, 1985; Probst, Coats, Martin, & Lonsbury-Martin, 1986). A significant characteristic of TEOAEs is that they have decreasing latencies, or time delays, with increasing stimulus frequency (Norton & Neely, 1987). This fact seems to be directly related to the tonotopic arrangement, or frequency map, of the basilar membrane of the inner ear. That is, cochlear sensitivity to specific sound frequencies occurs in a regular order in the primary structure of the cochlea, with higher frequencies causing a response at the basilar end, nearest the middle ear and earlier in time, and lower frequencies causing responses at the apex or upper end that occur later in time.

In order to record TEOAEs, a probe is positioned in the external auditory canal. The probe delivers the stimulus, which is a "click" that includes a broad range of frequencies, as well as records the ear canal sound pressure. The ear canal sound pressure is a combination of both the stimulus and the returning echo. This sound is then signal averaged and analyzed by FFT to obtain a frequency spectrum of the emission and validate the presence of a response.

TEOAEs have received a good deal of attention because of the insights that they give the auditory scientist into the workings of the cochlear analyzer and because of their clinical utility. The absence of TEOAEs suggests quite strongly that a hearing loss of at least 30–40 dB is present. In addition, TEOAEs have found their way into the newborn nursery as an effective and noninvasive hearing screening measure.

Intermodulation/Distortion Product Emissions

DPOAEs are recorded by presenting two stimulus tones (f1 and f2) to the ear. When f1 and f2 are presented to the ear, distortion known as interference occurs and combination tones result. While there may be a large number of combination tones present, the distortion product 2f1–f2 is of most interest to researchers and clinicians because it is believed that this distortion product emission results from outer hair cell biomechanics. It has been shown that the 2f1–f2 DPOAE occurs primarily in the frequency range of 500 to 8000 Hz, and its amplitude is dependent upon the frequencies and intensities of f1 and f2 (Martin, Probst, & Lonsbury-Martin, 1990). DPOAEs are normally measured in a manner that results in something that looks not unlike an audiogram and is referred to as a DP-gram.

To record a DP-gram, a probe must be sealed in the ear canal. The probe produces two sound outputs (f1 and f2) and contains a microphone to measure the sound pressure level in the external ear canal. The oscillators presenting f1 and f2 step across frequencies, and the microphone is coupled to a phase locked filter/analyzer that records the amplitude of the 2f1–f2 distortion product as well as the amplitude of f1 and f2. The presence of the distortion product at a level of approximately 3 dB above the noise floor is considered confirmation that the cochlea (specifically, outer hair cells) is functioning in a normal manner.

Stimulus Frequency OAEs

SFOAEs are emissions that are similar to transiently evoked emissions but are evoked with continuous pure tones instead of click stimuli. They have not been studied to the extent that the other emissions have but can be seen in the same frequency region as TEOAEs.

For SFOAEs, the eliciting stimulus is a low-amplitude continuous pure tone that is swept from a low frequency to a high frequency (e.g., 800–2800 Hz). As the stimulus is swept across frequencies, the energy from the ear canal can be tracked by a signal analyzer that spectrally averages the ear canal signal utilizing a narrow frequency bandwidth resolution. Any SFOAEs present in the ear canal will sum with the stimulus and result in an elevation of sound pressure of a particular frequency region. The SFOAE is typically represented by peaks and valleys superimposed upon the frequency response of the sound system. The SFOAE extraction process is more complex than with the transient evoked emission. This emission type has not found its way into the clinical setting.

Auditory Steady-State Response

Since the early 1970s, audiologists have employed the auditory brainstem response (ABR) as an "objective" test of auditory activity in the region beyond the cochlea. This neural response is evoked by repeated stimulation of the ear, and the electrical responses given off from neurons in the brainstem are recorded from surface electrodes. The response voltage is very small relative to the biological background noise and so must be signal averaged to reveal itself. The response is best recorded from a relaxed subject and shows a great deal of consistency both within a given listener and across the population.

The single greatest limitation of the ABR is the necessity to use very brief stimuli. While brief stimuli generally cause well-defined responses, they also have very broad spectrums. The broad spectrums make testing at specific frequencies all but impossible, and this limits audiometric application. For many years, researchers and clinicians have searched for a way to use the ABR in hearing assessment in a manner that would allow a frequency-specific audiometric stimulus.

While the steady-state response of the auditory system has been recognized for many years (Galambos, Makeig, & Talmachoff, 1981), it is only recently that the procedure has been developed to the extent that it can be considered a clinical tool. The primary phenomenon to be considered here is that while the ABR cannot be evoked by a long-duration (steady-state) pure tone such as is used in conventional audiometry, it can be evoked by an amplitude- or frequency-modulated pure tone. For example, a pure tone of 1000 Hz amplitude modulated at a rate of 80 Hz will cause the neural auditory system to respond to the modulated signal. With the proper analysis technique, the spectrum of the EEG output from the brain will show a peak at 80 Hz, thus indicating that the modulated 1000 Hz signal was heard. All four (500, 1000, 2000, 4000 Hz) standard audiometric test frequencies can be tested at the same time simply by modulating each of them at a slightly different rate. Four spectral peaks representing those modulation rates will then be seen in the neural output spectrum in the normal ear.

All four of these frequencies with their individual modulation rates can be presented at the same time in one complex signal. Furthermore, the same set of frequencies with slightly different modulation rates can be presented to the opposite ear at the same time. In a normal system, the EEG will show eight individual peaks corresponding to the eight different modulation rates. Thus, both ears can be assessed at the same time in very short order. In the current clinical configuration called MASTER (John and Picton, 2000), the developers (Bio-Logic Corporation) suggest that audiometry can be done in approximately one third to one half the time normally consumed doing standard ABR testing.

Automated Brainstem Evoked Response Screening

It is generally acknowledged that hearing loss occurring early in life can have long-lasting consequences on speech and language development. Even very mild hearing losses occurring before about 3 years of age can have lasting effects (Alberti, Hyde, Riko, Corbin, & Abramovich, 1983). Because of this, the Joint Committee on Infant Hearing (1991), which is composed of professionals from a variety of settings, has recommended that newborns at risk for hearing loss be screened in the hospital before being discharged.

The traditional methods of hearing screening have used a variety of behavioral techniques. However, newborns and young infants have limited ability to respond behaviorally to test stimuli. For this reason, the ABR has found favor as a primary method for screening hearing in an "objective" manner. The ABR is not without limitations, the major one being the lack of frequency specificity. Nevertheless, the technique has demonstrated good agreement with behavioral pure tone testing and has become accepted as a valid screening method.

A major issue in hearing screening involves when and where it is to be done and who is to do it. If, as suggested by the Joint Committee, the screening is to be done on newborns in the hospital, the issue of who is to perform the testing is a major consideration. There simply are not enough audiologists to go around in the nation's hospitals. This means that relatively untrained technicians and volunteers must perform these tests. Traditional ABR testing on newborns is quite difficult and would not be possible by volunteers in most instances. Because of this, a number of manufacturers have developed automated ABR screening systems. These systems require very little interaction with the examiner beyond the application of electrodes and the placement of ear phones. All of the testing is controlled by software, including the "reading" of results and the making of recommendations regarding pass/fail.

One system that has received a good deal of attention is the ALGO system by Natus Corporation. With this system, after the electrodes have been attached to the baby's scalp, and when the equipment decides that the testing conditions are correct, the screener automatically begins presenting 35 dB click stimuli to the baby's ears. The responses are accumulated in computer memory and compared with an internal template of a "typical" newborn ABR. If the baby's responses are a sufficient match to the template, the screener stops testing and pronounces that the baby has "passed" the screening test. If the screener does not detect a match, it decides that a "refer" decision is necessary. The baby must then be seen for further testing by a qualified and trained professional.

Tympanometry

Objective assessment of middle ear status is a decades-old concept, but recent technological applications give greater diagnostic utility when evaluating infants. The test is fairly simple and quick. It requires placing a probe in the ear canal for a few seconds, and it is based on the notion that the eardrum is designed to vibrate in response to sound pressure. If the eardrum fails to move because of middle ear fluid with an ear infection, for example, the ear canal probe will produce a "tympano-gram" that shows sound bouncing off the eardrum instead of being carried into the inner ear. Although this is not a test of hearing, it identifies impaired auditory mechanisms sufficiently for hearing loss to be nearly precisely estimated. Furthermore, it accurately identifies conditions of the middle ear that are usually treatable. Speech and language delay occur in children with untreated middle ear conditions, and such conditions are evident even at birth now because of recent improvements in biomedical instrumentation used for this purpose.

Infant Hearing Screening Electrophysiology Standards

Thorough assessment of infant hearing is proposed in a number of states following the lead provided by the United Kingdom and Canada. To be sure, the United States was well behind the early detection of hearing loss race for several decades, and now is adhering to a standard, in most states, long since established by Great Britain. Hearing screening has been universally conducted in the United Kingdom since the 1960s, and technologically advanced methods of AABR and OAE testing have been performed since the 1980s. The system of health care in the United Kingdom facilitates follow-up in a timely manner after initial hearing screening failure. The exemplary system well established overseas is now making its way throughout the United States, with most states performing similarly exemplary screening programs and other states developing protocols. These rather complicated protocols (described below) illustrate the extent to which technology and science have affected the field of audiology. Indeed, the most basic procedure performed by a licensed and certified audiologist is the hearing screening test of newborns. As is apparent in the following section, an audiologist cannot simply have expertise in pure tone audiometry in order to perform this basic element of clinical practice. Rather, thorough understanding of appropriate technology is fundamental to this methodology. Full understanding of the following protocols is essential for persons involved with infant hearing screening programs. Other professionals may find this information a useful reference. Again, the complexity of this information serves also to illustrate the technological depth implicit in identifying hearing loss in infants.

Hearing Screening Procedure

U.K. and Canadian Protocols

In the United Kingdom and now in most of the United States, OAE screening is conducted initially. If this test is failed, the infant is rescreened typically with the same method. If this test is also failed, AABR is usually performed, again following the U.K. standard. In Ontario, Canada, a more thorough protocol is used. ABR testing is done at 500 and 2,000 Hz, and also at 1,000 Hz if a greater than 30 dB threshold is found between the 500 and 2,000 Hz values. Also, 4,000 Hz threshold is determined if the 2,000 Hz threshold exceeds 40 dB. This protocol on the surface appears to be somewhat daunting. However, it represents something of a compromise between testing all frequencies always and testing important frequencies for speech communication. In addition, DPOAEs are determined (1,000–4,000) and tympanometry is measured. Finally, if no response is recorded using ABR but OAE responses are present, an ABR otoneurological procedure is performed. The Ontario Infant Hearing Program protocol is among the most comprehensive available.

U.S. Protocols

In the United States, Kansas has proposed a thorough infant hearing screening program that requires extensive ABR procedures if OAE screening is failed. This protocol includes tone-evoked ABR as well as bone conducted responses and high-volume-level ABR to measure waveform morphology and interpeak latencies. North Carolina has also proposed a comprehensive program and a protocol that describes measures to be taken that avoid sedating the infant during ABR testing. Such a procedure is desirable considering possible side effects from the commonly used sedative for this purpose, chloral hydrate. Side effects can range from nausea and vomiting and a 24-hour period of imbalance to far more extreme drug reaction, including death, which may occur in syndromic babies.

In sum, it is obvious that the melding of professions into audiology has affected even the most fundamental of all audiometric procedures, namely, newborn hearing screening. Failure to provide this vital service competently can be expected to adversely affect speech and language development in the child. Thus, poor training in the professional providing diagnostic and assessment services may lead to harm to the infant. While it may have been sufficient to know how to induce a startle response to loud sound from a baby decades ago, determining hearing status in infants now requires knowledge of appropriate technology, human physiology, and, to a limited extent, pharmacology. Characterizing individual hearing loss and deafness using modern technology and procedures is the next step after hearing screening has identified the condition.

ASSESSMENT PROCEDURES FOR CHARACTERIZING INDIVIDUAL HEARING LOSS AND DEAFNESS

Improved Middle Ear Assessment

Clinical diagnostic audiological procedures continue to affect the development of the child in areas of overall health and, indirectly perhaps, speech and language acquisition. For example, objective assessment of middle ear function was historically restricted to infants older than 7 months because of inappropriate tympanometric tools. As early as 1973 it was reported that infants 0–7 months of age could not be tested using tympanometry, an objective method of assessing eardrum and middle ear performance (Bluestone, Beery, & Paradise, 1973). False results reported on babies 30 years ago using tympanometry resulted in lack of confidence in this important procedure in evaluation of ear infections in this age group, which is at high risk for recurrent otitis media (middle ear infection). The undesirable impact of chronic or recurrent ear infections in early infancy on language delay in school-age children is well established (Grievink, Peters, van Bon, & Schilder, 1993; Klausen, Moller, Holmefjord, Reisaeter, & Asbjornsen, 2000; Schilder et al., 1993). Fluctuating mild hearing loss as a result of mild ear infections produces a measurable impact on speech development and language acquisition in children in their primary grades at school. Failing to identify this common condition in infancy via this vital screening device and diagnostic instrument delayed accurate diagnosis of ear infections and treatment in countless cases. Research in the technology of tympanometry within the past decade has resulted in changes in the instrumentation to permit tympanometric assessment of infant ear drums and middle ear status with the inclusion of a minor change in probe tone frequency. The adjustment to the biomedical instrumentation is negligible in cost, and the application diagnostically affects the testing of virtually every infant in the United States.

Neural Pathologies

Other aspects of diagnostic audiology have improved because of technology and research focus. For example, description of "auditory neuropathy" in the past decade has assisted in explaining unusual test outcomes unknown to medical science previously while also providing a new cause of deafness. This condition in extreme cases is a cause of "deafness," but the damage is to the central nervous system rather than the ear itself. The diagnosis is made with sensitive electrophysiological instrumentation, including ABR and OAE assessment. An extensive literature is available to the interested reader (available via Medline or Pubmed). In addition, application of other evoked potential procedures, including identification of middle latency response, may contribute to the early diagnosis of hearing loss in infants and may also have application for early determination of auditory processing disorder, which also affects language acquisition.

ABR Improvements

Improvement in auditory evoked potential instrumentation and procedures during the past decade have resulted in more accurate determination of the extent and pattern of hearing loss in infants and young children. Use of tone-evoked ABR assessment as follow-up to other screening methods defines severity of loss at important frequencies for speech acquisition. This early "mapping" of the hearing level necessarily precedes appropriate remediation and amplification. When profound deafness is determined using these techniques, language habilitation can begin without focus on the auditory channel and with no loss of advantage in utilizing critical periods for language development. This technology also enables determination of cochlear implant candidacy before a child is 6 months of age, enabling speech/language development via the auditory channel should this be the preference of the parents (see Nicholas & Geers, chapter 12 this volume).

INTRAOPERATIVE AND POSTOPERATIVE MONITORING APPLICATIONS

Surgical Monitoring

Another area of technological contribution to the field of audiology is the subspecialty of "intraoperative monitoring." Electrophysiological surgical monitoring by audiologists improves surgical outcomes because of the determination of neural performance during surgery. When this technology is applied to cochlear implantation, surgical outcomes are similarly improved.

Monitoring Cochlear Implant Surgery

Determining the viability of the auditory nerve may be achieved during surgery using electrical stimulation of the eighth cranial nerve or via neural response imaging (NRI) during cochlear implant surgical procedures. Recording of the ABR with this technique demonstrates the conduction of what will become an acoustic signal postsurgically. The technique may also assist in the placement of the implant within the coiled cochlea, and depth of penetration can be roughly measured with this monitoring technique. Therefore, the surgeon is informed of the performance of the cochlear implant while adjustments in the device placement can still be made with relative ease.

P300 and Treatment

One component of the typical evoked acoustic response is produced in the cerebral cortex and is called the P300, referring to positive polarity of the response as well as its occurrence with a latency of 300 ms after the stimulus. This response can be used to indicate processing of sound in the brain.

Evoked potential applications after cochlear implantation are also used habilitatively. Measurements of cortical evoked potentials such as the P300 response through the implant are used to show that treatment is having an effect. Increased amplitude of the P300 potential is reported to precede a noticeable improvement in speech understanding among cochlear implant users receiving speech/language therapy (Beynon, Snik, & van den Broek, 2002; Kileny, Boerst, & Zwolan, 1997). That is, monitoring the "growth" in amplitude of the P300 at intervals along months of therapy may give evidence that continuing the course of treatment may eventually have a favorable outcome. Although the measurement of the P300 response to acoustic stimulation is decades old, cochlear implant application shows promise to improve language acquisition of deaf children who utilize this technology.

Accurate Early Diagnosis of Hearing Loss and Genetic Factors

Genetic Deafness

Along with decreased age of diagnosis of hearing loss, improvements have occurred in the United States in identification of etiologies of deafness. Obvious genetic conditions are easily recognized when they affect embryonic development and show up externally as poorly formed ears, for example. Finding subtle inner ear origins of deafness due to genetic factors is occurring routinely now but may require expensive DNA testing when this is suspected. This important aspect to early detection of hearing impairment has implications for appropriate habilitation and follow-up. For example, when hearing loss is identified and genetic testing follows, conditions involving maldevelopment of the auditory nervous system would likely not suggest good cochlear implant outcomes. Further assessment using electrically evoked ABR, or NRI procedures, could verify poor stimulation potential of the auditory nerve. This result might indicate speech and language habilitation using more traditional therapy protocols such as speechreading and auditory training.

Viral Deafness

Also, not well understood decades ago were viral conditions such as cytomegalovirus and their result on hearing. Early detection of hearing loss and determination of the cause have led to improvements in screening for viral conditions known to affect the hearing of the fetus. Blood serum testing for cytomegolovirus as an active viral eruption during early pregnancy may indicate possible cytomegalic inclusion disease in the infant. Although treatment is not available for this common virus, diagnosis of an active infection in the infant has implications for the parents and care givers as well as the health care workers exposed to the child. Special precautions of active carriers of the virus and those in contact with the infant would minimize other transmissions. In addition, monitoring of the virus into a quiescent stage in the mother would indicate potential to have another child who would not be infected. Further, monitoring of the child in early development using evoked potential measurement can determine a delayed-onset hearing loss, which should be suspected in both congenital and acquired forms of the disease.

Autosomal Recessive Deafness

To be sure, discovery of autosomal recessive causes of deafness, such as the now commonly reported connexin genes, explains the high incidence of genetic deafness that is recessive (as high as 80% of genetic deafness). Also, with genetic factors accounting for at least 60% of hearing loss in newborns, recessive genes are clearly factors in a high percentage of newborn deafness.

Connexin 26: Autosomal Recessive Deafness in Newborns   Connexin 26 (Cx26)–related hearing loss has been studied extensively during the past 5 years. The incidence of Cx26 as a cause of hereditary hearing loss is reported to be extremely high. A recent report describes several mutations (35delG, 167delT, and 235delC) on the *GJB2/DFN1* gene (Cx26) that have been attributed to approximately 50% of severe to profound sensorineural hearing loss cases, making it the most common type of congenital deafness worldwide (Tekin, Arnos, & Pandya, 2001).

Mechanism of Cx26 Deafness   The precise mechanism for how Cx26 causes dysfunction to the inner ear is also understood. Studies describe how this mutation interferes with the intercellular ion channels found within the inner ear, disrupting how potassium is recycled through the stria vascularis. The stria vascularis is known to be a key manufacture site for endolymph, an important inner ear fluid. Without a potassium-rich environment provided by endolymph, the hair cells in the cochlea will quickly die, causing deafness (Green et al., 2003; McGuirt & Smith, 1999; Tekin et al., 2001).

Cx Vestibular Involvement Cx26, in conjunction with Cx32, is also expressed within the vestibular organs (Forge et al., 1999). It is assumed that these mutations also affect the inner ear balance organs (saccule, utricle, and semicircular canals) in addition to the known damage to the inner ear hearing organ (cochlea). However, reports in the literature are lacking concerning vestibular features associated with Cx26 mutations (Green et al., 2003). Cohn et al. (1999) analyzed the vestibular function (rotary chair) of 13 individuals with Cx26-related deafness. Two were found to have abnormal results. One of these was a premature infant (born at 31 weeks) tested at 7 months. Denoyelle et al. (1999) retrospectively analyzed data on 10 individuals with the Cx26 mutation 35delG, all of whom were found to have normal vestibular function. Preliminary findings of a study at Gallaudet University (Ackley & North, 2003) indicate asymmetry in vestibular evoked myogenic potential (VEMP) amplitude as well as reduced amplitude overall in Cx26 deafness. This preliminary outcome suggests possible damage to saccular hair cells, which are responsible for gravitational balance and balance when moving in a straight line (linear acceleration).

Vestibular Assessment in Children: Developmental Implications

Importance of Physiological Assessment

A possible application of the VEMP procedure as it relates to childhood testing is to corroborate cochlear damage test findings. Magnetic resonance imaging and computer-assisted tomography scan are incapable of determining viability of hair cell performance. These procedures provide a visual image of the general anatomy. These tests do not resolve to less than 0.5 mm and therefore are incapable of imaging microscopic hair cells in either the cochlea or vestibular system. To this end, physiological "imaging" via evoked potential procedures performed by audiologists provides the important physiology ingredient to the "anatomy" and "physiology" equation desired in all studies of the human body for diagnostic as well as normative purposes. Determination of cochlear hair cell response is achieved with ABR measurement, but until recently measurement of hair cells in the vestibular system eluded audiologists. This has been especially true when testing infants and children, and finding how widespread damage to inner ear hair cells might occur beyond the cochlea is desirable for two reasons: (1) Diagnostic confirmation of the extent of inner ear maldevelopment is only rendered when both cochlear and vestibular aspects of the inner ear are measured, and (2) poor vestibular response may indicate other congenital anomalies such as perilymphatic fistula, or leak of inner ear fluid, which can be treated. In addition, poor VEMP responses recorded in children gives evidence of poor vestibular capability, which may then direct therapeutic focus on the balance system. Clearly, aspects of development may be enhanced when all systems are developing somewhat in parallel. Therefore, improving balance and coordination therapeutically may influence the child's level of confidence to foster improved development toward other milestones, including speech and language.

IMPROVING SPEECH AND LANGUAGE DEVELOPMENT IN DEAF CHILDREN USING AUDITION

Hearing Aids and Assistive Technology

There is little doubt that the extent to which a child can monitor speech and spoken language production via the auditory channel will affect these important developmental milestones. Improvements in assistive listening technology, hearing aid circuitry, and cochlear implants in the past decade affect this important developmental process. The clarity of the speech signal is markedly improved in all categories of listening technology since the 1980s, as well as minimizing undesirable background noise interference with the target signal and reducing output effectively to reduce loudness tolerance complaints. Circuitry has advanced from analog to digital, that is, programmable, and includes such options as multimemory remote operation with switchable directional microphone capability in high-background-noise environments and selectable compression circuitry while retaining speech intelligibility.

These remarkable technological achievements in microcircuitry have enabled many severely hard of hearing users, as well as "medically" deaf (>90 dB hearing level) persons to use their residual hearing effectively. Although analog circuitry is still available in hearing aids and assistive devices, it is generally selected because of lower cost. This circuitry amplifies in a linear fashion. It can distort sounds more noticeably than does digital circuitry, and it is limited in its ability to filter unwanted background noise. On the other hand, digital instruments are programmed via computer and can access multiple channels; they analyze incoming sound and adjust the loudness based on preset parameters; they detect softer sounds of speech and raise loudness to suit the circumstance; and they do not amplify background noise to the same degree as the primary signal. The size of the instrument is of concern, and the least noticeable devices are favored. And for this reason, the completely in the canal (CIC) device is the generally preferred model just as contact lenses are preferable over glasses. Young children may be more tolerant of a "noticeable" instrument, but teenagers often prefer the CIC model.

Cochlear Implants

Technological improvements in digital and programmable circuitry have had a similar impact on the cochlear implant industry as has been realized in the hearing aid and assistive listening device industries. Cochlear implants have developed from a single-channel analog device in the 1960s into the early 1980s, when multichannel implants replaced the old standard. Currently, as many as 32 channels of discrete stimulation can be achieved, with each channel uniquely programmable, and the processors have become more miniature (Frijns, Frijns, Klop, Bonnet, & Briaire, 2003; Skinner, Arndt, & Staller, 2002). Thirty-two channels of input enable stimulation along the frequency band of neural input into the cochlea that mimics the normal ear. Although 32 channels will not replace the thousands of discrete frequencies resolved by the normal functioning cochlea, multichannel cochlear implantation is proving to provide sufficient frequency discrimination capability to allow understanding of conversation in a high percentage of cases (Kiefer, Hohl, Sturzebecher, Pfennigdorff, & Gstoettner, 2002). The standard by which most (adult) cochlear implant users judge the success of the device is an ability to use the telephone. This is not a common standard among children using implants, but when a child can understand speech over the phone, this is considered the ultimate implant success nonetheless.

The single-analog-channel cochlear implant of decades ago provided little more than sound awareness, prosody or rhythm of speech, and perhaps some improvement in speechreading ability. The benefit of the implant in those "dark ages" of the device sometimes gave a surprising advantage to the user. For example, the case of a college student who was on the golf team reported he only used the early analog device when hitting the golf ball. Hearing the impact seemed to improve his score. He reportedly did not use the device in other settings, including in the classroom or in conversation. This type of early account has changed dramatically with multiple-channel digital and programmable implant technology.

Candidacy for cochlear implantation has also been revised since the time of the early devices (see Nicholas & Geers, chapter 12 this volume). Profoundly deafened adults were the early cases, and the protocol extends to 6-month-old infants currently. Improvements in determining candidacy and subsequent neural stimulation are facilitated with NRI, which measures neural capability and replaces the need for young children to determine how well they hear certain sounds through the implant (Frijns, Klop, Bonnet, & Briaire, 2003). Improvements in programming software have reduced session times by up to 75%, and mapping strategies are taking decisions out of the child implant equation (Kiefer, von Ilberg, Rupprecht, Hubner-Egner, & Knecht, 2000).

Implanting early in development has advantages. Taking advantage of peak language acquisitions periods before 1 year of age through 3 or 4 years of age is desirable. Also, plasticity of neurons is more evident in childhood than in adults, which might enable neural viability with electrical stimulation of the implant. And reports of success with children who are implanted before 2 years of age are convincing (Dillon, Cleary, Pisoni, & Carter, 2004; but see Nicholas and Geers, chapter 12 this volume, for a critique of most existing studies). However, implanting babies is steeped in controversy. Reactions from the Deaf community when this protocol emerged ranged from "genocide of the Deaf culture" to "wait until the children are old enough to decide for themselves." The controversy may persist, but there are arguments to rebut the reactions from Deaf opponents. First, cochlear implants will not eliminate all causes and types of deafness, and so the Deaf culture will remain. Second, waiting until a child is old enough to make a decision to receive an implant misses the critical speech/language acquisition period when the most gain in this development could be realized. Nonetheless, cochlear implants will likely continue to be controversial, and unsuccessful cases of implanted children will feed the debate.

An advantage of the early single-channel implant protocol was the requirement of a team approach to device candidacy. The team involved a group of professionals that assessed several related aspects of success and orientation to the new device and lifestyle. The surgeon and audiologists determined the severity of hearing loss and likely stimulability of the auditory nerve and brainstem. Speech-language pathologists assessed probable performance in speech/language post-surgically. Psychologists assessed personality profile to determine suitable adjustment to the changes imposed by an implant. Other professionals included biomedical engineers, specialists in vestibular (re)habilitation, deaf educators, social workers, and family counselors. Indeed, the team approach is still favored but is no longer required by the U.S. Food and Drug Administration because the device has passed clinical trials, and implantation may now be performed in clinics where team services may be unavailable. To this end, cochlear implant services are generally superior in a major medical center than in a private clinic.

Generally, when the team approach to implantation is utilized and prognosis for success is indicated, the cochlear implant serves to improve the quality of life for the user. In the case of young children, this includes near normal development of speech and spoken language in many cases (see Geers, chapter 11 this volume). As such, the child would not function as a "deaf" child while using the device. In older children, the implant may serve to sustain quality speech and further development of linguistic capability. With improvements in digital circuitry, increasing channel input and programmability, outcomes will continue to improve in areas of speech and language development among young "deaf" children.

SUMMARY AND CONCLUSIONS

Advances in biomedical instrumentation and technique in audiology have clearly affected speech and spoken language development of deaf children. These gains are most obvious in amplification, including assistive listening technology and hearing aids that use digital and programmable circuitry. This technology has also greatly improved cochlear implants with the advent of multiple-channel devices with programming capability of each channel. Indeed, digital/programmable circuitry and microphone improvements have removed much of the distortion, background noise, and loudness tolerance issues that plagued amplification devices for decades. The area of early identification of hearing loss in the past decade has greatly facilitated early intervention and capturing of the peak acquisition period for speech and language acquisition in children. Technological improvements have enabled screening applications and diagnostic utility of OAE, ASSR, AABR, and tympanometry. In addition, movement toward nationwide adoption of infant hearing screening protocols and improvements in procedure and follow-up take full advantage of the contributions made by technology. Finally, improvements in clinical audiology diagnostic procedures and research efforts have improved test capability, leading to better enumerated etiological factors and more carefully constructed habilitative methods. Improvements in diagnosing the entire inner ear, and not only the cochlea, are improving the ultimate speech and language outcomes of the child.

Future research will likely result in improvements in amplification circuitry, cochlear implant speech processing, and infant hearing screening equipment and protocols, as well as overall improvements in diagnostic audiology. Prospective monitoring of children who are screened before 6 months of age and who receive early, appropriate, and sustained therapeutic intervention, including amplification or cochlear implantation, will provide the database for desired speech and language outcomes. Application of evoked potential measures, including measurement of cortical evoked potentials during speech and language acquisition, will enhance development in children who use amplification or a cochlear implant. Measurement of balance function in young children will emerge as a routine evoked potential test procedure during the coming decade. This will contribute significantly to a minimal database on vestibular physiology in this age group, but more important, the test results will accurately identify the extent of damage to the entire inner ear and not just the cochlea, as has been the clinical focus traditionally.

Finally, deaf and hard-of-hearing children will continue to be the most important beneficiaries of the improvements in the profession of audiology. Advances in technology have enabled identification of hearing loss earlier in life than imagined when audiology began, and this is affecting early speech and language development in young children. Technological advances in cochlear implants and hearing aids are enabling more thorough (auditory) access to spoken language among deaf and hard-of-hearing children. And equipment and procedures can now diagnose deafness and hearing loss conditions in children that were previously a mystery. The final outcome of these advances is an improvement in the way of life for deaf and hard-of-hearing children worldwide.

Because of the degree to which speech and language benefits accrue to deaf and hard-of-hearing children from early and accurate diagnosis and assessment, they will be among the primary beneficiaries of continued advances in professional training as well as technological advances.

REFERENCES

Ackley, R. S., & North, C. (2003, November). *Vestibular evoked myogenic potential assessment of deaf subjects*. Technical session presented at the American Speech-Language and Hearing Association National Convention, Chicago, IL.

Alberti, P. W., Hyde, M. L., Riko, K., Corbin, H., & Abramovich, S. (1983). An evaluation of BERA for hearing screening in high-risk neonates. *Laryngoscope, 93*, 1115–1121.

Beynon, A. J., Snik, A. F., & van den Broek, P. (2002). Evaluation of cochlear implant benefit with auditory cortical evoked potentials. *International Journal Audiology, 41*(7), 429–435.

Bluestone, C. D., Beery, Q. C., & Paradise, J. L. (1973). Audiometry and tympanometry in relation to middle ear effusions in children. *Laryngoscope, 83*(4), 594–604.

Bonfils, P., (1989) Spontaneous otoacoustic emissions: Clinical interest. *Laryngoscope, 99*, 752–756.

Cohn, E. S., Kelley, P. M., Fowler, T. W., Gorga, M. P., Lefkowitz, D. M., Kuehn, H. J., et al. (1999). Clinical studies of families with hearing loss attributable to mutations in the connexin 26 gene (GJB2/DFNB1). *Pediatrics, 103*(3), 546–550.

Denoyelle, F., Marlin, S., Weil, D., Moatti, L., Chauvin, P., Garabedian, E. N., & Petit, C. (1999). Clinical features of the prevalent form of childhood deafness, DFNB1, due to a connexin 26 gene defect: Implications for genetic counseling. *Lancet, 343*, 1298–1303.

Dillon, C. M., Cleary, M., Pisoni, D. B., & Carter, A. K. (2004). Imitation of nonwords by hearing-impaired children with cochlear implants: Segmental analyses. *Clinical Linguistic Phonology, 18*(1), 39–55.

Downs, M. P., & Sterritt, G. M. (1967). A guide to newborn and infant hearing screening programs. *Archives of Otolaryngology, 85*, 15–22.

Elberling, C., Parbo, J., Johnsen, N. J., & Bagi, P. (1985). Evoked acoustic emission: Clinical application. *Acta Otolaryngologica, 421*(Suppl.), 77–85.

Forge, A., Becker, D., Casalotti, S., Edwards, J., Evans, W. H., Lench, N., & Souter, M. (1999). Gap junctions and connexin expression in the inner ear. *Novartis Foundation Symposium, 219,* 135–156.

Frijns, J. H., Klop, W. M., Bonnet, R. M., & Briaire, J. J. (2003). Optimizing the number of electrodes with high-rate stimulation of the clarion CII cochlear implant. *Acta Otolaryngologica, 123*(2), 138–142.

Galambos, R., Makeig, S., & Talmachoff, P. J. (1981). A 40 Hz auditory potential recorded from the human scalp. *Proceedings of the National Academy of Sciences of the United States of America, 78,* 2643–2647.

Green, G., Mueller, R. F., Cohn, E. S., Avraham, K. B., Kanaan, M., & Smith, R. (2003). Audiological manifestations and features of connexin 26 deafness. *Audiological Medicine, 1,* 5–11.

Grievink, E. H., Peters, S. A., van Bon, W. H., & Schilder, A. G. (1993). The effects of early bilateral otitis media with effusion on language ability: A prospective cohort study. *Journal of Speech-Language and Hearing Research, 36*(5), 1004–1012.

John, M. S., & Picton, T. W. (2000). Human auditory steady-state responses to amplitude-modulated tones: Phase and latency measurements. *Hearing Research, 141,* 57–79.

Joint Committee on Infant Hearing. (1991). 1990 Position statement. American Speech-Language and Hearing Association, *33*(Suppl. 15), 3–6.

Kemp, D. T. (1978). Stimulated acoustic emissions from within the human auditory system. *Journal of the Acoustical Society of America, 64,* 1286–1391.

Kemp, D. T. (1979). Evidence of mechanical nonlinearity and frequency selective wave amplification in the cochlea. *Archives of Otorhinolaryngology, 224*(1–2), 37–45.

Kemp, D. T. (1986). Otoacoustic emissions, travelling waves and cochlear mechanisms. *Hearing Research, 22,* 95–104.

Kemp, D. T., Ryan, S., & Bray, P. (1990). A guide to the effective use of otoacoustic emissions. *Ear and Hearing, 11*(2), 93–105.

Kiefer, J., Hohl, S., Sturzebecher, E., Pfennigdorff, T., & Gstoettner, W. (2002). Comparison of speech recognition with different speech coding strategies (SPEAK, CIS, and ACE) and their relationship to telemetric measures of compound action potentials in the nucleus CI 24M cochlear implant system. *Audiology, 40*(1), 32–42.

Kiefer, J., von Ilberg, C., Rupprecht, V., Hubner-Egner, J., & Knecht, R. (2000). Optimized speech understanding with the continuous interleaved sampling speech coding strategy in patients with cochlear implants: Effect of variations stimulation rate and number of channels. *Annals of Otolology Rhinolology Laryngolology, 109*(11), 1009–1020.

Kileny, P. R., Boerst, A., & Zwolan, T. (1997). Cognitive evoked potentials to speech and tonal stimuli in children with implants. *Otolaryngology Head and Neck Surgery, 117*(Pt 1), 161–169.

Klausen, O., Moller, P., Holmefjord, A., Reisaeter, S., & Asbjornsen, A. (2000). Lasting effects of otitis media with effusion on language skills and listening performance. *Acta Otolaryngologica, 543*(Suppl.), 73–76.

Martin, G. K., Probst, R., & Lonsbury-Martin, B. L. (1990). Otoacoustic emissions in human ears: Normative findings. *Ear and Hearing, 11*(2), 106–120.

McGuirt, W. T., & Smith, R. (1999). Connexin 26 as a cause of hereditary hearing loss. *American Journal of Audiology, 8*, 41–49.

Norton, S. J., & Neely, S. T. (1987). Tone burst evoked otoacoustic emissions from normal hearing subjects. *Journal of the Acoustical Society of America, 81*, 1860–1872.

Probst, R., Coats, A. C., Martin, G. K., & Lonsbury-Martin, B. L. (1986). Spontaneous, click, and tone burst evoked otoacoustic emissions from normal ears. *Hearing Research, 21*, 261–275.

Schilder, A. G., Van Manen, J. G., Zielhuis, G. A., Grievink, E. H., Peters, S. A., & Van Den Broek, P. (1993). Long-term effects of otitis media with effusion on language, reading and spelling. *Clinical Otolaryngology, 18*(3), 234–241.

Skinner, M. W., Arndt, P. L., Staller, S. J. (2002). Nucleus 24 advanced encoder conversion study: performance versus preference. *Ear and Hearing, 23*(1 Suppl.), 2S–17S.

Tekin, M., Arnos, K. S., & Pandya, A. (2001). Advances in hereditary deafness. *Lancet, 358*, 1082–1090.

Ungan, P., & Yagcioglu, S. (2002). Origin of the binaural interaction component in wave P4 of the short-latency auditory evoked potentials in the cat: Evaluation of serial depth recording from the brainstem. *Hearing Research, 167*(1–2), 81–101.

Yoshinaga-Itano, C. (1999). Benefits of early intervention for children with hearing loss. *Otolaryngology Clinics of North America, 32*(6), 1089–1102.

5

Relationships Among Speech Perception and Language Measures in Hard-of-Hearing Children

Peter J. Blamey, Julia Z. Sarant, & Louise E. Paatsch

Spoken communication has long been seen as being at the core of human society and human cognitive development. As a consequence, the development of spoken language is usually seen to be of central importance to all children, including deaf and hard-of-hearing children. The question "How do children learn to make sense from the complex acoustic speech signal?" has interested psychologists, physiologists, and linguists over many years: Brown (1973), Cutler and Swinney (1987), Eimas and Corbit (1973), Jusczyk (1993), Klatt (1979), Mehler et al. (1988), Vihman (1996), and Werker and Tees (1984), to name but a few. How hard-of-hearing children learn to make sense from the complex acoustic speech signal is an even more complex question, and less is known about the answer. A recent summary from the present authors' perspective may be found in Blamey (2002). The main points are as follows:

- Children fall into three hearing categories for the purpose of spoken language development: *hearing* with pure-tone average (PTA) thresholds up to 25 dB HL (hearing level), *hard-of-hearing* with PTA thresholds between 25 and 90 dB HL; and *deaf* with PTA thresholds greater than 90 dB HL.
- Cochlear implants can move a child from the deaf group to the hard-of-hearing group.
- Within the hard-of-hearing category, most children develop spoken language in a similar systematic fashion but usually delayed relative to the hearing group.

- Within the hard-of-hearing group, the degree of hearing loss has surprisingly low correlation with the rate of spoken language development or delay.
- Reduced auditory experience is clearly at the root of spoken language delay for hard-of-hearing children, and therefore early intervention is an important (some would say critical) factor in maximizing the child's exposure to spoken language.

Despite our incomplete psycholinguistic knowledge of how children learn spoken language, families and teachers of hard-of-hearing children are faced with the very real problem of how to help them achieve spoken language at a normal rate. This chapter describes some of the authors' research to evaluate potential solutions to this problem. We have taken a pragmatic experimental approach rather than a theoretical one, going where the data have taken us rather than following any particular learning model, with one exception. We chose not to include children who use sign or other manual communication in our research, because we were less familiar with these communication methods. The inclusion of sign would also complicate both the assessment of spoken language and the description of the development process.

The basis of a pragmatic comparative approach to spoken language development is quantitative assessment using reliable, repeatable, normalized measures. Speech perception tests are commonly used by audiologists to assess the benefits derived from hearing aids and cochlear implants. Language measures are often used by speech pathologists and teachers to assess the spoken language development and educational needs or progress of hard-of-hearing children. If we are to assess the contributions of different devices and habilitation methods to language development, their effects need to be expressed in a common metric, hence the title of this chapter.

Speech perception and language measures are clearly related, and yet the results are often interpreted in different ways, according to the circumstances under which the test was conducted. Some comprehensive language measures (e.g., the Clinical Evaluation of Language Fundamentals [CELF]; Wiig, Secord, & Semel, 1992; Semel, Wiig, & Secord, 1995) include a speech perception subtest. It is ironic that the Recalling Sentences in Context subtest of the CELF is classified as an expressive language measure, while an identical measure could be used as a measure of speech perception in an audiological evaluation. Both points of view can be justified if certain prior conditions are satisfied—that is, the test is a test of perception if the person being tested has perfect adult language, and a test of expressive language if the person being tested has perfect hearing and perfect receptive language. Unfortunately, none of these conditions is likely to be satisfied for hard-of-hearing children, and so the interpretation is difficult to say the least. To interpret the results correctly, one needs to know the effects of both hearing loss and limited language capabilities on the measures being used. If the effects of the variables can be separated, one has a very effective and generally applicable tool for studying language development and the benefits of cochlear implants, hearing aids, and various educational strategies for hard-of-hearing children.

In this chapter we discuss two approaches to studying the relationships between speech perception and language measures: an empirical multivariate regression analysis of longitudinal data from a large group of children (Blamey et al., 2001), and a more analytical approach based on a few simple assumptions about the ways in which hearing, lexical knowledge, and speech production abilities might be combined to yield a predicted score for a speech perception test (Paatsch, Blamey, Sarant, Martin, & Bow, 2004). The two approaches lead to some strong hypotheses about the effectiveness of cochlear implants compared to hearing aids for some groups of children, and about the effectiveness of language-based habilitation on the speech perception of children with hearing loss. These hypotheses are being tested using clinical and experimental data.

RELATIONSHIPS AMONG SPEECH PERCEPTION, PRODUCTION, LANGUAGE, HEARING LOSS, AND AGE

In this first study, the relationships between speech perception, spoken language, hearing, and age-related measures were explored for a group of 87 children who were assessed annually in a longitudinal study (Blamey et al., 2001). Table 5.1 gives details of the children studied. Some of the children used hearing aids (HA group), and some used

Table 5-1: Details of Children Studied

	Cochlear Implant Users	Hearing Aid Users
Number of children	47	40
Number with congenital loss	39	34
Total number of evaluations	80	72
Hearing loss (dB HL)	106 (11) [77–125]	78 (17) [40–103]
Onset of hearing loss (years)	0.3 (0.7) [0–3.4]	0.4 (1.1) [0–4.6]
Age at device fitting (years)	3.5 (1.5) [1.2–8.2]	Not known
Age at evaluation (years)	7.7 (2.0) [4.3–13.0]	9.0 (2.4) [4.5–13.5]
Duration of deafness (years)	3.2 (1.5) [0.5–8.2]	Not applicable
Auditory experience (years)	4.2 (2.0) [0.9–9.2]	8.5 (2.5) [0.6–13.5]

For rows, data are mean (standard deviation) [range] for each group of children. From Blamey et al. (2001) Copyright by the American Speech-Language-Hearing Association. Reprinted with permission.

cochlear implants (CI group). All were enrolled in oral/aural primary-school programs for children with hearing loss in Victoria and New South Wales, Australia. At the time the data were analyzed, some of the children had been assessed once, some twice, and some three times.

Data for a wide variety of perception, production, and language measures were collected, but only an abbreviated set are reported here for clarity and consistency with the second study reported below: The speech perception test scores are for the Consonant-Nucleus-Consonant (CNC) word test (Peterson & Lehiste, 1962), the speech production measure is percentage consonants correct (PCC; Shriberg, Austin, Lewis, Sweeny, & Wilson, 1997), and the language measure is the Peabody Picture Vocabulary test (PPVT; Dunn & Dunn, 1981, 1997). The CNC word test consists of lists of 50 monosyllabic words each composed of an initial consonant, a vowel, and a final consonant. They were presented to the children with live voice at a level of 65 dB SPL (sound pressure level) at a distance of 1 m, either in the auditory alone (A) condition or auditory visual (AV) condition with lipreading and hearing together. The children were required to respond verbally, and a word was counted as correct if every phoneme in the word was correctly produced. The PCC measure was derived from spontaneous conversations that were videotaped and later transcribed by a linguist experienced in the transcription of similar speech samples from hard-of-hearing children. A narrow transcription method was used, and a consonant was considered correct only if it matched the target phoneme in the word and no diacritic marks were used in its transcription. Only singleton consonants (excluding consonants in clusters) were counted in the calculation of the PCC. The PPVT consists of single words that were presented in the AV condition, and the child was required to select one of four pictures that best represented the meaning of the word. Each score for the PPVT was converted to an equivalent age, the age at which typical hearing children score the same on average as the child whose language is being assessed.

Figures 5.1 and 5.2 show the CNC word scores in the A condition and the PPVT equivalent ages, respectively. Both figures show improvements in scores over time, and very little difference in the level of the scores or the trends for the CI and HA groups. The mean scores for the PCC measure were 68.7% (standard deviation, 10.5%) for the CI group and 69.0% (standard deviation, 10.5%) for the HA group.

The effects of time were allowed for with three variables: the age at "onset" of hearing loss, the period of "deafness" between the onset of hearing loss and implantation (CI group only), and the period of "experience" from implantation to the date of evaluation (CI group) or from the onset of hearing loss to the date of evaluation (HA group). The date of hearing aid fitting was not known for some children in the HA group and was assumed to be shortly after the onset of hearing loss.

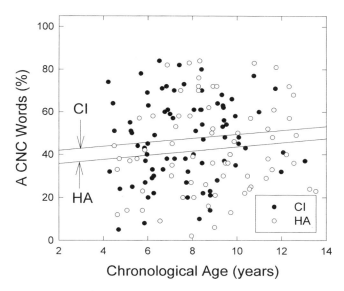

Figure 5-1. CNC word scores in the auditory condition versus chronological age for children using a cochlear implant (CI) or hearing aid (HA). From Blamey et al. (2001). Copyright by the American Speech-Language-Hearing Association. Reprinted with permission.

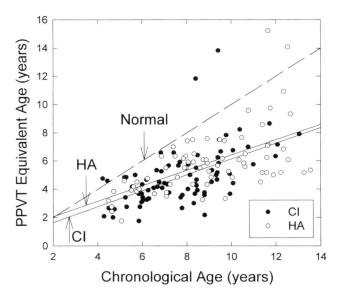

Figure 5-2. PPVT equivalent age versus chronological age for children using a cochlear implant (CI) or hearing aid (HA). The dashed line indicates average results for typical hearing children. From Blamey et al. (2001). Copyright by the American Speech-Language-Hearing Association. Reprinted with permission.

Multiple regression analyses were performed for all perception, production, and language measures as dependent variables, with onset,
deafness, experience, and PTA hearing loss as independent variables.
The regression equations are shown in table 5.2. Each equation shows
how children's scores on the various measures changed on average as a
function of time. For example, the second equation for the CI group
says that the average score for CNC words in the auditory-alone
condition increased by 3.60% for every year prior to the child's onset of
deafness, decreased by 2.37% for every year after the child became deaf
and before the cochlear implant operation, and then increased again by
3.24% for every year after the operation. This is consistent with the
gentle upward trend shown in figure 5.1. The same equation shows
that, on average, CNC word scores in the auditory-alone (A) condition
were lower by 0.38% for every decibel of hearing loss.

The effects of the time variables for the PPVT equivalent age analyses
were all statistically significant. For example, the PPVT equivalent age
for the CI group increased by 0.67 years for every year of chronological
age prior to the onset of deafness, by 0.57 years during the period between onset of deafness and cochlear implantation, and by 0.68 years
during the period following the implant operation. This corresponds to
strong language growth, as shown in figure 5.2, but unfortunately, the
average rate of growth is only about two thirds of the rate for hearing
children. This means that, on average, these deaf and hard-of-hearing
children were likely to enter secondary school (at about age 12) with
vocabulary knowledge equivalent to an 8-year-old hearing child.

**Table 5-2: Regression Analyses of Perception and Language Scores
as a Function of Age at Onset of Hearing Loss, Duration
of Deafness, Experience, and PTA Hearing Loss**

HA group

$\text{CNC AV} = 49.4^{***} + 7.52^{**}\ \text{onset} + 2.10^{*}\ \text{exp} - 0.12\ \text{PTA}$ $R^2 = .150$

$\text{CNC A} = 64.2^{***} + 5.89^{*}\ \text{onset} + 1.55\ \text{exp} - 0.48^{**}\ \text{PTA}$ $R^2 = .230$

$\text{PPVT} = 0.88 + 1.10^{***}\ \text{onset} + 0.53^{***}\ \text{exp} + 0.00\ \text{PTA}$ $R^2 = .405$

$\text{PCC} = 65.8^{***} + 3.71^{**}\ \text{onset} - 0.02^{*}\ \text{exp} + 0.02\ \text{PTA}$ $R^2 = .151$

CI group

$\text{CNC AV} = 103^{***} + 2.1\ \text{onset} - 1.47\ \text{deaf} + 4.66^{***}\ \text{exp} - 0.52^{*}\ \text{PTA}$ $R^2 = .221$

$\text{CNC A} = 81.7^{**} + 3.60\ \text{onset} - 2.37\ \text{deaf} + 3.24^{*}\ \text{exp} - 0.38\ \text{PTA}$ $R^2 = .180$

$\text{PPVT} = 4.17 + 0.67^{*}\ \text{onset} + 0.57^{***}\ \text{deaf} + 0.68^{***}\ \text{exp} - 0.04\ \text{PTA}$ $R^2 = .368$

$\text{PCC} = 75.2^{***} + 2.86\ \text{onset} - 1.16\ \text{deaf} + 1.87^{*}\ \text{exp} - 0.11\ \text{PTA}$ $R^2 = .174$

For CNC and PCC, units are percent for the scores and the constant coefficients, percent
per dB HL for PTA, and percent per year for onset, deafness, and experience coefficients. For
PPVT, the units are years for the equivalent age and the constant coefficients, and years per dB
HL for PTA. The coefficients for onset, deafness, and experience are dimensionless for the
PPVT equations.
$^{*}p < .05;\ ^{**}p < .01;\ ^{***}p < .001.$

It was hoped that the coefficients for the time variables in table 5.2 would all be significantly greater than zero, indicating that the children were improving in speech perception, vocabulary knowledge, and speech production accuracy over time. It was also expected that the coefficients for PTA would be significantly less than zero, indicating that the children with greater hearing loss had lower scores than children with lower hearing thresholds.

As shown by the asterisks in table 5.2, 12 of the 20 time coefficients were statistically significantly greater than zero, and two of the eight PTA coefficients were significantly less than zero. Despite these significant trends in the expected directions, the proportions of variance accounted for by the multiple regression analyses were less than or equal to 40.5% (see R^2 values in table 5.2). It is likely that much of the remaining variance is related to other variables not included in the regression equations of table 5.2. In the case of the CNC scores, the additional variables include the spoken language abilities of the child, as discussed in the introductory remarks to this chapter. Using the PPVT and PCC measures as additional independent variables in the analyses for CNC scores results in the regression equations of table 5.3. The PPVT equivalent age values used in these regression analyses were limited to a maximum of 7 years because it was found empirically that the perception scores reached a maximum at about this language level (Blamey et al., 2001). The coefficients of PPVT indicate the increase in percent score for each year of equivalent language age up to a maximum of 7 years. For example, the first regression equation indicates

Table 5-3: Regression Equations for Speech Perception Scores as a Function of Time, Hearing Loss, and Language and Speech Production

HA group
CNC AV $= -26.4 + 0.21$ onset $- 0.96$ exp $- 0.17$ PTA $+$
  9.76^{***} PPVT $+ 0.82^{***}$ PCC $R^2 = .677$
CNC A $= 5.2 + 0.21$ onset $- 0.77$ exp $- 0.51^{***}$ PTA $+$
  7.21^{***} PPVT $+ 0.65^{**}$ PCC $R^2 = .536$

CI group
CNC AV $= 27.8 - 3.07$ onset $- 1.90$ deaf $- 0.16$ exp $-$
  0.28 PTA $+ 4.80^{**}$ PPVT $+ 0.76^{***}$ PCC $R^2 = .522$
CNC A $= 0.61 - 2.21$ onset $- 4.07^{**}$ deaf $- 2.37$ exp $-$
  0.07 PTA $+ 6.28^{***}$ PPVT $+ 0.73^{***}$ PCC $R^2 = .573$

Units are percent for perception scores and constant coefficients; percent per year for onset, deafness, experience, and PPVT coefficients; and percent per dB HL for PTA. Units for the PCC terms are dimensionless because both the perception and production scores are percentages.
$^*p < .05$; $^{**}p < .01$; $^{***}p < .001$.

that the average CNC word score in the AV condition increased by 4.80% for the CI group as the children's equivalent age increased by 1 year. Similarly, the average score increased by 0.76% as the children's percentage of consonants correctly produced increased by 1%.

Comparison of tables 5.2 and 5.3 shows that the range of variance accounted for in the CNC analyses has increased from 15–23% in table 5.2 to 52–67% in table 5.3 when the language-based measures were introduced as additional independent variables. As expected, the coefficients for the PPVT and PCC measures are all significantly greater than zero in table 5.3. None of the 10 time coefficients (for onset, deafness, and experience) is significantly greater than zero. This means that all of the learning that contributed to increases in the CNC perception scores of these children was associated with spoken language improvements. Only one of the PTA coefficients was statistically significantly different from zero, meaning that perception scores were more significantly associated with linguistic performance than with hearing for all except the CNC A scores for the HA group.

No matter how strong an association may be between two measures, the association does not necessarily demonstrate a causal relationship one way or the other. It may be that children who have more hearing have better speech perception and therefore develop spoken language faster, or it may be that children who learn spoken language faster have higher speech perception scores. Whether the relationships are causal is of more than academic interest. If better hearing allows spoken language to develop faster, then children with hearing loss should be fitted with hearing aids or cochlear implants as early as possible. If spoken language performance is a major factor affecting speech perception, then habilitation should be directed at developing spoken language as quickly and effectively as possible, rather than concentrating entirely on improving hearing. It is possible, even probable, that both relationships are causal and better hearing makes it easier to learn spoken language, and better spoken language yields higher speech perception scores. In this case, when an individual child scores low for speech perception, one needs to know whether their performance is limited by their hearing, or their spoken language, or both, in order to provide the most effective habilitation program. This is the subject of the next section.

SEPARATING CONTRIBUTIONS OF HEARING, LEXICAL KNOWLEDGE, AND SPEECH PRODUCTION TO SPEECH PERCEPTION

In contrast to the multiple regression analysis in the previous section, the study of Paatsch et al. (2004) used a nonlinear mathematical model to describe the specific effects of hearing, lexical knowledge, and speech production on monosyllabic word perception scores. Thirty-three school children with hearing loss, fitted with hearing aids and/or cochlear implants, were evaluated using speech-perception, reading-aloud, speech-production, and language measures. These measures were incorporated into the mathematical model, which revealed that the word perception test scores in the auditory-alone mode were strongly dependent on residual hearing levels, lexical knowledge, and speech-production abilities. This is similar to the result described in the preceding section; however, the mathematical model also provided estimates of the separate effects of hearing and spoken language performance on the overall speech perception score for each child. This information is very important in optimizing the habilitation program for individual children.

Thirty-three children (16 boys and 17 girls) between 6 and 14 years of age participated in this study. Twenty of the children had a hearing loss greater than 90 dB HL, seven had a severe hearing loss (70–89 dB HL), and six had a moderate hearing loss (40–69 dB HL). Twenty-one of the children were fitted with behind-the-ear hearing aids by audiologists from Australian Hearing (An Australian government agency providing hearing aids to children throughout Australia). Twelve children were cochlear implant users who were implanted with the Nucleus 22 multichannel device (Clark et al., 1987) using the SPEAK speech processing strategy (Whitford et al., 1995). These children were managed by the Melbourne Cochlear Implant Clinic.

Table 5.4 shows the pure tone aided average thresholds at 500, 1000, and 2000 Hz for the better ear from the most recent audiogram, and the age for each child. None of the children in the study had an uncorrected visual impairment or known sensory dyslexia. During the selection process, one child was excluded for this reason. Children with very low reading levels (i.e., children who would have required assistance from the tester to read the monosyllabic words) were also excluded from the study. All 33 children attended mainstream primary and/or secondary schools where an oral/aural method of communication was used. Each school provided additional support for these children during mainstream classroom activities and within small group and/or individual sessions.

This study used evaluations of speech perception and spoken language that were very similar to those in the longitudinal study described above. Two lists of the CNC word test (Peterson & Lehiste, 1962) were presented to each child in the auditory-alone condition (listening without lipreading). Each participant also was required to read the two lists of CNC words presented in the auditory-alone condition plus an additional two lists. All CNC responses were videotaped, transcribed, and scored using the criteria that all three phonemes must be correctly produced for the word to be correct. A broad phonemic transcription

Table 5-4: Individual Scores for Percent Correct CNC Words in the Auditory Alone (A) and Read (R) Conditions ($n = 3$)

Participant	Age (yr:mo)	PTA (dB HL)	A Word Scores	R Word Scores	PPVT Age-Equivalent Score (yr:mo)	PCC
Cochlear implant users						
1	6:10	107	38	51	5:3	73
2	7:8	110	37	64	5:11	78
3	9:0	93	54	96	7:5	85
4	9:1	115	68	91	7:3	80
5	10:0	110	45	90	6:9	88
6	10:3	100	62	78	6:6	85
7	10:4	105	60	81	5:10	84
8	10:5	125	48	69	5:3	71
9	11:1	105	49	81	5:11	78
10	11:8	113	70	92	8:8	87
11	13:0	120	53	72	7:5	73
12	14:0	108	35	67	7:11	65
Hearing aid users						
13	7:6	97	20	57	4:10	84
14	8:8	60	70	98	7:7	92
15	8:10	85	50	84	6:1	84
16	8:11	45	72	75	7:7	78
17	8:11	90	13	77	5:3	77
18	9:4	62	84	97	7:11	89
19	9:10	68	37	94	6:11	84
20	10:0	83	89	99	7:6	92
21	10:6	102	24	76	5:10	75
22	10:10	88	47	56	6:1	73
23	11:0	68	76	88	5:9	91
24	11:4	102	25	50	6:1	75
25	11:5	88	27	73	8:3	79
26	12:8	103	23	93	8:2	84
27	12:8	70	76	87	10:7	87
28	12:10	97	23	51	5:8	74
29	13:2	75	24	37	5:2	74
30	13:4	40	55	88	9:1	76
31	13:5	90	29	97	14:9	84
32	13:6	92	23	90	5:4	78
33	13:7	78	71	97	8:10	82

was used in which each phone was transcribed as the nearest English phoneme without diacritics. Interlist variability was assessed by comparing the scores for the pairs of CNC word lists in each condition for each child. The standard deviation of the paired differences across all conditions was 5.45% for lists of 50 words. Table 5.4 includes the mean percentage words correct for the audition (A) and reading (R) conditions for each child.

Conversational speech samples were obtained from each participant by an experienced audiologist or teacher of the deaf. These samples were elicited using prompting questions about familiar topics. All conversations were videotaped. On average, a total of 60 utterances, which were representative of the child's conversational skills, were transcribed phonetically by two linguists. Both linguists had experience in listening to the speech of children with hearing loss. The rules used to separate utterances in these conversation samples included change of speaker, rising and falling intonation (indicating the end of an utterance), a pause of two or more seconds, and/or a single thought constituted as a single utterance. All utterances were transcribed using broad phonetic transcription so that productions of phonemes could be compared with those represented in the CNC words. PCC scores were based on singleton consonants only and excluded unintelligible parts of the conversation. The exclusion of consonants within clusters enabled a comparison of singleton consonants produced in spontaneous conversation with those produced in the elicited CNC word lists. The total number of phonemes produced by individual participants in the conversation samples ranged from 479 to 1,800 phonemes (mean = 1,050). The total number of words ranged from 200 to 739 words (mean = 437). Individual PCC scores are presented in table 5.4.

The PPVT III (Dunn & Dunn, 1997) was used to measure each participant's receptive vocabulary. PPVT equivalent age scores for each individual are presented in table 5.4.

The postulated mathematical model allows for three processes that occur when a child performs a word test with a verbal response: the sensory process that transmits phonetic information to the child's mental lexicon, the lexical access process that selects a word from the lexicon, and the production process in which the word is spoken. Different types of error may occur in each process. For example, incomplete or incorrect phonetic information could be heard, the word may be unknown or incorrectly stored in the lexicon, or the child may not have acquired the ability to say all of the phonemes in the word.

The model assumes that the probability of correctly completing each process is independent of the others. Thus, the probability of making a correct response can be expressed as the product of three probabilities representing correct processing of sensory information, correct processing of lexical information, and correct production of the word:

$$P_T = P_S \times P_L \times P_P \tag{5.1}$$

P_T is the total probability of a correct response, P_S is the probability of correct sensory information being transmitted to the lexicon, P_L is the probability of correctly identifying the word in the lexicon, and P_P is the probability of correct production of all phonemes. The model can be applied equally well to reading aloud or to auditory speech perception testing. There is a version of equation 5.1 for each sensory condition measured in the study:

$$P_{TA} = P_{SA} \times P_L \times P_P \quad (A = \text{auditory alone}) \qquad (5.2)$$
$$P_{TR} = P_{SR} \times P_L \times P_P \quad (R = \text{reading}) \qquad (5.3)$$

P_{TA} and P_{SA} are the total probability of a correct response and the probability of correct auditory information being transmitted to the lexicon in the auditory-alone condition, respectively. P_{TR} and P_{SR} are the total probability of a correct response and the probability of correct visual information being transmitted to the lexicon in the reading condition, respectively. Because of the visual acuity selection criteria for the participants, it was assumed that there were no sensory errors in the reading condition so that $P_{SR} = 1$. The probabilities of lexical correctness (P_L) and speech production correctness (P_P) were hypothesized to be the same in the A and R conditions.

Before the model was applied clinically, the assumptions and predictions of the model were tested rigorously using experimental data (Paatsch et al., 2004). In the interests of brevity and clarity, only the main points of the validation are covered in the following paragraphs. The validation of the model required the use of mathematically transformed data in order to cope with the nonlinear relationships between the variables; however, these transformations are not required for the clinical application of the model that will be described below. The statistical tool chosen to validate the model was multiple factor linear regression. This type of analysis requires a linear additive model rather than the nonlinear multiplicative one in equations 5.1–5.3. In order to separate the multiplicative terms in equations 5.2 and 5.3 into additive terms for the multiple linear regression, a logarithmic transform was applied to the data, as exemplified by the following equation for the auditory speech perception condition:

$$\log P_{TA} = \log(P_{SA} \times P_L \times P_P)$$
$$= \log P_{SA} + \log P_L + \log P_P \qquad (5.4)$$

The transformed model predicts that the linear regression analysis of $\log P_{TA}$ (logarithmically transformed total scores in the A condition) should have significant factors related to hearing ($\log P_{SA}$), lexical measures ($\log P_L$), and speech production measures ($\log P_P$). Similarly, the analysis of $\log P_{TR}$ (logarithmically transformed total scores in the R condition) should have significant factors related to lexical measures ($\log P_L$) and speech production measures ($\log P_P$) but not to sensory measures. It should be noted that the hypothesis that $P_{SR} = 1$ in the multiplicative model is equivalent to the hypothesis that $\log P_{SR} = 0$ in the transformed model. Furthermore, the regression coefficients for the lexical and speech production measures should be the same in the analyses of log P_{TA} and log P_{TR} because the terms log P_L and log P_P are common to both.

To assess these predictions, the measure of hearing ability was the PTA threshold, the lexical measure was PPVT equivalent age, and the production measure was PCC. These measures were used as the independent variables in multiple regression analyses where log P_{TA} and log P_{TR} were the dependent variables. Unlike the analyses in tables 5.2 and 5.3, the present analyses included children using hearing aids and children using implants within the same group, and thus a comparable measure of hearing was required for both devices. The concept of an equivalent hearing loss for cochlear implant users was introduced by Boothroyd and Eran (1994). An equivalent PTA for the cochlear implant users was derived from the results of Blamey et al. (2001), who reported that a group of 47 children using cochlear implants performed similarly on a broad range of speech perception and language measures to a group of 40 children with an average PTA of 78 dB HL using hearing aids. The equivalent PTA value of 78 dB HL takes into account the average improvement in hearing provided by the cochlear implant. As in the longitudinal study, the PPVT equivalent age was limited to 7 years because speech perception scores in the longitudinal study were not observed to increase further once this level was reached. Log PCC was used as the production measure, with the logarithmic transformation introduced to match the log P_P term in equation 5.4.

The top two sections of table 5.5 show the results of the linear regression analyses. All of the predictions of the model are satisfied by the experimental data. For the analysis of log P_{TA}, the regression coefficients corresponding to log PCC and PTA have values that are statistically significantly different from zero, and the PPVT coefficient is close to significance. For the analysis of log P_{TR}, the PPVT and log PCC factors have coefficients that are statistically significantly greater than zero, and PTA has a coefficient that is not statistically significantly different from zero. This pattern of significant factors indicates that auditory speech perception scores are associated with both hearing levels and spoken language performance as expected, and that reading scores do not depend on hearing levels. Comparing the analyses for log P_{TA} and log P_{TR}, the coefficients for PPVT and log PCC are within one standard deviation of one another, confirming that the lexical and production processes are the same in the auditory speech perception and reading conditions. Thus, the experimental results were consistent with the underlying assumptions of the mathematical model.

Having demonstrated the validity of the mathematical model experimentally, it can be used for its intended purpose, which is to separate the contributions of hearing and spoken language in the CNC

Table 5-5: Regression Analyses of Word Scores as a Function of PTA, PPVT, and log PCC

	PTA	PPVT	Log PCC
Log P_{TA}			
Coefficient	−.008	.079	.920
Standard deviation	.002	.040	.177
t	−4.14	1.99	5.20
p	.001*	.055	.001*
Log P_{TR}			
Coefficient	−.00042	.067	.783
Standard deviation	.001	.020	.089
t	−0.45	3.36	8.76
p	.659	.002*	.001*
Log P_{SA}			
Coefficient	−.0074	.012	.137
Standard deviation	.0020	.042	.189
t	−3.67	0.28	0.73
p	.001*	.780	.472

*Significant p-value.

word test scores for individual children. Dividing equation 5.2 by equation 5.3 and setting $P_{SR} = 1$ yields an estimate of the auditory-alone sensory contribution that has been separated from the linguistic processing components:

$$P_{SA} = (P_{SA} \times P_L \times P_P)/(P_L \times P_P)$$
$$= P_{TA}/P_{TR} \tag{5.5}$$

Equation 5.5 was used to calculate the percentage of hearing errors (P_{SA}) for each child from the data in table 5.4. This percentage is shown by the lighter gray portions of the bars in figure 5.3. The percentage of words correct in the auditory condition is shown by the darker gray portions of the bars. The central black portions of the bars represent the percentage of spoken language errors (lexical and production errors). The children with cochlear implants are to the left of the break in the graph, and the hearing aid users are to the right of the break. The hearing aid users have been sorted in order of increasing hearing loss from left to right.

As an additional check on the model, the logarithmically transformed P_{SA} values were subjected to a linear regression analysis, and the results are shown in the bottom section of table 5.5. As the model predicts, the coefficient for the hearing factor (PTA) is significantly different from zero, and the coefficients for PPVT and log PCC are not significantly different from zero. Thus, the model has been successful in separating the hearing component from the spoken language components.

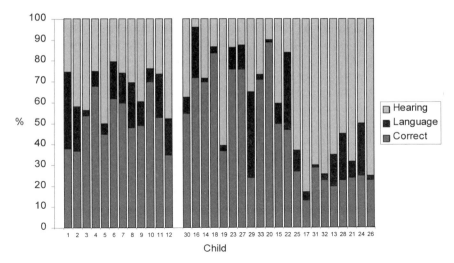

Figure 5:3. CNC word test results for individual children, partitioned into words correct, hearing errors, and spoken language errors.

Inspection of figure 5.3 shows that four children (1, 16, 22, and 29) made more language errors than hearing errors. These children will benefit most from language-based habilitation. Twenty-three of the children made language errors on 10% or more of the read words. These children would also benefit from language-based habilitation. Prior to the commencement of language-based habilitation, a complete psychological and language assessment might be appropriate to determine whether the child has more general learning difficulties and/or a specific language impairment in addition to their hearing loss.

The sensory score (P_{SA}) for the CI users averaged 66.6% with a standard deviation of 10.5%. Eight of the nine hearing aid users with the greatest hearing loss (greater than 88 dB HL) have sensory scores two standard deviations or more below the CI mean. These children (13, 17, 21, 25, 26, 28, 31, and 32) are likely to benefit most from using a cochlear implant instead of their hearing aids. Child 24 is a little less likely to benefit from a cochlear implant because her sensory score is already about the same as the lower range of sensory scores for the CI group. Note that there appears to be a fairly sudden drop in the sensory scores for hearing aid users at around 88 dB HL, separating the listeners with relatively good scores from those with relatively low scores. This boundary is close to the critical level of hearing separating deaf from hard-of-hearing children found in the longitudinal study data (Blamey, Paatsch, Bow, Sarant, & Wales, 2002).

One HA user stands out as different from the rest. Given his hearing loss of 68 dB HL and his relatively good spoken language performance, child 19 performed exceptionally poorly on the CNC word test in the auditory condition. There are several possible explanations for child 19's level of performance. It is possible that he would benefit from an improved hearing aid fitting. It is also possible that he has a condition known as auditory neuropathy that degrades the quality of hearing much more than would be expected from the audiometric thresholds (Rance, Cone-Wesson, Wunderlich, & Dowell, 2002), or that he has a fluctuating hearing loss, or the hearing aid was not working correctly on the day of the testing. The recommended response to this result would be an audiological assessment and hearing aid evaluation.

In addition to the diagnostic function illustrated above, the model may be useful in understanding the effects of specific habilitation methods on speech perception scores. The authors speculate that the hearing component is determined primarily by the hearing loss in combination with the assistive devices used and is not easily increased by training. If this is so, then auditory training will be effective only if it produces improvements in the lexical and/or production components. This is more likely to occur if the training is done using words in a meaningful context instead of nonsense syllables. Paatsch, Blamey, and Sarant (2001) found a similar effect in that phoneme production training was more effective in a meaningful context than in a nonmeaningful context. Further studies have found improvements in speech perception as a consequence of training the meanings of words (Sarant, Blamey, Bow, & Paatsch, 2004) and training of phonology and morphology (Bow, Blamey, Paatsch, & Sarant, 2004). These training studies support the causal nature of the association between language performance and speech perception scores. It remains to be shown that the improvements observed in speech perception were entirely due to increases in the linguistic terms and not in the sensory term of the detailed model. The model would also need to be elaborated further if it was to include the effects of morphology in addition to lexical knowledge and consonant production.

CONCLUSION

This chapter has outlined the empirical evidence supporting the need for specific language-oriented habilitation for deaf and hard-of-hearing children, whether they are using cochlear implants or hearing aids. Quantitative methods for assessing the effectiveness of the habilitation procedures and devices have also been outlined. These methods allow the effects of hearing abilities and devices to be separated from the effects of language performance. This is an essential step in optimizing the effectiveness of habilitation for deaf children in general and for individuals who may have specific needs that are different from the general population.

REFERENCES

Blamey, P. J. (2002). Development of spoken language by deaf children. In M. Marschark & P. Spencer (Eds.), *Oxford handbook of deaf studies, language, and education* (pp. 232–246). New York: Oxford University Press.

Blamey, P. J., Paatsch, L. E., Bow, C. P., Sarant, J. Z., & Wales, R. J. (2002). A critical level of hearing for speech perception in children. *Acoustics Research Letters Online, 3,* 18–23.

Blamey, P. J., Sarant, J. Z., Paatsch, L. E., Barry, J. G., Bow, C. P., Wales, R. J., et al. (2001). Relationships among speech perception, production, language, hearing loss, and age in children with impaired hearing. *Journal of Speech, Language, and Hearing Research, 44,* 264–285.

Boothroyd, A., & Eran, O. (1994). Auditory speech perception capacity of child implant users expressed as equivalent hearing loss. The Volta Review, 96(5), 151–167.

Bow, C. P., Blamey, P. J., Paatsch, L. E., & Sarant, J. Z. (2004). The effects of phonological and morphological training on speech perception scores and grammatical judgements in children with impaired hearing. *Journal of Deaf Studies and Deaf Education, 9,* 305–314.

Brown, R. (1973). *A first language: The early stages.* Cambridge, MA: Harvard University Press.

Clark, G. M., Blamey, P. J., Brown, A. M., Busby, P. A., Dowell, R. C., Franz, B. K.-H., Pyman, B. C., Shepherd, R. K., Tong, Y. C., Webb, R. L., Hirshonn, M. S., Kuzma, J., Mecklenburg, D. J., Money, D. K., Patrick, J. F., & Seligman, P. M. (1987). The University of Melbourne—Nucleus multi-electrode cochlear implant. *Advances in Oto-Rhino-Laryngology, 38,* 1–189.

Cutler, A., & Swinney, D. A. (1987). Prosody and the development of comprehension. *Journal of Child Language, 14*(1), 145–167.

Dunn, L. M., & Dunn, L. M. (1981). *Peabody Picture Vocabulary test—revised.* Circle Pines, MN: American Guidance Service.

Dunn, L. M., & Dunn, L. M. (1997). *Peabody Picture Vocabulary test* (3rd ed.). Circle Pines, MN: American Guidance Service.

Eimas, P. D., & Corbit, J. D. (1973). Selective adaptation of linguistic feature detectors. *Cognitive Psychology, 4,* 99–109.

Jusczyk, P. (1993). How word recognition may evolve from infant speech perception capacities. In G. T. M. Altmann & R. Shillock (Eds.), *Cognitive models of speech processing: The second Sperlonga meeting* (pp. 27–56). Hove: Lawrence Erlbaum.

Klatt, D. H. (1979). Speech perception: A model of acoustic-phonetic analysis and lexical access. *Journal of Phonetics, 7,* 279–312.

Mehler, J., Jusczyk, P., Lambertz, G., Halsted, N., Bertoncini, J., & Amiel-Tison, C. (1988). A precursor of language acquisition in young infants. *Cognition, 29,* 143–178.

Paatsch, L. E., Blamey, P. J., & Sarant, J. Z. (2001). Effects of articulation training on the production of trained and untrained phonemes in conversations and formal tests. *Journal of Deaf Studies and Deaf Education, 6*(1), 32–42.

Paatsch, L. E., Blamey, P. J., Sarant, J. Z., Martin, L. F. A., & Bow, C. P. (2004). Separating contributions of hearing, lexical knowledge and speech production to speech perception scores in children with hearing impairments. *Journal of Speech, Language, Hearing Research, 47*(4), 738–750.

Peterson, G. E., & Lehiste, I. (1962). Revised CNC lists for auditory tests. *Journal of Speech and Hearing Disorders, 27*, 62–70.

Rance, G., Cone-Wesson, B., Wunderlich, J., & Dowell, R. (2002). Speech perception and cortical event related potentials in children with auditory neuropathy. *Ear and Hearing, 23*, 239–253.

Sarant, J. Z., Blamey, P. J., Bow, C. P., & Paatsch, L. E. (2004). *Effects of vocabulary training on word knowledge and perception*. Manuscript submitted for publication.

Semel, E., Wiig, E., & Secord, W. A. (1995). *Clinical evaluation of language fundamentals* (3rd ed.). San Antonio, TX: Psychological Corporation, Harcourt Brace.

Shriberg, L. D., Austin, D., Lewis, B. A., Sweeny, J. L., & Wilson, D. L. (1997). The percentage of consonants correct (PCC) metric: Extensions and reliability data. *Journal of Speech, Language, and Hearing Research, 40*, 708–722.

Vihman, M. M. (1996). *Phonological development: The origins of language in the child*. Cambridge, MA: Blackwell Publishers.

Werker, J. F., & Tees, R. C. (1984). Cross-language speech perception: Evidence for perceptual reorganization during the first year of life. *Infant Behaviour and Development, 7*, 49–63.

Whitford, L. A., Seligman, P. M., Everingham, C. E., Antognelli, T., Skok, M. C., Hollow, R. D., Plaut, K. L., Genn, E. S., Staller, S. J., & McDermott, H. J. et al. (1995). (Evaluation of the Nucleus Spectra 22 processor and new speech processing strategy (SPEAK) in postlinguistically deafened adults. *Acta Otolaryngologica, 115*(5), 629–637.

Wiig, E., Secord, W. A., & Semel, E. (1992). *Clinical evaluation of language fundamentals—preschool*. San Antonio, TX: Psychological Corporation, Harcourt Brace.

6

The Oral Methods and Spoken Language Acquisition

Rod G. Beattie

Oralism is as much an attitude as it is a method.

—Colleague of W. G. Hardy in Connor, *Speech for the Deaf Child: Knowledge and Use*

The oral[1] methods discussed in this chapter all concern the development of spoken language skills for communication and learning and involve the production and reception of spoken language without the support of a visual-manual language or an artificially developed communication system. These methods have contributed to the rich, multicentury history pertaining to education of children who are deaf and hard of hearing. Unfortunately, this history has often been marked by acrimonious debate. It is not the intention to review this debate in this chapter, although it is certainly woven throughout the topic. Interested readers should consider Winefield (1987) or Vernon and Andrews (1990) for their reflections and summaries. Thus, disregarding much of the broader method debate, in this chapter I focus on the development of the oral methods, the different approaches that fall under the broad umbrella of the oral method, and what recent research has contributed to our knowledge about the use and effectiveness of oral methods.

WHAT LIES BEHIND THE ORAL METHODS OR APPROACHES?

Although "usable" audition has been exploited throughout the history of deaf education, the concept of exclusively using residual hearing emerged more recently. For example, Northern and Downs (2002), in describing

[1] In this chapter the single word "oral" represents the collection of methods that focus on using residual hearing and have development of oral speech and language as a goal.

educational methodologies, described auditory-verbal as a more recent
specialized approach that "is based on the expectation that young children who are deaf or hearing impaired can be educated through use of
their own residual hearing, however slight" (p. 358). Still, it should be
understood at the outset that the oral methods in their present forms were
not the result of recent personal epiphanies—romantic as that might be! In
reality, like most educational processes, a pattern of behaviors emerged
and the oral methods were refined as results were observed and knowledge was gained.

A Historical Developmental Sequence for Oral Methods

Although difficult to believe now, in past ages there was a common belief
that the congenitally deaf were people who were multiply disabled (see
Werner, 1932). Thus, a very early development that had a significant influence in promoting oral methods was the separation of the concepts of
deafness and mutism in those who had significant hearing impairments
from very early in life. In the topic of using residual hearing, and perhaps
to identify an originator of the oral method, Markides (1986) nominated
Archigenes, a Greek physician/scientist who lived in Rome around
100 A.D. Archigenes, who was hoping to cure deafness, suggested blowing
a trumpet in the patient's ear. Although drastic, the basic principle concerned residual hearing, and this focus on using residual hearing did
become the corner stone of all listening-based oral methods. Others continued the rather harsh experiments with trumpets and other loud devices
with interesting explanations. From the sixteenth century, Markides selected as examples Guido Cruidi's recommendation "that loud noises be
used to re-arouse the sensation of hearing" and Hieronymous Mercur-
ialis' conclusion that "the loud trumpet blast warmed the acoustic pas-
sages and stimulated hearing" (p. 58).

It was, however, 200 years ago that the collected tenants of modern
aural-oral programs were being laid down in a documented form.
Markides (1986) noted that Itard in 1821 discovered and recorded that
regular exposure to loud sounds improved speech perception in deaf
children. Itard reported particular success in teaching his charges to
differentiate vowels through audition if the auditory stimuli were used
consistently and persistently. In a defining or perhaps refining of the
understanding of the importance of the auditory feedback loop, Markides noted that Toynbee in 1858 wrote "that the great advantage of
calling forth the auditory power of the so-called deaf-mutes is 'they can
be enabled to hear their own voices and to modulate them'" (p. 58).

Around the end of the nineteenth century, Victor Urbantschitsch
(1982) in Austria became a well-known advocate of using hearing to
educate deaf children. It is around this time that the understanding of
"measurable" residual hearing was undergoing a change. The understanding concerned, in lay-audiological terms, how many people were

"stone" deaf, who had profound hearing losses but still heard some-thing under certain conditions, or who actually had a significant amount of useful residual hearing. Urbantschitsch's instruments (whistles) and his testing obviously had interesting links to modern audiological as-sessment. Perhaps his work fostered or sustained J. K. Love and A. G. Bell, who "concluded experimentally" that only a small percentage of people with hearing losses were totally deaf. Markides (1986) outlined a progression of many of these points by describing how Goldstein, before 1940, used ear trumpets and an acoustic stimulation program consisting of 15-minute daily sessions, which Goldstein believed brought about better speech comprehension and intelligibility.

In the late 1930s and in particular following the World War II, there was a significant impetus provided to oral education methods. The trio of developments concerned electroacoustic hearing aids, significant in-terest in theories of cognition, and concerted research. As important examples of this integration, Ewing and Ewing (1938) and colleague. T.S. Littler designed and built powerful group hearing aids and used them experimentally in schools—concluding that "the majority could derive very substantial help from the use of an electrical aid" (p. 24). Contemporaries Barczi in Hungary and Wedenberg in Sweden both "revived" other aspects of the work of Urbantschitsch but reduced the reliance on lipreading that the Ewings included. They also emphasized both early-childhood work and individualized programs based on meaningful material. In the mid 1940s to early 1950s, Huizing in Holland, Whetnall in Britain, and Wedenberg enhanced the general understand-ing of the importance of the early developmental period. Griffiths (1967) later captured a good example of the crystallized thinking from this period:

> The maturation period for learning to listen and learning to talk was between birth and three years of age.... If hearing aids were sup-plied to the deaf baby during this period, perhaps the brain would be able to utilize the amplified sound more effectively, and speech and language would be more readily acquired at this period than at any other later period. (p. 14)

Throughout the 1950s, 1960s, and 1970s improved hearing technol-ogy was certainly a factor in the development of oral educational pro-grams, but it is perhaps the time when modern-day proponents made the biggest contributions by publishing valuable information on their methods. Beebe (1953), Griffiths (1967), Pollack (1970), and Ling (1976) all produced volumes on educational structures or models, teaching sequences, and support materials. Interestingly, it is not uncommon that much good was overlooked because of other statements. Griffith's statement that "it now seems possible that the introduction of amplified sound is related to the reversal of loss in these infants" (p. 43), without reference to the context, was where many stopped reading. Similarly, the debate of the role of lipreading and to a degree "shielding" or using a "hand cue" that covers the mouth was defined by the following: "Both in home training and work done by the therapist, lipreading should be avoided as much as possible. Otherwise the child may easily become dependent upon lipreading and will not use his hearing" (Beebe, 1953, as cited in Markides, 1986, p. 61). Or, "[T]raining is concerned with awareness and interpretation of sounds hearing through the child's waking hours. [T]here can be no compromise because once emphasis is placed on 'looking' there will be divided attention, and vision, the unimpaired modality, will be victorious" (Pollack, 1964, as cited in Markides, 1986, p. 61).

Since the 1980s, technological advances have been much of the driving force behind oral methods. Advances in hearing aids have included miniaturization, binaural fittings, enhanced power and frequency range, enhanced microphones, wireless FM systems that improved the signal-to-noise ratio, better/longer lasting batteries, superior earmolds, and the move to digital from analog processing (see Ackley & Decker, chapter 4 this volume). Perhaps more than anything else, the development of the multichannel cochlear implant (CI) has energized practitioners of oral methods. There is now a significant collection of papers, reports, chapters, and books with such titles as *Learning to Listen With a Cochlear Implant* (Estabrooks, 1998). Many, like Estabrooks, open their texts with such enthusiastic statements as, "Never before in the history of education of children who are deaf has there been such potential for *listening*" (p. 72).

Implant technology continues to surge ahead—implant manufacturers compete for design enhancements or new developments and ultimately product sales. Equally exciting is the challenge for teachers and therapists to delivery effective programs to maximize the effectiveness of the equipment and the children's innate potential. It seems unlikely that this will "slow down" any time soon. Old test instruments of perception, comprehension, and production have been refined or new ones developed. New journals on CIs have emerged, some research based, others focused on habilitation or rehabilitation, and still others for the support of practitioners, parents, or implantees. Recently, it seems that "packaged" teaching programs and "clinical guides" have been the rage.

Underlying Philosophy, Aims, Goals, Motivations, or Shared Aspirations

Underlying all oral methods for educating those who are deaf or hard of hearing is the simple reality that having a hearing loss "disturbs" the natural learning of communication, language, and speech. As Fry (1964) summarized, the challenge for oral education of deaf and hard-of-hearing children is to give them sufficient experience with listening and speaking so that they have enough knowledge of the sound and structures of the language. Many have suggested and tried lipreading and literacy to compensate, but the limitations are generally understood. As Ling (2002) noted, the fragmentary nature of the information provided by speechreading is well understood (also see Woodward & Barber, 1960). While with literacy, the usual developmental pattern of a hearing child is back to front for the child who is deaf or hard of hearing. The hearing child has a sophisticated spoken language and then formally learns to read—the child with a hearing loss is usually in a deficit position.

Despite these challenges, Ling (1990) suggested that supporters of oral methods feel that there are very strong incentives to pursue the development of oral language skills. For the child with a hearing loss, "with spoken language, opportunities for higher education are less restricted, a more extensive range of careers is open, and there is greater employment security" (p. 9). Ling also suggested that those with intelligible speech and language will experience fewer restrictions in their social and personal lives. In a book intended for parents, Gatty (1996) proposed and responded to the question, "Why use an oral approach?" The reasons Gatty expanded upon mirrored those expressed by Ling, but had a different flavor:

1. A spoken/oral language "is the natural language of our culture, and, more specifically, of the parents of most deaf or hard of hearing children";
2. If a child "can use spoken language competently, confidently, and effectively, he is more likely to be able to participate in classes with hearing children"; and
3. It is possible more social, educational, and work opportunities will be available to him"... leading "to a more fulfilling and independent adult lifestyle" (p. 168).

Northern and Downs (2002) also identified the same points but provided a pragmatic explanation on the employment point: "[A]n employer is more inclined to hire a deaf person to whom he or she can give oral instruction rather that an equally capable deaf person to whom the employer must communicate in gestures and writing" (p. 358).

Watson (1998) elaborated on two points in support of oral methods— one educational and the second concerning choice. Both deserve consideration. The literacy argument concerned the assumption that students who are deaf or hard of hearing will be "able to use their development of spoken language both as a language of thought and a basis for developing literacy skills and achieving access to other curriculum areas" (p. 69). And the discussion about choice concerned the possibility that oral skills "offered deaf children a communication and cultural choice later in life" (p. 69).

One additional point that should be considered in a discussion of motivations for oral methods involves a shift from the pragmatic arguments to one couched in philosophy of normalization. Auditory-Verbal International state that their "philosophy supports the basic human right that children with all degrees of hearing impairment deserve an opportunity to develop the ability to listen and to use verbal communication within their own family and community constellations" (Estabrooks, 1994, p. 3).

ORAL METHODS: NAMES, CHARACTERISTICS, AND FEATURES

One would think that this section would be a relatively simple undertaking—list the oral methods and describe their shared characteristics and unique features. This, however, is not as easy is it would seem. With just a simple search, more than 20 names were identified in a very short time. Some method or intervention names involve single words like "oral," "aural," or "auditory." These were so common that it was impossible to identify a person responsible for the name. Similarly, the hyphenated names "auditory-oral method/intervention" and "aural-oral method/intervention" are nearly impossible to trace an origin. Some names have been "recycled," and the authors from a new generation may not be talking about exactly the same thing as their elders. There are also names like "Listen & Speak," "Listen & Talk," or "Hear & Say," many using creative fonts, but most of these seem location specific and are like commercial logos. To satisfy an itch about names, a 90-minute Internet search revealed more than a dozen linked method names and authors. The author with the earliest reference has been nominated for original credit in this instance:

Acoustic method (Goldstein, 1939)
Auditory training (Carhart, 1947)
Auditory approach (Fry & Whetnall, 1954)
Hearing treatment (Møller & Rojskjaer, 1960)
Sound-perceptive method (van Uden, 1960)
Verbertonal method (Guberina, 1964)
Acoupedics (Pollack, 1964)
Unisensory approach (Pollack, 1964)
Auditory habilitation (Connor, 1971)
Aural habilitation (Sanders, 1971)
Auditory learning (Ling, 1984)
Auditory-verbal therapy (Pollack, 1985)

The origin of some names and their attribution may not be correct—certainly the search was perfunctory, but even as it stands it is possible to argue that the "name game," if not harmful, is certainly a source of confusion. For example, for many current oral method teachers "auditory training" is an activity or component of what they do in their oral program. For others from an earlier era, auditory training *was* their oral program. When such transitions occurred is not always clear. Historical definitions for auditory habilitation and auditory training also illustrate possible confusion. Whetnall and Fry (1970) described auditory training as "the conscious provision for the deaf child of the conditions which enable the normally hearing child to learn to 'hear' in the full sense of the word and to produce speech" (p. 116). Contemporarily, Connor (1971) suggested that "the goal in auditory habilitation is the development of auditory attention and hearing perceptions leading to the dynamic use of residual hearing" (p. 317). Given these and many other later efforts to define the concepts in oral methods, it is not surprising that Cole and Gregory (1986) stated that "auditory training is a label for an ill-defined set of procedures related to the use of residual hearing in both children and adults" (p. 23). Certainly, name confusion will arise from problems associated with isolation or translation, but perhaps like in other areas of education of the deaf, unique names were adopted by their creators to differentiate their practice from that of others.

If nothing else came of this exercise, the search had value as it helped identify those names that are currently common parlance for oral methods. But Gatty's (1996) warning to parents about oral methods now can be seen to apply more widely: "[I]t is important for you to understand that there is really no single oral method of education but rather a group of methods which emphasize different aspects of the communication process" (p. 163). Indeed, in the oral method there is huge variation in the use of the existing nomenclature. In literature from the United Kingdom (see Royal National Institute for Deaf People, 2003; Watson, 1998), the common variations of oral methods described are auditory-verbal (AV), natural oralism/natural auralism (NO/NA), and the maternal reflective (MR) method. Meanwhile, in the literature from North America, the list of oral methods commonly includes auditory-verbal, auditory-oral, and cued speech (see Gatty, 1996; Northern & Downs, 2002).

Of these names, there is apparently contemporary transatlantic agreement on AV as an oral method—its lineage following from the unisensory/acoupedics entities of earlier times. For those approaches that take a more "liberal attitude" about the role of the visual channel in the oral method, NO/NA and auditory oral (AO), the differences are much more subtle even in theory and probably disappear completely in practice, even if treating them as different in this discussion is useful. The MR method will also be considered as an entity, but of the four, its current practice is seemingly the smallest. Since cued speech is addressed in another chapter (Hage & Leybaert, chapter 9 this volume), it is not included in this discussion of oral methods, although it is consistently acknowledged as such by educators.

An Aide-Mémoire

By using a linear continuum with highly auditory on the left and highly visual on the right, it is easy to visualize the methods used in educating children who are deaf or hard of hearing. See figure 6.1 illustrating the continuum of methods used in deaf education.

Using the same linear auditory/visual continuum it is possible to expand the oral method subheading to incorporate the range of contemporary oral approaches. On this basis, NO/NA and the AO methods have been assigned a central location on the continuum. While indeed they may not be perfectly centrally aligned on the continuum they do share many characteristics. The AV approach with its focus on audition places it furthest left on the audition continuum, while the MR approach, which includes significant components of visual input through literacy is located on the right. See figure 6.2 illustrating a continuum of oral methods of education students who are deaf or hard of hearing.

Auditory Verbal

Estabrooks has carefully repeated the definition of AV in a series of publications over the last decade or more: "Auditory-verbal therapy is the application and management of technology, strategies, techniques, and procedures to enable children with hearing impairments to learn to listen and understand spoken language in order to communicate through speech" (Estabrooks, 1994, p. 2). Pollack (1985) and others (Andrews, Leigh, & Weiner, 2004; Estabrooks, 1994; Simser, 1993) have consistently emphasized the exclusive focus upon listening and restricting a child's access to lipreading during therapy sessions, particularly in the early stages of listening and language development.

Besides the almost exclusive focus on listening, there are other characteristics that help define the AV approach. Most are not unique to AV

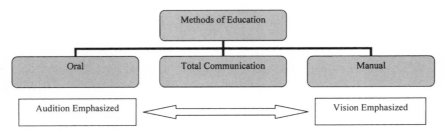

Figure 6-1. Continuum of general methods of education for students who are deaf or hard of hearing.

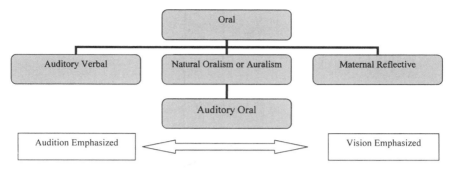

Figure 6-2. Continuum of oral methods of educating students who are deaf or hard of hearing.

but the may be emphasized more in AV than other approaches. In particular, the defining characteristics include (a) early input as soon as possible after diagnosis with a one-on-one diagnostic therapy perspective, (b) the best possible binaural amplification—consistently used and aggressively managed, (c) strong parental/family involvement and normalization of communicative input, and (d) integration of the child into family, neighborhood, school, and social activities. In the early stages of AV, Andrews et al. (2004) also commented that the "children attend private clinics at auditory-verbal centers" (p. 138). This center-based approach, if it is an established feature, is usually quickly bridged since mainstreaming is consistently stated as a goal of AV therapy (Goldberg & Flexer, 1993). Proponents of AV also see mainstreaming as a link between the communication approach and the preferred delivery model for the child's extended education.

Early identification, early fitting of assistive listening technology, and good audiological management underpin all AV programs. McCracken (2000) summarized this audiological focus in the early intervention program by saying that if children who are deaf or hard of hearing are to access residual hearing and use it to successfully to acquire spoken language, they must be accurately assessed and well fitted with sensory devices including hearing aids, FM aids, and CIs. McCracken continued by emphasizing that amplification is only as good as its management. Parents are trained to manage the equipment from the beginning, and there is an emphasis on regular aid checking and maintenance to ensure their child is maximizing their residual hearing. Concurrently or immediately following necessary audiological actions, diagnostic one-on-one AV therapy is started. Specifically, the child, parent, and therapist engage in appropriate play activities that the therapist is constantly evaluating to measure the child's abilities, identify future goals, and plan appropriate lessons.

All contemporary AV proponents emphasize the parents' primary role in the success of the AV approach. While parents are seen as partners in the one-on-one therapy sessions, their role is greater than that. Boucher Jones (2001) described how "parents learn to create good listening environments and to promote listening and auditory learning through the child's waking hours" (p. 18). The importance of learning that sounds have meaning is learned though daily routines and not isolated skill practice. Parents learn that audition, cognition, communication, language, and speech evolve concurrently—each following a familiar, but complexly interwoven developmental sequence. The therapists have a significant role in helping the parents understand these sequences and the activities that will promote their development.

In the AV approach, the topic of integration has a number of layers. Boucher Jones (2001) used the sentence: "Hearing is integrated into the child's total personality (Pollack, 1970); thus, the child is prepared to participate in the family's community" (p. 18). Ernst (2001) elaborated by quoting Hurzing, who in 1959 described the ultimate goal as one of "successful biosocial integration of the deaf child in a normal environment" (p. 20). Comprehensively, living and learning for the child involves hearing. The child develops awareness that sound has value and meaning and that it is stimulating. They eventually intuitively understand that hearing facilitates the meeting of human needs: physical, psychological, emotional, and social.

Auditory Oral

The basic features of the contemporary AO approach for children who are deaf or hard of hearing are the same as those described for the contemporary AV approach. There are, however, differences in degree or emphasis on most defining points by proponents aligned with other oral methods. To review, the key elements of AO involve the primacy of auditory input, early diagnosis and early invention, the early acquisition and use of the best possible hearing technology, a central role for parents, and the delivery of an effective educational program by qualified professionals.

To highlight the major differences between AV and AO, it would seem most researchers and educators would identify (a) the differences in degree to which audition and vision are used and (b) the differences in pedagogy with reference to both variety and location. Clark (1989), Cole (1992), and earlier Ling (1976), among many others, all suggest that historically the AO approach generally allow the child to lipread. Indeed, AO proponents from the past exploited the available phonologic/linguistic information from lipreading as much as possible, thus encouraging the children to develop their spoken language skills by combining auditory and visual cues. For most modern AO proponents there has been a subtle but important shift. Now, when the visual channel is considered, extraordinary efforts will not be taken to minimize exposure to lipreading or natural gestures, but then neither will attention be focused on them.

The other area where differences can be noted between the AV and AO approaches concern educational placement. While the AV approach has full-time placement in the neighborhood preschool, kindergarten, or school as its success definition, children who are following an AO approach may be found in a range of educational settings. The preschool setting may be a specialized one for children with hearing losses, if available, or the child may be placed in a reverse integration or regular preschool—again subject to availability. The school-age child may attend a special school for children who are deaf or hard of hearing, a co-enrollment model class/school, or a special unit or resource rooms or they may be partially or fully mainstreamed with or without the support of a visiting or itinerant teacher of the deaf. Indeed, many students following an AO approach experience several different educational environments over the years.

Another difference that may be drawn between AV and AO concerns the teaching of language. As mentioned above, AV focuses on the normal developmental sequences of audition/listening, communication/language/speech, and cognition. The acquisition process follows a natural or ecological one guided by diagnostic assessment. Historically, variations in the way language is developed in the AO approach emerged. Without returning to the minefield of devised and confusing names—the differences concerned the degree to which language may be taught in a structured fashion or learnt in a natural manner. In general, natural methods prevail, but more structured approaches emerge when a child's progress is slow or significantly delayed.

Natural Oralism/Natural Auralism

In the 1980s in Britain, idiosyncratic oral teaching practices spurred a group of teachers of the deaf to define a more contemporary oral approach that they first called "natural oralism" (Harrison, 1980). Later, NO came to be called "natural auralism" to emphasize hearing and listening, and now NA is often just called the "oral/aural" or "auditory/oral" approach/method (Watson, 1998).

Lewis (1996) reported that NA draws on learning principles of Jerome Bruner and "on descriptions of child language acquisition to support the case for hearing-impaired children being exposed to features of linguistic inputs and learning environments deemed facilitative for any child acquiring a first language" (p. 2). Lewis then added that "the essence of Natural Auralism is enshrined in the belief in two basic concepts: (1) maximal use of residual hearing and (2) the need for meaningful input" (p. 2). Lewis expanded upon the "linguistic input features" and "facilitative learning environments" points by quoting Harrison (1980):

Natural Auralists stress that the sequence of language development for hearing-impaired children albeit slower, "should be the same as that of the normal child, providing he receives the same kind of language experience from which to learn. . . . Natural Oralism would not set out to teach [correct in a structured fashion] incorrectly learnt syntax for it is firmly based on the belief that language and its rules have to be learnt by the child out of experience. . . . " (Lewis, 1996, p. 2)

Watson (1998) also expanded on the description of NA by including an extended quote by Lewis and Richards from 1988:

The word "aural" indicated the emphasis given to the use of residual hearing, while "natural" was seen as describing the approach to language development. Drawing on the work of writers such as Brown (1973), Wells (1986a and b) and others who have described the process of language acquisition in hearing children, the aim is to replicate for deaf children those conditions which have been identified as being facilitative in encouraging language development in young hearing children. Parents are encouraged to engage their child in meaningful conversational exchanges; to use features of motherese; to refrain from any attempt to force the child to talk or imitate while responding positively to every attempted vocalization made by the child. (p. 70)

Watson (1998) suggested that advances in audiology and technology have placed "the emphasis on the use of residual hearing" especially early detection, accurate diagnosis, and enhanced hearing aid design and performance (p. 71). Other descriptive points of NA include the following:

- "No child is precluded on the grounds of being too deaf" (p. 71).
- Lipreading and natural gesture are not denied, although no emphasis is placed on it. If possible "audition should take precedence over vision for the child" (p. 71).
- "There is no place within the approach for . . . enforced repetition of either words or sentences, or the inculcation of language structure rules" (p. 71). "The emphasis is placed on the exchange of meaning, and the rules and structures of language are assumed to be gradually learnt by the child through experiment in use, in much the same way as a young hearing child" (p. 71).
- Meta-linguistic awareness is encouraged because reflection on and the analyzing of already acquired language structures supports further development.
- Audiologically, key points concern careful attention to maintaining hearing aids to ensure peak working order, ensuring consistent daily wearing, and making extra efforts to provide favorable listening conditions.

- "Correction of speech sounds while the child is learning to talk is restricted to encouragement to listen carefully" (p. 72).
- "A further tenet of the approach is the promotion of an attitude towards communication in which the child is encouraged to be an active participant in attempting to receive and express meaning, using clues from context and their wider knowledge of the world to assist in the process" (p. 72).

As an educational extension, Lewis (1996) suggested that "Natural Auralists see the relationship between the written word and spoken language for hearing impaired children as being identical to that for hearing children" (p. 2). In NA, for the development of reading it is necessary that the child has had maximum experience with the controversial and creative elements of spoken language and has had the opportunity to reflect upon it.

Maternal Reflective Method

The MR method was described in van Uden (1977) in Holland and has been adopted by some schools in the United Kingdom. The role of the written form of the language is perhaps the feature of MR method that is most widely known. Providing an overview, Watson (1998) wrote:

> This approach is based upon conversational interaction between the deaf child and a more mature language user. The initial conversation is used as a "deposit" for discussion and analysis of grammatical structure. A central role is given with the approach to the use of the written form of language to support the development of spoken language. (p. 70)

Powers et al. (1999) reported that the MR method shares features with NA but is a distinct entity. Powers et al. identified the shared features of NA and the MR method as (a) the emphasis on the promotion of spoken language skills, (b) the stressed use of residual hearing, (c) the importance of audiological support, and (d) the belief that learning language occurs through a conversational approach. The distinct or key feature of MR method is the use of text from the very earliest stage.

Powers et al. (1999) elaborated on two elements that MR method teachers see as fundamental—the maternal element and the reflective element. In comparison to NA the first is a shared feature, while the second is distinct: "The maternal element is based on the notion that parents 'naturally use a different register' when speaking to babies and young children. This aspect of the approach has the same starting point of promoting interaction as natural auralism" (p. 121). In contrast, the reflective element of MR method is not featured or formally described by other methods:

Pupils are encouraged to reflect on language, considering such features as aspects of grammar, style, register and identifying forms of language such as colloquialisms. In order to achieve this reflection, the conversation is written down and prepared into a text by the teacher. The pupils are then required to analyse the text. The written form serves the dual function of preserving some of the features of spoken language which can easily be lost and of providing a text for analysis. (p. 121)

Integration

Having outlined the description of the four oral methods singled out for treatment, some readers may feel a bit bewildered or perplexed. Troubled, perhaps, because the similarities outweigh the differences. Indeed, there is much in common about the methods—now. This engendered feeling of dissatisfaction may reflect an interaction of the pressures of practice on theory and basic human nature. Considering this discussion of similarities, it is interesting to see that Moores (2001) has elected to keep the following paragraph in at least three editions of *Educating the Deaf*:

> Although the developers of acoupedic programs continually stress its unisensory nature, examination of their procedures clearly illustrates that they also rely heavily on visual and tactile modalities. In reality, human beings, including very young ones, function as integrated organisms. The young child relies on sensorimotor experience. Because hearing, vision, and touch constantly interact with and complement one another, it appears almost impossible to place total emphasis first on audition. (p. 272)

Rather than trying to list the similarities and differences of the oral methods, it may be more useful to reflect instead on some of the pressures that bring the methods into closer alignment.

New Technology

Although some professionals in the field of deaf education who use oral methods may harbor significant feelings of inadequacy in their ability to manage new hearing aids, FM systems, and CIs, the number who would reject the technological developments is probably negligible. Thus, as hearing technology improves, there is naturally an increase in the efforts or focus to exploit it by focusing on residual hearing.

Early Identification/Intervention

Over a significant period of time the benefits of early identification and intervention have been widely demonstrated and accepted. The importance and understanding of critical or optimal periods for learning have been a powerful motivation. Acknowledging data on critical or optimal periods has made the ethical obligations related to identification and intervention much clearer for teachers: Simply put, to know a child has a hearing loss after a neonatal screening program and to do nothing is unacceptable.

The Primacy of Parents

It would be a very naive teacher who would voice a position suggesting that he or she will have a greater influence in a young child's life than that of their parents. This acceptance of the central role that parents play in the development of their child and the interconnections with communication and language between a caregiver and child has now been taken as a given (see Brown & Nott, chapter 7 this volume).

Effectively Using Language Knowledge

Teachers now have a much greater understanding of the important role of the "motherese" dialect, the developmental milestones of child language acquisition, and the development of the social-linguistic perspective of language learning. With this knowledge trilogy, teachers are much better equipped to develop a comprehensive intervention program. Furthermore, their negative experiences with structured language programs continue to pressure them to embrace more natural options— reserving the structured approaches for specific cases and particular times.

RESEARCH FINDINGS

This section concerns the identification and consideration of a collection of contemporary research that has a connection to the central question: Are the oral methods effective for the development of receptive and expressive oral language such that they serve the functions of both communication and education effectively?

Although some would argue that this "big picture" question might be impossible to answer, it seems necessary to seek at least a better understanding of what the parameters of the answer might be by surveying the research literature. It also seems evident that there must also be a reconciliation of two important perspectives, one that is personal and social and often qualitative in nature, and another that concerns the reality of focused quantitative research findings.

Qualitative Concerns

It seems important to acknowledge that there is a stinging resentment and distrust in many people familiar with deafness and oral methods when they reflect on their personal experiences or careers. Echoes of the statement by Eric Greenway from 40 years ago in Great Britain can be still heard regularly in educational settings or found in the current literature:

> For almost a century we have witnessed the great oral experiment. . . . It cannot be denied that there have been some outstanding successes with an exclusive oral system, but for the majority it fails because it is unable to provide the fullest and most congenial means of communication. (cited in Northern & Downs, 2002, p. 361)

Whether Greenway's use of the word "majority" is presently accurate or not is beside the point being made—there are "others" who have not had the desired successful outcomes. The challenge, perhaps, is to better understand (a) who will likely experience success, (b) what can we do to improve oral methods to make them more encompassing, and (c) how do we effectively provide for those inadequately served.

Quantitative Concerns

It must also be acknowledged that there are studies like that of Weiss, Goodwin, and Moores (1975) that intensively evaluated children in seven well-known educational programs spanning the auditory-oral/ visual-manual continuum. Many of their points in recent research studies still hold true:

- Children who were mainstreamed were those who had better hearing and superior articulation before integration.
- Receptively, communication was received most efficiently via simultaneous speech and signs, followed by simultaneous speech and fingerspelling, then speechreading and audition, and least efficiently by audition alone.
- Expressively, better hearing students had better articulation scores. Articulation skill reflected an emphasis on auditory training and articulation in the program and not the overall method or approach.

Reflecting the "big picture" question and the illustrated qualitative/ quantitative concerns Watson (1998) suggested a different perspective for this research area: "The major issue facing professionals who wish to promote the new form of oralism is to demonstrate that the new oral/aural approach is fundamentally different from traditional oral approaches which served many pupils well but left others without any form of functional language" (p. 76). Watson acknowledged that there is a significant body of literature that describes individual oral programs (see Cole & Gregory, 1986; Ling, 1984) and a substantial bank of "how to" guides to assist teachers to implement both AO and AV approaches (see Clark, 1989; Estabrooks, 1994, 1998). Unfortunately, Watson also found that an examination of the literature in the area of effectiveness or outcomes for children who have been educated using an oral approach reveals a paucity of rigorous research.

Watson (1998) and Lynas (1999), among many others, have pondered this limitation. The basis for this limitation is generally taken to reflect the fact that most teachers of the deaf are fully involved with teaching, funding for research is restricted, and few educators have sufficient background to undertake studies in an area that is fraught with traps for even experienced researchers. As an example, Lynas, at the beginning of a longitudinal study exploring the impact of educational practice on outcomes of 11 profoundly deaf children, described the difficulties associated with establishing clear relationships between the communication approach, teaching practice, background factors, and the eventual educational outcomes.

Despite research with methodological challenges, there are a small number of relatively recent studies that have attempted to provide useful data. These studies focus on a range of outcomes: Some have a global nature considering educational success/placement; some concern general or specific language skills, while others focus on specifics such as auditory perception, discrimination, or literacy. P. E. Spencer (2002), recognizing that the skills of speech perception and production and language are all tightly intertwined with complex interactions, did not try to separate the studies for discussion. The reader's indulgence is requested as I include illustrative studies under the different headings in a desire to show a range of findings and trends in each area. The treatment, however, is knowingly not exhaustive.

Global Outcomes

Global outcome research has spurred interest in the oral methods for a long time, and some of these findings are now central to many oral programs. Connor (1971) reported on the work of Tervoort from the 1960s, who concluded "from longitudinal studies of young deaf children that, when appropriate acoustic stimulation is provided during the infant period of susceptibility to environment influence, it prevents development of an esoteric system of gesture communication on a purely visual basis" (p. 317). In the same era, Lenneberg (1967) noted that the time of amplification is the beginning of a child's "listening age." Besides the importance of this central tenet of all modern oral methods Lenneberg was also able to deliver an important warning about the importance of not rushing expressive language. Indeed, Lenneberg reported that the development of a child's inner language might be hindered by a premature expectation of expressive language.

Studying global outcomes a decade ago, Goldberg and Flexer (1993) found that a high proportion of a group of 157 AV-educated students were fully integrated in regular mainstream school settings and that 95% of the high school graduates had continued on to postsecondary education. Although an encouraging finding that reflects positively on the AV approach on the surface, little information was reported on the language and literacy skills of this group. Furthermore, since a stated goal of the AV approach is mainstream education, it is possible that families pursued this goal at any cost, making "percentage of student's mainstreamed" a dubious global outcome measure in a retrospective survey. More recently, Wray, Flexer, and Vaccaro (1997) examined the degree of appropriate mainstreaming and literacy levels for a group of 19 students who had participated in an AV early intervention program. In this instance, from the data collected the authors concluded that 16 of the 19 students were fully and appropriately included in mainstream classrooms and that those 16 read at or above grade level. With this information and careful consideration to student characteristics, some valuable points may be drawn for practitioners and researchers who are keen on replicating the results.

Communication/Language Outcomes

The interest in CIs has stimulated a great deal of research and many publications in the last 20 years. This research has often included hearing aids users as well—indeed, often they are offered as another comparison or reference group along with the hearing. Over the two decades, the focus of CI research has transitioned from the narrow perspective of speech perception to the broader issues of language and communication skills of children who are deaf and hard of hearing. In these studies, although the researchers may not have had a primary objective of investigating the effects of "method," it is frequently part of the broader discussion simply because many early protocols for implant candidacy urged or insisted on participation in an oral program for habilitation or rehabilitation. Unfortunately for the focus of this chapter, most of the method discussion focused on oral communication (OC) versus total communication (TC), and not the particular oral method that was followed.

Like most research areas in deafness, a couple consistent findings arise. Unfortunately, they are not the ones many readers desire: First, findings vary, and second, the direct comparison of studies is difficult or impossible. Various findings certainly hold true when communication-language outcomes and oral methods are considered. There are studies spanning positive to restrained conclusions, and each must be considered carefully so that the conditions, parameters, and implications are understood.

Findings Moving in a Positive Direction

Vermeulen, Hoekstra, Brokx, and van den Broek (1999) reported on the oral language acquisition of 12 children deafened by meningitis, initially fitted with conventional hearing aids, and then implanted at approximately 5 years of age. The authors reported that the CI reduced the rate of receptive language retardation and increased the rate of receptive language acquisition to a rate higher than that of hearing children. This finding encouraged the authors to predict that, over time, these children may catch up to the hearing children.

Robbins, Bollard, and Green (1999) studied 23 children with CIs and also found that, on average, the children "progressed at a rate that exceeded that of normal-hearing children (i.e., 9 months' receptive and expressive language growth in 6 months)" (p. 334). This result, the authors suggested, reflected the fact that the children were considerable younger when identified and implanted than were children from an earlier reported study. It was also interesting to note in this study that the authors found "no significant difference between the language performance of children who used OC or TC" (p. 334).

Rhoades and Chisolm (2000) in a study that focused on global language growth in 40 preschool children who received intensive AV intervention for a period of 1–4 years reached similar conclusions as those reported earlier. Rhoades and Chisolm reported that the subjects' yearly group performances on receptive and expressive language measures met the "expected average rate of growth" for each of the first 2 years of intervention and that the program "graduates" closed the gap between their chronological age and language age (p. 5).

Restraining Second Thoughts

In contrast to a growing body of very encouraging research literature, the sustaining of early language acquisition gains is brought into question by other studies. The study conducted by Blamey et al. (2001) is particularly interesting. These authors evaluated speech perception, speech production, and language skills for 47 children with profound hearing loss and CIs and 40 children with severe hearing loss and hearing aids over a 3-year period. All the children were educated in AO settings. At the conclusion of the study, the language skills were found to be very similar for the two groups suggesting that profoundly deaf children with CIs develop language skills similar to children with severe hearing losses who wear hearing aids. A strong relationship was observed between speech perception scores and language skills, suggesting a relationship between lexical knowledge and speech perception measures, although no relationship was observed between language measures and pure tone average. The authors suggested that other factors including visual access to lipread information, reading and writing, and intrinsic factors such as intelligence have a strong influence upon language development. The regression model developed from the data suggested that children with severe hearing loss who use hearing aids and children with profound hearing loss who use CIs will have an average language delay of 4–5 years by the age of 12 years. This study concluded that there is a strong need for intensive language-based habilitation to enable these children to understand material that will be presented to them in secondary school.

Although Bell, Hickson, Woodyatt, and Dornan (2001) present only a single case study, it is a particularly interesting one concerning child potential and intervention methods. Bell et al. (2001) examined the speech and language skills of monozygotic twins, one with a profound hearing loss and a CI and one with normal hearing. The deaf twin was diagnosed with a profound hearing loss at 4 months and fitted with high-powered hearing aids. She was originally enrolled in a TC program soon after diagnosis but also received intensive AV therapy prior to receiving a CI at 2 years 2 months of age. Assessment of cognition, speech, language, and voice were conducted for both twins at 4 years 4 months and 4 years 11 months of age. At the time of the last assessment, both children had cognitive skills within normal limits (WNL). Speech and language skills were also found to be WNL when the twins were assessed using formal-standardized tools. Discourse analysis, however, showed some subtle differences between the twins that were not observed in the formal language tests. Even though the implanted twin was performing WNL on the language tests, her hearing twin sister was performing above average with scores consistently higher than the deaf twin. This suggests that the deaf child may still have a language delay when compared to her genetic potential. The study concluded that this child, with a profound prelingual hearing loss, is one of a small group of children who achieved age appropriate speech and language within 2–3 years of CI use. The authors suggested that her success might be attributable to her early implantation, intensive AV therapy, the good speech perception skills afforded by the CI, and, significantly, her age–appropriate signing skills and strong language base prior to implantation.

Focused Outcomes

Research in three specific areas, speech perception, speech production, and literacy, with reference to the effects of program or method are surveyed in this section.

Speech Perception

Hodges, Ash, Balkany, Butts, and Schloffman (2000) studied speech perception ability in very young children with CIs. Of particular interest in this chapter is that they focused on the effects of the educational setting—TC, AO, or AV. While the oral group (AO and AV) achieved mean scores that were significantly better than the TC group on all test measures, the data showed "that the two groups of orally trained children perform similarly on speech perception measures" (p. 252). The authors suggested that their single-center study allowed them to control a number of variables such as surgery, implant program, parent counseling, and school support. In a balanced manner, however, they also acknowledged that other factors such as socioeconomic status, effects of bilingualism, child's cognitive ability, parent's motivation, or the quality of teaching were possible causes of the disparity in the results.

Speech Production

Robbins (2000) reported that most parents seeking a CI for their child have improved speech skills as a common desire. This same statement surely holds true for parents choosing an oral method as well. Robbins, citing research in the mid 1990s (Osberger et al., 1994; Tobey et al., 1994; Tye-Murray et al., 1995), concluded that the collective results suggested that "cochlear implants enhance speech production ability to a degree that was not possible with conventional hearing aids" (Robbins, 2000, p. 342). Serry and Blamey (1999) qualified this positive agreement by reporting research that found implanted children needed an average of 15 months from first recognizing a speech sound to using it correctly in their phonetic repertoire at least half of the time. The authors of the collective research, however, acknowledge varied individual speech performance and nominated communication methodology and rehabilitation along with age at onset of deafness and time of implantation as possible factors affecting receptive and expressive speech outcomes.

Literacy

Against the backdrop of reported literacy achievement results at the third or fourth grade level by students who have hearing losses (Schildroth & Karchmer, 1986; see also Traxler, 2000), Geers and Moog (1989) investigated the literacy levels for 100 profoundly deaf students who were 16 or 17 years old enrolled in oral programs in the United States and Canada. Geers and Moog concluded that the students had "a much higher potential for literacy than . . . previously reported and that the primary predictor for literacy was English language competence" (p. 69). Although most of the participants did not achieve reading levels equal to their peers by the end of high school, they did find that between 24% and 36% reached "this level on the various reading measures administered" (p. 84). Geers and Moog suggested that vocabulary development was a major limiting factor. Even with 88% of the group demonstrating practical proficiency with spoken English, as determined by a language proficiency interview, their average oral and reading vocabulary scores at the sixth and seventh grade level fell well below their general language proficiency. Although these improved results are encouraging, it has been suggested that this group of participants may not be representative of other deaf students, since they came from higher socioeconomic backgrounds with earlier hearing aid fitting, higher than average IQ, and involved parents.

More recently, Lewis (1996, 1998) in the United Kingdom has also reported higher levels of literacy attainment among pupils educated within an NA approach. Lewis (1998) reported mean reading levels of approximately 13 years for students who left deaf school from the NA programs, with a quarter of the sample reading at or above their chronological age. In reference to the improved outcomes, when compared to earlier benchmark reports by researchers like Conrad (1979), Lewis chose not to revisit old efficacy arguments about oral versus other approaches. Instead, Lewis, first in 1996 and then again in 1998, explored aspects and practices that appeared "to contribute to higher literacy attainment in reading with deaf children within auditory/oral approaches" (Lewis, 1996, p. 101).

In 1996, Lewis nominated two important links between NA and improved literacy outcomes. First, NA seeks to consciously "replicate the facilitative styles and contingent behaviour in adults that are linked to positive linguistic progress, initiative and creative thinking in children" (p. 6). And second,

> [i]f spoken language skills, experience and reading skills are intricately interwoven in hearing children (Wells, 1985) then it is not surprising to find that an approach which pays careful attention to conversational opportunities and meaningful experience (including auditory experience) when trying to maximise both educational and reading progress in hearing-impaired children is apparently more successful in supporting reading development. (p. 6)

By 1998 Lewis suggested that NA and the interactive reading approach facilitate development because they help to fulfill a number of important conditions:

1. A basic level of linguistic understanding was established before formal reading programs were introduced.
2. The integrity of reading as a receptive process was preserved.
3. The language and ideas that are used to promote deaf children's earliest reading insights were accessible to them.

RESTRICTIONS, CLARIFICATIONS, AND LIMITATIONS

Outcomes from methods, programs, and research of the same should be viewed carefully. The parameters influencing outcome success are complex and involve both intrinsic and external characteristics of the student, parents, educators, methodology, and the program (see Waltzman, 2000, for an expanded list of parameters for success with those using CIs.) Consideration of these complex parameters of success probably influenced Gatty (1996) to caution parents who are contemplating using an oral approach for their children to scrutinize reported results of oral programs. In summarizing for parents, Gatty reported that the "results of using an oral approach varied widely" (p. 169). It was acknowledged that some students complete fully mainstreamed secondary and tertiary education programs. Others, however, were not as successful in these mainstream environments and found it necessary to change to programs or approaches that use more visual means of communication. Gatty also suggested that parents should understand (a) the importance of parental involvement in the child's education, (b) the need for a strong focus on spoken and written language skill development, (c) the need for a robust academic curriculum, and (d) widely held high expectations for achievement. Gatty also foreshadowed for the parents that the reality remains that most deaf students in oral programs also go on to develop some sign language skills at some time in their life.

Musselman, Wilson, and Lindsay (1989) highlighted the variability of outcome research, when factors such as communication method, educational placement or program type, and subject/family characteristics are considered in a study. They compared 131 severely and profoundly deaf children in a range of programs, including TC classes, AO classes, and AO programs where the children received individualized instruction from a teacher of the deaf and were integrated into regular schools. Speech and language skills and other factors relating to the performance of the three groups were examined. To understand the findings, however, differences in the children in the different programs needed to be carefully considered. The children in the individualized AO programs were found to have higher IQs, had more hearing, and had better educated parents than those in other programs. Not surprisingly, on the outcome measures of speech and language skills the individualized AO program children were found to have significantly higher speech and language scores than the other groups of children in either the AO or TC classes. The results for the children in the AO classes, on the measures of language skill in particular, were lower than the children from the TC classes or those in individualized AO programs. As a communication/placement explanation of this finding, Musselman et al. (1989) hypothesized that opportunities for interaction with peers may be responsible. The AO students in individualized programs had more opportunity for interaction with hearing peers, which fostered their spoken language development, while the TC group had more opportunity to interaction with peers via sign communication. In this instance, the students in the AO classes were thought to experience the effects of interdependent hurdles of weaker language skills, ease of communication, and restricted opportunities for peer communication.

Other studies have used outcome studies as the starting point to improve practice by attempting to unravel the factors that influence high levels of spoken language performance for deaf children. Not surprisingly, these studies also serve to illustrate the complex, interrelated nature of the success factors. Musselman and Kircaali-Iftar (1996), in a small study, which means statistical power must be considered, selected children from a large existing data base to attempt to explain the "unexplained variance" for success (p. 108). They compared 10 children with high levels of spoken language skills (HS) and 10 children with low levels of skills (LS), where skill level was determined by considering the combined results of seven measures of speech and language relative to hearing loss, age, and intelligence. In analyzing the data, no differences were observed in degree of hearing loss, socioeconomic status, or age of hearing aid fitting in the two groups. The children in the HS language group, however, were more likely to have been placed in an AV or AO setting, to have received more individualized instruction at home and at school to support spoken language development, and to have had more direct instruction from parents. Interestingly, parental attitude toward deafness was also found to differ. Musselman and Kircaali-Iftar indicated that the "HS families viewed deafness as a challenge to be overcome, while most LS families viewed it as a difference to be accommodated" (p. 119). Yet the parents in both groups reported satisfaction with their children's programs. Summarizing those features that enhance higher skills in spoken language, Musselman and Kircaali-Iftar indicated that their quantitative analysis nominated "A/O communication, individual instruction, integrated placement, and direct instruction by parents," and these, the authors indicated, are "variables which, in fact, comprise part of the A/V philosophy" (p. 117). Overall, this study contributed to the understanding of what it is possible to achieve with an oral approach with a favorable set of factors operating.

ADVANCES AND CONTRIBUTIONS TO GOOD PRACTICE

Themes relating to good practice and success emerge from reviews of the research literature. The three highlighted here are positive performance parameters, the "before 6 months" target and the decibel partition, and progress and pacing.

Positive Performance Parameters

An easily identified good practice theme when oral methods are the focus concerns positive performance parameters. That is, it is possible for children who are deaf or hard of hearing to achieve good spoken language and literacy levels provided a favorable set of factors or conditions are operating. Indeed, Geers and Moog (1989) contend that 90% of deaf children can achieve proficiency in spoken language communication under optimal conditions when the child has strong family support, an average intellectual ability, and exposure to a quality educational program.

There are, however, many other positive performance parameters for consideration. There are child-related factors—hearing factors (age at onset, degree, early identification, assistive hearing equipment, limited bouts of otitis media, etc.), innate abilities (intelligence, language-learning inclination, attention/concentration ability, attitude, etc.), and concomitant considerations (no other disability, good general health, number of siblings, birth order, etc.). There are also parent factors such as education level, communication attitude, commitment, resiliency, financial resources, support systems, and mental and physical health, among others. Important "outside the family" factors have to be considered as well, including availability of an intensive individualized program; quality medical, audiological, and educational professionals; available high-quality services and schools at early childhood, preschool-kindergarten, and secondary school levels; and the opportunity to interact with hearing children on a regular basis.

The "Before 6 Months" Target and the Decibel Partition

Another overlapping theme that is always in the success mix for language learning by a child with a hearing loss concerns the degree of hearing loss and the importance of early identification and intervention to take advantage of recognized sensitive or critical periods for developing communication, language, and speech. Since the mid 1990s Yoshinaga-Itano, in a series of publications (see Yoshinaga-Itano, chapter 13 this volume), has raised optimism by reporting results where most children with hearing loss are achieving language skills in the normal range if the loss is identified before 6 months of age, a hearing device is fitted, and effective early intervention is started immediately. In particular, Yoshinaga-Itano (2003) indicated that the distribution of language quotients for children in the Colorado program overlaps but does not match that of hearing children—the average falling in the low average range of development category. Still, the awareness of the importance of the "before 6 months" target has spread widely and is certainly continuing to influence the planning of universal neonatal hearing screening and habilitation programs. Caution, however, should still be recognized because it is also important to understand that language levels achieved according to a "group mean" for students with a hearing loss in a research study cannot be assumed to reflect the likely outcome for an individual child.

Blamey (2003) delivered another caution when reflecting on the difference between deaf and hard-of-hearing children—specifically the decibel partition. Blamey suggested "there is a critical level of hearing, about 90 dB HL, which separates the deaf and hard-of-hearing groups fairly clearly in terms of their auditory speech perception performance, but not so clearly in terns of their overall spoken language performance"

(p. 242). This difference in deaf and hard-of-hearing children may also reflect Grosjean's concerns (as cited in Aquiline, 2000):

> Despite considerable effort on the part of deaf children and of the professionals that surround them, and despite the use of various technological aids, it is a fact that many deaf children have great difficulties producing and perceiving an oral language in its spoken modality. Having to wait several years to reach a satisfactory level that might never be attained, and in the meantime denying the deaf child access to a language that meets his/her immediate needs (sign language), is basically taking the risk that the child will fall behind in his/her development, be it linguistic, social or personal. (pp. 2–3)

Progress and Pacing

The last theme that emerges from the literature and selected for mention here relates to the need for a degree of caution when rates of progress and pacing, either narrowly focused or broadly based, are considered. The exciting results of some very young children with positive performance parameters including advantaged positions of early programs and better hearing should not become the basis for complacency or extended performance projections. To start with, it would be interesting to know the numbers or percentage of very young children who actually experience these parameters in different locations.

In the meantime, the reports of progress and pacing of older children should also be reviewed. In particular, the growing collection of studies of gains in language levels (e.g., Bell et al., 2001; Rhoades & Chisolm, 2000; Robbins et al., 1999) with younger children should be contrasted with the studies of Blamey et al. (2001) of school-age children. The young child who is or becomes a "star" in preschool may not retain that status throughout grade and secondary school. As a result of their study, Blamey et al. emphasized the need for ongoing intensive language instruction for all children with significant hearing loss throughout primary and into secondary education so that they attain language levels sufficient to access the secondary school curriculum. To this point, however, Moores's (2001) warning seems particularly appropriate for these periods of transitions. By providing ongoing language support, educators must acknowledge that there is a basic trade-off between time spent in academic subjects and time spent developing language skills.

SUMMARY AND CONCLUSIONS

While the history of oral methods of education children who are deaf and hard of hearing is long, the effectiveness of the methods over time has been challenged by poorly defined programs, a plethora of confusing names, and mixed long-term results. Still, this did not stop the oral juggernaut. The reasons for the longevity and vitality of oral programs are diverse. Certainly, the documentation of individual children who have successfully achieved spoken language skills has been important, but so has the recognized oral method successes (by research or otherwise). Other factors include an amazing number of charismatic oral method teachers and practitioners, many substantive technological developments, the influence of the normalization/integration movement, and the undeniable demographic reality that most children with a hearing loss have hearing parents who desire their child to use oral language.

The oral programs have certainly received impetus from the production of educational materials and ongoing teacher/practitioner education. Specifically, many oral program support materials have now been updated largely in response to technological developments and described in detail by organizations and master practitioners or teacher-trainers (see, e.g., Cochlear, 2003; Estabrooks & Marlow, 2000; Ling, 2002; McCormick & Archbold, 2003; Pollack, Goldberg, & Caleffe-Schenck, 1997; Royal National Institute for Deaf People, 2003; St. Gabriel's Auditory-Verbal Early Intervention Centre, 2001). Additionally, some oral approaches such as AV have self-initiated quality control systems as it applies to the skills or skill development of their practitioners (see Estabrooks, 1994, for a summary).

There is certainly a growing collection of recent research findings reporting generally better outcomes for children who are deaf and hard of hearing compared with past research reports. Some reported results are very encouraging, while others are more modest. Although research parameters must be carefully considered before applying the results to others, the encouraging reported trends include improved appropriate and successful mainstream placements and academic success, faster language-learning rates, and higher overall levels of language development. More focused results such as improved levels of literacy skills, better receptive abilities through audition (with particular reference of CI use), and improved speech/intelligibility (again reflecting CI use) are also encouraging.

From a qualitative perspective, one might wonder if there are also subtle indications of more positive outcomes for children educated using oral methods. In the 1960s Greenway was quoted using the phrase "some outstanding successes... but for the *majority* it fails" (cited in Northern & Downs, 2002, p. 360) when commenting about the results with an exclusive oral system. In the year 2000, the quoted material of Grosjean seems more moderate in tone. In this instance, when Grosjean was discussing the deaf child's ability to perceive and process oral language in its spoken modality, the phrase "it is a fact that *many* deaf children have great difficulties" was used (cited in Aquiline, 2000). Is this change in the choice of descriptive words "majority" to "many" suggesting that there has been an improvement trend in the effectiveness of oral methods? Perhaps or perhaps not, but it does raise interesting research questions.

Creative research programs focusing on oral methods should be pondered and developed by both researchers and teacher-practitioners. Placements, programs, practitioners, and practice could be improved with targeted research. It is a reality that experimental studies with random assignment to treatment are seldom possible. Indeed, even studies with reasonably large numbers are difficult in the low-incident reality of deafness and hearing impairment. Longitudinal studies, albeit with smaller numbers of participants, could and should be undertaken. More quasi-experimental and descriptive studies of groups and individual cases are certainly of value and should not be abandoned. But creatively, can we do more? Perhaps researchers should more aggressively consider the benefits of single-subject research designs. It is perhaps surprising that the experimental rigor of these designs has not become a common choice of researchers in areas of deafness and especially for those who are interested in evaluating the effects of treatments regimes (i.e., specific oral methods). Similarly, it seems remarkable that researchers have not exploited the statistical power of structural equation modeling using LISREL (analysis of linear structural relationships) to test the causal relationships between the important variables that the advocates of oral methods have suggested. Perhaps they soon will.

In the epigraph to this chapter on oral methods and spoken language acquisition, I used a "twice-removed" quote: a statement by an unknown colleague of W. G. Hardy in Connor (1971), "Oralism is as much an attitude as it is a method" (p. 337). The quote was selected because it serves an interesting counterpoint to a data-based or factual understanding of the efficacy of the oral methods. It was also selected because it was unlikely to offend readers the same way that a religious faith metaphor might if used to illustrate one of the bases for using the oral methods in the education of the deaf and hard of hearing. The quote contained much truth—much of which still holds today. In the future, maybe the conscientious application of good research and good practice reviews may allow us to clarify the relative roles and weightings for attitude and data-driven knowledge. Logically, then, the winners will be the deaf children for whom these programs were designed in the first place.

REFERENCES

Andrews, J. F., Leigh, I. W., & Weiner, M. T. (2004). *Deaf people: Evolving perspectives from psychology, education, and sociology.* Boston: Pearson.

Aquiline, C. (2000, July). *World Federation of the Deaf: Towards a policy on Deaf education.* Paper presented to the International Congress of Educators of the Deaf, Sydney, Australia.

Beebe, H. (1953). *A guide to help the severely hard of hearing child*. New York: Basel-Karger.

Bell, B., Hickson, L., Woodyatt, G., & Dornan, D. (2001). A case study of the speech, language and vocal skills of a set of monozygous twin girls: One twin with a cochlear implant. *Cochlear Implants International, 2*(1), 1–16.

Blamey, P. J. (2003). Development of spoken language by deaf children. In M. Marschark & P. E. Spencer (Eds.), *Deaf studies, language, and education* (pp. 232–246). Oxford: Oxford University Press.

Blamey, P. J., Sarant, J. Z., Paatsch, L. E., Barry, J. G., Bow, C. P., Wales, R. J., et al. (2001). Relationships among speech perception, production, language, hearing loss, and age of children with impaired hearing. *Journal of Speech, Language and Hearing Research, 44*(2), 264–285.

Boucher Jones, M. (2001). Response to question 4: Does the auditory-verbal approach differ from the auditory-oral approach and/or traditional aural habilitation? In W. Estabrooks (Ed.), *50 frequently asked questions about auditory-verbal therapy* (pp. 17–19). Toronto: Learning to Listen Foundation.

Brown, R. (1973). *A first language: The early stages*. Cambridge, MA: Harvard University Press.

Carhart, R. (1973). Auditory training. In H. Davis (Ed.). *Hearing and deafness: A guide for layman* (pp. 276–299). New York: Staples Press.

Clark, M. (1989). *Language through living for hearing-impaired children*. London: Hodder and Stoughton.

Cochlear. (2003). *Listen learn and talk*. Lane Cove West, NSW: Cochlear.

Cole, E. B. (1992). *Listening and talking: A guide to promoting spoken language in young hearing-impaired children*. Washington, DC: A. G. Bell Association for the Deaf.

Cole, E. B., & Gregory, H. (Eds.). (1986). *Auditory learning*. Washington, DC: Alexander Graham Bell Association for the Deaf.

Connor, L. E. (Ed.). (1971). *Speech for the deaf child: Knowledge and use*. Washington, DC: Alexander Graham Bell Association for the Deaf.

Conrad. R. (1979). *The deaf school child*. London: Harper and Row.

Ernst, M. (2001). Response to question 5: Why is "integrating hearing into the personality" of the auditory-verbal child so important? In W. Estabrooks (Ed.), *50 frequently asked questions about auditory-verbal therapy* (pp. 20–22). Toronto, ON: Learning to Listen Foundation.

Estabrooks, W. (1994). *Auditory-verbal therapy*. Washington, DC: Alexander Graham Bell Association for the Deaf.

Estabrooks, W. (1998). Learning to listen with a cochlear implant: A model for children. In W. Estabrooks (Ed.), *Cochlear implants for kids* (pp. 72–88). Washington, DC: Alexander Graham Association for the Deaf.

Estabrooks, W., & Marlow, J. (2000). *The baby is listening: An educational tool for professionals who work with children who are deaf or hard of hearing*. Washington, DC: Alexander Graham Bell Association for the Deaf.

Ewing, I. R., & Ewing, A. W. G. (1938). *The handicap of deafness*. London: Longmans Green.

Fry, D. B. (1964). Speech. In the *Report of the Proceedings of the International Congress on Education of the Deaf* (pp. 183–191). Washington, DC: U.S. Government Printing Office.

Fry, D. B., & Whetnall, E. (1954). The auditory approach in the training of deaf children. *Lancet, 1,* 583–587.

Gatty, J. (1996). The oral approach: A professional point of view. In S. Schwartz (Ed.), *Choices in deafness: A parents' guide to communication options* (2nd ed., pp. 162–171). Bethesda, MD: Woodbine House.

Geers, A., & Moog. J. (1989). Factors predicting the development of literacy in profoundly hearing-impaired adolescents. *Volta Review, 91*(2), 69–86.

Goldberg, D. M., & Flexer, C. (1993). Outcomes survey of auditory-verbal graduates: A study of clinical efficacy. *Journal of the American Academy of Audiology, 4,* 189–200.

Goldstein, M. A. (1939). *The acoustic method for the training of the deaf and hard of hearing child.* St. Louis, MO: Laryngoscope Press.

Griffiths, C. (1967). *Conquering childhood deafness: A new technique for overcoming hearing problems in infants and children.* New York: Exposition Press.

Guberina, P. (1964). Verbotonal method and its application to the rehabilitation of the deaf. In the *Report of the Proceedings of the International Congress on Education of the Deaf* (pp. 279–293). Washington, DC: U.S. Government Printing Office.

Harrison, D. (1980). Natural oralism—a description. *Journal of the British Association of Teachers of the Deaf, 4*(4).

Hodges, A. V., Ash, S. H., Balkany, T. J., Butts, S. L., & Schloffman, J. J. (2000). Speech perception abilities in pediatric cochlear implant recipients receiving total communication, oral, and auditory-verbal training. In S. B. Waltzman & N. L. Cohen (Eds.), *Cochlear implants* (pp. 251–252). New York: Thieme.

Lenneberg, E. H. (1967). *Biologic foundations of language.* New York: Wiley.

Lewis, S. (1996). The reading achievement of a group of severely and profoundly hearing-impaired school leavers educated within a natural aural approach. *Journal of the British Association of Teachers of the Deaf, 20*(1), 1–7.

Lewis, S. (1998). Reading and writing within an oral/aural approach. In S. Gregory, P. Knight, W. McCracken, S. Powers, & L. Watson. (Eds.), *Issues in deaf education* (pp. 101–110). London: David Fulton Publisher.

Ling, D. (1976). *Speech and the hearing impaired child: Theory and practice.* Washington, DC: Alexander Graham Bell Association for the Deaf.

Ling, D. (Ed.). (1984). *Early intervention for hearing-impaired children: Oral options.* San Diego, CA: College-Hill Press.

Ling, D. (1990). Advances underlying spoken language development: A century of building on Bell. *Volta Review, 92*(4), 8–20.

Ling, D. (2002). *Speech and the hearing impaired child: Theory and practice* (2nd ed.). Washington, DC: Alexander Graham Bell Association for the Deaf.

Lynas, W. (1999). Identifying effective practice: A study of a small sample of profoundly deaf children. *Deafness and Education International, 1*(3), 155–171.

Markides, A. (1986). The use of residual hearing in the education of hearing-impaired children—a historical perspective. *Volta Review, 88*(5), 57–66.

McCormick, B., & Archbold, S. (2003). *Cochlear implants for young children: The Nottingham approach to assessment and rehabilitation.* London: Whurr.

McCracken, W. (2000, July). A review of good practice: Audiological management. In *Congress 2000: Achieving in the 21st Century. Proceedings of the 19th International Congress on Education of the Deaf* [CD], Sydney: Quilcopy Audio Recording Services.

Møller, T. T., & Rojskjaer, C. (1960). *Injury to hearing through hearing treatment (acoustic trauma)*. Fifth Congress, International Society of Audiology. Bonn, Germany.

Moores, D. F. (2001). *Educating the deaf: Psychology, principles, and practices* (5th ed.). Boston: Houghton Mifflin.

Musselman, C., & Kircaali-Iftar, G. (1996). The development of spoken language in deaf children: Explaining the unexplained variance. *Journal of Deaf Studies and Deaf Education, 1*(2), 108–121.

Musselman, C. R., Wilson, A. K., & Lindsay, P. H. (1989). Factors affecting the placement of preschool deaf children. *American Annals of the Deaf, 134*, 9–13.

Northern, J. L., & Downs, M. P. (2002). *Hearing in children* (5th ed.). Philadelphia: Lippincott Williams & Wilkins.

Osberger, M. J., Robbins, A. M., Todd, S. L., & Riley, A. I. (1994). Speech intelligibility of children with cochlear implants. *Volta Review, 96*, 169–180.

Pollack, D. (1964). Acoupedics: A uni-sensory approach to auditory training. *Volta Review, 66*, 400–409.

Pollack, D. (1970). *Educational audiology for the limited-hearing infant*. Springfield, IL: Charles C. Thomas.

Pollack, D. (1985). *Educational audiology for the limited-hearing infant and preschooler* (2nd ed.). Springfield, IL: Charles C. Thomas.

Pollack, D., Goldberg, D., & Caleffe-Schenck, N. (1997). *Educational audiology for the limited-hearing infant and preschooler* (3rd ed.). Springfield, IL: Charles C. Thomas.

Powers, S., Gregory, S., Lynas, W., McCracken, W., Watson, L., Boulton, A., et al. (1999). *A review of good practice in deaf education*. London: Royal National Institute for Deaf People (RNID).

Rhoades, E. A., & Chisolm, T. H. (2000). Global language progress with an auditory-verbal approach for children who are deaf or hard of hearing. *Volta Review, 102*(1), 5–24.

Robbins A. M. (2000). Rehabilitation after cochlear implantation. In J. K. Niparko, K. I. Kirk, N. K. Mellon, A. M. Robbins, D. L. Tucci, & B. S. Wilson (Eds.), *Cochlear implants: Principles and practices* (pp. 323–363). Philadelphia: Lippincott Williams & Wilkins.

Robbins, A. M., Bollard, P. M., & Green, J. (1999). Language development in children implanted with the CLARION cochlear implant. *Annals of Otology, Rhinology, and Laryngology, 177*(Suppl.), 113–118.

Royal National Institute for Deaf People. (2003). *Working with children with cochlear implants: Educational guidelines project*. London: Author.

Sanders, D. A. (1971). *Aural rehabilitation*. Englewood Cliffs, NJ: Prentice-Hall.

Schildroth, A. N., & Karchmer, M. A. (Eds.). (1986). *Deaf children in America*. San Diego, CA: College-Hill Press.

Serry, T. A., & Blamey, P. J. (1999). A 4-year investigation into phonetic inventory development in children with cochlear implants. *Journal of Speech and Hearing Research, 42*, 141–154.

Simser, J. (1993). Auditory-verbal intervention: Infants and toddlers. *Volta Review, 95*(3), 217–229.

Spencer, P. E. (2002). Language development of children with cochlear implants. In J. B. Christiansen & I. W. Leigh, *Cochlear implants in children: Ethics and choices* (pp. 222–249). Washington, DC: Gallaudet University Press.

St. Gabriel's Auditory-Verbal Early Intervention Centre. (2001). *A curriculum for the development of audition, language, speech, and cognition.* Castle Hills, NSW: St. Gabriel's School for the Hearing Impaired.

Tobey, E., Geers, A., & Brenner, C. (1994). Speech production results: Speech feature acquisition. *Volta Review, 96,* 109–1129.

Traxler, C.B. (2000). Measuring up to performance standards in reading and mathematics: Achievement of selected deaf and hard-of-hearing students in the national norming of the 9th Edition Stanford Achievement Test. *Journal of Deaf Studies and Deaf Education, 5,* 337–348.

Tye-Murray, N., Spencer, L., & Woodworth, C. G. (1995). Acquisition of speech by children who have prolonged cochlear implant experience. *Journal of Speech and Hearing Research, 38,* 2327–2337.

Urbantschitsch, V. (1982). *Auditory training for deaf mutism and acquired deafness* (S. R. Silverman, Trans.). Washington, DC: Alexander Graham Bell Association for the Deaf. (Original work published 1895.)

van Uden, A. (1960). A sound-perceptive method. In A. W. G. Ewing (Ed.), *Modern educational treatment of deafness* (pp. 19/3-19/12). Manchester: Manchester University Press.

van Uden, A. (1977). *A world of language for deaf children.* Lisse, The Netherlands: Swets and Zeitlinger.

Vermeulen, A., Hoekstra, C., Brokx, J., & van den Broek, P. (1999). Oral language development in children assessed with the Reynell Developmental Language Scales. *International Journal of Pediatric Otorhinolaryngology, 47,* 153–155.

Vernon, M., & Andrews, J. (1990). *The psychology of deafness: Understanding deaf and hard-of-hearing people.* New York: Longman.

Waltzman, S. B. (2000). Variables affecting speech perception in children. In S. B. Waltzman & N. L. Cohen (Eds.), *Cochlear implants* (pp. 199–205). New York: Thieme.

Watson, L. (1998). Oralism: Current policy and practice. In S. Gregory et al. (Eds.), *Issues in deaf education* (pp. 69–76). London: David Fulton Publisher.

Wedenberg, E. (1951). Auditory training for deaf and hard of hearing children. *Acta Otolaryn Suppl., 94,* 1–130.

Weiss, K. L., Goodwin, M. W., & Moores, D. F. (1975). *Characteristics of your deaf children and early intervention programs* (Research Rep. 91). Washington, DC: Department of Health, Education, and Welfare, Bureau of Education for the Handicapped.

Wells, G. (1985). *Language, learning and education.* Windsor, NFER/Nelson.

Wells, G. (1986a). *The meaning makers.* London: Hodder & Stoughton.

Wells, G. (1986b). *Language development in the pre school years.* Cambridge: Cambridge University Press.

Werner, H. (1932). *History of the problem of deaf-mutism until the 17th century* (C. K. Bonning, Trans.). London: Royal National Institute for Deaf People RNID.

Whetnall, E., & Fry, D. B. (1970). *Learning to hear* (R. B. Niven, Ed.). London: William Heinemann.

Winefield, R. (1987). *Never the twain shall meet: Bell, Gallaudet and the communications debate.* Washington, DC: Gallaudet University Press.

Woodward, M. F., & Barber, C. G. (1960). Phoneme perception in lipreading. *Journal of Speech and Hearing Research, 3*, 213–222.

Wray, D., Flexer, C., & Vaccaro, V. (1997). Classroom performance of children who learned spoken language communication through the auditory-verbal approach: Evaluation and treatment efficacy. *Volta Review, 99*(2), 107–120.

Yoshinaga-Itano, C. (2003). From screening to early identification and intervention: Discovering predictors to successful outcomes for children with significant hearing loss. *Journal of Deaf Studies and Deaf Education, 8*(1), 11–30.

7

Family-Centered Practice in Early Intervention for Oral Language Development: Philosophy, Methods, and Results

P. Margaret Brown & Pauline Nott

Over the past 30 years there has been significant change in the philosophy underpinning early intervention practice in developed countries. This change has arisen from a number of factors. Perhaps the most important of these has been a deeper understanding of how a child develops; what factors affect and, more specifically, promote that development; and the importance of early childhood as a foundation for later cognitive, academic, linguistic, and social competence (Brooks-Gunn, Berlin, & Fuligni, 2000). This perspective has been particularly useful in understanding and promoting language development in deaf children.

Currently, child development theory is strongly influenced by the work of Vygotsky (1986), and his perspective on development highlights three critical points. First, he suggested that early development and learning best take place within the context of the child's cultural group, usually the family. As Gauvain (1999) suggested, development "relies in critical ways on children's participation in the activities and practices of the community in which growth occurs" (p. 173). In contrast to Piaget (1945/1962), who viewed development as the outcome of the internal processes of assimilation and accommodation as the child encounters and interacts with the outside world, Vygotsky placed heavier emphasis on the child's engagement in activities with others. In this view of development, the focus is more on the child in context rather than the child as an individual (Farver, 1999). The second point raised by Vygotsky is that these learning experiences are supervised and mediated through interaction with a more expert individual, commonly an adult and especially the parent or primary caregiver. Third, Vygotsky proposed the idea of a zone of proximal development (ZPD). The ZPD is defined as the developmental distance between what the child can do independently and what the child can accomplish with the assistance of the expert individual, or tutor. For effective learning, therefore, the tutor should target support to that zone lying just beyond the skills already mastered by the child. This requires several important attributes of the tutor: sensitivity to the child's current state of development; knowledge of the next step in development; knowledge of the child's everyday experiences, interests, strengths, and motivations; and a range of effective teaching strategies to draw upon.

Turning specifically to theories of child language acquisition, a similar trend emerged in the 1970s and 1980s. Research became focused on interactions between parents and infants with the aim of identifying specific aspects of the interaction that affected the rate of child language acquisition (Bruner, 1983; Snow, 1984; Stern, 1977). These included the degree of maternal topic control (Nelson, 1973), expansions of the child's communicative behavior (Cross, 1977), and directive syntax such as interrogatives (McDonald & Pien, 1982). Collectively, then, emerging views of child development and child language acquisition pointed to the importance of the parents as tutors and to the family and its activities as the primary learning context in early childhood. At this time, a number of researchers also began to study interactions between parents and infants with hearing loss (Schlesinger & Meadow, 1972; Spencer & Gutfreund, 1990). This was particularly important for two reasons. First, investigations of these special populations would possibly provide corroboration for strategies that were universally effective for promoting children's language growth. Second, the discovery of differences among parents and their children both in the quality of the interaction and in strategies might provide clues to more effective intervention.

This emerging orientation on child development from the child-in-context perspective influenced those seeking to support children with special needs, and the philosophy of "family-centered practice" emerged in the literature (Dunst, Trivette, & Deal, 1988). In 1995, these principles became incorporated into law in the United States in as Public Law 99–957, Part C of the Early Intervention Program for Infants and Toddlers, under the Individuals with Disabilities Education Act. Family involvement in early intervention programming for deaf children was further recommended by the Joint Committee on Infant Hearing (2000). Powers et al. (1999) also endorsed this philosophy specifically in relation to early intervention for children with hearing loss, highlighting family empowerment and parent–professional partnerships as key elements in their review of good practice in the United Kingdom. Programs in many developed countries declare that they have now embraced and acted upon this philosophy. Before we can evaluate whether this is the case, it is important to understand what is meant by family-centered practice and what underpins good practice.

WHAT IS FAMILY-CENTERED PRACTICE?

Family-centered practice is variously described as a philosophy (Bruder, 2000), a set of guidelines for practice (Dunst, 1997), and a set of values (Bruder, 2000) that is now recognized as the most appropriate model of early intervention for children with special needs, including children with hearing loss. As Bruder notes, family-centered intervention places an emphasis on the strengths of families rather than their deficits, promotes choice and decision-making control, and values intervention that is based on collaboration between the family and professional. Dunst (1997) identified other characteristics such as sensitivity and responsiveness to diversity, flexibility and individualized support, intervention that capitalizes on the family's cultural context, and intervention that is competency enhancing to strengthen the functioning of the family, particularly the parents. Further, services for families should take place in the settings in which the child is cared for and taught, the child's "natural" environment (Harbin, McWilliam, & Gallagher, 2000, p. 389). Seen in this way, the goals of family-centered practice relate not only to developmental outcomes for the child but also to parent and family benefits.

A critical element of family-centered practice is the collaboration between the parent and professional to develop a plan for the care and education of the child: the individualized family service plan. Within a family-centered model, the focus shifts from direct intervention with the child by the professional to promotion of a context that will promote optimal development in the child. The child and the family are central to the context, so in this sense, the intervention is also child centered. To do this, professionals need to be aware of the family's daily routines, capacities, needs, concerns, and priorities. This seems a far cry from the traditional role of the early interventionist. The orientation away from direct intervention with the child by the professional and toward the adults who have responsibility for the child requires significant changes in attitude, practice, and skills. Rather than early childhood educators, early interventionists in family-centered programs now need to see themselves as adult educators (Klein & Gilkerson, 2002). Apparently, however, it is difficult for early interventionists to do this. As McBride and Peterson (1997) found, despite current knowledge of family-centered practice, many early intervention teachers continued to focus their teaching directly with the children. They speculated that this may be because of insufficient training in parent-focused intervention, an inability to accept that children with special needs learn in the same manner as children with typical development, or possibly doubt about the efficacy of parent-focused intervention.

Dunst (2002) argued that family-centered practice has both a relational and a participatory component. The relational component relates to the professional's skills, beliefs and attitudes. The participatory component relates to the flexibility, responsiveness, and individualized nature of the professionals' involvement with the family and the opportunities they provide for the family to be empowered in decision making and action. Using these criteria, Dunst and his colleagues developed a measure of early intervention practices along a continuum from professionally centered, to family allied, to family focused, and then family centered. Despite the claims of family centeredness made by many programs, Dunst and his colleagues found that most preschool programs were located at the other end of the continuum. In addition to this, programs that were developmental and educational were more likely to be family allied, family focused, or family centered, whereas therapy-based programs were more likely to be family allied or professionally centered. Ernest (cited in Dunst, 2002) argued that parents see family-centered practice as the ideal although the evidence suggests that the majority of programs are not family centered in their orientation (Dunst & Brookfield, cited in Dunst, 2002).

FAMILY-CENTERED EARLY INTERVENTION IN ORAL PROGRAMS FOR CHILDREN WITH HEARING LOSS

What should be the components and practices of family-centered early intervention using an oral approach to promoting spoken language development of children with hearing loss? It is most likely that these terms mean different things to different people. For instance, while "oral" may be easily defined generally, there are differences between specific approaches to oral intervention, such as auditory oral (AO), auditory verbal (A-V), and so on (see Beattie, chapter 6 this volume). Even within these specific methodologies there will be differences in implementation of the practice. Moreover, identifying what is meant by family-centered practice may be elusive because it is now widely accepted that the values, beliefs, and practices underpinning the role parents play in the early tutoring of their children differ among cultural groups (Farver, 1999; Johnston & Wong, 2002; Kermani & Brenner, 2000). But here's the trick: It is precisely this recognition of the uniqueness of cultural groups, especially individual families, that lies at the core of family-centered practice. Understanding the family's routines and important events, keeping the intervention focused around these, directing intervention at the capacities of the parents to interact appropriately with their child during these activities, understanding next steps in development, and having skills in teaching parents effective scaffolding techniques are the ingredients of family-centered practice.

Many early interventionists working in oral programs would argue that their work is family centered. But is it really? And, if so, how well is it being done? These are difficult questions to answer. What we need are detailed descriptions of practice and processes, and these need to be coupled with measures of outcomes. Specifically, within a family-centered model, further descriptions need to address such questions as whether teachers focus their intervention efforts on parent–child interactions in typical settings, whether the targets for the intervention curriculum are driven or sourced from the individual needs of families and children in particular, whether the primary goal is to facilitate communication between the parent and child rather than the achievement of specific targets in speech and language, and whether the teacher values the potential expertise of the parent and sees the parent as the primary agent of change.

MEASURING OUTCOMES OF FAMILY-CENTERED EARLY INTERVENTION FOR YOUNG CHILDREN WITH HEARING LOSS

In reviewing the literature, descriptions of actual of family-centered practice with families of children with hearing loss are inadequate, and studies measuring the outcomes are few. Then there is the vexing question of what we should measure as outcomes. Most studies have traditionally used vocabulary counts and language outcomes as their measure of the efficacy of early language intervention, and while these are of course useful measures, arguably there are other measures that may be equally important. These include measures of the overall development of the child, including social-emotional competence, literacy, educational achievement, and quality of life. Given that we have accepted the notion of family-centered practice, it seems logical that we should also be measuring the effects of our intervention on the family as a whole (i.e., family functioning; Dunst et al., 1988). Further, we need measures of change in parents, particularly along such parameters as competence, confidence, coping, level of satisfaction with services, quality of interaction, and relationship with the child (Dunst, 2002).

At what point or points should measurements take place? Researchers most commonly have gathered data at exit from early intervention or shortly after that. It may be that some effects of early intervention are immediate while others are more gradual. Gathering evaluative information throughout the period that intervention is occurring may help to establish general trends or patterns of change. Duration and size of effect are other issues that need to be considered.

A third issue is how we can account for variability in practice. Programs offering spoken language intervention vary considerably in the ways in which intervention is designed and implemented. There are differences not only in specificity (the types of strategies used) and intensity (how often intervention takes place) but also in quality (how well the strategies are implemented; Mayne, Yoshinaga-Itano, Sedey, & Carey, 1998). In addition to these internal differences, there also will be outside influences such as the effects of earlier diagnosis and the changing technology of assistive devices.

A fourth important issue is the ever-changing context in which data are collected. At publication, results of studies are soon rendered less relevant to the current climate. For example, Calderon and Naidu (1998) reported early intervention data collected between 1989 and 1994. Given the significant and rapid changes in technology and practice since 1989, the issues for today's practitioners may be different from those they addressed.

A final difficult issue is the problem of dealing with the conflict that arises out of the need for large population studies from which to make generalizations and the need for detailed descriptions of strategies that work. Carney (1996) suggested that a large homogeneous population of participants is required in order to draw conclusions. However, the population of deaf individuals is not homogeneous when we factor in cultural differences, degrees of hearing loss, communication methods, models of intervention, modes of delivery, and quality of intervention practice. From a purely practical point of view, large-scale studies tend to use gross measures of progress, ignoring potentially important variables. On the other hand, although detailed case study data may have the potential to uncover the benefits of particular interventions, the results cannot be generalized to larger populations. Another alternative is compilation of carefully controlled single subject studies. This methodology seems to have great promise but is used comparatively rarely in the field.

Child Language Outcomes

To date, outcomes of family-centered oral intervention are largely unknown. A review of the literature indicates that outcome measures in oral early intervention programs have focused on child language and that research results are fraught with difficulties in interpretation. First, researchers have generally failed to separate out the communication modality variable. The participants in the research are often grouped together regardless of the whether they are using AO or total communication (TC) approaches (Musselman & Kircaali-Iftar, 1996; Strong, Clark, & Walden, 1994), although some studies have reported results from A-V therapy (Rhoades & Chisholm, 2000). Second, the studies are contaminated by the inclusion of children with hearing losses ranging from mild to profound (Stokes & Bamford, 1990). In addition to this, some researchers have used vocabulary counts as estimates of language acquisition (Mayne et al., 1998; Nott, Cowan, Brown, & Wigglesworth, 2003), and while these measures have norms, at best they give an incomplete picture of a child's communicative ability. Having said this, such studies appear to be revealing a trend toward more rapid vocabulary acquisition.

An early study by Griswold and Cummings (1974) of children in a TC program found that at 36–48 months of age, the mean vocabulary count of the participants was 142 words and that this increased to 156 at 48–60 months. In comparison to hearing children, this would indicate a severe language delay in these children. More recently, however, Mayne et al. (1998) reported 31 signed or spoken words using the MacArthur Communicative Development Inventories (Fenson et al., 1993) when children were between 23 and 25 months of age and 217 words between 35 and 37 months of age. Mayne et al. (1998) further suggested that rate of vocabulary growth in their participants was similar to that of hearing children although the onset of the vocabulary "spurt" seen in hearing children was delayed by about 6 months. Unfortunately, the above two studies involved both children using spoken language and TC, and it is impossible to ascertain how the results apply to oral programming alone. In addition, no information is given about how family-centered the programs were. Even so, these two studies hint that language outcomes have significantly improved (see figure 7.1).

In terms of language development, Strong et al. (1995) investigated rates of receptive and expressive language development of 2,519 children from birth to 60 months of age over the duration of their involvement in the family-centered SKI*HI program. The authors found that the mean gains from pre- to postintervention were 11.8 months for expressive language and 12.8 months for receptive language. On

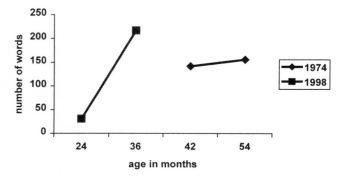

Figure 7-1. Comparison of Expressive Vocabulary Studies: 1974 (Griswold & Cummings 1974) and 1998 (Mayne et al. 1998).

average, the duration of intervention was 13.4 months, indicating that although delayed, the children were progressing at a rate close to that of hearing children. A similar result apparently was obtained by Calderon and Naidu (1998), who found mean pre- to postintervention gains of 17.1 months for expressive language and 9.9 months for receptive language in 80 children entering early intervention between birth and 36 months of age, although no data were presented indicating the mean duration of family-centered intervention. Both of these studies, however, failed to separate out critical variables such as degree of hearing loss and type of programming.

Stokes and Bamford (1990) investigated early language acquisition in four children with moderate to profound hearing losses enrolled in a parent-focused AO early intervention program. The children were diagnosed and fitted with hearing aids between 4 and 18 months of age. Despite the degree of hearing loss, all four children made the transition from intentional communication to spoken words between 15 and 21 months of age, indicating only a short language delay at this developmental point. Again, however, little is known about how family centered the program was.

Rhoades and Chisholm (2000) tracked the expressive and receptive language progress of 40 children receiving between 1 and 4 years of A-V therapy. A-V therapy had been initiated between the ages of 4 and 100 months, with a mean initiation age of 44 months. The participants were separated into four cohorts according to the number of years of intervention. Annual assessments of expressive and language progress were made that were then converted to rate of language growth. Results indicated that, for each age cohort, rate of development was about equivalent to or in excess of the expected rate. It is difficult, however, to separate out the effects of the approach on age of entry into the program. This is an important issue in determining the appropriateness of the intervention for infants or as a remedial therapy for older children with significant language delay.

Musselman and Kircaali-Iftar (1996) investigated a number of factors that they hypothesized were related to spoken language outcomes of early intervention: audiological characteristics of the child, demographic characteristics of the family, child educational history, and family orientation to deafness. They contrasted two groups of 10 children with either high or low language performance who attended AO, A-V, or TC programs. Results showed that there was greater parental involvement in the child's education in the high-scoring group and that intervention was more likely to be purely oral (AO or A-V). Whether this was because this group of children had a greater propensity for spoken language or was an effect of the intervention is difficult to unravel. Parents of the higher scoring children were more involved in their child's program in terms of time and commitment and implemented teaching sessions with the child. Despite these differences, it is noteworthy that there was no difference between high- and low-scoring groups for degree of parental satisfaction, suggesting that parents either adjust well over time or place less value on language acquisition alone as the desired outcome.

Moeller (2000) investigated the association between age of the child at enrollment in early intervention and degree of family involvement in the program. The group of participants included almost equal numbers of children using either oral or TC approaches. Moeller found that the children who performed best on language measures (within the average range for vocabulary) were those who were identified by 11 or 12 months of age and whose mothers were highly involved in the child's program. High level of family involvement was found to be a stronger predictor of language outcomes than either age of the child at entry to early intervention or degree of hearing loss.

In summary, there is evidence that language outcomes for children with hearing loss are better in recent studies than in older ones. Although it is difficult to draw conclusions from existing literature, this seems to be the case when spoken as well as signed language is considered and when oral as well as TC programs are considered. One contributing variable, however, that seems to emerge from these studies is the degree of involvement of parents regardless of the type of intervention. Further investigation of interventions that have strong parental involvement is needed to corroborate this finding.

Academic Performance of Children With Hearing Loss Who Participate in Early Intervention Programs

Degree of family involvement in early intervention also emerged as an important variable in two other studies. Acting on Carney and Moeller's (1998) suggestion that we need to measure outcomes other than communication and language, Martineau, Lamarche, Marcoux, and Bernard (2001) investigated the academic achievement (reading/writing scores, mathematics scores, and academic delay) of 112 children with hearing losses ranging from mild to profound. Irrespective of degree of hearing loss, the students with less academic delay were those who used oral communication, had strong parental support, and parental involvement in their program. A further positive association was found between early parent-focused services and higher scores in reading/writing and mathematics.

Watkins (1987) investigated the language and educational achievements of 92 children who had been involved in the SKI*HI program. Although this study did not separate out communication modality, it showed that home-based intervention, in which parents were guided in their interactions with the child, was a more effective model than an intensive preschool program.

Parent Expectations and Children's Developmental Progress

Wu and Brown (2004) investigated parents' and teachers' expectations of A-V therapy and the child's language development. Data were collected by questionnaires that were distributed to parents and teachers at three early intervention centers. These centers either used A-V therapy exclusively or had teachers on staff who used A-V therapy with particular families. Twenty matching questionnaires were completed and returned. The authors found that the child's expressive language development was predicted by a factor composed of age of diagnosis, age of device fitting and entry into early intervention, and the teachers' expectations of the child. These measures also predicted child receptive language with the addition of the parents' expectations of the teacher's use of A-V therapy. The results suggest that parents invest a great deal of faith in professionals and that the presence of harmonious expectations between the teacher and the family is a powerful force.

Dromi and Ingber (1999) investigated expectations from early intervention of 50 mothers of children with hearing losses ranging from mild to profound. They sought information about the mothers' expectations about the nature of the program and the professionals they were dealing with. There were some expectations common to all the mothers, such as their need for information, professional guidance, and emotional support and their expectation of the attributes of the professionals and their own level of involvement. There were, however, clear differences in how the mothers envisaged their own role in the intervention program. Four different groupings were identified: independent decision makers; well-socialized; minimalist, relinquishing responsibility; and full collaborators. Although this study did not connect these categories with any child outcome data, it underscores the need to fashion the early intervention program around the individual perceptions and capacities of parents regarding their own engagement with the intervention.

In summary, the degree of parent involvement in the child's program and the collaborative relationship between parent and professional may be powerful ingredients in family-centered practice. Given the variability in the individual perceptions and capacities of parents, professionals need to recognize that each partnership will be unique, making differing demands on the partnership and requiring flexibility of response.

THEORETICAL UNDERPINNINGS OF FAMILY-CENTERED ORAL EARLY INTERVENTION

It has already been established that oral programs are not generic; in fact, they are extremely diverse the world over. The concept of family-centered practice also lends itself to diversity in interpretation, and while

Dunst (1997) has outlined some "core practices" of family-centered intervention, these practices are couched in broad philosophical terms. The literature identifies several elements that are fundamental: working alongside parents, quality of interaction, amount of interaction, ability to capitalize on everyday experiences, and effective guidance based on parent–child interaction. Nevertheless, there still remains a lack of detail in how a family-centered approach translates into recommended practice in the field of early intervention in general, especially for oral services supporting children with hearing loss.

Working With Parents

It is now common practice to involve the parents of a child with hearing loss in teaching sessions with their children during early intervention. The particular role assigned to the parent by the teacher, and the nature of the teaching approach itself, may or may not be family centered. It has been recognized that the daily interactions of parents with their children provide both the context and the ingredients important in communication development (e.g., Koester, Papoušek, & Smith-Gray, 2000). Mahoney and Wheedan (1997) argue that if a teaching approach is based upon the parent–child interaction literature, then it will be "truly effective at accomplishing the goals of family-centered philosophy" (p. 165). Further, family–teacher relationships need to reflect collective empowerment rather than a more traditional relationship where the professional had "power over the family" (Turnbull, Turbiville, & Turnbull, 2000).

There are two aspects of parent–child interaction research that are particularly relevant to a family-centered model for the child with a hearing loss. First, important features of the interaction between hearing children and their parents that promote communication development have been identified, and second, research has highlighted effective intervention approaches that are based upon parent–child interaction.

Features of Parent–Child Interaction That Promote Communication Development

A significant theoretical and research base has been developed as researchers have concentrated increasingly on aspects of early child development in the family context. Summaries follow that address aspects of parent–child interaction that have been found to be important by researchers focused on interactions in hearing dyads and may therefore be expected to be of importance in dyads in which young deaf children are accruing spoken language experiences.

Joint Attention

Since the late 1970s, theorists such as Bruner (1978) have argued for the importance of mother–child "routines" in scaffolding the child's early language development. Bruner postulated that joint attention under-pinned learning in these early routines. Evidence for the pivotal role of joint attention in language learning began to emerge in the 1980s and centered around a series of studies by Tomasello and colleagues (Tomasello & Todd, 1983; Tomasello & Farrar, 1986). Tomasello investigated the association between joint attention and early lexical development, videotaping hearing mother–hearing child dyads engaged in play with a set of novel toys when the children were between 12 and 18 months old. He found that the amount of time the dyads spent in joint attention was positively related to the child's vocabulary size at 18 months. This finding was replicated in a number of subsequent studies by Tomasello and Farrar (1986) and others (Baldwin, 1995). Saxon (1997) investigated the association between joint attention at 6 and 8 months and language competency as measured on the MacArthur Communicative Development Inventories (Fenson et al., 1993) at 17 and 24 months. Joint attention at 6 months was positively associated with language levels at both 17 and 24 months.

Joint attention is clearly important in the early language development of babies and infants. But how is joint attention achieved? What strategies does a parent use to gain and maintain joint attention, and do these change as the child's language competency grows? Research by Smith, Adamson, and Bakeman (1988) sheds some light upon these questions. While Smith et al. found that joint attention was one of two aspects of a mother's behavior that predicted 40% of the variance in vocabulary size at 18 months, it is the type of strategies mothers employed to establish joint attention that is of interest here. Smith et al. found that the more time mothers spent in attentional strategies of the conventional type, the more time their infants spent in joint object play and the larger was their infant's productive vocabulary. Conventional strategies were defined as actions that utilized the typical shared situation between the parent and child and involved pointing, ritualized activities such as book reading, or discreet verbal direction. Literal strategies that involved moving objects or using sound makers to establish attention were not associated with rate of language acquisition.

Work by Dunham, Dunham, and Curwin (1993) also found that early lexical development was facilitated in infants of 18 months of age when the caregiver followed rather than led the infant's focus of attention. Saxon (1997), however, compared the effects of verbal following (where the mother refers to a toy the child is already focused upon) with verbal redirecting (where the mother refers to a toy different from the one the child is focused on). Saxon found that parental verbal redirecting of the child's attention when the child was 6 months of age was also positively correlated with joint attention, concluding that early joint attention was not frustrated by maternal redirection. The types of strategies parents employ to engage their child, therefore, appear to differ according to the age and attentional capacities of the child. In considering the way that professionals currently work with families, is joint attention considered to be a core component of the intervention? Do teachers guide parents in implementing appropriate strategies to maintain joint attention with their child?

Responsiveness

For some time now, researchers have been interested in the relationship between what is termed "responsive" parenting and child development in a number of domains, including cognitive and socioemotional development. More recently, Tamis-LeMonda, Bornstein, and their colleagues have investigated the predictive relationship between responsive parenting and child language outcomes. Bornstein (1989) defined responsiveness as the prompt, contingent, and appropriate responding by mothers to children's exploratory and communicative behavior. Responsiveness incorporates the notion of verbal sensitivity where positive and meaningful changes in the mother's verbal behavior are seen in response to a child's vocal and exploratory behavior.

Bornstein and Tamis-LeMonda (1997) examined the relationship between verbal sensitivity, verbal intrusiveness, and hearing children's verbal comprehension. Forty mother–child dyads were videotaped at home in free play when the children were 9 and 13 months of age. Child comprehension was assessed in maternal interviews in which mothers were asked about their child's understanding of words and phrases using a checklist. Bornstein and Tamis-LeMonda found that maternal sensitivity, and not intrusiveness, at 9 months predicted child comprehension at 13 months of age and that this relationship was particularly strong for children who were initially lower in verbal comprehension.

In a later study, Bornstein, Tamis-LeMonda, and Haynes (1999) investigated the relationship between verbal responsiveness and vocabulary growth. Thirty hearing mother-child dyads were videotaped at home in both a play and mealtime context when the children were 13 and 20 months of age. Productive vocabulary of both the child and mother was assessed as well as the mother's verbal responses to their child's exploratory and vocal behavior. Bornstein et al. found that mother's verbal responsiveness predicted child vocabulary growth and that maternal vocabulary did not. Interestingly, child vocabulary level was also found to be predictive of maternal responsiveness suggesting that responsiveness is influenced by the reciprocal nature of mother–child interactions.

Tamis-LeMonda, Bornstein, and Baumwell (2001) examined the relationship between responsive parenting and the timing of achievement in language milestones as opposed to the level of achievement. Forty mother-child dyads were videotaped in free play with a standard set of toys when the children were 9 and 13 months of age. Child achievement on five early language milestones was assessed in weekly telephone interviews in which a range of inventories were used to probe the child's language level. From these interviews, ages were calculated for when the child used first imitations, first words, 50 words in expressive language, combinatorial speech, and language to talk about the past. Tamis-LeMonda et al. found maternal responsiveness at both 9 and 13 months predicted all five language milestones over and above the children's own activities. Of interest, however, was the finding that particular maternal responses (e.g., affirmations, descriptions, vocal imitations, expansions, and questions) were more predictive than others, depending upon the child's developmental level, reflecting what Tamis-LeMonda et al. termed the "multidimensional" nature of maternal responsiveness.

Clearly, maternal responsiveness is important in child language acquisition. In terms of oral family-centered intervention, do the teaching approaches used assist parents to be responsive to their child's spontaneous communicative attempts? What techniques do teachers use to help parents become more responsive?

Child-Directed Speech

Child-directed speech (CDS) is a term that describes a range of communicative behaviors that adults, especially parents, use when talking to their children. Also known as "motherese," "parentese," or "baby talk," features of CDS include slower rate of speech, exaggerated intonation, shorter utterance length, topics limited to the here and now, more restricted vocabulary that is usually object centered, more contextual support, more repetitions, and more questions and imperatives. Theorists have argued about the role of CDS in promoting communication development. There are those who propose that CDS serves to support the child's limited conversational competence, some argue that it supports the child's limited processing capacities, and others suggest that CDS is a powerful tool for maintaining the child's attention (Owens, 2001).

One of the major criticisms of the facilitating role of CDS in language development is the fact that not all features of CDS are found across all languages and cultures. It is argued that if CDS is necessary for language acquisition, then it should be evident in all languages. At the same time, however, this does not mean that CDS may not be helpful in promoting language development. Gallaway and Richards (1994) review the evidence in support of CDS and, while they concluded that there are problems with much of the research attempting to identify a causal link between CDS and subsequent child language development, they also point out that some evidence is emerging for the facilitating role of specific aspects of parent input.

Amount of Talk

The notion that children who hear more talk will talk more themselves seems perfectly logical. Evidence demonstrating the importance of the amount of talk that parents direct to their children has emerged from two studies. First, Huttenlocher, Haight, Seltzer, and Lyons (1991) studied the verbal input of mothers to their 18–29-month-old hearing children in the home while engaged in activities such as mealtime, dressing, and play. It was found that the children of mothers who talked more during these everyday activities had larger vocabularies than did children whose mothers talked less.

These results were further supported in a longitudinal study by Hart and Risley (1995), who observed the everyday interactions of 42 parents and their 1–3-year-old children. The participants came from a range of socioeconomic and at-risk populations. Hart and Risley found that a number of features of parenting were significantly associated with children's language skill at 3 years of age, including the amount of parent-to-child talk. Importantly, it was the amount of talk within the context of conversations that Hart and Risley postulate was so powerful in language learning. Do current oral teaching approaches allow the child with hearing loss to take advantage of the volume and richness of language in everyday interactions, or do these approaches inadvertently limit these qualities in parent–child interactions?

Everyday Life Experiences

The studies by Huttenlocher et al. (1991) and Hart and Risley (1995) underline the importance of the child's everyday life experiences in providing an appropriate context for language learning. Wolery (2000) suggests that programs for young children with disabilities should seek to influence positively a major proportion of the child's interactions each day. Dunst and his colleagues (Dunst, Hamby, Trivette, Raab, & Bruder 2000; Dunst et al., 2001) have been prominent in developing a body of research to improve our understanding of the learning opportunities afforded by everyday life experiences and how this affects intervention practices for children with disabilities.

What is meant by everyday learning experiences? In an extensive survey of more than 3,000 parents of children with or at-risk for developmental delay, Dunst et al. (2000) identified 50 activities in 11 categories that constituted the learning opportunities of family life and the same number of activities in community life. It was found that family life was made up of a broad range of activities, including "family routines, parenting activities, child routines, socialization activities, family rituals and celebrations, physical play and literacy activities and play and entertainment activities" (p. 160). While parents identified learning opportunities in all 22 categories of family and community life, Dunst et al. found parents varied in which activities they nominated as most important to their child's learning.

The value of everyday experiences to promote learning in children with special needs was the subject of a subsequent study by Dunst et al. (2001). Sixty-three caregivers and their young children participated in an intervention study in which an activity setting matrix was used to identify the activities in which targeted behaviors could be promoted. This was coupled with contingent responsiveness and/or incidental teaching to support children's learning in these contexts. Dunst et al. were interested in the effect of particular characteristics of the activity setting, namely, the people involved and the development-enhancing characteristics of the activity upon child outcomes. Dunst et al. described activity settings as development enhancing when they were based upon the child's interest and provided opportunities for engagement, exploration, practice, and mastery of a skill. It was found that the presence of development-enhancing characteristics in everyday learning opportunities were the best predictors of positive and prosocial child functioning. Further, participation in a larger variety of these everyday learning opportunities was associated with increased social responsiveness and positive affect.

It is evident that the experiences of everyday life provide numerous learning opportunities for all children, including those with special needs. In considering children requiring intervention in the communicative domain, these activities provide opportunities for the child to experience language repeatedly in the same or similar contexts, thus reducing the child's cognitive effort and facilitating the learning process. While some experiences are common to all children, others are not. It is important, therefore, that the teacher is familiar with the activities embedded in the life of each family and includes these activities as part of the intervention.

Teaching Approaches Based on Parent–Child Interaction

For some time now researchers have called for the adoption of teaching approaches that take advantage of the facilitating features of parent child interaction outlined above. Despite such calls, there seems a reluctance in some quarters to give credence to these approaches for the child with hearing loss, in favor of more curriculum-driven approaches. Since the 1970s, we have seen the evolution of a group of interventions including "incidental language teaching," "milieu teaching," and "responsive interaction" that are collectively known as "naturalistic" teaching approaches (Kaiser, Hancock, & Hester, 1998). While each approach is different, they share common principles that include meaningful conversation as the basis of language acquisition, parental responsiveness (following the child's lead, modeling, expansions), environmental arrangement, and everyday life experiences as the context for learning language (Kaiser et al., 1998).

Over the past 20 years, Kaiser and her colleagues have conducted a series of studies investigating the effectiveness of naturalistic teaching approaches with a range of children with communication disorders and their parents. It has been consistently found that parents are able to implement naturalistic approaches effectively (Kaiser et al., 1996) and that these approaches are effective in promoting language development (Kaiser & Hester, 1994). While this research has focused upon children with disabilities other than hearing loss, some data are beginning to emerge on the effectiveness of naturalistic teaching in promoting communication skills in children who are deaf or hard of hearing.

Byrne (2000) studied the effect of parent- and teacher-implemented naturalistic approaches in promoting spoken language development in a primary-school–age child with severe to profound hearing loss. Four naturalistic approaches were used across three teaching conditions: teacher alone, parent alone, or joint teacher and parent implementation. Byrne found that the child participant was more likely to achieve the language goals in spontaneous language when the parent implemented teaching alone or in conjunction with the teacher, while language teaching in the teacher alone condition was less effective. Byrne further found that the parent was able to provide more opportunities than was the professional for the child to experience the language goal during sessions across all naturalistic approaches.

Parent–child interaction continues to challenge researchers in their struggle to understand and explain its role and contribution to child language learning. It is evident, however, that the parent, the child, their interaction, and the everyday context in which these interactions occur are all important in language learning, even though the mechanisms by which they promote language are not yet fully understood. It is also evident that particular characteristics of parent–child interactions act to support and promote language development such as responsiveness, contingency, and engagement. What place does parent–child interaction have in a family-centered, early intervention program for children with hearing loss?

A MODEL OF FAMILY-CENTERED PRACTICE IN EARLY INTERVENTION

Below is a proposed model of family-centered practice for young children with hearing loss and their families. It was specifically designed to incorporate aspects of parent–child interaction research with hearing children outlined above. An important question is whether it is valid to use research based upon interaction with hearing dyads in a model for intervention with children with hearing loss. It is argued here that hearing loss affects a child's communication learning essentially by reducing the overall experience of language. Put simply, the child does not hear as much of the language directed to and used around her as does the hearing child. The intervention task is therefore essentially one of finding ways to maximize the child's experience of language, both hearing and using it, in everyday situations.

With the advent of universal neonatal screening programs and subsequent reduction in the age of identification (Apuzzo & Yoshinaga-Itano, 1995) and significant improvements in hearing aid and cochlear implant technology, a child with hearing loss now has a much improved ability to hear speech at a very young age. Modern hearing devices mean that young children are able to access a better quality of speech signal and hear more of it. It is now possible for babies with hearing loss to participate and engage in interactions with their parents and their wider family in a manner similar to that of hearing children. This allows deaf and hard-of-hearing children to take advantage of the many learning opportunities that parent–child interactions provide. As such, research into interactions with hearing dyads should logically form the basis of an intervention model for the child with hearing loss.

SOLAR

In this section we propose a new model of early intervention for children with hearing loss based on the principles of family-centered practice. The SOLAR model (Brown & Nott, 2003) was developed primarily to document and clarify the changing role of teachers who work in an AO early intervention program that is family centered. The model, shown in figure 7.2, has three orbits: the inner, outer, and SOLAR orbit (the region in which the teacher uses skills and competencies to support the child, parent, and family).

Inner Orbit

The inner orbit is central to the philosophy underpinning the SOLAR model—that is, as is the case with hearing children, interactions between children with hearing loss and their parents provide the foundations for spoken communication development. It is argued that the child learns to converse by being actively involved in conversations. Children learn by doing and by being supported as active participants in what it is they are attempting to learn. We see examples of the "learning by doing" approach to teaching across many fields. For instance, it is well accepted that children learn a second language more effectively when immersed in situations that place responsibility on them to act "as if" they understand and give the impression that they can use the language (Locke, 1993). Immersion creates a genuine motivation for the child to acquire a language in authentic situations. The need to learn is

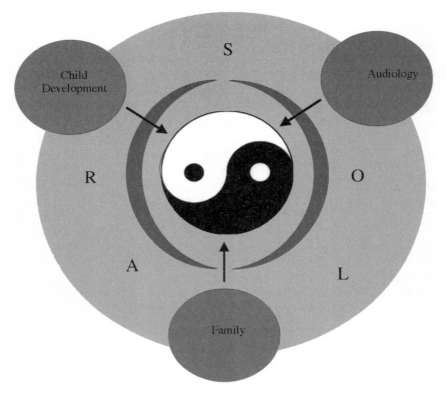

Figure 7-2. The SOLAR model. S = Setting the scene; O = Observing; L = Listening; A = Assessing; R = Responding.

motivated by the desire to engage in meaningful interactions with others. The same principle applies to the young child with a hearing loss. The child is motivated to attend, listen to, and ultimately understand what others are saying by his desire to engage with others.

The interaction between parent and child is at the core of the model and is represented by the Yin Yang symbol to convey the reciprocal, responsive, and dynamic nature of this relationship. In this model, parent–child interaction is considered as providing the context, the motivation, and the ingredients to promote spoken communication development.

Outer Orbit

In the outer orbit there are three "planets," each representing a source of knowledge and information that teachers must consider when trying to promote communication skills in a child with hearing loss. These sources of knowledge include the child's current developmental status, the audiological characteristics and environment of the child, and the family's roles, routines, and special events that comprise the daily life of the child. Each source of information affects the interaction between parent and child, as denoted by the arrows directed to the inner orbit in figure 7.2.

The SOLAR Orbit

The SOLAR orbit represents the tasks of the teacher of the deaf. This orbit is positioned around the interaction between the parent and child to indicate that the teacher's role is primarily one of supporting, nurturing, enhancing, and thus strengthening the interaction by empowering the parent. The teacher does not typically have a role in direct interaction with the child within the SOLAR model, particularly in the early years of language acquisition. The SOLAR orbit is also intersected by the arrows from the outer orbit to denote that knowledge of child development, audiology, and the family are pivotal to effective implementation of the teaching role.

SOLAR is an acronym for a framework that teachers can use when planning and implementing a teaching session that is based on parent–child interaction. There are five teaching tasks: setting the scene (S), observing (O), listening (L), assessing (A), and responding (R). These tasks are ordered in this fashion purposefully to convey that each session should begin with a plan and clearly identified goal, and the room is set up in a way that will target the goal. As the session proceeds, the teacher observes, listens to, and assesses both the child and parent in relation to the established goals and responds appropriately.

The SOLAR orbit is represented as a cycle indicating that the five teaching tasks are dynamic and interrelated and may be revisited any number of times in a session. Changes to the set up will occur for a variety of reasons, and of course observation, listening, and assessment of the revised set up should then follow. The O, L, and A tasks will not necessarily occur in this order; however, it is assumed that all three are important sources of information that a teacher uses to plan what, when, and how to respond. The R in SOLAR has to do with the strategies the teacher uses to promote and enhance parent–child interaction. There are two distinct roles for the teacher of the deaf in the SOLAR orbit: an *executive* role performed in collaboration with the family involving the S, O, L, and A tasks, and a *coaching* role performed in partnership with the family involving the R task.

The Executive Role of the Teacher in SOLAR

The executive role is so named to represent the "decision-making" role undertaken by teachers in collaboration with parents. Decisions are made about child skills and family strengths, about plans and goals, about the type and design of activities, and about responses and reactions to goals. The first four SOLAR tasks are elaborated below with a focus upon issues related to family-centered practice.

Setting the Scene   In setting the scene, the teacher needs to consider the family environment, including routine activities, special events, the affective environment of the child and the family's skills, competencies, and knowledge, particularly those of the parents. In working closely with the family, teachers need to consider the effect of their presence, behavior, and most important, their communication about the child and with the parents. This is a critical issue, particularly in a home-visiting kind of service.

A critical role of the teacher is to suggest interactive activities that will promote the agreed goals of the session as outlined in the individual family service plan. Importantly, these activities should be family centered and of interest and relevance to the family's unique and everyday life experiences. Teachers should embed activities in the family's culture and experiences rather than attempt to introduce activities that do not "fit" either with the child, the parent, or the family. The advantages of this approach are that it demystifies the process of spoken language acquisition for parents and stresses the potency of their own involvement in the intervention, thus enhancing their feelings of confidence and competence.

It is critical for the child's engagement in the interaction that both routine and play activities are selected and arranged in a way that is developmentally appropriate. Knowledge of what children typically engage with at particular ages, and more important, how they engage in such activities is fundamental to achieving developmental appropriateness. Having said this, such knowledge does not necessarily take account of the individual preferences of children or indeed their parents. In relation to parents, each has a unique relationship with the child, built around particular routines and activities. While these activities are often part of most family experiences, the way both partners engage in these routines is idiosyncratic to each parent–child dyad. When teachers incorporate this uniqueness into their choice of activity, they are more likely to be family centered.

Observing, Listening, Assessing   When working alongside a child and parents the aim of the teacher is to gather information about the child, the interactions between the parent and the child, and the family in order to develop a plan with the parents based on this information. Formal assessments of the child's level of functioning can provide useful information, but it is contended here that the most important information is provided by careful observation of typical, real-life interactions. Observing contingent responsiveness between parent and child, the amount of joint attention, and how this is created and maintained by both partners, and listening to and recording the communicative output of both parent and child yield information that is critical for ongoing planning with the parents.

In order to plan appropriate goals, the teacher must continually establish a picture of the child's communication ability, including listening and attending behavior, oral receptive and expressive language skills, phonological skills, and the child's ability to use communication functionally. In the young child, gaining accurate and representative data about such skills is not easy, and increasingly, the value of parents as a reliable source of data about their child is becoming more accepted. Assessment tools that incorporate parent report such as the Rossetti Infant-Toddler Language Scale (Rossetti, 1990), the MacArthur Communicative Development Inventories (Fenson et al., 1993), and the Diary of Early Language (Nott et al., 2003) are examples of such tools. Formal assessments are often combined with sampling of the child's skill using videotapes of the child engaged in activities with the parents in a clinical setting. With the young child, however, these assessments may well underestimate what the child is actually capable of. It is well known that a child's emerging communication skills are often embedded in and supported by specific routines (Harris, Barrett, Jones, & Brookes, 1988) and, as such, are much more likely to be observed in the home environment. A single home visit may provide the teacher with information that could take several visits to a clinic or center to obtain.

Parents are a valuable source of information about their child, and their observations and judgments should be included in the data collection phase of the assessment. It is important that there is continual monitoring of whether there is a good fit between what the teacher observes and what the parent considers that their child can do. An assessment based upon data the parent does not believe in is of little value to the parent and a poor foundation for planning and implementing teaching goals. Discrepancies in how teachers and parents view a child's skills should therefore be discussed and clarified, so that a consensual view of the child's skill is reached. Working collaboratively with parents during this phase will promote empowerment and ensure a positive relationship between the teacher and parent.

The triad of "observing, listening to, and assessing" also provides an approach to facilitating parent–child interaction. Kaiser et al. (1998) epitomize the role of parent–child interaction in the following statement: "[T]he interaction defines the teachable moment and the content of teaching" (p. 48). This is a major departure from other oral teaching approaches that seek to teach children predetermined, individual, targets for later use in conversation. The approach implies that the targets and the context are inextricably intertwined and the teacher cannot be prescriptive about what, when, and how to teach. In an approach founded on parent–child interaction, it is essential for the teacher of the deaf to learn how each parent and child typically, but uniquely, interact. Ideally, home visits provide the teacher with the most authentic data about the interaction and give the teacher crucial insights into the individual nature of the interaction.

What is it the teacher is looking for when observing, listening to, and assessing an interaction? The aim is to identify strengths in the interaction and the individual nature of each interaction. Research informs us that joint attention, parental responsiveness including contingency, CDS, volume and richness of input, and everyday family experiences are important in facilitating oral language learning. These features are sometimes incorporated into rating scales or checklists to guide the teacher in promoting language development. The Checklist for Caregivers: Communication-Promoting Behaviors (Cole, 1992) is an example of one such checklist. While helpful, however, such checklists typically fail to capture the diversity of interactions both within and across cultures (McCollum & McBride, 1997). A family-centered approach would value and be responsive to the individual differences in how parents and their children interact.

It is also important to observe, listen to, and assess family experiences related to their deaf children's language learning. There is a wealth of information about the family that will enhance the teacher's ability to work in a way that is both appropriate and relevant to each individual family. This includes knowledge of the home environment, the family members, when and where the child and parent spend time together, what routines the parent and child engage in, what scripts they use in these routines, and what the child's activity preferences are. Other important sorts of information are what the parents typically do and/or enjoy doing with their child and what rules and expectations govern the daily routines of family life.

Answers to these questions can readily be gained through observation and listening in the child's home environment. In addition, a "talking map" (Brown & Nott, 2003) can provide detailed information about who interacts with the child at home and the context and scripts of these interactions. The talking map is an assessment tool based upon work by Farver (1999), who used "activity settings" to analyze the "who, what, where, when and why of daily life" (p. 102). Farver argued that these activity settings provide the context in which all children learn. The talking map should be completed by the teacher and parent collaboratively. It provides the teacher with a picture of each individual child's communication environment, by identifying who communicates with the child and when. Each talking map is different, to reflect the individual and unique ways in which families interact and communicate. Information from the map is useful in identifying the existing contexts of a family's everyday experience that can be used to promote oral language development. As such, it is particularly useful in the demystification of the process of language acquisition and empowering parents as the primary agents of change in their child's development.

Collectively, information is shared with the parents and used to make decisions about goals and plans. The implementation of these plans is the final phase of the SOLAR model.

The Coaching Role of the Teacher in SOLAR

The coaching role of the teacher of the deaf is so named to convey the idea that, in family-centered intervention, the teacher does not work directly with the child but supports the parent to do so. So, what qualities make a good coach? Using the analogy of, say, an athletics coach, the effective coach has qualities that are very special. The first of these qualities is that the coach has a mental picture of the "ideal" in performance and a determination to develop strengths in the athlete to achieve this level of performance. In many cases, a good coach does not perform the task as well as the athlete. What the coach brings, however, is the understanding of the nature of the task to be done, detailed analysis of the strengths and needs of the athlete, and support. In the coaching role, the teacher knows what the ultimate goal is, analyzes the strengths and needs of the dyad, shares this information with the parent, and provides opportunities for the parent to practice and refine their skills.

Having gathered information about the child and the family, completed appropriate assessments, and established plans, the teacher of the deaf must now respond and continue to engage in the SOLAR cycle. There are several critical tasks for the teacher when responding, and the responses need to be made sensitively and without jeopardizing the confidence of the parent. Remembering that interactions with another are the substance of our relationship with that person, these interactions need to be acknowledged and treated with deep respect. Consideration also should be given to the fact that these interactions also fit somewhere along continua from routine to intimate and from universal to culturally specific.

In responding to parents, the teacher should be able to convey to the parent not only the current cognitive and social developmental status of the child, but also how the child is working toward achieving phonological, semantic, syntactic, and pragmatic proficiency. This requires that the teacher understand in depth the associations and dependencies between major domains of development and be able to present these to parents at a level the parent can understand. Knowledge and ability to communicate the next step are fundamental to ensuring that parent and teacher are working in the ZPD. Judging the degree and type of support the child needs requires the adult to be vigilant. When more support is needed for the child, strategies can include designing activities for predictability, repetition, giving extra contextual support, and tagging the unknown to the known. When the child is succeeding with the task, parents can be encouraged to add in new language, withdraw contextual support, increase the complexity of the activity, and show expectation of task completion.

SUMMARY AND CONCLUSIONS

In this chapter we have attempted to describe the current status of family-centered practice in oral early intervention for children with hearing loss. As has been shown, the definition of family-centered practice is elusive and open to a range of interpretations. Certainly it would appear that, in early childhood intervention in general, while teachers believe that they are working in a family-centered manner, the research suggests that this is not necessarily the case. This is also likely to apply to oral early intervention for children with hearing loss, given the diversity of programs.

Research is still needed to ascertain whether family-centered oral early intervention is effective. Most recent research is contaminated by an inability to separate out variables such as degree and type of hearing loss, age of identification, type of oral programming, degree of involvement of the family in the program, and the extent to which the program is family centered in its orientation. Further limitations apply to the research in terms of the limited outcome variables, and the application of the findings to the design of programs for parents wanting their child to listen and use spoken language.

Clearly, teachers of the deaf working in oral early intervention programs require comprehensive training in audiological management. However, it is suggested that the traditional method of teacher training that uses a child-focused perspective to promote oral language development does not reflect current knowledge of child language acquisition. A reorientation in training is required toward understanding early language acquisition from a parent–child interaction perspective, incorporating knowledge about the cognitive and social-emotional processes underpinning language acquisition, and the importance of everyday settings. Probably the most critical issue in all of this is the understanding that a child's first language is the tool for the enculturalization of that child into the family group. If parents choose the spoken language modality, teachers of the deaf need to be expert at coaching them in scaffolding techniques in that language mode. Further, training as adult educators is essential to effective implementation of family-centered practice. The SOLAR model of practice presented here articulates the interaction between parent and child as the core, with the teacher fulfilling executive and coaching functions with the family both in collaboration and in partnership.

Clearly, large-scale and detailed studies of the efficacy of family-centered practice in oral early intervention are required. We need to understand the long-term effects of family-centered practice, not only regarding children's language and communication outcomes, but also regarding academic outcomes, the quality of relationships within the family, and ultimately the quality of life for the child on maturity.

REFERENCES

Apuzzo, M. L., & Yoshinaga-Itano, C. (1995). Early identification of infants with significant hearing loss and the Minnesota Child Development Inventory. *Seminars in Hearing, 16*(2), 124–139.

Baldwin, D. A. (1995). Understanding the link between joint attention and language. In C. Moore & P. Dunham (Eds.), *Joint attention: Its origin and role in development* (pp. 131–158). Hillsdale, NJ: Lawrence Erlbaum.

Bornstein, M. H. (1989). *Maternal responsiveness: Characteristics and consequences. New directions for child development.* San Francisco, CA: Jossey-Bass.

Bornstein, M. H., & Tamis-LeMonda, C. S. (1997). Maternal responsiveness and infant mental abilities: Specific predictive relations. *Infant Behavior and Development, 20*(3), 283–296.

Bornstein, M. H., Tamis-LeMonda, C. S., & Haynes, O. M. (1999). First words in the second year: Continuity, stability, and models of concurrent and predictive correspondence in vocabulary and verbal responsiveness across age and context. *Infant Behavior and Development, 22*(1), 65–85.

Brooks-Gunn, J., Berlin, L. J., & Fuligni, A. S. (2000). Early childhood intervention programs: What about the family? In J. P. Shonkoff & S. J. Meisels (Eds.), *Handbook of early childhood intervention* (pp. 549–588). Cambridge: Cambridge University Press.

Brown, P. M., & Nott, P. (2003, January). *Reaching for the stars: A SOLAR model of early intervention.* Paper presented at the Australian and New Zealand Conference for Educators of the Deaf, Perth, Australia.

Bruder, M. B. (2000). Family-centered early intervention: Clarifying our values for the new millenium. *Topics in Early Childhood Special Education, 20*(2), 105–115.

Bruner, J. (1978). From communication to language: A psychological perspective. In I. Markova (Ed.), *The social context of language* (pp. 255–287). New York: Wiley.

Bruner, J. (1983). *Child's talk.* New York: W. W. Norton.

Byrne, M. R. (2000). Parent-professional collaboration to promote spoken language in a child with severe to profound hearing loss. *Communication Disorders Quarterly, 21*(4), 210–223.

Calderon, R., & Naidu, S. (1998). Further support for the benefits of early identification and intervention for children with hearing loss. *Volta Review, 100*(5), 53–84.

Carney, A. E. (1996). Early intervention and management of the infant with hearing loss: What's science got to do with it? *Seminars in Hearing, 17*(2), 185–195.

Carney, A. E., & Moeller, M. P. (1998) Treatment efficacy: Hearing loss in children. *Journal of Speech, Language and Hearing Research, 41*, 561–584.

Cole, E. B. (1992). *Listening and talking. A guide to promoting spoken language in young hearing-impaired children.* Washington, DC: Alexander Graham Bell Association of the Deaf.

Cross, T. G. (1977). Mother's speech adjustments: The contributions of selected child listener variables. In C. E. Snow & C. A. Ferguson (Eds.), *Talking to children: Language input and acquisition* (pp. 151–188). Cambridge: Cambridge University Press.

Dromi, E., & Ingber, S. (1999). Israeli mothers' expectations from early intervention with their preschool deaf children. *Journal of Deaf Studies and Deaf Education, 4*(1), 50–68.

Dunham, P. J., Dunham, F., & Curwin, A. (1993). Joint–attentional states and lexical acquisition at 18 months. *Developmental Psychology, 29*(5), 827–831.

Dunst, C. J. (1997). Conceptual and empirical foundations of family-centered practice. In R. Illback., C. Cobb, & J. H. Joseph (Eds.), *Integrated services for children and families: Opportunities for psychological practice* (pp. 75–91). Washington, DC: American Psychological Association.

Dunst, C. J. (2002). Family-centered practices: Birth through high school. *Journal of Special Education, 36*(3), 139–147.

Dunst, C. J., Bruder, M. B., Trivette, C. M., Hamby, D., Raab, M., & McLean, M. (2001). Characteristics and consequences of everyday natural learning opportunities. *Topics in Early Childhood Special Education, 21*(2), 68–92.

Dunst, C. J., Hamby, D., Trivette, C. M., Raab, M., & Bruder, M. B. (2000). Everyday family and community life and children's naturally occurring learning opportunities. *Journal of Early Intervention, 23*(3), 151–164.

Dunst, C., Trivette, C., & Deal, A. (1988). *Enabling and empowering families: Principles and guidelines for practice.* Cambridge, MA: Brookline Books.

Farver, J. A. (1999). Activity setting analysis: A model for examining the role of culture in development. In A. Goncu (Ed.), *Children's engagement in the world. Sociocultural perspectives* (pp. 99–127). Cambridge: Cambridge University Press.

Fenson, L., Dale, P., Reznick, J. S., Thal, D., Bates, E., Hartung, J., Pethick, S., et al. (1993). *MacArthur Communicative Development Inventories: User's guide and technical manual.* San Diego, CA: Singular Publications.

Gallaway, C., & Richards, B. J. (1994). *Input and interaction in language acquisition.* Cambridge: Cambridge University Press.

Gauvain, M. (1999). Everyday opportunities for the development of planning skills: Sociocultural and family influences. In A. Goncu (Ed.), *Children's engagement in the world: Sociocultural perspectives* (pp. 173–201). Cambridge: Cambridge University Press.

Griswold, E., & Cummings, J. (1974) The expressive vocabulary of preschool deaf children. *American Annals of the Deaf, 119,* 16–28.

Harbin, G. L., McWilliam, R. A., & Gallagher, J. J. (2000). Services for young children with disabilities and their families. In J. P. Shonkoff & S. J. Meisels (Eds.), *Handbook of early childhood intervention* (pp. 387–415). Cambridge: Cambridge University Press.

Harris, M., Barrett, M., Jones, D., & Brookes, S. (1988). Linguistic input and early word meaning. *Journal of Child Language, 15,* 77–94.

Hart, B., & Risley, T. R. (1995). *Meaningful differences in the everyday experience of young American children.* Baltimore: P. H. Brookes.

Huttenlocher, J. W., Haight, A. B., Seltzer, M., & Lyons, T. (1991). Early vocabulary growth: Relation to language input and gender. *Developmental Psychology, 27*(2), 236–248.

Johnston, J. R., & Wong, M-Y. A. (2002). Cultural differences in beliefs and practices concerning talk to children. *Journal of Speech, Language, and Hearing Research, 45*(5), 916–926.

Joint Committee on Infant Hearing (2000). Year 2000 Position Statement: Principles and guidelines for early hearing detection and intervention programs. *American Journal of Audiology, 9,* 9–29.

Kaiser, A. P., Hancock, T. B., & Hester, P. P. (1998). Parents as cointerventionists: Research on applications of naturalistic language teaching procedures. *Infants and Young Children, 10*(4), 46–55.

Kaiser, A. P., Hemmeter, M. L., Ostrosky, M. M., Fischer, R., Yoder, P., & Keefer, M. (1996). The effects of teaching parents to use responsive interaction strategies. *Topics in Early Childhood Special Education, 16*(3), 375–406.

Kaiser, A. P., & Hester, P. P. (1994). Generalized effects of an enhanced milieu teaching. *Journal of Speech and Hearing Research, 37,* 1320–1340.

Kermani, H., & Brenner, M. E. (2000). Maternal scaffolding in the child's zone of proximal development across tasks: Cross-cultural perspectives. *Journal of Research in Childhood Education, 15*(1), 30–52.

Klein, N. K., & Gilkerson, L. (2002). Personnel preparation for early childhood intervention programs. In J. P. Shonkoff & S. Meisels (Eds.), *Handbook of early childhood intervention* (2nd ed., pp. 454–483). Cambridge: Cambridge University Press.

Koester, L. S., Papoušek, H., & Smith-Gray, S. (2000). Intuitive parenting, communication, and interaction with deaf infants. In P. E. Spencer, C. J. Erting & M. Marschark (Eds.), *The deaf child in the family and at school* (pp. 55–71). Mahwah, NJ: Lawrence Erlbaum.

Locke, J. L. (1993). *The child's path to spoken language.* Cambridge, MA: Harvard University Press.

Mahoney, G. J., & Wheedan, C. A. (1997). Parent child interaction—the foundation for family centred early intervention practice: A response to Baird and Peterson. *Topics in Early Childhood Special Education, 17*(2), 165–184.

Martineau, G., Lamarche, P., Marcoux, S., & Bernard, P. (2001). The effect of early intervention on academic achievement of hearing-impaired children. *Early Education and Development, 12*(2), 275–288.

Mayne, A. M., Yoshinaga-Itano, C., Sedey, A. L., & Carey, A. (1998). Expressive vocabulary development of infants and toddlers who are deaf or hard of hearing. *Volta Review, 100*(5), 1–28.

McBride, S. L., & Peterson, C. (1997). Home-based early intervention with families of children with disabilities: Who is doing what? *Topics in Early Childhood Special Education, 17,* 209–233.

McCollum, J. A., and McBride, S. L. (1997). Ratings of parent-infant interaction: Raising questions of cultural validity. *Topics in Early Childhood Special Education, 17*(4), 494–519.

McDonald, L., & Pien, D. (1982). Mother conversational behaviour as a function of interactional intent. *Journal of Child Language, 9,* 337–358.

Moeller, M. P. (2000). Early intervention and language development in children who are deaf and hard of hearing. *Pediatrics, 106*(3), 1–9.

Musselman, C., & Kircaali-Iftar, G. (1996). The development of spoken language in deaf children: Explaining the unexplained variance. *Journal of Deaf Studies and Deaf Education, 1*(2), 108–121.

Nelson, K. (1973). *Structure and strategy in learning to talk* (Monograph No. 38). Society for Research in Child Development. Chicago: University of Chicago Press.

Nott, P., Cowan, R., Brown, P. M., & Wigglesworth, G. (2003). Assessment of language skills in young children with profound hearing loss under two years of age. *Journal of Deaf Studies and Deaf Education, 8*(4), 401–421.

Owens, R. E. (2001). *Language development*. Needham Heights, MA: Allyn and Bacon.

Piaget, J. (1962). *Play, dreams, and imitation in childhood*. New York: Norton. (Original work published 1945)

Powers, S., Gregory, S., Lynas, W., McCracken, W., Watson, L., Boulton, A., et al. (1999). *A review of good practice in deaf education*. London: Royal National Institute for Deaf People.

Rhoades, E. A., & Chisholm, T. H. (2000). Global language progress with an auditory-verbal approach for children who are deaf or hard of hearing. *Volta Review, 102*(1), 5–25.

Rossetti, L. (1990). *The Rossetti Infant-Toddler Language Scale*. East Moline, IL: Linguisystems.

Saxon, T. F. (1997). A longitudinal study of early mother-infant interaction and later language competence. *First Language, 17*, 271–281.

Schlesinger, H., & Meadow, K. (1972). *Sound and sign: Childhood deafness and mental health*. Berkeley, CA: University of California Press.

Smith, C. B., Adamson, L. B., & Bakeman, R. (1988). Interactional predictors of early language. *First Language, 8*, 143–156.

Snow, C. (1984). Parent–child interaction and the development of communicative ability. In R. Schiefelbusch & J. Pickar (Eds.), *The acquisition of communicative competence* (pp. 69–108). Baltimore: University Park Press.

Spencer, P. E., & Gutfreund, M. (1990). Characteristics of "dialogues" between mothers and prelinguistic hearing-impaired and normally-hearing infants. *Volta Review, 92*, 351–359.

Stern, D. N. (1977). *The first relationship*. Cambridge, MA: Harvard University Press.

Stokes, J., & Bamford, J. (1990). Transition from prelinguistic to linguistic communication in hearing-impaired infants. *British Journal of Audiology, 24*, 217–222.

Strong, C. J., Clark, T. C., & Walden, B. E. (1995). The relationship of hearing-loss severity to demographic, age, treatment, and intervention-effectiveness variables. *Ear and Hearing, 15*(2), 126–137.

Tamis-LeMonda, C. S., Bornstein, M. H., & Baumwell, L. (2001). Maternal responsiveness and children's achievement of language milestones. *Child Development, 72*(3), 748–767.

Tomasello, M., & Farrar, J. M. (1986). Joint attention and early language. *Child Development, 57*, 1454–1463.

Tomasello, M., & Todd, J. (1983). Joint attention and lexical acquisition style. *First Language, 4*, 197–212.

Turnbull, A. P., Turbiville, V., & Turnbull, H. R. (2000). Evolution of family-professional partnerships: Collective empowerment as the model for the early twenty-first century. In J. P. Shonkoff & S. Meisels (Eds.), *Handbook of early childhood intervention* (2nd ed., pp. 630–650). Cambridge: Cambridge University Press.

Vygotsky, L. S. (1986). *Thought and language.* Cambridge, MA: MIT Press. (Originally published in Russian in 1934 as Myschlenie i rech' [Thinking and speech])

Watkins, S. (1987). Long term effects of home intervention with hearing-impaired children. *American Annals of the Deaf, 132,* 267–271.

Wolery, M. (2000). Behavioural and educational approaches to early intervention. In J. Shonkoff & S. Meisels (Eds.), *Handbook of early childhood intervention* (2nd ed., pp. 179–203). Cambridge: Cambridge University Press.

Wu, C. D., & Brown, P. M. (2004). Parents' and teachers' expectations of auditory-verbal therapy. *Volta Review, 104*(1), 5–20.

8

Speech Production and Spoken Language Development of Children Using "Total Communication"

Linda J. Spencer & J. Bruce Tomblin

A variety of methods have been used to support deaf children's spoken language development. These methods have employed a host of educational techniques, with input modes that range from exclusively using visual input for language development to input modes that provide solely auditory/aural input. One particular educational philosophy has attempted to combine input modalities to provide information from visual/aural modalities. This approach has been dubbed the total communication (TC) approach.

The purpose of this chapter is threefold. The first objective is to provide a background explanation of the TC educational approach that will lay a framework for viewing the acquisition of speech and spoken language skills of children who are educated with this philosophy. This will include an evolutionary account of the primary factors leading to the implementation of this approach and a description of the philosophy that underlies the reasons for instituting TC within the educational system. This background should illustrate the difficulty inherent in providing a standardized methodology for studying the TC population regarding outcomes. Second, with that caveat in mind, we present a review of studies that outline achievement profiles of children who have been educated in the TC setting. Within these profiles, the topics of oral articulation proficiency and how it relates to speech intelligibility are discussed, as well as spoken and written language developmental patterns found in this population. Finally, areas where there is a need for more research are highlighted.

HISTORICAL USE OF MULTIPLE MODALITIES

The idea of using multiple modalities to communicate with deaf individuals may be thought of as a recent development by some, yet this practice can be traced back at least as early as the 1600s when Juan Pablo Bonet published a one-handed manual alphabet. Bonet's educational methodology included oral articulation training that was based on written and fingerspelled information (Evans, 1982). Approaches that combined modalities for education also were described by Charles Michel de L'Epée in Paris 1776; Henry Guyot in Groningen, Holland, in 1790; Abbé Roch Bébian in France circa 1825; and Andrew Wright in England in 1891. In the United States, the "combined system" that included signing, fingerspelling, speech, and lipreading was utilized at Gallaudet College in the late 1800s.

The preference of the use of multiple modalities for educating deaf students has waxed and waned over time, as has the use of oral/aural practice. Throughout the first half of the twentieth century, several different philosophies of communication with deaf individuals were used within the United States. By the middle of the twentieth century there was a strong preference among deaf educators to use oral approaches. Also at this time, however, there was a burgeoning line of study concerning sign language development. Stokoe (1960/1978) outlined specific features of American Sign Language (ASL) that included location, shape, and movement, which he called "cheremes." These features were defined as relating to signs as sounds or phonemes relate to spoken words. Additional work of researchers such as Bellugi and her colleagues (e.g., Bellugi & Fischer, 1972; Klima & Bellugi, 1979) led to the acknowledgment of the legitimacy of signed languages, such as ASL and British Sign Language, as full and sufficient natural languages.

This was also a period in which there was an increase in the knowledge of the advances in linguistic theory and of the language acquisition process in hearing children. For example, researchers began to document the age and order of acquisition of English grammatical structures (Berko, 1958; Brown, 1964; Cazden, 1968). This knowledge heightened awareness of the need to expose children to a full and complete language in their formative years. In this context, Lenneberg (1967) stated his concern that deaf children begin to learn language after "the most important formative period for language establishment is already on the decline." Research that documented the status of English language skill acquisition of deaf children seemed to validate these concerns, demonstrating delayed development of vocabulary, grammar, and syntax (Cooper, 1967; Crandall, 1978; Heider & Heider, 1941; Presnell, 1973).

Concurrently, studies that investigated the achievement levels of deaf children educated in "oral" programs were reporting that reading achievement scores of the graduates of these programs for the deaf were hovering at the fourth and fifth grade level (DiFrancesca, 1972; Furth, 1966; Goetzinger and Rouzey, 1957). Similarly, in 1970, Markides found that speech intelligibility of deaf children who were educated via oral education practices was below 20%. These results were found despite evidence that the range of intelligence for the population, given no other disability, was commensurate with that of the hearing population (Vernon, 1968).

The dissatisfaction with the language, speech, and academic achievement levels of children with severe to profound hearing loss initiated a movement toward incorporating signed language once again into the educational curriculum for deaf children in the late 1960s and early 1970. To facilitate this while continuing to provide spoken language input, small groups of educators and linguists created new systems for producing signs with the order and, to some extent, the morphology of spoken English (Clarke, 1972; Gustason & Zawolkow, 1999). It is about this time that the term "total communication" began to come into the literature especially within the United States.

The TC Philosophy

Total communication is a philosophy of communication that is utilized in educational settings and in home environments and is not necessarily a communication method (Scouten, 1984). For the purpose of this chapter, "total communication" refers to "the combined use of aural, manual and oral modalities in communicating with and teaching hearing impaired individuals" (Garretson, 1976, p. 89). There is much misunderstanding of this term, and as a result, it is not always clearly defined within the literature. A frequent misuse of the term "total communication" occurs when authors describe a communication method and interchange the method with the philosophy. The delineation must be made, however, between the philosophical nature of TC and the *methods* of communication used *within* the TC philosophy. For example, sometimes the terms TC and simultaneous communication (SC) are used interchangeably (Caccamise, Ayers, Finch, & Mitchell, 1997). SC indicates that signs and spoken words and morphemes are produced simultaneously and, therefore, in the same order of the grammar of the spoken language. Thus, SC in its pure form actually incorporates little of the flexibility inherent in the TC philosophy. Variable use of the TC and SC labels, and variability in the degree to which either approach is implemented, causes confusion and complicates the ability of researchers to control for aspects of language input in studies of the outcomes. Figure 8.1 provides a schematic model of TC, showing that the umbrella term of "total communication" covers a host of concepts contained under the broad construct. At the core of this philosophy is the goal of providing an amalgam of input and flexible opportunities for output that maximize the child's ability to communicate.

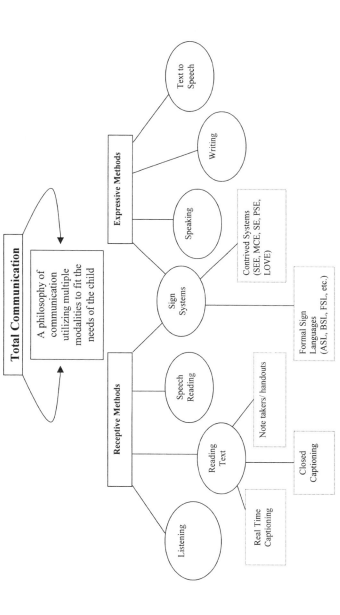

Figure 8-1. Schematic model of the "total communication" philosophy. BSL, British Sign Language; SEE = Signed Exact English; SE = Signed English; PSE = Piegin Signed English; LOVE = Linguistics of Visual English; FSL = French Sign Language.

The TC approach, therefore, is meant to be fluid, individualized, and context and situation dependent. For example, it would not be uncommon to observe a child in a TC program being taught via an English-based signing system (probably accompanied by spoken language as in SC) during a language lesson, in order to target the development and understanding of specific word endings, yet in a subsequent lesson to be taught via ASL for a literature presentation. Alternatively, from the TC perspective, it would also be possible for a child to start out utilizing a signed language as a primary modality for communication during the preschool years, using more and more voice as speaking skills mature, and, finally, reaching a point in the middle school years where a signed system is used only for receptive purposes during school lectures. Sometimes sign language is phased out entirely and gradually replaced by real-time captioning or even listening alone. At other times, signing becomes the sole or at least the primary communication modality used by a child. Common themes in programs that have adopted the TC philosophy thus include the following, as outlined by Davis and Hardick (1981, pp. 315–316) and Knauf (1978, p. 561):

1. The child will be able to make use of audition and vision as useful sources of information.
2. Any given child will make use of one or both sources (modalities) in a way that fits his or her individual needs and skills during a particular communication instance.
3. Flexibility and adaptability in use of modality of communication method used yield a larger number of potential audiences and an increased access to communication partners.
4. There can be an evolution of communication modality used as a particular child develops skills within a certain modality area.
5. The language of the hearing community serves as the linguistic basis for the sign system used.

The decision for more educational programs to institute a TC philosophy leads to the question of which manual communication system(s) (or languages) should be used (Caccamise et al., 1997). The answer to this question is long and complicated, and there appears to be a discrepancy between what people think *should* be used and what *is* in use regarding sign systems. According to Caccamise et al. (1997), there are three main categories of systems that are used within the TC philosophy: ASL, manually coded English (MCE), or a combination of ASL and MCE. Although the purpose of this chapter is not to critique any particular manual method, it is important for the reader to be aware that there are a variety of manual systems used within the TC approach.

ASL is a complete, natural language having developed over time by a community of users. Reflecting its visual-gestural base, ASL differs from English in grammar and, to some degree, in semantic boundaries.

Unlike English, ASL is characterized by topicalization (with both sign order and nonmanual indicators marking a "fronted" topic). In addition, morphemes can be "overlain" and simultaneously expressed in ASL through use of grammatically specific facial expressions (Siple & Fischer, 1991) and incorporation of manner and direction and even grammatical role (subject, object, etc.) into the expression of verbs (Supala, 1991). Phrase boundaries can also be marked in ASL by the location and the manner of placement of the sign on the body (Neidle & MacLaughlin, 2002), and Conlin, Hagstrom, and Neidle (2003) describe how particle formation using the question sign "what" can be used in ways that differ from the English use of particle formation. Additionally, ASL uses specific signals for turn taking besides those that are used in spoken English. ASL also has its own set of idioms, and in fact, signers find the meaning of most English idioms to be opaque (Marschark, 2004). Because of all of these structural differences between ASL and spoken English, it is virtually impossible to produce them simultaneously.

On the other hand, artificial sign systems known collectively in the United States as MCE are contrived systems for representing English visually. Such systems were developed with the premise that signs can be effectively produced and processed if they follow rules for English word order and grammatical morphemes. Indeed, MCE was developed to provide both a visual and auditory model of English simultaneously. Thus in MCE, signs are borrowed from ASL, and words are inflected using invented signs that are combined with the base sign, in the sequence in which they would occur in spoken English. The idea was that these contrived signed English sign systems would provide the opportunity for SC via both talking and signing. Initially, one of the goals of MCE was to improve literacy, based on the logic that if deaf children developed proficiency in English, they would have an advantage when they began to learn to read (Gustason & Zawolkow, 1999). However, the evidence in this regard remains inconsistent at best.

The Arguments for and the Limitations of Using Total Communication

The advocates of TC stress that the flexibility in philosophy yields a potential for the child to communicate with a variety of people in a variety of situations using a choice of modalities (Hawkins & Brawner, 1997). Many parents are concerned with the cultural implications of deafness for their children. They feel that in order to gain a cultural identity, it is important to be able to communicate with others in the Deaf culture. Given that the language of the Deaf community in the United States is ASL, many feel it is important for a child to develop an ability to communicate using a signed modality in order to be able to share in the rich traditions of the Deaf culture (Baker, 1994). However, while the TC philosophy may attempt to foster a use of signs, many critics point out that if a formal signed language such as ASL is not taught early on, mastery of that language may not take place. Thus, TC, which usually involves using voice plus MCE, may not assure a deaf person's full participation in the Deaf cultural group.

The TC premise allows for communication to take place in an unlimited number of situations. Sign can be used in cases where amplification or technology use is not possible or helpful, where background noise interferes with the signals provided by amplification, during instances of technology breakdowns, or simply when preferred. In situations where parents are unable or not wanting to commit to one modality of communication, TC allows for a combination of choices. In many families, one parent may feel comfortable learning and utilizing a signed language, whereas another parent may be unable to achieve an adequate comfort or proficiency level with the signed language. The TC philosophy is able to accommodate these types of situations and is felt by many to be an attractive option. Vernon and Andrews (1990, pp. 82–86) offer a host of references to support the notion that TC yields positive developmental, psychosocial, linguistic, and academic benefits regarding the education of deaf children.

Yet the very flexibility inherent in the TC philosophy is often criticized as being one of the major limitations of this approach. The concern has been raised that humans have a "limited attentional capacity" or a "limited cognitive capacity" (Wood, 1992), which could limit a deaf child's ability to benefit from receiving two different modalities of language input. Aural habilitation textbooks have pointed out that critics of TC speculate that children learn through *either* the visual channel *or* the auditory channel (Knauf, 1978). The argument is that if one channel is not optimal, the stronger channels will prohibit the use of the weaker one, and the child will choose the path of least resistance. Critics use the rationale that sign, which uses the visual medium, is more salient than is the speech signal for the deaf child. If the child has easy access to communication via sign, she may not develop listening, lipreading, or speaking skills. For these reasons, opponents of TC warn against the introduction of sign, whether ASL or MCE, because they feel it will inhibit the development of spoken English or speech reading skills (Watson, 1976). Ultimately, they argue the brain is unable to process both signs and speech together. Alternatively, the argument is that in the presence of sensory deprivation (e.g., deafness), the visual modality will be enhanced to the point that visual attention will become superior in deaf individuals such that they will form a reliance on visual signals for the processing of information (Bosworth & Dobkins, 2002). It should be noted, however, that there are no substantial data that support these concerns, and there is no convincing evidence that deaf children form any kind of exclusive reliance on, or develop an advantage in, visual attention or processing tasks (Proksch & Bavelier, 2002; Tharpe, Ashmead, & Rothpletz, 2002).

Aside from the arguments pertaining to attention and processing, the suitability of many aspects of the "created" MCE systems to the visual modality has been called in question. Whereas speech is processed by the auditory modality in the temporal continuum, natural sign languages also are able to exploit the simultaneous spatial (visual) display of information. For example, in studying the natural language of ASL, Bellugi and Fisher (1972) found that although it may take longer to produce a specific sign than it does to say a specific word, it is possible to convey the same amount of information in the same time in ASL and spoken English. This is because in a signed utterance it is possible to convey several linguistic features concurrently through inflections that change the spatial location of the sign, its direction of movement, the facial expressions and postures accompanying it, and so on. In speech, the speaker must order the meaning units in sequence, which takes more time.

There are additional concerns regarding the contrived signed systems used within the TC philosophy. Some argue that the use of contrived signed systems, especially in SC, may prevent the development of a full and complete language system because when hearing teachers or parents use both speech and sign modalities simultaneously, they use incomplete and inconsistent sign input (Kluwin, 1981; Marmor & Petitto, 1979). Swisher (1985; Swisher & Thompson, 1985) found that mothers who were learning how to use MCE with their children omit between 8% and 26% of what they say, particularly function words that are grammatically specific to English. An important point with these criticisms, however, may lie in the proficiency level of the user. These levels are typically not formally measured. This, plus the small numbers of participants in most available studies, should lead to cautious interpretation of results. For example, Marmor and Petitto (1979) utilized just two hearing teachers who had used MCE for more 3 years, even if they had been judged to have "exceptionally good command of Manual English" by a school administrator (not necessarily the most appropriate judge). This subjective description was not corroborated with any objective measure, and the study did not describe where or how the teachers obtained their training. Other researchers, meanwhile, have been somewhat more specific in their evaluation of participants' signing and have provided more positive estimates of adults' abilities to provide TC language input. For example, Luetke-Stahlman (1988) and Woodlinger-Cohen (1991) both reported that teachers matched as much as 90% of what they said and what they signed. In short, because of a lack of specificity and control of variations in language input to children in TC or SC programs using MCE, it is not clear whether questions that remain about its efficacy arise because it is inherently an incomplete and restricted model of input, or whether there is a failure in the system to assure that teachers and parents utilize the system in a complete and accurate manner. Variability in the language models provided should be considered when supposed "results" of exposure to TC are discussed.

A final and practical limitation of the TC philosophy is that it is not always implemented within the theoretical framework as intended. For example, school districts are not always able to afford the number of sign language interpreters needed, and the training of the mainstream teachers may not be adequate to match the needs of a child placed within the classroom. There can be a mismatch between the sign systems used from year to year, due to differences in educator backgrounds. Similarly, if a child is ready to utilize real-time captioning, the school district will need to utilize a proactive approach in order to be able to invest in the training of personnel and equipment to make this possible. Sometimes there is resistance to adopting new technology that requires training, which leads to conflict between the professionals and families involved. Additionally, there could be differences between the linguistic levels of children who are grouped together out of practical necessity, leading to mismatches in modalities presented and utilized within the classroom. In short, it is a tremendous educational challenge to provide the level of individualization that is called for within a TC philosophy.

Research Challenges in TC

The eclectic nature of TC has implications when reviewing literature on outcome research, because the sign systems used within the research base investigating TC are not standardized, nor is the amount of time devoted to speech production or auditory training consistent across programs. Given the premise that the purpose of the TC approach is to meet the individual communication needs of each child served within the program, it holds that there is no way to keep constant or quantify the amount of auditory training, speech production training, or type of sign communication system a particular child receives. Indeed, it is sometimes impossible to qualify what sign system is used. This is an inherent point of contention and ambiguity within this field of study. The amount of aural/oral input and type of sign system used within a TC program is not the main research question with this population, however. Instead, it would be more worthwhile to investigate general outcomes in this very heterogeneous population of children who are educated under the umbrella term of this method.

Unfortunately, as the TC philosophy developed, there was no systematic implementation of the method and no systematic way to quantify the extent to which the philosophy was utilized within many programs or research designs. In fact, none of the studies mentioned in this chapter reported using any type of screening instrument to verify or to describe the extent to which a TC philosophy was utilized within a program studied. With this in mind, we turn to outcome studies involving children who have been purported to use this educational approach. This review allows us to show how these children are able to utilize "total communication" input to support spoken language development. Once again, however, it is important to emphasize that spoken language development is not the only objective of this educational approach.

ACHIEVEMENT PROFILES OF TC USERS

Models of Speech Presented

One of the initial concerns regarding the education of children using the TC approach was how this method would effect the development of speech skills (Wilbur, 1979). Some authors have suggested that there are qualitative differences in the models of speech presented to children in TC programs and the models presented in the mainstream or oral programs (Huntington & Watton, 1986). Other investigators have documented substantial acoustical differences in the articulation characteristics of the speech of hearing individuals under situations where they used speaking alone versus using speech while signing. For example, speakers producing speech while signing tend to have longer sentence durations and longer pause times between words (Whitehead, Schiavetti, Whitehead, & Metz, 1997) as well as increased word, vowel, and diphthong durations (Whitehead, Schiavetti, Whitehead, & Metz, 1995; Wilbur & Petersen, 1998). Although these distortions would appear to result in an aberrant speech model being presented to deaf children, some have suggested that the rate of speech used during signing and speaking (Schiavetti, Whitehead, Metz, Whitehead, & Mignerey, 1996; Whitehead et al., 1995) mirrors the types of changes in the speech that is presented to young hearing children by their parents (Owens, 1992) or in the "clear speech" (Picheny, Durlach, & Braida, 1986) techniques that are advocated for use with hard-of-hearing individuals. "Clear speech" is a way people modify their speech patterns when they are in noisy situations. These modifications include using a slower rate of speaking, using a wider range of pitch and loudness levels, and speaking with a mildly exaggerated pattern of articulation for sounds such as /p/, /b/, /g/, /k/, /t/, /d/, as well as vowels. "Clear speech" has been shown to be more intelligible than conversational speech for both hard-of-hearing and hearing individuals when listening conditions are not optimal (Payton, Uchanski, & Braida, 1994; Uchanski, Choi, Braida, Reed, & Durlach, 1996). Whether these differences enhance or impede the acquisition of speech in deaf and hard-of-hearing children has not yet been investigated.

Oral Articulation Skills of Deaf Children

Some investigators have looked at how the oral articulation skills of children educated in TC programs develop. In examining the literature on articulation and intelligibility development in this population, one must take into consideration the following factors: What was the unit measured (phonemes, words, phrases, sentences), how it was measured (subjective or objective measures), and who did the measuring (naive listeners, experienced listeners). In addition to these factors, it is worthwhile to know whether the study design is comparative, descriptive, cross-sectional, or longitudinal. In the case of comparative studies, it is important to know whether the study design has controlled for extrinsic variables that could have an effect on intelligibility. These variables may include socioeconomic status (SES), the amount of educational emphasis placed on the development of speech production and listening skills, the type of programming (public school, private school), and hearing level (Geers, Moog, & Schick, 1984). Geers et al. (1984) argued that there is no "established relation" between SES and the ability to speak intelligibly, but they note that higher SES may allow for more therapy and more resources for therapy and could be related to parental involvement and "aspiration" level. Additional factors pertaining to hearing level may include the type and fit of amplification. If a child uses a cochlear implant (CI), it is important to know what type of CI technology was used and whether or not the insertion was complete or incomplete. In the last decade, a major trend in the published research pertaining to articulation proficiency in those who use TC has concentrated on the population of children who utilize CIs, yet it is important to consider the articulation proficiency outcomes of children with profound hearing loss who wear hearing aids as well.

Studies of Children Prior to the Advent of TC

A historical, descriptive perspective gives the impression that for children with profound hearing loss, developing intelligible speech is formidable task. There is little documentation of the types of educational programs and language modalities in the oldest group of studies presented here, including some as late as the 1970s. However, given the philosophy of the time, it is probably safe to assume that programs either used oral language only or that only a minimal amount of signed language was used—and that the programs could not be considered to use "total communication." Early studies revealed that the intelligibility of children with significant hearing loss was extremely poor (Hudgins & Numbers, 1942; John & Howarth, 1965; Markides, 1970; Monsen, 1978). One of the earliest studies (Hudgins & Numbers, 1942) found the average scores of intelligibility for a group of deaf and hard-of-hearing children between the ages of 8 and 20 years to be between 9% and 21%

words intelligible on average. Thirty years later Smith (1975) reported remarkably similar results: Average listeners could identify 18.7% of the words spoken by her group of children. Common phonetic errors included substituting one vowel or consonant for another, changing a vowel to sound like /uh/ and confusing voice–voiceless sounds (e.g., /b/ for /p/ or /k/ for /g/), or omitting sounds or producing them in a distorted way.

Several researchers examined the speech characteristics of hard-of-hearing children 8 years or older in either cross-sectional or longitudinal studies. Both Hudgins and Numbers (1942) and Smith (1975) found little improvement in speech as a function of age. McGarr (1987) studied children longitudinally between the ages of 11 and 14 years. She found little change in the average number and types of vowel and diphthong errors over time.

The Transition to Use of TC in Educational Programs

Many studies describing the speech skills of children who used manual communication have indicated that the programs utilized TC, yet the caveat is that the children may have not received substantive therapy regarding speech production skills (e.g., Wilbur, 1979). Often, little documentation of the components of the education program was provided in the methods section of the studies reviewed. Delaney, Stuckless, and Walter (1984), for example, documented the effects that the introduction of a TC curriculum into an aural/aural school had on several performance areas including speech development. This study was limited in that it addressed the teaching staff's perception of the effect sign language had on speech development, and there were no empirical data collected to support the perceptions. During the transition period 1 year before introduction of TC, 79% of the faculty reported they felt positively about the introduction of TC. Two years later, 75% of the faculty still felt positively; however, by 10 years after the introduction of TC, only 60% of the faculty reported a positive perception the effect of TC on speech development. Thus, the promise of fully intelligible speech in TC classrooms has not been achieved. Hyde and Power (1992) found that even teachers who were familiar with the speech patterns of their 10–17-year-old TC students never assigned a rating of "wholly intelligible" for their students, and only 13% of their students were rated as "fairly easy to understand" whereas a total of 67% of students had speech that was rated as "about half understandable."

Comparative Studies

Historically, even some comparative studies failed to provide a clear description of the population from which the samples were drawn. This may be one reason that in general these comparative studies are equivocal on the topic of whether children educated in oral environments outperformed children educated in total communication environments regarding speech production skills.

In an early study, Stuckless and Birch (1966) matched 38 pairs of deaf children with respect to age, hearing levels, sex, IQ, and SES to yield two groups of children. One group utilized a combined manual and oral method of communication and the other group utilized oral communication. Speech production was assessed via a 50-word intelligibility index, assigned by three listeners who had experience with listening to the speech of deaf individuals. The listeners attempted to identify the words produced by each speaker. Results indicated there was no statistical difference in intelligibility between the two groups of children. Similar findings were reported by Montgomery (1966) who studied 55 prelingual, profoundly deaf children who graduated from several schools throughout Scotland. Speech intelligibility was assessed through one objective measure, which was the percentage of phonemes produced correctly during a spontaneous speech sample. In addition, teachers completed a 10-point subjective rating scale to indicate the speech intelligibility of each of the participants. Finally, the teachers completed subjective rating scales to indicate each student's degree of proficiency with manual communication. Montgomery found no evidence of a negative impact of signed communication on speech intelligibility, and he concluded that exposure to manual communication did not have a deleterious effect on speech production. This study did not provide demographic data other than degree of hearing loss, age, and sex, however, and thus it is unclear whether other factors such as IQ, parental income, or age at amplification had an effect on outcomes of this study.

Meadow (1968) investigated the lipreading and speech production skills of pairs of deaf children and their parents who were matched on age, sex, IQ score, and father's occupation. One group included 46 pairs of deaf children of deaf parents, educated in an environment that utilized sign language and speech, whereas the other group included 51 pairs of deaf children who had hearing parents and were educated in a spoken language environment. Results of this study were generally in agreement with those above, in that there was no evidence that the use of sign language prevented acquisition of lipreading skills, as there was not a statistical difference in the lipreading performance between groups. Speech performance was evaluated via a 3-point rating scale that was completed by three different professionals. Again, there were no significant differences between the two groups of children.

Vernon and Koh (1971) studied 79 students from the California School for the Deaf who were categorized as signers and compared their speech production performance with 190 children who did not use sign. From these two participant pools, 32 pairs matched for grade level in school were constructed. All children had greater than 70 dB loss across the speech frequency range (500–2000 Hz). Speech production was retrospectively assessed via school records based on a teacher rating scale of 1–3 (good, fair, or poor speech intelligibility). Results indicated there were no differences found between the two groups in speech reading and speech intelligibility skills (oral group average score was 2, [standard deviation, 0.82], and the TC group average score was 2.71 [standard deviation, 0.81]). Unfortunately, this study did not provide detailed background information on demographic variables such as age at onset of deafness, consistency of hearing-aid use, or amount of speech therapy received, and very little description of the speech skills was provided beyond the subjective ratings.

In contrast with the findings of the above studies, Yoshinaga-Itano and Sedey (2000) found an effect for language modality when they investigated factors that influenced speech development in a group of 147 children who had varying degrees of hearing loss (see Yoshinaga-Itano, chapter 13 this volume). These children differed from those in the above studies in that they represented a recent cohort of deaf children who benefited from earlier age of identification of hearing loss and access to modern amplification technology. In addition, this study looked at a variety of demographic and developmental variables including age of child, degree of hearing loss, maternal education, gender, ethnicity, expressive language ability, mode of communication, and secondary disabilities and their effects on the development of phoneme inventories and speech intelligibility. Results indicated that *age* was the strongest predictor of speech ability, with older children producing more phonemes correctly. Additional predictors included degree of hearing loss and mode of communication as determined by whether or not the child and the parent used sign language during a videotaped child interaction. Children with lesser degrees of hearing loss, and those using oral-only communication, scored higher on the speech measure. In addition, speech skills appeared to be influenced by the children's language quotient, as measured by the expressive language subscale of the Minnesota Child Developmental Inventory (Ireton & Thwing, 1974). Children who had higher language skills also tended to have better speech skills. However, the authors did not indicate whether there were any modifications made in the test administration to account for the language modality used in this parent-report measure of child expressive language. Additionally, the researchers did not report whether there was a relationship between degree of hearing loss and type of language modalities used. Although they recognized that children who utilized oral communication exclusively during the speech sampling procedure tended to produce more intelligible speech and a larger phonemic repertoire than did the children who used TC, they stressed that their regression analysis did not provide a causal explanation of the results.

Studies of Children Using Cochlear Implants

The reader will note that very few comparative studies completed before the 1990s controlled for variables subsequently known to affect intelligibility, and few studies completed after the year 2000 consider the use of TC in children using CIs.

Articulation or Intelligibility Studies Where TC Participants Utilized CIs

Several studies have demonstrated that the use of CIs facilitates the development of speech production skills in children who have prelingual hearing losses. This section limits discussion to studies that included participants who utilized TC.

Initially, investigators began to describe speech production outcomes and attempted to explain variability in outcome. Tye-Murray, Spencer, and Woodworth (1995) examined the intelligibility of CI users. Intelligibility was determined by having the children imitate sentences and retell a story. A speech pathologist transcribed the utterances, and the percentage of phonemes produced correctly and the percentage of total words produced correctly were derived. In addition, listeners who were unfamiliar with the speech of deaf individuals rated how well they were able to understand the speech that was produced by the children. The participants in this study utilized TC and were educated in public school programs.

Tye-Murray et al. (1996) found that children who received their implants before 5 years of age progressed at a faster rate regarding speech production skills than did those receiving implants at later ages. They also found that within the entire group there was a large range in articulation performance. On average, the entire participant group produced 53% of their phonemes correctly, but the range of performance was between 14% and 92% correct. Although this study reported that cochlear implantation enhanced speech development as measured by sounds correctly produced, this did not always ensure that listeners understood what the children were saying. Listeners rated the speech of these children quite low, assigning them an average of 2.5 on a 10-point rating scale, where 1 was low and 10 was high. In addition, there was a significant correlation between how well participants recognized speech while wearing their CIs and their ability to produce speech sounds. Finally, the researchers found that signing did not disappear following implantation. In fact, it was observed that children continued to produce both speech and sign in more than 80% of their utterances during the story retell task.

Osberger, Robbins, Todd, and Riley (1994) examined the speech intelligibility of children with prelingual hearing loss after an average of 3 years of CI experience. Nine of the children used oral communication and nine of the children used total communication. Participants were matched for age at onset, age at implantation, and experience with the device. Participants' speech production was audio recorded as they imitated sentences. The sentences were played to listeners who wrote down what they heard. The number of words that were correctly identified was reported as the percentage of words understood. Results indicated that children in the oral group fared significantly better than those in the TC group. The average intelligibility score of the oral group was 48% while the score of the TC group was 21.5%; however, there was no control for SES, intelligence, or sex differences in this study, and there was no control for initial intelligibility levels. Therefore, it is unclear whether the oral group started off with higher intelligibility scores than the TC group. Tobey, Geers, Brenner, Altuna, & Gabbert (2003) studied the sentence production skills of 181 children between 8 and 9 years of age with an average of 5.5 years of CI experience. The participants were enrolled in educational programs that utilized a range of communication modes from TC to auditory-oral. The sentences the children produced were played to listeners who wrote down what they thought the children said. These listeners were able to identify 63.5% of key words spoken (SD = 31.5%; range, 0–98%). The authors then looked to see what contributed to variability in sentence production skills. They looked at child and family characteristics (e.g., age, age at onset and implantation, IQ, family size, SES, and gender), implant characteristics (e.g., technology, number of electrodes), and educational characteristics (therapy hours, clinician experience, parent involvement, and classroom placement) and entered them into a multiple regression model. Results indicated that the important contributors to the variability of ultimate speech intelligibility included IQ, size of the family, duration of using newer implant technology, the number of electrodes that were active, and the way the implant was programmed. Secondary contributors to intelligibility were classroom placement and communication mode, which accounted for 12% of the variance. Thus, children in mainstream classrooms who used auditory-oral speech modes achieved higher speech production scores. Speech intelligibility levels of all of these long-term CI users were considerably higher than users who had less than 3 years of implant experience.

In contrast with findings from the above studies, Connor, Hieber, Arts, and Zwolan (2000) demonstrated that the consonant production skills of CI recipients using TC were not significantly different from those of deaf children who used the oral communication if they utilized advanced implant technology and if they received their implants no later than 5 years of age. It is not known how consonant production skills relate to overall word intelligibility within this group of children, however. Furthermore, although participants were matched on intelligence ability, SES and sex differences were not analyzed.

Geers, Spehar, and Sedey (2002) utilized a subset of children from the later-published Tobey et al. (2003) study to provide insight into the variability in performance of TC users. These researchers examined the speech production skills of 27 CI users who were between 8 and 9 years of age. All had received CIs before age 3 and subsequently utilized TC for at least 3 years after implantation. Speech intelligibility was assessed via a sentence production task that was recorded and played to naive listeners, who then wrote down the number of words they understood. The mean percentage of words correctly identified for this group of children was 59%, with an SD of 34% and a range of 0–98%. A conversational language sample also was elicited with each child by an examiner who used "simultaneous speech and sign" in order to determine what communication modality the child used. Results for this portion of the study noted that in a conversational context, for this group of identified TC users, 9 of 27 children used only speech as their mode of communication, 6 of 27 used sign, and 12 of 27 used both speech and sign to communicate. The results of this study suggest that a TC placement does not preclude the development of speech production skills. There was a significant relationship between the amounts of speech a child used in a conversational sample and their speech perception skills as well as with the development of intelligibility.

Intelligibility skills are even higher in children with more implant experience, as documented in a recent study of the subjective and objective intelligibility of long-time CI users (Peng, Spencer, & Tomblin, 2004). This study examined the speech of 24 children who had 84 months of CI experience; 23 of 24 of the participants were educated in TC programs. The participants imitated sentences, and their productions were recorded. Subsequently, listeners who were not experienced with the speech patterns of deaf individuals listened to and wrote down what they thought the children were saying. The mean percentage of words correctly identified was 71.54%, with an SD 29.9% and a range of 6–100%. The average intelligibility rating (the subjective measure) was 3.03 on a scale where 4 was the highest score possible. Younger age at implantation and the use of the multipeak coding strategy (a particular type of sound processing used in some advanced CIs) were associated with higher levels of intelligibility.

Overall, the studies reviewed in this section demonstrate that the goal of developing intelligible speech is possible for children who utilize CI technology and TC. While there is still variability in ultimate articulation proficiency, more and more of these children are developing speaking skills that allow them to communicate with listeners who are not familiar with the speech patterns of deaf individuals. In the past, when (at best) hearing-aid technology was used with profoundly deaf individuals, the average number of words these children produced that were understandable to a listener ranged between 10% and 40%. The most current studies of CI users are yielding numbers that range between 59% and 72%.

From the evidence at hand, it is apparent that the use of TC does not preclude the development of intelligible speech, nor does it guarantee the development of intelligible speech. There are some differences in the outcomes of studies that have compared the intelligibility and articulation performance of TC users with users of other communication methods, but there is no evidence to indicate that one and only one philosophy of communication guarantees the development of intelligible speech. There does appear to be evidence, however, that certain factors can maximize the opportunity for the development of intelligible speech in children with profound hearing loss. The specific components of an educational program that can optimize the opportunity for this development include the following: (1) The program promotes early identification and intervention. (2) The program ensures that amplification or cochlear implantation is completed with the most updated technology possible and/or adequate surgical placement of the device. (3) The program fosters the development of listening skills. (4) The program targets the development of speech production skills.

The components that help to ensure optimal speech development have also been investigated regarding spoken language achievement in TC users. The next section reviews studies of the development of English language skills.

STUDIES OF LANGUAGE ACHIEVEMENT IN TC USERS

The challenges of developing intelligible speech for prelingually deaf children who utilize TC are not the only barriers to communication; lexical and grammatical skills are needed for the development of spoken languages such as English. The development of English also poses a formidable learning task for these children (Quigley, Power, & Steinkamp, 1977). Again, we see, however, that technological advances with modern hearing aids and CIs have ameliorated the effects of hearing loss on English language development.

Researchers have documented that the main obstacle to the development of spoken language in individuals who are deaf and who use TC is a lack of an appropriate model of language presented, specifically, a lack of consistent, complete, and adequate visual or auditory input. For example, Marmor and Petitto (1979) documented that classroom teachers in TC environments tend to present a predominance of ungrammatical signed utterances that followed neither the rules of English nor those of ASL. Additionally, many teachers often omitted inflected endings when using signed English (Kluwin, 1981; Marmor & Petitto, 1979).

An additional factor that compounds the lack of consistent sign input for endings is that many deaf children cannot hear the low-intensity, high-frequency sounds such as /s,z/ and low-frequency, low-intensity sounds such as /m,n,ng/ that tend to occur at the end of English words.

For example, many deaf hearing-aid users are unable to articulate an /s/ or distinguish between /t/ and /d/ (Smith, 1975). As a consequence, research has documented that deaf children who used hearing aids and who were educated in TC settings have difficulty knowing when the endings occur in everyday speech. These students tend to omit morphological endings or use them inappropriately (Crandall, 1978; Quigley & Paul, 1984).

Bornstein, Saulnier, and Hamilton (1980) investigated the mode of communication (i.e., signed, spoken, or both) that TC-educated children used during the administration of a standardized language test. They reported that after 2 years of being in a school system (about age 6), the children produced 34% of their words with sign and speech, 1% of the words using speech-only modality, and 18% of their words in sign-only modality. After 4 years of being in school, all but two children produced 100% of their words with both speech and sign. The use of inflectional endings by 20 young hearing-aid users over a 4-year time period was also investigated. At an average age of 47.6 months, the children used no endings in either modality. Four years later, the percentage of inclusion was better, albeit delayed. The children were least likely to use third-person singular endings (11% of the time when use would be appropriate), and most were likely to use regular plural endings (67% of the time). There is some evidence that the developmental order for morpheme endings may be the same for deaf children who use MCE and for hearing children, although deaf children may be less consistent in their use (Crandall, 1978; Schick & Moeller, 1992).

Geers et al. (1984) studied deaf children who were educated in TC programs and analyzed their oral, manual, and combined productions of English language structure. This study found that deaf children who were between 5 and 9 years of age scored lower than typical hearing 4-year-old children on a task that was designed to elicit simple language structures such as articles, prepositions, conjunctions, and negation. Additionally, there was a discrepancy between the spoken and signed accuracy in the population studied, with a higher rate of accuracy found in the signed productions. These authors concluded that the use of inflectional endings in MCE did not ensure that the inflections would be produced in the spoken modality.

On the other hand, Schick and Moeller (1992) reported that certain language properties, such as syntactic ordering rules, could be developed despite having an inconsistent input. They confirmed that there were other language properties that were more vulnerable to receiving a degraded input. They replicated previous findings that deaf TC users did not consistently use auxiliary and copula verbs and that they used fewer morpheme endings than did their hearing peers who use English. Schick and Moeller also found that deaf TC participants tended to begin using these morphemes when they were much older than their hearing peers.

There is evidence that the use of CI technology can affect language achievement, especially with respect to TC users and their inclusion of grammatical morphemes. Spencer, Tye-Murray, and Tomblin (1998) documented that children with prolonged experience with CIs used inflected endings in conversation significantly more often than a group of similarly aged children with profound hearing loss who used hearing aids. Both CI and hearing-aid users marked plurals most commonly, followed by present progressives, possessives, third-person singular, and regular past tense, demonstrating a similar progression in their mastery of endings. Additionally, although the primary mode of communication used to express a majority of words within conversation for both hearing-aid users and CI users was voice and sign, the mode used to express bound morphemes for CI users was usually voice only. When hearing-aid users produced bound morphemes, they usually did so only in sign. This contrast in modality suggested that the CI offers acoustic access to the sounds used to produce morpheme endings, and that CI users who use TC are able to incorporate them into their phonology and in their spoken morphology.

Tomblin, Spencer, Flock, Tyler, and Gantz (1999) studied the English language achievement of 29 prelingually deaf children who were educated in TC programs and provided further evidence of spoken language improvement in CI users in TC programs. These children had 3 or more years of CI experience, and their language achievement levels were compared to a similar group of prelingually deaf children who did not have CI experience. The Rhode Island Test of Language Structure (Engen & Engen, 1983), a measure of signed and spoken sentence comprehension, was administered to the CI users, and it was found that the CI users achieved significantly better scores than their agemates who used hearing aids. The Index of Productive Syntax (Scarborough, 1990) was used as a measure of expressive (signed and spoken) English grammar, and again it was found that CI users performed significantly better than their agemates who were deaf and who wore hearing aids. Furthermore, these investigators found that deaf children with CI experience had higher English grammatical achievement levels than did their peers who had hearing-aid experience. The more CI experience children have, the better is their language achievement.

Connor et al. (2000) studied the relationship between educational program (oral communication or TC) and receptive and expressive vocabulary development in a group of CI users. They found a complex relationship between performance with a CI, age at implantation, and educational program. The authors reported that there were no significant differences between *rate* of improvement over time on receptive vocabulary scores between their TC group and children who utilized spoken communication. The authors did find, however, that if children in the TC group received their implants early (before age 5), their receptive vocabulary scores were higher than those of children in the spoken language group. This reflects a generally larger vocabulary at time of implantation for the TC users. There were no differences in receptive vocabulary scores, however, if the implants were received in the elementary school years.

Finally, Spencer, Barker, and Tomblin (2003) offered additional evidence that deaf children who receive CIs and who are educated in a mainstream educational environment utilizing a TC approach have excellent potential to perform favorably relative to their age-matched hearing peers on various language and literacy measures. In this study, 16 pediatric CI users' language and literacy skills were evaluated and then compared to those of a reference group of 16 age-matched, hearing children. All 32 participants were educated in mainstream classes within the public school system in the Midwest. The Sentence Formulation and Concepts and Directions subtests of the Clinical Evaluation of Language Fundamentals–3 (Semel, Wiig, & Secord, 1995) test were used to evaluate receptive and expressive language skills. Reading comprehension was evaluated with the Paragraph Comprehension subtest of the Woodcock Reading Mastery Test (Woodcock, 1987). Performance measures for the writing analyses included productivity, complexity, and grammaticality measures. Although there were significant differences between CI users and their hearing peers in the ability to correctly utilize grammatical structures such as conjunctions and correct verb forms when they were required to formulate written and oral sentences, the CI users performed within one SD of their hearing peers on language comprehension, reading comprehension, and writing accuracy measures.

In summary, as also described above in the section on the development of intelligible speech of TC users, we find that there is a tremendous amount of variability in reports about how these children develop language skills. Much of the research has focused on how children learn to form grammatically correct sentences and include word endings. In general, we see that these skills follow the typical pattern of development of hearing children, albeit in a delayed fashion. The areas at greatest risk for difficulty include morphological structure and the ability to implement the grammatical structures of conjunctions and verb forms. There seems to be an intricate relationship between the age of identification, the quality of technology implemented, and the consistency of exposure to a fully developed language system.

SUMMARY, CONCLUSIONS, AND IMPLICATIONS FOR FUTURE RESEARCH

The studies presented above regarding speech and language development offer no convincing evidence that the use of sign within a TC program precludes the development of spoken language skills. Rather, we have seen that advances in technology have been associated with increased levels of spoken language development within the group of deaf and hard-of-hearing children who use TC. Variability of both speech and language results is the hallmark of many of the findings, and the reasons for this variability continue to be the subject of much discussion.

In any case, the extent to which the TC philosophy is implemented in a consistent manner throughout educational programs is unclear, and there continues to be a need in the field of deaf education to continue to evaluate the quality of the TC programs that are established. It is likely that the way TC is used will change in the upcoming years with the advent of early identification of hearing loss and early intervention, yet it is even more probable that the current studies regarding the outcomes of spoken language development will soon be outdated. For the first time in the history of the education of deaf individuals, achievements in speech and language development in this population are changing faster than researchers can keep up. This is an exciting and challenging time in the field, but before we can begin to know where this current generation is going, it would be prudent to look at the previous generation of children who have been educated in the TC system throughout their school years. This group has now reached young adulthood, graduated from high school, and either begun postsecondary education or entered the job market. We do not have a good sense of what the outcomes are for this group of individuals, nor do we have a way to even measure the extent to which they were educated in a true TC philosophy. It is important to develop a way to evaluate the integrity of the TC program used and then to ascertain how well children who have been educated with this philosophy have integrated into society and to find out whether TC users identify with hearing people or with Deaf culture, or whether they feel comfortable going between these groups.

Additionally, it is unclear whether children who begin their language learning using a TC philosophy as infants and toddler continue to utilize this modality in later years. Early indications suggest that after the first 3 years after receiving a CI, these children continue to use signed English for both their expressive and receptive communication needs (Tye-Murray et al., 1996). Yet, with the advent of newborn hearing screening, and the trend toward earlier implantation, these results may change. The cohort of children who have been products of this system is just beginning to reach the elementary school age. In the upcoming years, it will be important to continue to investigate whether infants who began learning language with signed support continue to rely on sign or whether they become auditory learners who eventually abandon their use of signed English. Potentially, these children could become facile code switchers, who utilize sign with deaf peers and speech with hearing peers.

REFERENCES

Baker, S. (1994). *A resource manual of deafness.* Sulphur, OK: Oklahoma School for the Deaf.

Bellugi, U., & Fischer, S. (1972). A comparison of sign language and spoken language. *Cognition, 1,* 173–200.

Berko, J. (1958). The child's learning of English morphology. *Word, 14,* 150–177.

Bornstein, H., Saulnier, K., & Hamilton, L. (1980). Signed English: A first evaluation. *American Annals of the Deaf, 125,* 467–481.

Bosworth, R., & Dobkins, K. (2002). The effects of spatial attention on motion processing in deaf signers, hearing signers, and hearing nonsigners. *Brain and Cognition, 49,* 152–169.

Brown, R. B. U. (1964). Three processes in the child's acquisition of syntax. *Harvard Educational Review, 39,* 133–152.

Caccamise, F., Ayers, R., Finch, K., & Mitchell, M. (1997). Signs and manual communication systems selection, standardization, and development. *American Annals of the Deaf, 142*(3), 90–105.

Cazden, C. B. (1968). The acquisition of noun and verb inflections. *Child Development, 39,* 433–448.

Clarke, R. B. (1972). Total communication. *Canadian Teacher of the Deaf, 2,* 22–30.

Conlin, F., Hagstrom, P., & Neidle, C. (2003). A particle of indefiniteness in American Sign Language. *Linguistic Discovery, 2*(1). Retrieved April 29, 2004, from http://journals.dartmouth.edu/webobjbin/WebObjects/Journals.woa/1/xmlpage/1/archive

Connor, C. M., Hieber, S., Arts, H. A., & Zwolan, T. A. (2000). Speech, vocabulary, and the education of children using cochlear implants: Oral or total communication? *Journal of Speech, Language, and Hearing Research, 43*(5), 1185–1204.

Cooper, R. (1967). The ability of deaf and hearing children to apply morphological rules. *Journal of Speech and Hearing Disorders, 10,* 77–86.

Crandall, K. E. (1978). Inflectional morphemes in the manual English of young hearing-impaired children and their mothers. *Journal of Speech and Hearing Research, 21*(2), 372–386.

Davis, J. M., & Hardick, E. J. (1981). *Rehabilitative audiology for children and adults.* New York: John Wiley and Sons.

Delaney, M., Stuckless, E. R., & Walter, G. G. (1984). Total communication effects: A longitudinal study of a school for the deaf in transition. *American Annals of the Deaf, 129*(6), 481–486.

DiFrancesca, S. (1972). *Academic achievement test results of a national testing program for hearing-impaired students.* Washington, DC: Gallaudet College.

Engen, E., & Engen, T. (1983) *Rhode Island Test of Language Structure.* Baltimore: University Park Press.

Evans, L. (1982). *Total communication.* Washington, DC: Gallaudet College Press.

Furth, H. G. (1966). A comparison of the reading test norms of deaf and hearing children. *American Annals of the Deaf, 111,* 461–462.

Garretson, M. D. (1976). Total communication. In R. Frisna (Ed.), *A Bicentennial Monograph on Hearing Impairment*: Trends In the USA (pp. 88–95).

Geers, A., Moog, J., & Schick, B. (1984). Acquisition of spoken and signed English by profoundly deaf children. *Journal of Speech and Hearing Disorders, 49*, 378–388.

Geers, A., Spehar, B., & Sedey, A. (2002). Use of speech by children from total communication programs who wear cochlear implants. *American Journal of Speech-Language Pathology, 11*(1), 50–58.

Goetzinger, C. P., & Rouzey., C. L. (1957). Educational achievement of deaf children. *American Annals of the Deaf, 104*, 221–231.

Gustason, G., & Zawolokow, E. (1999). *Signing exact English.* Los Alamitos, CA: Modern Sign Press.

Hawkins, L., & Brawner, J. (1997). *Educating children who are deaf and hard of hearing: Total communication* (ERIC Digest No. 559). Reston, VA: ERIC Clearinghouse on Disabilities and Gifted Education.

Heider, F., & Heider, G. (1941). A comparison of sentence structure of deaf and hearing children. *Volta Review, 43*, 357–360; 536–540; 599–604.

Hudgins, C. V., & Numbers, G. C. (1942). An investigation of the intelligibility of the speech of the deaf. *Psychology Monographs, 25*, 289–392.

Huntington, A., & Watton, F. (1986). The spoken language of teachers and pupils in the education of hearing-impaired children. *Volta Review, 88*(1), 5–19.

Hyde, M., & Power, D. (1992). The use of Australian Sign Language by deaf people. *Sign Language Studies, 75*, 167–182.

Ireton, H., & Thwing, E. (1974). *Minnesota Child Development Inventory.* Minneapolis, MN: Behavior science systems, Inc.

John, J. E., & Howarth, J. N. (1965). The effect of time distortions on the intelligibility of deaf children's speech. *Language and Speech, 8*, 127–134.

Klima, E., & Bellugi, U. (1979). *The signs of language.* Cambridge, MA: Harvard University Press.

Kluwin, T. (1981). The grammaticality of manual representations of English in classroom settings. *American Annals of the Deaf, 126*, 417–421.

Knauf, V. (1978). Language and speech training. In J. Katz (Ed.), *Handbook of clinical audiology* (pp. 549–564). London: Williams & Wilkins.

Lenneberg, E. H. (1967). *Biological foundations of language.* New York: John Wiley & Sons.

Luetke-Stahlman, B. (1988). SEE-2 in the classroom: How well is English grammar represented? In G. Gustason (Ed.), *Signing English: Exact or not? A collection of articles* (pp. 128–131). Los Alamitos, CA: Modern Sign Press.

Markides, A. (1970). The speech of deaf and partially hearing children with special references to factors affecting intelligibility. *British Journal of Disorders of Communication, 5*, 126–140.

Marmor, G. S., & Petitto, L. (1979). Simultaneous communication in the classroom: How well is English grammar represented? *Sign Language Studies, 23*, 99–136.

Marschark, M. (2004) Metaphor in sign language and sign language users: A window into relations of language and thought. In H. Colston & A. N. Katz (Eds.), *Figurative language comprehension: Social and cultural influences* (pp. 309–334). Mahwah, NJ: Lawrence Erlbaum.

McGarr, N. S. (1987). Communication skills of hearing-impaired children in schools for the deaf. *ASHA monographs*, Oct (26), 91–107.

Meadow, K. P. (1968). Early manual communication in relation to the deaf child's intellectual, social, and communicative functioning. *American Annals of the Deaf, 113*(1), 29–41.

Monsen, R. B. (1978). Toward measuring how well children speak. *Journal of Speech and Hearing Research*(21), 197–219.

Montgomery, G. W. G. (1966). The relationship of oral skills to manual communication in profoundly deaf adolescents. *American Annals of the Deaf, 111*(4), 557–565.

Neidle, C., & MacLaughlin, D. (2002) The distribution of functional projections in ASL: Evidence from overt expressions of syntactic features. In G. Cinque (Ed.), *Functional structure in the DP and IP: The cartography of syntactic structures* (Vol. 1, pp. 105–224). New York: Oxford University Press.

Osberger, M. J., Robbins, A. M., Todd, S. L., & Riley, A. I. (1994). Speech intelligibility of children with cochlear implants. *Volta Review, 96*(5), 169–180.

Owens, R. (1992). *Language Development: An introduction.* New York: Merrill.

Payton, K. L., Uchanski, R. M., & Braida, L. D. (1994). Intelligibility of conversational and clear speech in noise and reverberation for listeners with normal and impaired hearing. *Journal of the Acoustical Society of America, 95*(3), 1581–1952.

Peng, S. C., Spencer, L., & Tomblin, J. B. (2004). Speech intelligibility of pediatric cochlear implant recipients with seven years of device experience. *Journal of Speech Language and Hearing Research, 47*(6), 1227–1235.

Picheny, M. A., Durlach, N. I., & Braida, L. D. (1986). Speaking clearly for the hard of hearing II: Acoustic characteristics of clear and conversational speech. *Journal of Speech and Hearing Research, 29,* 434–446.

Presnell, L. (1973). Hearing-impaired children's comprehension and production of syntax in oral language. *Journal of Speech and Hearing Research, 16,* 21–21.

Proksch, J., & Bavelier, D (2002). Changes in the spatial distribution of visual attention after early deafness. *Journal of Cognitive Neuroscience, 14*(5), 687–701.

Quigley, S. P., & Paul, P. V. (1984). ASL and ESL? *Topics in Early Childhood Special Education, 3*(4), 17–26.

Quigley, S. P., Power, D., & Steinkamp, M. W. (1977). The language structure of deaf children. *Volta Review, 79*(2), 73–84.

Scarborough, H. S. (1990). Index of Productive Syntax. *Applied Psycholinguistics 11,* 1–22.

Schiavetti, N., Whitehead, R. L., Metz, D. E., Whitehead, B. H., & Mignerey, M. (1996). Voice onset time in speech produced during simultaneous communication. *Journal of Speech and Hearing Research, 38,* 565–572.

Schick, B., & Moeller, M. P. (1992). What is learnable in manually coded English sign systems? *Applied Psycholinguistics, 13*(3), 313–340.

Scouten, E. (1984). *Turning points in the education of deaf people.* Danville, IL: Interstate Printers and Publishers, Inc.

Semel, E., Wiig, E., & Secord, W. (1995). *Clinical evaluation of language fundamentals* (3rd ed.). San Antonio, TX: Psychological Corporation, Harcourt Brace.

Siple, P., & Fischer, S. (1991). Introduction. In P. Siple & S. Fischer (Eds.), *Theoretical issues in sign language research* (Vol. 2, pp. 1–8). Chicago: University of Chicago Press.

Smith, C. (1975). Residual hearing and speech production in deaf children. *Journal of Speech and Hearing Research, 18,* 795–811.

Spencer, L., Barker, B., & Tomblin, J. B. (2003). Exploring the language and literacy outcomes of pediatric cochlear implant users. *Ear and Hearing, 24*(3), 236–247.

Spencer, L., Tye-Murray, N., & Tomblin, J. B. (1998). The production of English inflectional morphology, speech production, and listening performance in children with cochlear implants. *Ear and Hearing, 19*(4), 310–318.

Stokoe, W. C. (1978). *Sign language structure: An outline of the visual communications systems*. Silver Spring, MD: Linstok Press. (Original work published as Studies in Linguistics Occasional Papers, No. 8, 1960, Buffalo, NY: Department of Anthropology and Linguistics, University of Buffalo)

Stuckless, E. R., & Birch, J. W. (1966). The influence of early manual communication on the linguistic development of deaf children: II. *American Annals of the Deaf, 111*(3), 499–504.

Supalla, S. (1991). Manually coded English: The modality question in signed language development. In P. Siple & S. Fischer (Eds.), *Theoretical issues in sign language research* (Vol. 2. pp. 85–110). Chicago: University of Chicago Press.

Swisher, V. (1985). Signed input of hearing mothers to deaf children. *Language Learning, 34*(63), 99–125.

Swisher, M. V. & Thompson, M. (1985) Mothers learning simultaneous communication: The dimensions of the task. *American Annals of the Deaf, 130*(3), 212–217.

Tharpe, A. M., Ashmead, D., & Rothpletz, A. (2002). Visual attention in children with normal hearing, children with hearing aids, and children with cochlear implants. *Journal of Speech, Language and Hearing Research, 45*, 403–413.

Tobey, E. A., Geers, A. E., Brenner, C., Altuna, D., & Gabbert, G. (2003). Factors associated with development of speech production skills in children implanted by age five. *Ear and Hearing, 24*(1), 36S–45S.

Tomblin, B., Spencer, L., Flock, S., Tyler, R., & Gantz, B. (1999). A comparison of language achievement in children with cochlear implants and children with hearing aids. *Journal of Speech, Language, and Hearing Research, 42*, 497–511.

Tye-Murray, N., Spencer, L., & Woodworth, G. G. (1995). Acquisition of speech by children who have prolonged cochlear implant experience. *Journal of Speech and Hearing Research, 38*(2), 327–337.

Uchanski, R., Choi, S., Braida, L., Reed, C., & Durlach, N. (1996). Speaking clearly for the hard of hearing: IV. Further studies of the role of speaking rate. *Journal of Speech and Hearing Disorders, 39*, 494–509.

Vernon, M. (1968). Fifty years of research on the intelligence of the deaf and hard of hearing: A survey of the literature and discussion of implications. *Journal of Rehabiliation of the Deaf, 1*, 1–11.

Vernon, M., & Andrews, J. (1990). *Psychology of deafness*. New York: Longman.

Vernon, M., & Koh, S. D. (1971). Effects of oral preschool compared to early manual communication on education and communication in deaf children. *American Annals of the Deaf, 116*(6), 569–574.

Watson, T. J. (1976). *Methods of communication currently used in the education of deaf children*. London: Royal National Institute for the Deaf, pp. 3–8.

Whitehead, R. L., Schiavetti, N., Whitehead, B. H., & Metz, D. E. (1995). Temporal characteristics of speech in simultaneous communication. *Journal of Speech and Hearing Research, 38*(5), 1014–1024.

Whitehead, R. L., Schiavetti, N., Whitehead, B. H., & Metz, D. E. (1997). Effect of sign task on speech timing in simultaneous communication. *Journal of Communication Disorders, 30*(6), 439–455.

Wilbur, R. B. (1979). *American Sign Language and sign systems*. Baltimore, MD: University Park Press.

Wilbur, R. B., & Petersen, L. (1998). Modality interactions of speech and signing in simultaneous communication. *Journal of Speech Language and Hearing Research, 41*(1), 200–212.

Wood, D. (1992). Total Communication and the education of deaf children. *Developmental Medicine and Child Neurology, 34*(2), 266–269.

Woodcock, S. (1987). *Woodcock Reading Mastery Tests—revised*. Circle Pines, MN: American Guidance Service.

Woodlinger-Cohen, R. (1991). The manual representation of speech by deaf children, their mothers, and their teachers. In P. Siple & S. D. Fischer (Eds.), *Theoretical issues in sign language research: Vol. 2. Psychology* (pp. 149–169). Chicago: University of Chicago Press.

Yoshinaga-Itano, C., & Sedey, A. (2000). Early speech development in children who are deaf or hard of hearing: Interrelationships with language and hearing. *Volta Review, 100*(5), 181–209.

9

The Effect of Cued Speech on the Development of Spoken Language

Catherine Hage & Jacqueline Leybaert

Cued Speech (CS) was developed by Orin Cornett in 1966 (Cornett, 1967) and now has been adapted to more than 40 languages and major dialects. CS is neither a sign language nor a manually coded system that uses signs from a sign language in spoken language word order. Instead, it is a mode of communication for visually conveying traditionally spoken languages at the phonemic level (i.e., the same linguistic level conveyed via speech to hearing individuals). In CS, the speaker complements lip gestures of speech with manual cues. A cue is made of two parameters: a hand shape and a hand location around the mouth.

The American English form of CS uses eight hand shapes corresponding to groups of consonants and four hand locations to convey vowels and diphthongs (see figure 9.1). Groups of phonemes that are distinguishable by lipreading (e.g., /p/, /d/, and /Z/) are coded by a same hand shape or at the same location. Conversely, phonemes that have similar lip shape are coded with different hand shapes (e.g., /p/, /b/, and /m/) and hand locations (e.g., /i/ and /e/). Information given by the cues and information given by lipreading are thus complementary. Each time a speaker pronounces a consonant-vowel (CV) syllable, a cue (a particular hand shape at a specific position) is produced simultaneously. For example, when saying the words "bell" and "bowl," two different hand locations would be used to distinguish between the two vowels; when saying the words "but" and "putt," two different hand shapes would be used to code the initial consonant. Syllabic structures other than CV are produced with additional cues. For example, a vowel-only syllable is represented by the neutral hand

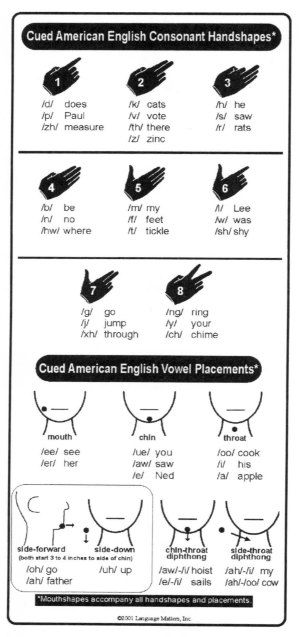

Figure 9-1. Hand shapes and locations in English cued speech.

shape at the location corresponding to that vowel. Syllables including consonant clusters, or codas, are coded using the hand shape corresponding to the additional consonant at the neutral position.

The hand shapes and hand locations used in CS—unlike those of fingerspelling—are not, by themselves, interpretable as language. Instead, the visual information provided by lipreading is also necessary. The integration of labial and manual information points to a single, unambiguous, phonological percept that deaf children could not have obtained from either source alone. They thus can interpret a spoken message as a reliable visual language in which the gestures (i.e., the combination of lip movements and manual cues) are now entirely specified, both at the syllabic and at the phonemic levels. Each syllable (and phoneme) corresponds to one and only one combination of labial and manual information, and vice versa, a characteristic that makes CS (at least in theory) entirely functional for speech perception.

EFFECT OF CS ON THE DEVELOPMENT OF SPOKEN LANGUAGE THROUGH THE VISUAL MODALITY

Traditional oral approaches to language development in deaf children are often unsuccessful because children with significant hearing losses do not have full access to all necessary linguistic contrasts. Indeed, the information they get through speechreading, residual hearing, or the combination of the two is neither sufficiently precise nor sufficiently reliable to allow them to detect the regularities at the root of the phonology and grammar of the language. Yet, it is precisely these qualities that are at the root of the generative system of language (Locke, 1997) and that are at stake in the linguistic development of the deaf child, whatever the modality of language (spoken or signed, with or without information from lipreading). Before considering the effect of CS on the development of phonology and syntax, it is therefore important to evaluate whether CS enhances speech perception.

Effects of CS on Speech Perception

Deaf people's comprehension of spoken language is usually poor. Most speechreaders understand only about one fourth of what is said even in one-on-one conversations (Liben, 1978). However, large improvements of deaf children's speech reception skills have been demonstrated both for English- and French-speaking children when cues from the CS system are added to information from lipreading (Alegria, Charlier, & Mattys, 1999; Nicholls & Ling, 1982; Périer, Charlier, Hage, & Alegria, 1988). Nicholls and Ling (1982), for example, found that the speech reception scores of profoundly deaf children taught at school using CS for at least 3 years increased from about 30% for both syllables and words with lipreading alone, to more than 80% given lipreading plus cues.

Périer et al. (1988) assessed the improvement offered by CS cues on the understanding of sentences having simple subject–verb–object syntactic structure and three levels of speechreading difficulty. This design allowed them to determine the effects of CS on the disambiguation of speechread sentences that do not present linguistic challenges. Children had to choose a picture corresponding to the spoken sentence from among a set of four alternatives (the target and three distractors), all of which appeared identical via speechreading alone. The results showed that perception was enhanced by the addition of cues, with a larger enhancement when the choice between the sentence and the other three distractors was more difficult. The enhancement was also larger for children whose parents used CS intensively to communicate with them at home, from an early age, than for children who benefited from CS later, only at school, usually from the age of 6.

The differential benefit displayed by the early and late CS users may be explained in two ways: Early CS-users might be more familiar with words presented in CS, or, due to their CS exposure, they might have developed a more efficient phonological processor (i.e., that depends on the quality of the mental representations of the phonemes). Alegria et al. (1999) found that early CS users displayed a larger improvement than did later users from the addition of cues in the perception of both words and pseudowords (pronounceable nonwords). Because pseudowords were unfamiliar for both groups of children, these results support the suggestion that early experience with CS enhances the efficiency of the processing of pure phonological information. This result is interesting because the capacity to process "new" phonological information may be at the root of the development of lexical and even morphosyntactic aspects of language, allowing for the efficient combination of multiple meaningful parts in word creation.

Effects of CS on Morphosyntactic Development

Given the above findings, the next question is whether the information provided by CS helps the *linguistic* development of deaf children. Should this be the case, the effect of CS might be more marked in grammar, one of the domains most difficult to master by deaf children, and, more particularly, morphosyntax. Morphosyntactic ability involves combining morphemes to modulate and add grammatical meaning to lexical items and typically is learned naturally, via early language interactions, rather than being specifically taught at school.

Some studies have suggested that the difficulties in acquiring aspects of grammatical morphology can be greater than for semantic aspects of language. This may be so because morphologically significant features are generally short items, such as closed-class words or affixes (e.g., inflections) attached to words. They generally are produced rapidly and with low stress in normal, fluent language. Grammatical morphemes can be picked up in lipreading, but only with difficulty, either because they are affixed to words' ends (e.g., plural markers in English or French) or because they are short, unaccented morphemes (e.g., prepositions and articles). A deaf speaker of a language like French or English thus often fails to perceive and encode these morphemes, and, with such a degraded input, deaf children have fewer opportunities to develop mastery of morphological rules.

Taeschner, Devescovi, and Volterra (1988) reported the case of a congenitally deaf woman who had acquired a high level of competence in spoken and written Italian. Despite achievements in lexical and syntactic competence similar to those of a hearing native speaker who was selected as a comparison case, she had a specific impairment of morphosyntactic ability, in particular in the use of free-standing function words such as prepositions. Her morphological deficiencies thus cannot be ascribed to a general linguistic deficit, but are clearly more specific.

Because CS provides unambiguous information that indicates the presence of even unstressed syllables, it may help to ameliorate the challenge deaf children face in the development of morphosyntax. Kipila (1985) recorded language samples of a child exposed to CS since the age of 18 months that support this suggestion. This child was profoundly deaf and received a cochlear implant (CI) before the age of 4 years. One year later, the mean length of his utterances was 4.5 morphemes, corresponding to the mean number of morphemes of hearing children before the ages of 4 or 5 years. The focus of the study, however, was the acquisition of the 14 grammatical morphemes identified by Brown (1973) for English-speaking hearing children:

- present progressive—verb + ing
- the preposition "in"
- the preposition "on"
- plural inflections (e.g., -s, -es)
- past inflections on irregular verbs
- possessive inflections (e.g., the dog's ball)
- uncontractible copula ("is," "am," and "are")
- articles ("the," "a," "an")
- past inflections on regular verbs (e.g., -ed)
- regular third person forms (e.g., s as in "He writes well")
- irregular third person forms (e.g., "has," "does")
- uncontractible auxiliary forms (e.g., "did")
- contractible copula (e.g., -'s and -'re)
- contractible auxiliary forms (e.g., -'d)

Kipila found that the percentage of correct use was 100% for the seven first morphemes normally acquired and varied between 50% and 80% for the seven later-acquired morphemes (see Brown, 1973, for discussion). These observations, although indicating a delay in the development of some aspects of morphosyntax, reveal linguistic development in children who receive CS to be different from that of deaf children exposed to traditional oral approaches (Kipila, 1985) in that some in the latter group never reach the level of control of these morphemes shown by the CS children.

Périer, Bochner-Wuidar, Everarts, Michiels, and Hage (1986) have documented the French linguistic development of S., a profoundly deaf child exposed since the age of 11 months to "complete signed and cued French," a new method combining CS and Signed French (see Charlier, 1992). The parents of S. offered him more and more CS as his linguistic level increased. S. demonstrated a rapid and regular linguistic development. Language samples at 4 years 6 months showed a correct use of morphosyntactic markers (e.g., *"Je m'appelle Cathy comme toi . . . non parce que aujourd'hui c'est samedi . . . non, je ne vais pas manger dans le salon, je vais manger au GB . . . "*). The syntactic structures were correctly used, as were the adverbs such as *aussi* ("too"), *comme* ("like"), and *parce que* ("because"). Use of negative forms, first person pronouns, reflexive pronouns, prepositions, and articles was also correct.

Hage (1994; see also Hage, Alegria, & Périer, 1991) conducted a large "paper-and-pencil" study on different aspects of French morphosyntax involving 202 children from different educational backgrounds. The researchers wanted to assess the effect of deaf children's exposure to a linguistic model on the development of prepositions and grammatical gender, the most arbitrary aspects of morphosyntax in French. Indeed, the initial case studies indicated a favorable linguistic development for children exposed early to CS (i.e., before 18 months of age). However, these early observations did not allow separation of the effects of CS per se from parental involvement. If involvement is not controlled, any comparison between a CS group and a non-CS, oral group could be confounded. A particular effort, therefore, was made to select among the children with profound deafness those whose parents were most motivated and convinced about their choice of method of education. It was decided that participation in early intervention (i.e., before 3 years of age) was an indicator of parent involvement, and therefore the sample was limited to such families. Early intervention, in this case, refers to diagnosis of hearing loss, fitting with hearing aids, and commencement of early linguistic stimulation. The study thus compared children exposed to CS from an early age and children educated orally, also from an early age. In addition, factors of degree of hearing loss, deafness occurring before or after the age of 2 years, lack of other handicaps, and exposure to a single language both at home and at school were considered. A subsample of 98 participants fit these criteria.

A first, multiple-choice lexical test (vocabulary) involved presenting children with a target word and four alternatives. The participants had to choose the item that was best related to the target word, for example, *savon* (target word: soap): *laver* (to wash), *nager* (to swim), *fuir* (to avoid), or *regarder* (to watch). Phonological and morphological relations between the target and the response alternatives were avoided. The second test assessed children's knowledge of the grammatical gender of familiar words. Participants were asked to underline the article *le* or *la* corresponding to familiar words presented as drawings, while the experimenter spoke the word without cueing. Pronouncing the word (requiring speech-reading) was done in order to avoid confusions like *vélo* (masculine) and *bicyclette* (feminine), which could be represented with the same drawing but are of different grammatical gender. The third test aimed at assessing the knowledge of prepositions and determiners (prepositions and quantifiers). Children received sentences like *Papa est parti* [*en, au, de, sur*] *avion* (Daddy has gone [by, on, with] plane) or *Marc mange* [*le, de, un, de la*] *tarte* and had to underline the correct determiner.

The assumption was that CS offers the necessary information to internalize these arbitrary aspects of the language, those that are less sensitive to explicit teaching. Therefore, children who are exposed to CS were expected to show an advantage for these aspects. The characteristics of the subjects and their results in the three tests are shown in table 9.1.

Comparison of performance in the two groups' vocabulary and grammatical gender items just failed to reach statistical significance ($p = .052$), but the two groups differed significantly on preposition items ($p < .001$). These results indicate that the two groups differed more strongly on knowledge of prepositions than on vocabulary or grammatical indications of gender, although there was also a trend for CS children to also perform higher on these two measures.]

It appears in table 9.1 that both groups had a fairly good knowledge of grammatical gender. The next questions, therefore, were how this knowledge was acquired and whether the manner of acquisition was similar in both groups. The effect of age was examined, because a strong

Table 9-1: Characteristics of the Participants Exposed to an Oral Method of Education or to Cued Speech and Mean Percentage of Correct Responses in Vocabulary, Grammatical Gender, and Preposition Tests

	Oral	Cued Speech
n	41	27
Mean age (years; months)	14;4	12;0
Range	8;8–20;3	7;6–17;8
% Correct responses		
Vocabulary	82	93
Grammatical gender	82	96
Prepositions	71	89

effect of age would be indicative of a training effect through explicit instruction by the parents, the school, or speech therapists. Each experimental group was divided into two age groups, above or below 11 years.

Analyses indicated reliable main effects of age and of method of communication (p values < .001). Although the age by method of communication interaction was not significant, the effect of age did not seem to be the same for children in the oral and the CS groups. Among the oral participants, performance increased dramatically with age, while there was little effect of age in the CS group, where children younger than 11 years already demonstrated performance near ceiling for the three tests. The data of table 9.2 indicate that the participants from the oral group older than 11 years reached the same performance as those in the CS group who were younger than 11 years in the three tests. The oral group thus needed more time to reach the same level of performance. However, their performance on the preposition test remained limited.

Grammatical gender is one of the most important aspects of the French language. Indeed, most utterances have at least one noun that possesses grammatical gender. The determiners around that noun (articles, adjectives) take the gender and the number of the noun. The consequence of this is that children are frequently exposed to gender in French language, but most of the time gender is semantically arbitrary, for example, *la table* ("table," feminine) and *le mur* ("wall," masculine). Gender marking may be acquired as an associative learning process via gender-marked articles, pronouns, adjectives, and particular lexical items. However, phonology also allows one to guess the gender in some cases, but only in a probabilistic way. Thus, nearly all the names ending with /et/ are feminine (e.g., *bicyclette, raclette, poussette*), while names ending with /o/ are often masculine (e.g., *bateau, râteau, manteau*). Some endings, such as /wa/, could be masculine or feminine (e.g., *la loi, le*

Table 9-2: Characteristics of the Participants as a Function of Age Group and Communication Method, and Mean Percentage of Correct Responses in the Vocabulary, Grammatical Gender, and Preposition Tests

	Oral		Cued speech	
	<11;0 years	>11;0 years	<11;0 years	>11;0 years
Mean age (year; month)	10;0	15;4	9;5	13;5
% correct responses				
Vocabulary	73	91	89	97
Grammatical gender	74	90	93	99
Prepositions	61	82	85	93

foie). In order to construct a productive competence of gender mor-phophonology, children need to establish a link between the cue de-livered by the end of the word and other gender markers such as articles and other determiners.

Karmiloff-Smith (1979) has established that 3-year-old hearing chil-dren have a productive knowledge of grammatical gender in French, meaning that they are able to correctly guess the grammatical gender of words they do not know on the basis of suffixes. This is extremely difficult for deaf children to acquire because the critical information for gender prediction (in those cases where it is possible) involves relations between spelling regularities at the ends of words and the unstressed nature of determiners, articles, and pronouns. Both of these charac-teristics are difficult for deaf children to perceive. Moreover, because it is highly arbitrary, grammatical gender is not taught at school but is allowed to develop naturally through language use.

The observations included in table 9.2 show that children from the CS group and those from the oral group in the Hage (1994) study produced the correct gender for common words. However, the fact that the CS group had an earlier knowledge of gender than did children from the oral group leads one to wonder whether the same processes are at the root of the knowledge developed by the two groups. Exposure to cued speech might favor the development of a sensitivity of grammatical gender related to phonology, while children with oral training but no CS may acquire gender more on the basis of learning associations be-tween gender-marked morphemes (articles, pronouns, adjectives) and particular lexical items.

In order to explore this issue, Hage (1994) selected frequent and in-frequent French words that ended either with a masculine ending (*manteau, lapin, trumeau, troussequin*), a feminine ending (*cigarette, tartine, girouette, mezzanine*), or a neutral ending, meaning that the ending did not allow prediction of the grammatical gender (*poire, foyère, verre, sar-cloir*). She asked the children to produce a determiner for nouns re-presented by drawings. The nouns were given by speech alone (without cues). Two groups of deaf participants were included, one with children educated orally and the other with children educated with CS.

Mean percentage of correct attribution of grammatical gender for infrequent words is shown in table 9.3. The difference between items with neutral endings and items with endings that appropriately indicate masculine or feminine (called "marked" items) was significant in both groups ($p < .0001$). However, the data did not show a larger capacity of the CS group to exploit the words' endings to generate grammatical gender. Actually, the mean percentage of correct responses for the neutral words was above chance for the CS group (66% instead of nearly 50%), indicating that the participants of this group already knew some of these words. Therefore, in a second analysis, only the children who

Table 9-3: Characteristics of the Participants as a Function of Communication
Method, and Mean Percentage of Correct Attribution
of Grammatical Gender for Infrequent Nouns' Neutral
and Marked (Masculine and Feminine) Endings

	Oral	Cued Speech
n	21	32
Mean age (range [year; month])	13;8 (10;10–17;9)	11;3 (6;11–17;8)
Neutral % correct	48	66
Marked % correct	61	75

had less than 60% correct responses for the neutral condition were selected.

Table 9.4 shows that participants of both groups succeeded better at
producing grammatical gender when items had the appropriate ending
to indicate masculine or feminine (i.e., were marked) than when they
were neutral ($p < .0001$). However, a marginal interaction ($p < .10$) between group and type of items was observed because scores of children
in the CS group increased more than did those in the oral group when
items were marked for gender.

The relative difficulties of the oral group apparently are not due to a
reduced adult input. Although parents' speech was not measured in this
study, parents of the oral children likely did not produce fewer gender-
marked morphemes (articles, pronouns, adjectives) than did parents of
children in the CS group. Children from both groups also likely had
similar difficulties in hearing the small, unstressed articles *le* and *la*, and
pronouns *son* and *sa*. What makes the input difference is that these determiners are produced manually in CS by the parents and can be picked
up visually by the children of the CS group. Children receiving CS thus
appear to develop an implicit knowledge of word gender. Children receiving exposure to spoken language (without CS), by contrast, noun

Table 9-4: Number of Participants and Mean
Percentage of Correct Attribution
of Grammatical Gender for Infrequent
Nouns With Neutral and Marked (Masculine
and Feminine) Endings as a Function
of Communication Method

	Oral	Cued speech
n	19	15
Neutral % correct	46	56
Marked % correct	60	78

gender is probably largely learned via associating a particular lexical item with a gender-marked determiner. If the word is less frequent, the strength of the particular article–noun will be weaker and the attribution of gender will be at risk. These results indicate a role played by CS in the acquisition of grammatical gender based on phonology.

THE EFFECT OF CS ON THE DEVELOPMENT OF SPOKEN LANGUAGE THROUGH USE OF CIs

Since fitting young deaf children with a CI has become widespread, we are confronted with new questions about CS. For example, does CS, which stimulates the visual channel, cease to be useful or even be contraindicated for such children either pre- or after implantation (Descourtieux, Groh, Rusterholz, Simoulin, & Busquet, 1999)? Given that CIs only give degraded acoustic information, and it may still be difficult for children to reliably discriminate fine phonetic differences created by place of articulation and voicing (Pisoni, 2000), CS may help a young deaf child with a CI to perceive these fine phonetic differences. This leads to the prediction that profoundly deaf children who are CS users would do better in auditory word identification than those who are not CS users. This, in turn, could help the development of morphosyntax and of accurate phonological representations in CS users. Speech production might be another ability where the information provided by CS and by the CI would converge. Children who receive auditory feedback through a CI might learn to adjust their oral productions in relation to the reference points created by CS. In the rest of this chapter we examine whether CS affords a benefit to children with CIs. The variability of these benefits and the problems encountered are also discussed.

Is CS Useful for Speech Identification for CI Users?

The introduction of pediatric CIs has changed the situation of profoundly deaf children raised with CS, because improvement in their hearing has an effect on strategies of perception of oral language. Many children may learn to understand speech without having to look at the speaker—and reliance on speechreading and CS is reduced. However, the reception of oral language, although more natural than without a CI, remains often imprecise and incomplete. Children may continue to have confusions between word sounds (e.g., *manteau* with *chapeau*), which will create confusions between meanings. Perception of auditory information through CIs is also difficult in the context of noise. With the CI, oral communication is more spontaneous and production intelligibility may increase, but language comprehension may still be less than perfect, and both lexical and syntactic development may be delayed accordingly.

The usefulness of CS for children who were raised with it and also have received CIs has been investigated by Descourtieux (2003). The sample consisted of 55 children from 3 to 16 years of age, including 42 who had CIs. Open set perception of words was assessed in three modalities: auditory alone (A), auditory and speechreading (A + SR), and speechreading and CS (SR + CS), without sound. Performance in the A condition increased with age from 3 to 12 years. Participants between 13 and 16 years of age had lower auditory performance than did the other groups, but they represent the "classical" population of children raised with CS, who perceive language through vision and not audition due to having gotten CIs at relatively late ages. For age groups at 5–8 years, 9–12 years, and 13–16 years, visual information seemed to provide important assistance. Performance in A + SR and SR + CS con- CS conditions was higher than 80% correct. However, the SR + CS conditions showed a slight advantage over the A + SR conditions. Speechreading may enhance speech perception for two reasons: It de- livers phonetic information, and it enhances the receiver's attention to the incoming auditory information. These two possible effects of speech- reading are present in both of the conditions. The slight advantage offered by the SR + CS modality, however, may indicate that there remains a certain amount of phonological information that is perceived more precisely through the CS modality than through the A + SR modality.

In short, although the auditory modality appears to support speech understanding by children with CIs, and development of spoken com- munication seems to be possible along much the same developmental trajectory as in hearing children, the auditory channel continues to provide less than full access to spoken messages. Even in the group of younger children (3–4 years old) who were implanted before 3 years of age, CS seems to remain an efficient tool for perceiving spoken lan- guage.

The Effect of CS Exposure on Word Identification by CI Users

Consider the case of Vincent, a deaf child who received a CI at 2 years, 9 months (Descourtieux et al., 1999). Before implantation, Vincent had accurate phonetic discrimination and a rich lexical comprehension of words delivered through CS and used cues to express himself. What would be the prediction for his word understanding, through audition, after implantation? Will he be able to understand auditorally the words he previously understood visually; that is, will he *transfer* his word identification competence from one modality to the other? Or, will he experience the same difficulties as children implanted at the same age but not previously exposed to CS? Clinical observations showed that Vincent functioned quite well with the CI: "[A]fter 6 months of CI use, Vincent understood by audition alone the words of his already extensive vocabulary. After 2 years of CI use, he can follow a conversation without lipreading. He speaks with intelligible speech" (Descourtieux et al., 1999, p. 206).

What about group observations? Cochard (2003) assessed the development of auditory speech comprehension and recognition of words in closed sets and sentences in both closed sets (SCS) and open sets (SOS) in a group of deaf children, from 3 months until 5 years after implantation. Before implantation, the children were in an oral setting, a signed French setting, or a CS setting. Children who were raised in a CS setting had better results than did those of the other two modes of communication, but this effect was modulated by time of measurement and type of material. For words and sentences in closed sets, CS users showed an advantage over children from the other two groups at 1 and 3 years after implantation. This advantage vanished at 5 years after implantation, presumably because children from the three groups had ceiling results at this point of measurement. Interestingly, for sentences in open sets, the advantage of children raised with CS was maintained at 3 and 5 years after implantation. At 5 years after implantation, Cochard found the performance of the CS children to be near 100% correct, while the performance of the other two groups was around 60% correct.

The Effect of CS Exposure on the Development of Speech Production/Intelligibility

Vieu et al. (1998) studied a group of 12 French children who had received CIs at a mean age of 7 years, 2 months. The children were assigned to three groups according to their communication mode before implantation: four used auditory-oral communication, four used CS, and the other four used sign language. Word intelligibility was assessed before implantation and at 1, 2, and 3 years after implantation. The scores (number of words correctly pronounced from a set of 20 pictures) steadily improved with more experience with the CI. In the oral group, scores averaged 18.9% before implantation and 55.5% 3 years after implantation. In the sign group, scores averaged 12.5% before implantation and 41.2% 3 years after implantation. In the CS group, scores were 22.5% before implantation and 66.8% 3 years after implantation.

Cochard (2003) found that at 1 year after implantation, children raised with signed French, with CS, or orally did not show any difference in their speech intelligibility scores. Scores for all groups were below 2.0 on a scale from 1 (completely unintelligible speech) to 5 (speech intelligible to everyone). At 3 and 5 years after implantation, children whose mode of communication before implantation was CS had better intelligibility scores (between 4.0 and 5.0) than did those of the signed French group (below 3.0) or the oral group (below 3.0 at 3 years and below 4.0 at 5 years).

Linguistic Development of Children With CS and CIs

In their study, Vieu et al. (1998) presented an open set of 15 sentences, in an open set auditory-alone condition, and the children repeated each sentence following the stimulus. The responses were scored as correct or incorrect for each category of words (i.e., determiners, nouns, verbs, adjectives, and pronouns), and an error score was calculated for each child. By 3 years after implantation, children who used CS demonstrated a tendency for higher scores than did those in the auditory-oral or sign language groups, although the differences were not statistically significant. Vieu et al. also assessed the language level of sentences in spontaneous speech, by recording the storytelling of the children at 3 years after implantation in response to pictures showing various activities. Speech was scored either as an unintelligible production, production of isolated words or approximated words ("cot" for "cat"), production of associated words ("cat gray"), production of pseudosentences (e.g., subject–complement–verb, "cat milk drink"), or production of full sentences (e.g., "the cat drinks the milk"). The results show that by 3 years after implantation, all children receiving CS or auditory-oral instruction produced sentences or pseudosentences, but none of the children in the sign language group did. The authors concluded that syntax had a tendency to be more advanced in the CS group than in the sign language or auditory-oral groups. It must be remembered, however, that the children of this study received their CIs at a relatively late age (around 7 years). Therefore, CS education prior to implantation appears to be a good tool for promoting syntactic development, in this case allowing children to acquire normal sentence structure.

Cochard (2003) classified children according to three "profiles of evolution" as a function of their delay in the development of the different linguistic abilities after implantation, according to the analysis designed by Le Normand (1997). Only those children who were congenitally or prelingually deaf and fitted with a CI before the age of 4 years 5 months were included in the study. Some of these children had experienced rapid and continuous progress since their implantation. They had begun to demonstrate lexical development at 3–8 months after implantation, morphosyntactic development at 11–20 months after implantation, and metalinguistic development at 36 months after implantation. These were labeled the "profile 1" children. "Profile 2" children had experienced a less rapid progression. Their access to the lexical system had required a longer period of 6–24 months after implantation. Their morphosyntactic development started 20–31 months after implantation, and their metalinguistic development began 60 months after implantation. Finally, "profile 3" children were those whose lexical development started at 36 months after implantation or later and who did not reach morphosyntactic development.

The aim of the research was to search for predictors related to the mode of communication used that could be related to the linguistic evolution of these children. A smaller group of 19 children was selected from among the 53 children, who were followed at least since the age of 48 months. This sample included children belonging to profile 1 or profile 2. Children corresponding to profile 3 were deliberately discarded from the study because of the existence of associated disabilities/learning challenges.

Cochard's results showed that profile 1 children and profile 2 children did not differ in the age at which they began auditory education. Profile 1 children belonged, in most cases (90%), to families who felt they had a good communication with their child, while profile 2 children belonged to families whose parents felt limited in their communication because of a lack of efficiency in their method of communication. The families of the profile 1 children used oral communication (20%) or oral communication with CS (80%), and 60% of the families of children in the profile 1 group were reported to use CS "intensively." The families of the profile 2 group used signed French with CS (56%), oral communication and CS (33%), or French Sign Language (11%). The use of CS thus seems to contribute to better linguistic development in children fitted with a CI. Also relevant here is the length of time CS was used relative to time of implantation. Cochard found that before implantation, 60% of the families of the profile 1 group already used CS, while only 11% of the families of the profile 2 group did. Forty percent of the families of the profile 1 group and 55% of the families of the profile 2 group began to use CS during the year of implantation. Two years after implantation, all the families of the profile 1 group still used CS, while 88% of the families of the profile 2 group used it. Four years after implantation, CS had been abandoned by nearly 40% of the families of the profile 1 group and 80% of the families of the profile 2 group. According to Cochard, the reasons for dropping CS were different in the two groups: The families of the profile 1 group felt that the receptive and linguistic progress of their children did not necessitate supplemental coding of auditory information. These children made few perceptual confusions, and they also had a good comprehension of the linguistic messages without speechreading. They did not watch their parents' lips, and the parents had gradually stopped cuing for them. The families of the profile 2 group, in contrast, had less training in CS than the families of the profile 1 group. Cuing required a considerable effort and was slow and frustrating. Therefore, children rapidly stopped watching the code. Taken together, these observations suggest that CS remains a very good tool to help the linguistic development of children fitted with a CI. However, the code seems to be difficult to acquire by some families.

Le Normand (2003) examined the factors at the root of the heterogeneity of the results observed after implantation in the development of language. She assessed 50 French-speaking children, who had received

CIs between 21 and 78 months of age, at 6, 12, 18, 24, and 36 months after implantation. She found that the socioeconomic status of the families and gender were two important predictors of the variability observed among children in her study. She also investigated the mode of communication used by the children: no particular mode, CS alone, CS + signed French + French Sign Language, CS + signed French, CS + French Sign Language, and signed French + French Sign Language. Although there was no significant impact of the mode of communication upon the total number of words produced, the children who used CS alone produced a higher number of content words and function words than did those educated with the other modes of communication. These data must be interpreted with caution because the effect of mode of communication was not significant, possibly because of (uncontrolled) links between mode of communication and other variables, such as socioeconomic level.

Negative Evidence

It is well recognized that not all children who undergo cochlear implantation before the age of 4 years develop near normal language within 2 or 3 years after implantation. Szagun (2001), for example, reported that 55% of the children in her study who received CIs before the age of 4 years remained at the stage of two-word utterances even after 3 years of language development after implantation. Thus, the question is raised of how to support those children who are not acquiring language normally. Szagun (2001) suggested that for children who are trained aurally (which is the favored method in Germany, e.g.),

> a program of total communication—as is practised in countries such as U.S.A., Great Britain, or Israel—would be of benefit. Using gestures or sign language would promote the use of symbols, which is an essential component of cognitive development, and could prevent a possible negative influence of insufficient symbol use on cognitive development. (p. 297)

Szagun also argued for a strong link between vocabulary and grammar, in that children must have a sufficiently large vocabulary in order to learn grammar (Kelly, 1996). We would like to suggest the use of CS as another alternative. CS could help to disambiguate the information children get through the CI, which could help in the development of vocabulary and, subsequently, of grammar. The combination of CI and CS allows deaf children to interpret the audiovisual input as a reliable language in which the gestures are entirely specified and could be related to meaning.

In a more recent study, Szagun (2004) showed that children with CIs made errors of gender and omissions on articles. To explain this observation, she argued that "due to their hearing impairment, these children frequently miss unstressed pronominal articles in incoming speech (which) would lead to a reduced frequency of actually processed article input" (p. 26), and that

> [t]he difficulties hearing-impaired children experience in constructing a case and gender system are due to processing limitations. While such processing limitations may have their root in a perceptual deficit, they may become a linguistic cognitive deficit during the children's developmental history. (p. 27).

On the basis of the data summarized above, we suggest that the use of CS might help to overcome this "perceptual deficit" in CI children by transmitting complete information about these unstressed elements of language and might help to avoid the development of a "cognitive deficit" during the child's developmental history of language.

CONCLUSIONS

Data collected in the 1980s and the 1990s demonstrated that the use of CS can be a powerful tool for language development by profoundly deaf children equipped with hearing aids. CS enhances speech perception through the visual modality, the acquisition of vocabulary and morphosyntax, and metalinguistic development (Charlier & Leybaert, 2000), as well as the acquisition of reading and spelling (Leybaert, 2000; Leybaert & Lechat, 2001), at least for children acquiring French.

More recent data seem to indicate that children who have received CIs benefit from previous exposure to CS. However, use of CS before implantation is likely to become more and more rare. Indeed, most children are now fitted with a CI around the age of 1 year. We believe that during the first months or years of CI use, auditory perception of an implanted child remains imperfect. Therefore, the identification of new words would still benefit from the addition of CS to the signal delivered by the CI. Oral comprehension does not develop exclusively by the auditory channel but necessitates audiovisual integration (Schwartz, Berthommier, & Savariaux, 2002). Children fitted early with a CI thus would benefit from multimodal input during the development of phonological representations. These phonological representations then would serve as the platform from which phonological awareness, reading, and spelling acquisition could be launched.

The use of CS by children with CIs is a challenge. Children may not often look at a speaker's lips and hands, and they may tend to rely on auditory information alone. Parents may lose their motivation to cue, feel discouraged, or simply abandon coding with the hands. Therefore, it would be important to assess regularly whether cuing remains necessary and under what circumstances after implantation. It is likely that after some period of auditory rehabilitation, children fitted with a CI will be capable of learning new words by auditory means alone (see Geers, chapter 11 this volume).

Continued attention, nonetheless, should be devoted to the development of morphosyntax after cochlear implantation. This domain of language acquisition is particularly important and sensitive to a lack of precise input, as Szagun's (2004) data show. The capacity to develop morphosyntax easily in response to a well-specified input also tends to diminish with age, although the limits of a precise "sensitive period" cannot be fixed at present (for different views on this point, see Locke, 1997; Szagun, 2001). In short, the benefit and limits of the use of CS with children with CI remain to be investigated more extensively. In particular, data from languages other than French are urgently needed.

REFERENCES

Alegria, J., Charlier, B., & Mattys, S. (1999). The role of lip-reading and cued-speech in the processing of phonological information in French-educated deaf children. *European Journal of Cognitive Psychology, 11*, 451–472.

Brown, R. (1973). *A first language: The early stages*. Cambridge, MA: Harvard University Press.

Charlier, B. (1992). Complete signed and cued French: An original signed language-cued speech combination. *American Annals of the Deaf, 137*, 331–337.

Charlier, B. L., & Leybaert, J. (2000). The rhyming skills of deaf children educated with phonetically augmented speechreading. *Quarterly Journal of Experimental Psychology, 53A*(2), 349–375.

Cochard, N. (2003). Impact du LPC sur l'évolution des enfants implantés. *Actes des Journées d'études Nantes, 40*, 65–77.

Cornett, O. (1967). Cued Speech. *American Annals of the Deaf, 112*, 3–13.

Descourtieux, C. (2003). Seize ans d'expérience pratique à CODALI: Evaluation—evolutions. *Actes des Journées d'études Nantes, 40*, 77–88.

Descourtieux, C., Groh, V., Rusterholz, A., Simoulin, I., & Busquet, D. (1999). Cued Speech in the stimulation of communication: An advantage in cochlear implantation. *International Journal of Pediatric Otorhinolaryngology, 47*, 205–207.

Hage, C. (1994). *Développement de certains aspects de la morpho-syntaxe chez l'enfant à surdité profonde: Rôle du langage parlé complété*. Unpublished doctoral dissertation, Université Libre de Bruxelles.

Hage, C., Alegria, J., & Périer, O. (1991). Cued Speech and language acquisition: The case of grammatical gender morpho-phonology. In D. S. Martin (Ed.), *Advances in cognition, education and deafness* (pp. 395–399). Washington, DC: Gallaudet University Press.

Karmiloff-Smith, A. (1979). *A functional approach to child language*. Cambridge: Cambridge University Press.

Kelly, L. (1996). The interaction of syntactic competence and vocabulary during reading by deaf students. *Journal of Deaf Studies and Deaf Education, 1*, 75–90.

Kipila, B. (1985). Analysis of an oral language sample from a prelingually deaf child's cued speech: A case study. *Cued Speech Annals, 1*, 46–59.

Le Normand, M.-T. (1997). Early morphological development in French children. In A. Olofsson & S. Stromqvist (Eds.), *Cross-linguistic studies of dyslexia and early language development* (pp. 59–79). Luxembourg: Office for Official Publications of the European Communities.

Le Normand, M.-T. (2003). Acquisition du lexique chez l'enfant implanté. *Actes des Journées d'études Nantes, 40*, 97–108.

Leybaert, J. (2000). Phonology acquired through the eyes and spelling in deaf children. *Journal of Experimental Child Psychology, 75*, 291–318.

Leybaert, J., & Lechat, J. (2001). Variability in deaf children's spelling: The effect of language experience. *Journal of Educational Psychology, 93*, 554–562.

Liben, L. S. (1978). The development of deaf children: An overview of issues. In L. S. Liben (Ed.), *Deaf children: Developmental perspectives* (pp. 3–40). New York: Academic Press.

Locke, J.L. (1997). A theory of neurolinguistic development. *Brain and Language, 58*, 265–326.

Nicholls, G., & Ling, D. (1982). Cued Speech and the reception of spoken language. *Journal of Speech and Hearing Research, 25*, 262–269.

Périer, O., Bochner-Wuidar, A., Everarts, B., Michiels, J. & Hage, C. (1986). The combination of cued speech and signed French to improve spoken language acquisition by young deaf children. In B. Tervoort (Ed.), *Signs of life: Proceedings of the Second European Congress on Sign Language Research* (pp. 194–199). Amsterdam. (Reprinted in *Cued Speech Journal, 4*(7), 1990).

Périer, O., Charlier, B., Hage, C., & Alegria, J. (1988). Evaluation of the effects of prolonged cued speech practice upon the reception of spoken language. In I. G. Taylor (Ed.), *The education of the deaf: Current perspectives* (Vol. 1) (pp. 47–59). London: Croom Helm.

Pisoni, D. B. (2000). Cognitive factors and cochlear implants: Some thoughts on perception, learning, and memory in speech perception. *Ear and Hearing, 21*, 70–78.

Schwartz, J. L., Berthommier, F., & Savariaux, C. (2002). Audio-visual scene analysis: Evidence from a "very-early" integration process in audio-visual speech perception. In *Proceedings of ICSLP 2002* (pp. 1937–1940).

Szagun, G. (2001). Language acquisition in young German-speaking children with cochlear implants: Individual differences and implications for conceptions of a "sensitive phase." *Audiology and Neuro-otology, 6*, 288–298.

Szagun, G. (2004). Learning by ear: On the acquisition of case and gender marking by German-speaking children with normal hearing and with cochlear implants. *Journal of Child Language, 31*, 1–30.

Taeschner, T., Devescovi, A., & Volterra, V. (1988). Affixes and function words in written language of deaf children. *Applied Psycholinguistics, 9*, 385–401.

Vieu, A., Mondain, M., Blanchard, K., Sillon, M., Reuillard-Artières, F., Tobey, E., et al. (1998). Influence of communication mode on speech intelligibility and syntactic structure of sentences in profoundly hearing impaired French children implanted between 5 and 9 years of age. *International Journal of Pediatric Otorhinolaryngology, 44*, 15–22.

10

A Computer-Animated Tutor
for Language Learning:
Research and Applications

Dominic W. Massaro

This volume documents how successfully humans learn and use language without adequate auditory input. Sign language parallels spoken language in acquisition, use, and communication, but even oral language can serve communication when the auditory input is degraded or even absent. Lipreading (speechreading because it involves more than just the lips) allows these individuals to perceive and understand oral language and even to speak (Bernstein, Demorest, & Tucker, 2000; Kisor, 1990; Mirrelles, 1947). Speechreading seldom disambiguates all of the spoken input, however, and other techniques have been used to allow a richer input. Cued speech, for example, is a recent deliberate solution to having a limited auditory input and consists of hand gestures while speaking that provide the perceiver with disambiguating information in addition to what is seen on the face. Other devices such as vibratory aids that transduce the auditory speech into tactile input have also been used (Bernstein, Demorest, Coulter, & O'Connell, 1991; Waldstein & Boothroyd, 1995) For hard-of-hearing individuals, however, processing oral language from the voice and face is a natural solution to handling two limited input channels. This situation is the focus of this chapter, and the technology, research, and pedagogy described here support the premise that all humans easily exploit multiple sensory inputs in language processing.

The need for language tutoring is pervasive in today's world. Millions of individuals have language and speech challenges, and these individuals require additional instruction in language learning. For example, it is well known that hard-of-hearing children have significant deficits in both spoken and written vocabulary knowledge (Breslaw, Griffiths, Wood, & Howarth, 1981; Holt, Traxler, & Allen, 1997). A similar situation exists for autistic children, who lag behind their typically developing cohort in language acquisition (Tager-Flusberg, 2000). Currently, however, these needs are not being met. One problem that the people with these disabilities face is that there are not enough skilled teachers and professionals to give them the one-on-one attention that they need. So they resort to other resources, such as books or other media, but these are not easily personalized to the students' needs, lack the engaging capability of a teacher, are rather expensive, and are relatively ineffective.

In addition to these individuals with specific language challenges, many other persons must learn a new language. Given the highly mobile society, individuals of all walks of life find themselves in situations in which successful business and social interactions require use of a nonnative language. As an obvious example, English is becoming increasing necessary and desirable worldwide, and the number of people in the world who are learning English is increasing at a rapid rate. One of our goals is to apply the knowledge that has been obtained in speech science and related disciplines to several domains of language learning. These include the learning of vocabulary and grammar as well as the perception and production of speech.

This goal was facilitated or even created by our serendipitous relationship with a computer-animated talking head, Baldi® (Dominic W. Massaro, Santa Cruz, CA, USA). We first incorporated Baldi in order to control the visible speech presented to participants in our research on multisensory or multimodal speech perception. Baldi's versatility soon convinced us that he had potential value as an embodied conversational agent who could guide students through a variety of exercises designed to teach vocabulary and grammar and to develop linguistic and phonological awareness. We believe this vocation for Baldi holds promise for all children with language challenges and even for typically developing children. Baldi is now used in the Language Wizard and Tutor program (described in Bosseler & Massaro, 2003), which encompasses and implements developments in the pedagogy of how language is learned, remembered, and used.

Given this context, this chapter continues with the evidence for the value of multimodal linguistic input followed by a theoretical description of multimodal speech perception. The technology behind Baldi's attractive exterior is described, as well as his development and the evaluation of his effectiveness in simulating a naturally talking person. The case is then made for the importance of vocabulary in cognitive development, the value of the direct teaching of vocabulary and grammar, and the development and evaluation of the Language Wizard/Tutor for language tutoring.

MULTIMODAL SPEECH AND ITS VALUE
FOR LANGUAGE TUTORING

Speech science evolved as the study of a unimodal auditory channel of communication because speech was viewed as solely an auditory event (e.g., Denes & Pinson, 1963). There is no doubt that the voice alone is usually adequate for understanding and, given the popularity of mobile phones, might be the most frequent medium for today's communication. However, speech should be viewed as a multimodal phenomenon because the human face presents visual information during speech production that is critically important for effective communication. Experiments indicate that our perception and understanding are influenced by a speaker's face and accompanying gestures, as well as the actual sound of the speech (Massaro, 1987, 1998, 2000, 2004; Summerfield, 1987).

In face-to-face communication, visible speech from the talker's face (or from a reasonably accurate synthetic talking head) improves understanding. For many individuals with severe or profound hearing loss, understanding visible speech is essential to orally communicating effectively with others. Even for typically hearing individuals, the face is valuable because many communication environments involve a noisy auditory channel, which degrades speech perception and recognition. Visible speech is also an important oral communication channel for individuals with specific limitations in processing auditory information, or with other types of language challenges. One of the central themes of our research is that viewing speech as a multimodal experience can also improve language tutoring, an important challenge for applications of speech science.

BALDI AND THE VALUE OF VISIBLE SPEECH

The value of visible speech in face-to-face communication was the primary motivation for the development of Baldi, a three-dimensional computer-animated talking head, shown in figure 10.1. Baldi provides realistic visible speech that is almost as accurate as a natural speaker (Cohen, Beskow, & Massaro, 1998; Massaro, 1998, ch. 13). Baldi's visible speech can be appropriately aligned with either synthesized or natural auditory speech. Baldi also has teeth, a tongue, and a palate to simulate the inside of the mouth, and the tongue movements have been trained to mimic natural tongue movements (Cohen et al., 1998). We have also witnessed that the student's engagement is enhanced by face-to-face interaction with Baldi (Bosseler & Massaro, 2003; Massaro & Light, 2003).

Our software can generate a talking face (with an optional body) in real time on a personal computer, and Baldi is able to say anything at

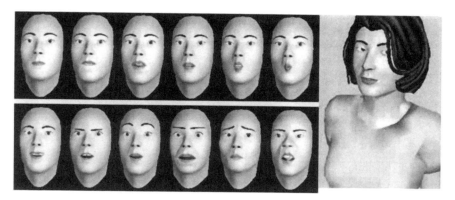

Figure 10-1. Baldi, our three-dimensional computer-animated talking head, has realistic speech as well as convincing emotions. The top panel shows six phoneme articulations, and the bottom panel, six basic emotions. In addition, Baldi has a sister, Baldette, who has both hair and a body with appropriate gestures of oral language.

any time in our applications. Baldi can be thought of as a puppet controlled by a set of strings that move and modify its appearance. In the algorithm for the synthesis of visible speech, each speech segment is specified with a target value for each string or what we call a facial control parameter. Critical components of the animation are to blend the successive segments together and to implement coarticulation, which is defined as changes in the articulation of a speech segment due to the influence of neighboring segments. The algorithm for animating coarticulation is based on a model of speech production using rules that describe the relative dominance of the characteristics of the speech segments (Cohen & Massaro, 1993; Massaro, 1998).

A central and somewhat unique quality of our work is the empirical evaluation of the visible speech synthesis, which has been carried out hand-in-hand with its development. The quality and intelligibility of Baldi's visible speech have been repeatedly modified and evaluated to accurately simulate naturally talking humans (Massaro, 1998). The gold standard we use is how well Baldi compares to a real person. Given that viewing a natural face improves speech perception, we determine the extent to which Baldi provides a similar improvement. We repeatedly modify the control values of Baldi in order to meet this criterion. We modify some of the control values by hand and also use data from measurements of real people talking (Cohen, Massaro, & Clark, 2002; Ouni, Massaro, Cohen, & Young, 2003). Versions of Baldi now speak a variety of languages, including Arabic (Badr; Ouni et al., 2003), Spanish (Baldero), Mandarin (Bao), Italian (Baldini; Cosi et al., 2002), German (Balthasar), and French (Baladin).

Value of Face-to-Face Input

There are several reasons why the use of auditory and visual information from an accurate talking head like Baldi is so successful, and why it holds so much promise for language tutoring (Massaro, 1998). These include (a) the information value of visible speech, (b) the robustness of visual speech, (c) the complementarity of auditory and visual speech, and (d) the optimal integration of these two sources of information. We review evidence for each of these properties in this chapter and begin by describing an experiment illustrating how facial information increases recognition and memory for linguistic input.

Information Value of Visible Speech

In a series of experiments, we asked 71 typical college students to report the words of sentences presented in noise (Jesse, Vrignaud, & Massaro, 2000/01). On some trials, only the auditory sentence was presented (unimodal condition). On some other trials, the auditory sentence was accompanied by Baldi, which was appropriately aligned with the auditory sentence (bimodal condition). The test items consisted of 65 meaningful sentences from the database of Bernstein and Eberhardt (1986), for example, "We will eat lunch out." The sentences were three, four, and five syllables in length and consisted of 43 statements, 17 questions, and 5 imperatives.

Figure 10.2 gives the proportion of words correctly reported for the unimodal and bimodal conditions for each of the 71 participants. As can be seen in figure 10.2, the talking face facilitated performance for everyone. Performance was more than doubled for those participants performing particularly poorer given auditory speech alone. Although a unimodal visual condition was not included in the experiment, we know that participants would have performed significantly lower than the unimodal auditory condition. Thus, the combination of auditory and visual speech has been described as synergistic because their combination can lead to accuracy that is significantly greater than accuracy on either modality alone.

Similar results are found when noise-free speech is presented to persons with limited hearing. Erber (1972) tested three populations of children (adolescents and young teenagers) strictly defined by their amount of hearing: normal hearing (NH), severely impaired (SI), and profoundly deaf (PD). The test consisted of a videotaped speaker pronouncing the eight consonants /b/, /d/, /g/, /p/, /t/, /k/, /m/, and /n/ spoken in a bisyllabic context /aCa/, where C refers to one of the eight consonants. Although all three groups benefited from seeing the face of the speaker, the SI group revealed the largest performance gain in the bimodal condition relative to either of the unimodal conditions

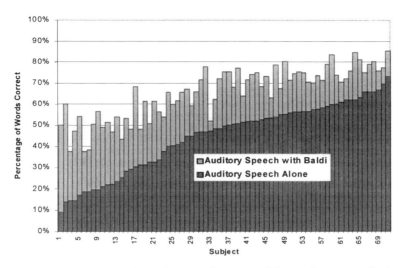

Figure 10-2. Proportion of words correctly reported for auditory speech alone and auditory speech with Baldi conditions for each of the 71 participants in the task (after Jesse et al., 2000/01).

(Massaro & Cohen, 1999). The NH group had very good auditory information, so the face could not contribute much, whereas the PD group had very poor auditory information, so the voice could not contribute much. The SI group, on the hand, had a reasonable degree of both auditory and visual information. As noted in the following discussion of complementarity and optimal integration, perception of speech can be very good when some hearing is present and the face of the speaker can be seen.

Finally, the strong influence of visible speech is not limited to situations with degraded auditory input, whether due to a noisy signal or hearing loss. Even with high-quality auditory input, a perceiver's recognition of an auditory-visual syllable can reflect the contribution of both sound and sight. For example, if the ambiguous auditory sentence "My bab pop me poo brive" is paired with the visible sentence "My gag kok me koo grive," the perceiver is likely to hear "My dad taught me to drive." Two ambiguous sources of information are combined to create a meaningful interpretation (Massaro, 1998).

Robustness of Visible Speech

Empirical findings indicate that speechreading, or the ability to obtain speech information from the face, is robust; that is, perceivers are fairly good at speechreading in a broad range of viewing conditions. To obtain information from the face, the perceiver does not have to fixate directly on the talker's lips but can be looking at other parts of the face or even somewhat away from the face (Smeele, Massaro, Cohen, & Sittig, 1998). Furthermore, accuracy is not dramatically reduced when the facial image is blurred (because of poor vision, e.g.), when the face is viewed from above, below, or in profile, or when there is a large distance between the talker and the viewer (Massaro, 1998; Munhall & Vatikiotis-Bateson, 2004). These findings indicate that speechreading is highly functional in a variety of nonoptimal situations. The robustness of the influence of visible speech is illustrated by the fact that people naturally integrate visible speech with audible speech even when the temporal occurrence of the two sources is displaced by about a one fifth of a second (Massaro & Cohen, 1993). Light and sound travel at different speeds, and the dynamics of their corresponding sensory systems also differ (the retina transduces a visual stimulus much more slowly than the cochlea transduces an auditory one). Thus, a cross-modal integration should be relatively immune to small temporal asynchronies (Massaro, 1998, ch. 3).

Complementarity of Auditory and Visual Information

A visual talking head allows for complementarity of auditory and visual information. Auditory and visual information are complementary when one of these sources is most informative in those cases in which the other is weakest. Because of this, a speech distinction between segments is differentially supported by the two sources of information. That is, two segments that are robustly conveyed in one modality are relatively ambiguous in the other modality (Massaro & Cohen, 1999). For example, the difference between /ba/ and /da/ is easy to see but relatively difficult to hear. On the other hand, the difference between /ba/ and /pa/ is relatively easy to hear but very difficult to discriminate visually. The fact that two sources of information are complementary makes their combined use much more informative than would be the case if the two sources were noncomplementary, or redundant (Massaro, 1998, ch. 14).

Optimal Integration of Auditory and Visual Speech

The final value afforded by a visual talking head is that perceivers combine or integrate the auditory and visual sources of information in an optimally efficient manner (Massaro, 1987; Massaro & Cohen, 1999; Massaro & Stork, 1998). There are many possible ways to treat two sources of information: use only the most informative source, average the two sources together, or integrate them in such a fashion that both sources are used but that the least ambiguous source has the most influence. Perceivers in fact integrate the information available from each modality to perform as efficiently as possible (Massaro, 1998). The best evidence for optimal integration comes from an important manipulation that systematically varies the ambiguity of each source of information in terms of how much it resembles each syllable (Massaro, 1998). In a series of experiments, the properties of the auditory stimulus were varied to give an auditory continuum between the syllables /ba/ and /da/. In analogous fashion, properties of our animated face were varied to give a continuum between visual /ba/ and /da/. Five levels of audible speech varying between /ba/ and /da/ were crossed with five levels of visible speech varying between the same alternatives. In addition, the audible and visible speech also were presented alone for a total of $25 + 5 + 5 = 35$ independent stimulus conditions. This so-called expanded factorial design has been used with 82 participants who were repeatedly tested, giving 24 observations at each of the 35 stimulus conditions for each participant. These results have served as a database for testing models of pattern recognition (Massaro, 1998).

The proportion of /da/ responses for each of the stimulus conditions was computed for each participant. The results of one representative participant are presented in figure 10.3 to illustrate the nature of the data analysis and model testing. Figure 10.3 gives the observed (points) proportion of /da/ judgments as a function of the auditory and visual stimuli in the unimodal and bimodal conditions. Although figure 10.3 might seem somewhat intimidating at first glance, a graphical analysis of this nature can dramatically facilitate understanding of the underlying processes. Only two levels of visible speech are shown in the graph for pedagogical purposes. Notice that the columns of points are spread unevenly along the x-axis. The reason is that they are placed corresponding to the influence of the auditory speech (at a value equal to the marginal probability of a /da/ judgment for each auditory level of the independent variable). This spacing thus reflects relative influence of adjacent levels of the auditory condition.

The single modality (unimodal) auditory curve (indicated by the open circles) shows that the auditory speech had a large influence on the judgments. More generally, the degree of influence of this modality when presented alone would be indicated by the steepness of the response function. The unimodal visual condition is plotted at .5 (which is considered to be completely neutral) on the auditory scale. The influence of the visual speech when presented alone is indexed by the vertical spread between the two levels of the visual condition.

The other points give performance for the auditory-visual (bimodal) conditions. This graphical analysis shows that both the auditory and the visual sources of information had a strong impact on the identification judgments. The likelihood of a /da/ identification increased as the auditory speech changed from /ba/ to /da/, and analogously for

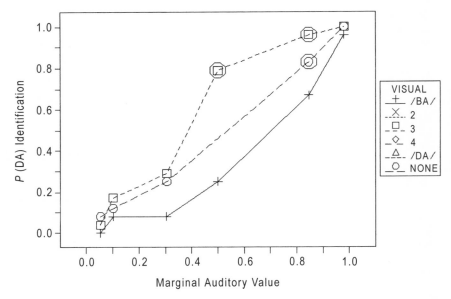

Figure 10-3. The points give the observed proportion of /da/ identifications in the unimodal and factorial auditory-visual conditions as a function of the five levels of synthetic auditory and visual speech varying between /ba/ and /da/. Only two levels of visible speech are shown in the graph for pedagogical purposes. The columns of points are placed at a value corresponding to the marginal probability of a /da/ judgment for each auditory level on the independent variable. The auditory alone conditions are given by the open circles. The unimodal visual condition is plotted at .5 (completely neutral) on the auditory scale. The predictions of the FLMP gave an RMSD of .051. (RMSD is Root Mean Square Deviations) Results shown are for participant 30.

the visible speech. The curves across changes in the auditory variable are relatively steep and also spread out from on another with changes in the visual variable. By these criteria, both sources had a large influence in the bimodal conditions.

Finally, the auditory and visual effects are not additive in the bimodal condition, as demonstrated by a significant auditory-visual interaction. The interaction is indexed by the change in the spread among the two bimodal curves across changes in the auditory variable. This vertical spread among the two curves is much greater toward the middle than at the ends of the auditory continuum. It means that the influence of one source of information is greatest when the other source is neutral or ambiguous. To understand multimodal speech perception, it is essential to understand how the two sources of information are used in perception. This question is addressed in the next section.

Evaluation of How Two Sources Are Used

To address how the two sources of information are used, three points are circled in figure 10.3 to highlight the conditions involving the fourth level of auditory information (A4) and the third level of visual information (V3). When presented alone, P(/da/ | A4) (i.e., the probability of perceiving /da/ at A4) and P(/da/ | V3) are both about .8. When these two stimuli occur together, P(/da/ | A4 V3) is about .95. This so-called synergistic result (the bimodal is more extreme than either unimodal response proportion) does not seem to be easily explained by either the use of a single modality during a given presentation or a simple averaging of the two modalities. In order to systematically evaluate theoretical alternatives, however, formal models must be proposed and tested against all of the results, not just selected conditions. It therefore is useful to understand how one formalizes two competing models and test them against the results.

According to nonintegration models, any perceptual experience results from only a single sensory influence. Thus, the pattern recognition of any cross-modal event is determined by only one of the modalities, even though the influential modality might vary from one categorization event to the next. This idea is in the tradition of selective attention theories according to which only a single channel of information can be processed at any one time (Pashler, 1998). According to the single-channel model (SCM), only one of the two sources of information determines the response on any given trial. Formalization of the SCM is given in Massaro (1998).

The Fuzzy Logical Model of Perception

According to integration models, multiple sensory influences are combined before categorization and perceptual experience. The fuzzy logical model of perception (FLMP) assumes that the visible and audible speech signals are integrated. Before integration, however, each source is evaluated (independently of the other source) to determine how much that source supports various alternatives. The integration process combines these support values to determine how much their combination supports the various alternatives. The perceptual outcome for the perceiver will be a function of the relative degree of support among the competing alternatives.

Figure 10.4 illustrates three major operations during pattern recognition in the FLMP. Features are first independently evaluated (as sources of information) in terms of the degrees to which they match specific object prototypes in memory. Each feature match is represented by a common metric of fuzzy logic truth-values that range from 0 to 1 (Zadeh, 1965). In the second operation, the feature values corresponding to a given prototype are multiplied to yield an overall (absolute) goodness of match for that alternative. Finally, the goodness of

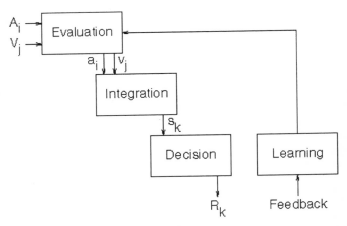

Figure 10-4. Schematic representation of the FLMP to include learning with feedback. The three perceptual processes are shown to proceed left to right in time, to illustrate their necessarily successive but overlapping processing. These processes make use of prototypes stored in long-term memory. The sources of information are represented by uppercase letters. Auditory information is represented by A_i, and visual information by V_j. The evaluation process transforms these sources of information into psychological values (indicated by lowercase letters a_i and v_j) These sources are then integrated to give an overall degree of support, s_k, for each speech alternative k. The decision operation maps the outputs of integration into some response alternative, R_k. The response can take the form of a discrete decision or a rating of the degree to which the alternative is likely. The feedback during learning is assumed to tune the prototypical values of the features used by the evaluation process.

match for each alternative is compared relatively to the sum of the support for all relevant alternatives (the relative goodness rule; Massaro, 1998).

To explain pattern recognition, representations in memory are an essential component. The current stimulus input has to be compared to the pattern recognizer's memory of previous patterns. One type of memory is a set of summary descriptions of the meaningful patterns. These summary descriptions are called prototypes, and they contain a description of features of the pattern. The features of the prototype correspond to the ideal values that an exemplar should have if it is a member of that category. To recognize a speech segment, the evaluation process assesses the input information relative to the prototypes in memory.

The FLMP takes a strong stance on the question of discrete versus continuous information processing. Information input to a stage or output from a stage is continuous rather than discrete. Furthermore, the transmission of information from one stage to the next is assumed to occur continuously rather than discretely. The three processes shown in figure 10.4 are offset to emphasize their temporal overlap. Evaluated information is passed continuously to integration while additional evaluation is taking place. Although it is logically the case that some evaluation must occur before integration can proceed, the processes are assumed to overlap in time. Similarly, integrated information is continuously made available to the decision process.

Given the FLMP framework, we are able to make an important distinction between "information" and "information processing." The sources of information from the auditory and visual channels make contact with the perceiver at the evaluation stage of processing. The reduction in uncertainty effected by each source is defined as information. In the fit of the FLMP, for example, the degree of support for each alternative from each modality corresponds to information. The predicted response probability in the unimodal condition is predicted to be a direct measure of the information given by that stimulus. These values represent how informative each source of information is. Information processing refers to how the sources of information are processed. In the FLMP, this processing is described by the evaluation, integration, and decision stages.

Across a range of studies comparing specific mathematical predictions (Massaro, 1988, 1989, 1998; Massaro, Weldon, & Kitzis, 1991), the FLMP has been more successful than other competitor models in accounting for the experimental data (Massaro, 1989, 1998; Massaro & Friedman, 1990). It is worthwhile to address two important issues related to the integration of auditory and visual speech.

Why Integration

One might question why perceivers integrate several sources of information when just one of them might be sufficient. Most of us do reasonably well in communicating over the telephone, for example. Part of the answer might be grounded in our ontogeny. Integration might be so natural for adults even when information from just one sense would be sufficient because, during development, there was much less information from each sense and therefore integration was all the more critical for accurate performance (Lewkowicz & Kraebel, 2004).

Underlying Neural Mechanism

If we really want to understand speech processing in deaf as well as hearing individuals, a natural question concerns the neural mechanism underlying the integration algorithm specified in the FLMP. An important set of observations from single-cell recordings in the cat's brain could be interpreted in terms integration of the form specified by the FLMP (Meredith, 2004; Stein, Jiang, & Stanford, 2004; Stein & Meredith, 1993). A single hissing sound or a light spot can activate neurons in the superior colliculus. A much more vigorous response is produced, however, when both signals are simultaneously presented from the same location. These results parallel the outcomes we have observed in unimodal and bimodal speech perception.

As proven elsewhere, the FLMP is mathematically equivalent to Bayes's theorem (Massaro, 1998, ch. 4), which is an optimal method for combining two sources of evidence to test among hypotheses. Anastasio and Patton (2004) propose that the brain can implement a computation analogous to Bayes's rule and that the response of a neuron in the superior colliculus is proportional to the posterior probability that a target is present in its receptive fields, given its sensory input. The authors also assume that the visual and auditory inputs are conditionally independent given the target, corresponding to our independence assumption at the evaluation stage. They show that the target-present posterior probability computed from the impulses from the auditory and visual neurons is higher given sensory inputs of two modalities than it is given input of only one modality, analogous to the synergistic outcome of the FLMP.

A Universal Principle and Its Implications for Language Learning

The FLMP has proven to be a universal principle of pattern recognition (Campbell, Schwarzer, & Massaro, 2001; Massaro, 1998, 2002; Massaro, Cohen, Campbell, & Rodriguez, 2001; Movellan & McClelland, 2001). In multisensory texture perception, for example, there appears to be no fixed sensory dominance by vision or haptics, and the bimodal presentation yields higher accuracy than either of the unimodal conditions (Lederman & Klatzky, 2004). In many cases, these sources of information are ambiguous and any particular source alone does not usually specify completely the appropriate interpretation. Parenthetically, it should be emphasized that these processes are not necessarily conscious or under deliberate control. Most important, we have found that typically developing children integrate information from the face and voice (Massaro, 1984, 1987, 1998) as well as do deaf and hard-of-hearing children (Massaro & Cohen, 1999) and autistic children (Massaro & Bosseler, 2003; Williams, Massaro, Peel, Bosseler, & Suddendorf, 2004).

Our early research indicated that preschool as well as school children integrate auditory and visual speech (Massaro, 1984). More recently, we have shown that both hard-of-hearing children and autistic children appear to integrate information from the face and the voice. Massaro and Bosseler (2003) tested whether autistic children integrate information in the identification of spoken syllables. An expanded factorial design was used in which information from the face and voice was presented either unimodally or bimodally, and either consistent with one another or not. After training the children in speechreading to enhance the influence of visible speech from the face, the identification task was repeated. Children behaved similarly in the two replications, except for a larger influence of the visible speech after training in speechreading. The FLMP gave a significantly better description of performance than the SCM, supporting the interpretation that autistic children integrate vocal and facial information in speech perception.

There is evidence that hard-of-hearing and deaf children also integrate auditory and visual speech. Erber (1972) tested three populations of children under auditory, visual, and bimodal conditions. The FLMP was applied to the results of all three groups and gave an excellent description of the identification accuracy and confusion errors of all three groups of children (Massaro, 1998, ch. 14). Erber's results also reveal a strong complementarity between the audible and visible modalities in speech, which is discussed more fully in Massaro (1998, ch. 14). These results from typically developing children as well as deaf and hard-of-hearing and autistic children indicate that multisensory environments should be ideal for speech and language learning.

LANGUAGE TUTORING BY COMPUTER-BASED INSTRUCTION WITH BALDI

Computer-based instruction is an emerging method to train and develop vocabulary knowledge for both native- and second-language learners (Druin & Hendler, 2000; Wood, 2001) and individuals with special needs (Barker, 2003; Heimann, Nelson, Tjus, & Gilberg, 1995; Moore & Calvert, 2000). An incentive to employing computer-controlled applications for training is the ease with which individually-tailored instruction, automated practice and testing, feedback, and branching can be programmed. Another valuable component of computer-based instruction is the potential to present multiple sources of information, such as text, sound, and images in sequence or in parallel (Chun & Plass, 1996; Dubois & Vial, 2000). Incorporating text and visual images of the vocabulary to be learned along with the actual definitions and spoken words facilitates learning and improves memory for the target vocabulary. Dubois and Vial (2000), for example, found an increase in recall of second-language vocabulary when training consisted of combined presentations of spoken words, images, written words, and text relative to only a subset of these formats.

Computer-based instruction can easily be made available to the child most hours of a day and most days of the year. Having continual access to the instruction is valuable because learning and retention are positively correlated with the time spent learning. Take, for example, an autistic boy who has irregular sleep patterns. He could conceivably wake in the middle of the night and participate in language learning with Baldi as his friendly guide. The instruction would be tailored exactly to his strengths and needs. Other benefits of this program could include spoken and written language and provide a semblance of a game-playing experience while actually learning. More generally, we have found that the students enjoy working with Baldi because he offers extreme patience, he does not become angry, tired, or bored, and he is always there (Bosseler & Massaro, 2003).

We hypothesized that language-learning applications with animated tutors perceived as supportive and likeable will engage children with special needs as well as foreign language learners (Massaro, 2000). Given that education research has shown that children can be taught new word meanings by using direct instruction (Beck, McKeown, & Kucan, 2002), we developed a multimedia application to teach vocabulary and grammar.

Language Wizard/Tutor

Our early experience with the use of our initial software applications was disconcerting but highly informative.[1] The initial goal was to provide so-called easy-to-use tools to teachers to develop their own instructional applications across all of their teaching domains (Massaro et al., 2000). Much to our disappointment, however, we found that only one of the teachers, who already was using other software products and writing his own applications, was successful in creating lessons. We thus embarked on the development of a wizard and tutor that would be useful to everyone involved in the educational process (Massaro & Bosseler, 2003; Massaro & Light, 2004a).

Our Language Wizard is a user-friendly application that allows a coach or even a student to compose lessons with minimal computer experience and instruction. Although slightly more complex than, for example, your typical installation wizards because of the many more options, the program has wizardlike features that direct the coach to explore and choose among the alternative implementations in the creation of a lesson. The evolving design of this pedagogy is based on educational principles to optimize learning, which are not always intuitive. The Language Wizard allows the coach to tailor the lesson to the needs of the student, to seamlessly meld spoken and written language, to bypass repetitive training when student responses indicate that material is mastered, to provide a semblance of a game-playing experience while actually learning, and to lead the child along a growth path that always bridges his or her current "zone of proximal development."

The Language Tutor, although relatively mellow by video game standards, has enough engaging interactive features to engage the

[1]The development of this application was carried out in collaboration with the Center for Spoken Language Understanding at the Oregon Health Sciences University and the Tucker Maxon Oral School, both in Portland, Oregon.

student in mastering the lesson. We have found that mimicking various aspects of video games enhances learning effectiveness (Gee, 2003). Some of these properties include (1) providing information when needed, (2) operating at the outer edge of the student's competence, (3) rewarding commitment of the learner's self, and (4) challenging the student to think about the relationship among the things being learned. The resulting lessons encompass and instantiate the developments in the pedagogy of how language is learned, remembered, and used. Figure 10.5 gives a computer screen from a vocabulary lesson on fruits and vegetables.

One of the psychological principles that we exploit most is the value of multiple sources of information in perception, recognition, learning, and retention. An interactive multimedia environment is ideally suited for learning (Wood, 2001). Incorporating text and visual images of the vocabulary to be learned along with the actual definitions and sounds of the vocabulary facilitates learning and improves memory for the target vocabulary and grammar. Many aspects of our lessons enhance and reinforce learning. For example, the existing program makes it

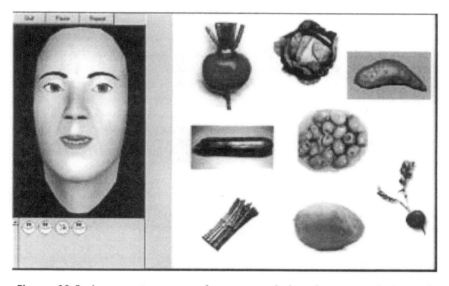

Figure 10-5. A computer screen from a vocabulary lesson on fruits and vegetables, illustrating the format of the Language Tutor. Each lesson contains Baldi, the vocabulary items and written text (not present in this exercise), and "stickers." For example, Baldi says "Click on the beet." The student clicks on the appropriate region, and feedback is given for each response, in the form of Baldi's spoken reaction and stickers (e.g., happy and disgusted faces). After Massaro and Light (2004a).

possible for the students to (1) observe the words being spoken by a realistic embodied conversational agent (Baldi), (2) experience the word as spoken as well as written, (3) see visual images of referents of the words, (4) click on or point to the referent or its spelling, (5) hear themselves say the word followed by a correct pronunciation, (6) spell the word by typing, and (7) observe and respond to the word used in context. Table 10.1 gives a description of the eight application exercises in the Language Wizard/Tutor. We now justify the importance of the direct teaching of vocabulary.

Essential Role for Vocabulary Knowledge in Language Development

Vocabulary knowledge is central for understanding the world and for language competence both in spoken language and in reading (Gupta & MacWhinney, 1997). Empirical evidence indicates that very young normally-developing children more easily form conceptual categories when category labels are available than when they are not (Waxman, 2002). Once the child knows about 150 words, there is a sudden increase in the rate at which new words are learned and the emergence of grammatical skill (Marchman & Bates, 1994). Even children experiencing language delays because of specific language impairment benefit once this level of word knowledge is obtained. Vocabulary knowledge is positively correlated with both listening and reading comprehension (Anderson & Freebody, 1981; Stanovich, 1986; Wood, 2001) and predicts overall success in school (Vermeer, 2001). It follows that increasing the pervasiveness and effectiveness of vocabulary learning offer a promising opportunity for improving conceptual knowledge and language competence for all individuals, whether or not they are disadvantaged because of sensory limitations, learning disabilities, or social condition.

Validity of the Direct Learning of Vocabulary

There are important reasons to justify the need for direct teaching of vocabulary. Although there is little emphasis on the acquisition of vocabulary in typical school curricula, research demonstrates that some direct teaching of vocabulary is essential for appropriate language development in normally-developing children (Beck et al., 2002). Contrary to a common belief that learning vocabulary is a necessary outcome of reading in which new words are experienced in a meaningful context, context seldom disambiguates the meaning of a word completely. As an example, consider a passage from *The Fir Tree* by Hans Christian Andersen:

> Then two servants came in rich livery and carried the Fir Tree into a large and splendid drawing-room. Portraits were hanging on the walls, and near the white porcelain stove stood two large Chinese vases with lions on the covers.

Table 10-1: Description of the Eight Application Exercises in the Language Wizard/Player

Application Exercise	Description
Pretest	Baldi instructs the student to "click on the zucchin," and the student is required to drag the computer mouse over the item that was just presented and click on it. Feedback can be given about the student's response via a happy or sad face. Items can be randomly presented a variable number of times.
Presentation	One image becomes highlighted, and Baldi tells the student, "This is a zucchini" (for example). The written label of the vocabulary item can appear on the screen below the canvas of images. Baldi then instructs the student, "Show me the zucchini," and the student is required to drag the computer mouse over the highlighted image and click on it. Feedback can be given. This is to reinforce that the student knew which image was being described. Items can be randomly presented a variable number of times.
Identification	Baldi instructs the student, "Click on the zucchini" (for example), and the student is required to drag the computer mouse over the item that was just presented and click on it. Feedback can be given. If the student chose the wrong item, the correct item is highlighted and Baldi tells the student that the word they chose was not the zucchini and that the item that is highlighted is the zucchini. Items can be randomly presented a variable number of times.
Reading	The written text of all of the vocabulary items is presented below the images. Baldi instructs the student to click on the word corresponding to the highlighted image. Feedback can be given. Items can be randomly presented a variable number of times
Spelling	One of the images is highlighted while Baldi asks the student to type the corresponding word. Feedback can be given. If the student is incorrect, the correct spelling of the vocabulary item appears above the student's attempt and Baldi reads the word and spells it out to the student.
Imitation	One of the images is highlighted, and Baldi names the item. The student is instructed to repeat what Baldi had just said after the tone. The student says the word, and his or her voice is recorded and played back. Baldi can then say the word again to reinforce the child's pronunciation. Items can be randomly presented a variable number of times.

(continued)

Table 10-1: (continued)

Application Exercise	Description
Elicitation	One of the images is highlighted, and Baldi asks the student to name it. Independent of the student's production response, Baldi can then say the word again to reinforce the child's pronunciation. Items can be randomly presented a variable number of times.
Posttest	Baldi instructs the student, "Click on the zucchini," and the student is required to drag the computer mouse over the item that was just presented and click on it. Feedback can be given about the student's response via a happy or sad face. Items can be randomly presented a variable number of times.

Most of the words in this passage are not disambiguated by context. The meaning of livery, portraits, porcelain, and vases, for example, cannot be determined from the context of the story alone. Research by Beck et al. (2002) and Baker, Simmons, and Kameenui (1995) provides some evidence that hearing children more easily acquire new vocabulary by direct intentional instruction than by other incidental means (see also McKeown, Beck, Omanson, & Pople, 1985; Pany & Jenkins, 1978; Stahl, 1983). Although there does not appear to be any analogous research with deaf and hard-of-hearing children, the same advantage of direct instruction presumably would exist for them or other children with language challenges.

Direct instruction is also valuable because knowing a word is not an all-or-none proposition. A single experience with a word (even if the correct meaning of the word is comprehended) is seldom sufficient for mastering that word. Acquiring semantic representations appears to be a gradual process that can extend across several years (McGregor, Friedman, Reilly, & Newman, 2002). Words are complex multidimensional stimuli, and a person's knowledge of the word will not be as complete or as accurate as its dictionary entry. Semantic naming errors are more likely to occur with those items that have less embellished representations. Thus, it is important to overtrain or continue vocabulary training after the word is apparently known and to present the items in a variety of contexts in order to develop rich representations. Picture naming and picture drawing are techniques that can be used to probe and reinforce these representations (McGregor et al., 2002). Qian (2002) found that the dimension of vocabulary depth (as measured by synonymy, polysemy, and collocation) is as important as that of vocabulary size in predicting performance on academic reading. Therefore, a student can profit from the repeated experience of practicing new words in multiple contexts during the direct teaching of vocabulary.

The Language Wizard/Tutor with Baldi encompasses and instantiates the developments in the pedagogy of how language is acquired, remembered, and used. Direct teaching of vocabulary by computer software is possible, and an interactive multimedia environment is ideally suited for this learning (Wood, 2001). The Language Tutor provides a learning platform that allows optimal conditions for learning and the engagement of fundamental psychological processes such as working memory, the phonological loop, and the visual-spatial scratchpad (Atkins & Baddeley, 1998). Evidence by Baddeley and colleagues (Baddeley, Gathercole, & Papagno, 1998; Evans et al., 2000) supports the strategy of centering vocabulary learning in spoken language dialogs. There is also some evidence that reading aloud activates brain regions that are not activated by reading silently (Berninger & Richards, 2002). Thus, the imitation and elicitation activities in the Language Tutor should reinforce learning of vocabulary and grammar. Experimental tests of the effectiveness of the Language Wizard/Tutor with hard-of-hearing children are described next.

Effectiveness of Language Wizard/Tutor

Hard-of-hearing children have significant delays in both spoken and written vocabulary knowledge (Breslaw et al., 1981; Holt et al., 1997). One reason is that these children tend not to overhear other conversations because of their limited hearing and are thus shut off from an opportunity to learn vocabulary. These children often do not have names for specific things and concepts and therefore communicate with phrases such as "the window in the front of the car," "the big shelf where the sink is," or "the step by the street" rather than "windshield," "counter," or "curb" (Barker, 2003). In an initial independent evaluation carried out by Barker (2003), 13 teachers successfully used the Language Wizard to compose individually tailored lessons for their hard-of-hearing students, and the students learned and retained new vocabulary from these lessons.

Students photographed surroundings at home. Pictures of 10–15 objects were then incorporated in the lessons. Students practiced the lessons about 10 minutes a day until they reached 100% on the posttest. They then moved on to another lesson. They were also retested about 1 month after each successful (100%) posttest. Ten girls and nine boys 8–14 years old participated; 16 were hard-of-hearing children, and 3 were hearing children.

Figure 10.6 gives the average results of these lessons for three stages: pretest, posttest, and retention after 30 days. The items were classified as known, not known, and learned. Known items are those children knew on the pretest before the first lesson. Not known items are those

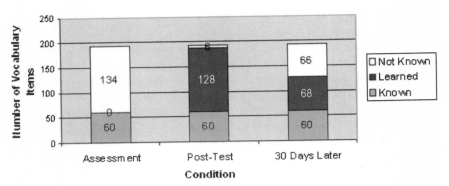

Figure 10-6. Results of word learning at the Tucker-Maxon Oral School using the Language Wizard/Tutor. The results showed significant vocabulary learning, with more than 50% retention of new words after 30 days.

children were unable to identify in the pretest. Learned items are those not-known items identified correctly in the posttest. Students knew about half of the items without any learning; they learned the other half of the items and retained about one half of the newly learned items when retested 30 days later.

Since no control groups were used in the evaluation described above, it was possible the children were learning the words outside of the Language Tutor environment. In addition, the results do not give the rate of vocabulary acquisition. It would also be valuable to measure production of the words, given that only identification was measured previously.

To study these questions, we used a within-student multiple baseline design (Baer, Wolf, & Risley, 1968; Horner & Baer, 1978), where certain words were continuously tested while others were tested and trained (Massaro & Light, 2004a). Although the teachers and speech therapists agreed not to use these words during our investigation, it is still possible that the words could be learned outside of the Language Tutor environment. The single-student multiple-baseline design monitors this possibility by providing a continuous measure of the knowledge of words that are not being trained. Thus, any significant differences in performance on the trained words and untrained words can be attributed to the Language Tutor training program itself rather than some other factor. In addition, this design tracks the rate of learning of each child.

Eight hard-of-hearing children, two males 6 and 7 years old and six females 9 and 10 years old, were recruited with parental consent from the Jackson Hearing Center in Palo Alto, California. Table 10.2 gives a description of the children and their hearing. Using the Language Wizard, the experimenter developed lessons with a collection of

Table 10-2: Age of the Participants at the Midpoint of the Study and Individual and Average Aided Auditory Device Thresholds (dB HL) at Four Frequencies for the Eight Students Studied in Massaro and Light (2004a)

S#	Age (year; month)	500 Hz	1,000 Hz	2,000 Hz	4,000 Hz	PTA	ULE	URE
1	7; 2	40	35	47	55	41	78	80
2	6; 11	35	30	35	43	33	80	85
3	10; 7	25	35	40	45	33	35	35
4	9; 3	30	33	45	68	36	95	42
5	11; 0	40	35	40	50	38	—	—
6	10; 0	50	52	55	60	52	95	95
7	9; 4	25	15	25	35	21	90	80
8	9; 11	30	35	40	60	35	110	60
Mean	9; 3	34	34	41	52	36	83	68

Participants 1 and 2 were in grade 1, and the others were in grade 4. Participant 7 had a cochlear implant, and the seven other children had binaural hearing aids, except for participant 8, who had just one aid. The participant numbers (S#) correspond to those in the results; PTA is pure tone average; ULE ad URE are unaided thresholds for left and right ears, respectively (which are not available for S5).

vocabulary items customized to each student. Each collection consisted of 24 items to provide three lessons of eight items for each child. Images of the vocabulary items were shown on the screen next to Baldi as he spoke. As can be seen in table 10.1, one exercise asked the child to respond to Baldi's instructions such as "click on the cabbage" by clicking on the item. Other exercises asked the child to recognize or type the written word. The production exercises asked the child to repeat the word after Baldi named the highlighted image or to name the image prior to Baldi naming it.

Figure 10.7 gives the accuracy of identification and production for one of the eight students. These results are typical because the outcome was highly consistent across the eight students. Identification performance was better than production because a child would be expected to recognize an object in order to pronounce it correctly. There was little knowledge of the test items without training, even though these items were repeatedly tested for many days. Once training began on a set of items, performance improved quickly until asymptotic knowledge was obtained. This knowledge did not degrade after training on these words ended and training on other words took place.

A reassessment test given about 4 weeks after completion of the experiment revealed that the students retained the items that were learned. The results show that the Language Tutor application is effective in teaching new vocabulary, there is a fast rate of learning given

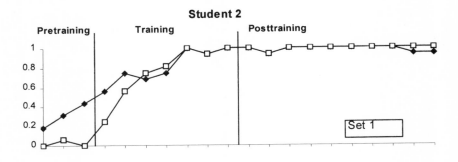

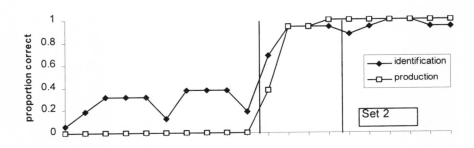

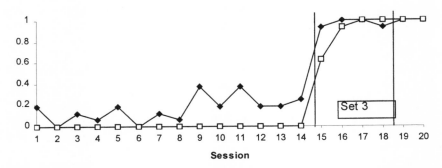

Figure 10-7. Proportion of correctly identified items (diamonds) and correctly produced items (squares) across the testing sessions for student 2. The training occurred between the two vertical bars. The figure illustrates that once training was implemented identification performance increased dramatically, and remained accurate without further training.

instruction, and the knowledge is retained at least a month after training is completed.

Development and Evaluation of a Speech Training Tutor

We have extended previous approaches to spoken language intervention for deaf children (e.g., Ling, 1976; Ling & Ling, 1978) by viewing speech learning as a multisensory experience (Massaro et al., 1999, Massaro, Cohen, Tabain, Beskow, & Clark, in press), and we have tested the idea that Baldi can function effectively as a language tutor to teach speech perception and production. Baldi has a tongue, hard palate, and three-dimensional teeth, and his internal articulatory movements have been trained with electropalatography and ultrasound data from natural speech (Cohen et al., 1998; Massaro et al., in press). Although previous approaches have used palatometry (Fletcher, Dagenais, & Critz-Crosby, 1991) and electropalatography (Hardcastle & Gibbon, 1997) as a form of visual feedback, Baldi can display a more representative view of the actual articulation. Baldi can demonstrate articulation by illustrating a midsagittal view, or the skin on the face can be made transparent to reveal the internal articulators, as shown in figure 10.8. In addition to simply showing the actual articulation, the area of contact between the tongue and palate and teeth can be highlighted.

The orientation of the face can be changed to display different viewpoints while speaking, such as a side view or a view from the back of the head (Massaro, 1998). As an example, a unique view of Baldi's internal articulators can be presented by rotating the exposed head and vocal tract to be oriented away from the student. It is possible that this back-of-head view would be much more conducive to learning language production. The tongue in this view moves away from and toward the student in the same way as the student's own tongue would move. This correspondence between views of the target and the student's articulators might facilitate speech production learning. One analogy is the way one might use a map. We often orient the map in the direction we are headed to make it easier to follow (e.g., turning right on the map is equivalent to turning right in reality).

Figure 10-8. Various views of Baldi that can be used in speech and language tutoring.

Baldi's auditory and visual speech can also be independently controlled and manipulated, permitting customized enhancements of the
informative characteristics of speech. These features offer novel approaches in language training, permitting Baldi to pedagogically illustrate appropriate articulations that are usually hidden by the face. Baldi
can be made even more informative by embellishing of the visible
speech with added features. Distinguishing phonemes that have similar
visible articulations, such as the difference between voiced and voiceless
segments, can be indicated by vibrating the neck. Nasal sounds can be
marked by making the nasal opening red, and turbulent airflow can be
characterized by lines emanating from the mouth during articulation.
These embellished speech cues could make the face more informative
than it normally is. Based on reading research, we expected that these
additional visible cues would heighten the child's awareness of the articulation of these segments and assist in the training process.

Children with hearing loss require guided instruction in speech
perception and production. Some of the distinctions in spoken language cannot be heard with degraded hearing—even when the hearing
loss has been compensated by hearing aids or cochlear implants. To test
whether the Baldi technology has the potential to help individuals with
hearing loss, Massaro and Light (2004b) carried out a speech training
study. Seven students (two male and five female) from the Jackson
Hearing Center and JLS Middle School in Los Altos, California, participated in the study. Table 10.3 gives a description of the children and
their hearing.

The students were trained to discriminate minimal pairs of words
bimodally (auditorily and visually) and were also trained to produce

Table 10.3: Individual and Average Unaided and Aided Auditory Thresholds (dB HL) for Four Frequencies for the Seven Students Studied in Massaro and Light (2004b)

Student No.	Aids	500 Hz	1000 Hz	2000 Hz	4000 Hz	Age (years)
1	Binaural	60/25	60/15	75/30	85/45	12
2	Binaural	6028	80/25	85/30	80/30	11
3	Binaural	85/50	90/55	85/55	80/55	8
4	Binaural	45/15	60/35	65/45	60/50	11
5	CI-I- left ear	95/40	110/25	115/25	105/35	13
6	Binaural	65/30	95/30	100/35	110/70	13
7	Right ear	65/30	55/35	65/40	70/60	8
Average		68/31	79/31	84/37	84/49	11

Unaided Aided Auditory Thresholds (dB HL)

CI, Cochlear implant.

Production Ratings as a function of Category Involved

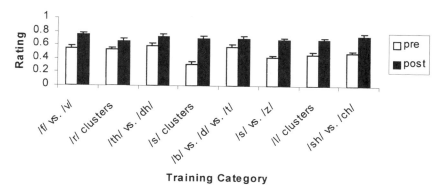

Figure 10-9. Intelligibility ratings of the pretest and posttest word productions (and standard error bars) for each of the eight training categories.

various speech segments by visual information about how the inside oral articulators work during speech production. The articulators were displayed from different vantage points so that the subtleties of articulation could be optimally visualized. The speech was also slowed down significantly to emphasize and elongate the target phonemes, allowing for clearer understanding of how the target segment is produced in isolation or with other segments. Each student completed eight training lessons of approximately 45 minutes for a total of 6 hours of training.

Figure 10.9 shows that the students' ability to accurately perceive and produce words involving the trained segments improved from pretest to posttest. Intelligibility ratings of the posttest productions were significantly higher than pretest productions, indicating significant learning. It is always possible that some of this learning occurred independently of our program or was simply based on routine practice. To test this possibility, we assessed the students' productions 6 weeks after training was completed. Although these productions were still rated as more intelligible than the pretest productions, they were significantly lower than posttest ratings, indicating some decrement due to lack of continued participation in the training program. This is evidence that at least some of the improvement must have been due to the program.

SUMMARY AND CONCLUSIONS

Perceivers expertly use multiple sources of information to identify and interpret the language input. Auditory and visual speech is seamlessly evaluated and integrated to facilitate understanding in face-to-face communication. This behavior is accurately described by a fuzzy logical model of perception (FLMP). Given the value of face-to-face interaction, our persistent goal has been to develop, evaluate, and apply animated agents to produce realistic and accurate speech. Baldi is an accurate three-dimensional animated talking head appropriately aligned with either synthesized or natural speech. Baldi has a tongue and palate, which can be displayed by making his skin transparent. Based on this research and technology, we have implemented computer-assisted speech and language tutors for hard-of-hearing and autistic children. Our language-training program utilizes Baldi as the conversational agent, who guides students through a variety of exercises designed to teach vocabulary and grammar, to improve speech articulation, and to develop linguistic and phonological awareness. Some of the advantages of the Baldi pedagogy and technology include the popularity and effectiveness of computers and embodied conversational agents, the perpetual availability of the program, and individualized instruction. The science and technology of Baldi hold great promise in language learning, dialog, human–machine interaction, and education.

ACKNOWLEDGMENTS

This work was supported in part by grants from the National Science Foundation (CHALLENGE grant CDA-9726363 and grant BCS-9905176), a grant from the Public Health Service (PHS R01 DC00236), cooperative grants from the Intel Corporation and the University of California Digital Media Program (D97-04), and grants from the University of California, Santa Cruz.

REFERENCES

Anastasio, T. J., & Patton, P. E. (2004). Analysis and modeling of multisensory enhancement in the deep superior colliculus. In G. Calvert, C. Spence, & B. E. Stein (Eds.), *Handbook of multisensory processes* (265–283). Cambridge, MA: MIT Press.

Anderson, R. C., & Freebody, P. (1981). Vocabulary knowledge. In J. T. Guthrie (Ed.), *Comprehension and teaching: Research perspectives* (pp. 71–117). Newark, DE: International Reading Association.

Atkins, P. W. B., & Baddeley, A. D. (1998). Working memory and distributed vocabulary learning. *Applied Psycholinguistics, 19*, 537–552

Baddeley, A. D., Gathercole, S. E., & Papagno, C. (1998). The phonological loop as a language learning device, *Psychological Review, 105*, 1, 158–173.

Baer, D, M., Wolf, M. M., & Risley, T. R. (1968). Some current dimensions of applied behavior analysis. *Journal of Applied Behavior Analysis, 1*, 91–97.

Baker, S. K., Simmons, D. C., & Kameenui, E. J. (1995). *Vocabulary acquisition: Synthesis of the research*. Eugene, OR: National Center to Improve the Tools of Educators.

Barker, L. J. (2003). Computer-assisted vocabulary acquisition: The CSLU vocabulary tutor in oral-deaf education. *Journal of Deaf Studies and Deaf Education, 8*, 187–198.

Beck, I. L., McKeown, M. G., & Kucan, L. (2002). *Bringing words to life: Robust vocabulary instruction*. New York: Guilford Press.

Berninger, V. W., & Richards, T. L. (2002). *Brain literacy for educators and psychologists*. San Diego: Academic Press.

Bernstein, L. E., Demorest, M. E., Coulter, D. C., and O'Connell, M. P. (1991). Lipreading sentences with vibrotactile vocoders: Performance of normal-hearing and hearing-impaired subjects. *Journal of the Acoustical Society of America, 90*, 2971–2984.

Bernstein, L. E., Demorest, M. E., & Tucker, P. E. 2000. Speech perception without hearing. *Perception and Psychophysics, 62*, 233–252.

Bernstein, L. E., & Eberhardt, S. P. (1986). *Johns Hopkins lipreading corpus videodisk set*. Baltimore, MD: Johns Hopkins University.

Bosseler, A., & Massaro, D. W. (2003). Development and evaluation of a computer-animated tutor for vocabulary and language learning for children with autism. *Journal of Autism and Developmental Disorders, 33*, 653–672.

Breslaw, P. I., Griffiths, A. J., Wood, D. J., & Howarth, C. I. (1981). The referential communication skills of deaf children from different educational environments. *Journal of Child Psychology, 22*, 269–282.

Campbell, C. S., Schwarzer, G., & Massaro, D. W. (2001). Face perception: An information processing perspective. In M. J. Wenger & J. T. Townsend (Eds.), *Computational, geometric, and process perspectives on facial cognition: Contexts and challenges* (pp. 285–345). Mahwah, NJ: Lawrence Erlbaum.

Chun, D. M., & Plass, J. L. (1996). Effects of multimedia annotations on vocabulary acquisition. *Modern Language Journal, 80*, 183–198.

Cohen, M. M., & D. W. Massaro (1993). Modeling coarticulation in synthetic visual speech. Models and Techniques in Computer Animation. In D. Thalmann and N. Magnenat-Thalmann (Eds) *Models and techniques in computer animation* (pp. 141–155). Tokyo: Springer-Verlag.

Cohen, M. M., Beskow, J., & Massaro, D. W. (1998, December). *Recent developments in facial animation: An inside view*. Paper presented at Auditory Visual Speech Processing ''98, Sydney, Australia.

Cohen, M. M., Massaro, D. W., & Clark, R. (2002, October). Training a talking head. In *Proceedings of ICMI'02, IEEE Fourth International Conference on Multimodal Interfaces* (pp. 499–504). Piscataway, NJ: IEEE Computer Society.

Cosi, P., Cohen, M. M., & Massaro, D. W. (2002). Baldini: Baldi speaks Italian. In *Proceedings of 7th International Conference on Spoken Language Processing (ICSLP'02)* (pp. 2349–2352). Denver, CO.

Denes, P. B., & Pinson, E. N. (1963). *The speech chain. The physics and biology of spoken language*. New York: Bell Telephone Laboratories.

Druin, A., & Hendler, J. (Eds.). (2000). *Robots for kids: Exploring new technologies for learning*. San Francisco: Morgan Kaufmann.

Dubois, M., & Vial, I. (2000). Multimedia design: The effects of relating multimodal information. *Journal of Computer Assisted Learning, 16*, 157–165.

Erber, N. P. (1972). Auditory, visual, and auditory-visual recognition of consonants by children with normal and impaired hearing. *Journal of Speech and Hearing Research, 15*, 423–422.

Evans, J. J., Wilson, B. A., Schuri, U., Baddeley, A. D., Canavan, A., Laaksonen, R., et al. (2000). A comparison of "errorless" and "trial and error" learning methods for teaching individuals with acquired memory deficits. *Journal of the International Neuropsychological Society, 10,* 67–101.

Fletcher, S. G., Dagenais, P. A., & Critz-Crosby, P. (1991). Teaching consonants to profoundly hearing-impaired speakers using palatometry. *Journal of Speech and Hearing Research, 34,* 929–942.

Gee, J. P. (2003). *What video games have to teach us about learning and literacy.* New York: St. Martin's.

Gupta, P., & MacWhinney, B. (1997). Vocabulary acquisition and verbal short-term memory: Computation and neural bases. *Brain and Language, 59,* 267–333.

Hardcastle, W. J., & Gibbon, F. (1997). Electropalatography and its clinical applications. In M. J. Ball & C. Code (Eds.), *Instrumental clinical phonetics* (pp. 149–193). London: Whurr.

Heimann, M., Nelson, K., Tjus, T., & Gilberg, C. (1995). Increasing reading and communication skills in children with autism through an interactive multimedia computer program. *Journal of Autism and Developmental Disorders, 25,* 459–480.

Holt, J. A., Traxler, C. B., & Allen, T. E. (1997). *Interpreting the scores: A user's guide to the 9th Edition Stanford Achievement Test for educators of deaf and hard-of-hearing students.* Washington, DC: Gallaudet Research Institute.

Horner, R. D., & Baer, D. M. (1978). Multiple-probe technique: A variation of the multiple baseline. *Journal of Applied Behavior Analysis, 11,* 189–196.

Jesse, A., Vrignaud, N., & Massaro, D. W. (2000/01). The processing of information from multiple sources in simultaneous interpreting. *Interpreting, 5,* 95–115.

Kisor, H. (1990). *What's that pig outdoors? A memoir of deafness.* New York: Hill and Wang.

Lederman, S. J., & Klatzky, R. L. (2004). Multisensory texture perception. In G. Calvert, C. Spence, & B. E. Stein (Eds.), *Handbook of multisensory processes* (pp. 107–122). Cambridge, MA: MIT Press.

Lewkowicz, D. J., & Kraebel, K. S. (2004). The value of multisensory redundancy in the development of intersensory perception. In G. Calvert, C. Spence, & B. E. Stein (Eds.), *Handbook of multisensory processes* (pp. 655–678). Cambridge, MA: MIT Press.

Ling, D. (1976). *Speech and the hearing-impaired child: Theory and practice.* Washington, DC: Alexander Graham Bell Association for the Deaf.

Ling, D., & Ling, A. (1978). *Aural habilitation: The foundation of verbal learning in hearing-impaired children.* Washington, DC: Alexander Graham Bell Association for the Deaf, pp. 129–130, 211.

Marchman, V., & Bates, E. (1994). Continuity in lexical and morphological development: A test of the critical mass hypothesis. *Journal of Child Language, 21,* 339–366.

Massaro, D. W. (1984). Children's perception of visual and auditory speech. *Child Development, 55,* 1777–1788.

Massaro, D. W. (1987). *Speech perception by ear and eye: A paradigm for psychological inquiry.* Hillsdale, NJ: Erlbaum.

Massaro, D. W. (1988). Ambiguity in perception and experimentation. *Journal of Experimental Psychology: General, 117,* 417–421.

Massaro, D. W. (1989). Testing between the TRACE model and the fuzzy logical model of speech perception. *Cognitive Psychology, 21*, 398–421.

Massaro, D. W. (1998). *Perceiving talking faces: From speech perception to a behavioral principle.* Cambridge, MA: MIT Press.

Massaro, D. W. (2000, August). From "speech is special" to talking heads in language learning. In *Proceedings of Integrating Speech Technology in the (Language) Learning and Assistive Interface* (pp. 153–161).

Massaro, D. W. (2002). Multimodal speech perception: A paradigm for speech science. In B. Granstrom, D. House, & I. Karlsson (Eds.), *Multilmodality in language and speech systems* (pp. 45–71). Dordrecht: Kluwer.

Massaro, D. W. (2004). From multisensory integration to talking heads and language learning. In G. Calvert, C. Spence, & B. E. Stein (Eds.), *Handbook of multisensory processes* (pp. 153–176). Cambridge, MA: MIT Press.

Massaro, D. W., Beskow, J., Cohen M. M., Fry, C. L., & Rodriguez, T. (1999). Picture My Voice: Audio to Visual Speech Synthesis using Artificial Neural Networks. In *Proceedings of Auditory-Visual Speech Processing (AVSP'99)* (pp. 133–38). Santa Cruz, CA.

Massaro, D. W., & Bosseler, A. (2003). Perceiving speech by ear and eye: Multimodal integration by children with autism. *Journal of Developmental and Learning Disorders, 7*, 111–144.

Massaro, D. W., & Cohen, M. M. (1993). Perceiving asynchronous bimodal speech in consonant-vowel and vowel syllables. *Speech Communication, 13*, 127–134.

Massaro, D. W., & Cohen, M. M. (1999). Speech perception in hearing-impaired perceivers: Synergy of multiple modalities. *Journal of Speech, Language, and Hearing Science, 42*, 21–41.

Massaro, D. W., Cohen, M. M., Beskow, J., & Cole, R. A. (2000). Developing and evaluating conversational agents. In J. Cassell, J. Sullivan, S. Prevost, & E. Churchill (Eds.), *Embodied conversational agents* (pp. 286–318). Cambridge, MA: MIT Press.

Massaro, D. W., Cohen, M. M., Campbell, C. S., & Rodriguez, T. (2001). Bayes factor of model selection validates FLMP. *Psychonomic Bulletin and Review, 8*, 1–17.

Massaro, D. W., Cohen, M. M., Tabain, M., Beskow, J., & Clark, R. (in press). Animated speech: Research progress and applications. In E. Vatiokis-Bateson, G. Bailly, & P. Perrier (Eds.), *Audiovisual speech processing.* Cambridge, MA: MIT Press.

Massaro, D. W., & Friedman, D. (1990). Models of integration given multiple sources of information. *Psychological Review, 97*(2), 225–252.

Massaro, D. W., & Light, J. (2003, August). *Read my tongue movements: Bimodal learning to perceive and produce non-native speech /r/ and /l/. Eurospeech 2003-Switzerland (Interspeech).* In Proceedings of the 8th European Conference on Speech Communication and Technology, (Eurospeech 2003/Interspeech 2003) (CD-Rom, 4 pages). Geneva, Switzerland.

Massaro, D. W., & Light, J. (2004a). Improving the vocabulary of children with hearing loss. *Volta Review, 104*(3), 141–173.

Massaro, D. W., & Light, J. (2004b). Using visible speech for training perception and production of speech for hard of hearing individuals. *Journal of Speech, Language, and Hearing Research, 47*(2), 304–320.

Massaro, D. W., & Stork, D. G. (1998). Sensory integration and speechreading by humans and machines. *American Scientist, 86,* 236–244.

Massaro, D. W., Weldon, M. S., & Kitzis, S. N. (1991). Integration of orthographic and semantic information in memory retrieval. *Journal of Experimental Psychology: Learning, Memory, and Cognition, 17,* 277–287.

McGregor, K. K., Friedman, R. M., Reilly, R. M., & Newman, R. M. (2002). Semantic representation and naming in young children. *Journal of Speech, Language, and Hearing Research, 45,* 332–346.

McKeown, M., Beck, I., Omanson, R., & Pople, M. (1985). Some effects of the nature and frequency of vocabulary instruction on the knowledge and use of words. *Reading Research Quarterly, 20,* 522–535.

Meredith, M. A. (2004). The neural mechanisms underlying the integration of cross-modal cues: Single neurons, event-related potentials and models. In G. Calvert, C. Spence, & B. E. Stein (Eds.), *Handbook of multisensory processes* (pp. 343–355). Cambridge, MA: MIT Press.

Moore, M., & Calvert, S. (2000). Vocabulary acquisition for children with autism: Teacher or computer instruction. *Journal of Autism and Developmental Disorders, 30,* 359–362.

Munhall, K., & Vatikiotis-Bateson, E. (2004). Spatial and temporal constraints on audiovisual speech perception. In G. Calvert, C. Spence, & B. E. Stein (Eds.), *Handbook of multisensory processes* (pp. 177–188). Cambridge, MA: MIT Press.

Ouni, S. Massaro, D. W., Cohen, M. M., Young, K., & Jeese, A. (2003). Internationalization of a Talking Head. In *Proceedings of the 15th International Congress of Phonetic Sciences (ICPhS'03).* Universitat Autonoma de Barcelona, Barcelona, Spain.

Pany, D., & Jenkins, J. R. (1978). Learning word meanings: A comparison of instructional procedures and effects on measures of reading comprehension with learning disabled students. *Learning Disability Quarterly, 1,* 21–32.

Pashler, H. E. (1998). *The psychology of attention.* Cambridge, MA: MIT Press.

Qian, D. D. (2002). Investigating the relationship between vocabulary knowledge and academic reading performance: An assessment perspective. *Language Learning, 52,* 513–536.

Smeele, P. M. T., Massaro, D. W., Cohen, M. M., & Sittig, A. C. (1998). Laterality in visual speech perception. *Journal of Experimental Psychology: Human Perception and Performance, 24,* 1232–1242.

Stahl, S. (1983). Differential word knowledge and reading comprehension. *Journal of Reading Behavior, 15*(4), 33–50.

Stanovich, K. E. (1986). Matthew effects in reading: Some consequences of individual differences in the acquisition of literacy. *Reading Research Quarterly, 21,* 360–406.

Stein, B. E., & Meredith, M. A. (1993). *The merging of the senses.* Cambridge, MA: MIT Press.

Stein, B. E., Jiang, W., & Stanford, T. R. (2004). Multisensory integration in single neurons of the midbrain. In G. Calvert, C. Spence, & B. E. Stein (Eds.), *Handbook of multisensory processes* (pp. 243–264). Cambridge, MA: MIT Press.

Summerfield, Q. (1987). Some preliminaries to a comprehensive account of A/ V speech perception. In B. Dodd & R. Campbell (Eds.), *Hearing by eye: The psychology of lipreading* (pp. 3–51). Hillsdale, NJ: Lawrence Erlbaum.

Tager-Flusberg, H. (2000). Language development in children with autism. In L. Menn & N. Bernstein Ratner (Eds.), *Methods for studying language production* (pp. 313–332). Mahwah, NJ: Erlbaum.

Vermeer, A. (2001). Breadth and depth of vocabulary in relation to L1/L2 acquisition and frequency of input. *Applied Psycholinguistics, 22,* 217–234.

Waldstein, R. S., & Boothroyd, A. (1995). Speechreading supplemented by single-channel and multi-channel tactile displays of voice fundamental frequency. *Journal of Speech and Hearing Research, 38,* 690–705.

Waxman, S. R. (2002). Early word-learning and conceptual development: Everything had a name, and each name gave birth to a new thought. In U. Goswami (Ed.), *Handbook of childhood cognitive development* (pp. 102–126). Malden, MA: Blackwell Publishing.

Williams, J. H. G., Massaro, D. W., Peel, N. J., Bosseler, A., & Suddendorf, T. (2004). *Visual-auditory integration during speech imitation in autism. Research in developmental disabilities 25,* 559–575.

Wood, J. (2001). Can software support children's vocabulary development? *Language Learning and Technology, 5,* 166–201.

Zadeh, L. A. (1965). Fuzzy sets. *Information and Control, 8,* 338–353.

11

Spoken Language in Children
With Cochlear Implants

Ann E. Geers

Children with prelingual profound hearing loss who receive oral training and conventional amplification develop spoken language, on average, at about half of the rate of hearing children (Blamey et al., 2001;
Boothroyd, Geers, & Moog, 1991). They demonstrate average delays in
language development of 4–5 years by the time they enter high school
(Blamey et al., 2001; Geers & Moog, 1989). This language delay is not
reduced in children whose educational program includes manually
coded English (Geers & Moog, 1992; Geers, Moog, & Schick, 1984; Schick,
2003). The frequently reported low literacy levels among students with
severe to profound hearing impairment are, in part, due to the discrepancy between their incomplete spoken language system and the demands of reading a speech-based system (Perfetti & Sandak, 2000).
Cochlear implant technology is designed to provide the most critical
information contained in the auditory speech signal to permit improved
access to speech at an early age. This potential, together with appropriate
intervention, may provide a young deaf child with a better chance to
develop competence in spoken language. Language competence that is
closer to the level of hearing peers should be exhibited in phonology,
vocabulary, syntax, and discourse-level skills.

The advent of cochlear implant technology is a relatively recent
phenomenon. The first multichannel cochlear implant system provided
by Cochlear Corporation (the Nucleus-22 device) was introduced in
1984. There are currently three companies in the United States producing
cochlear implant systems approved by the U.S. Food and Drug Administration (FDA): Advanced Bionics Corporation, Cochlear Americas,

and MED-EL Corporation. All three manufacturers are continually implementing more sophisticated processing strategies and updating the hardware. As these enhancements take place, the devices have improved, children with greater amounts of residual hearing are being implanted, and the average age at implantation has decreased dramatically. In the United States, current FDA guidelines permit cochlear implantation in children as young as 12 months of age with profound deafness (i.e., PTA thresholds of 90 dB HL or greater). Children 2 years and older with severe deafness may also be considered for cochlear implantation (i.e., PTA threshold of 70 dB HL or greater).

The currently available cochlear implant systems share many common characteristics. They all require surgery to place the stimulating electrode array inside the cochlea and a magnet under the skin to maintain contact between the externally worn hardware and the implanted electronic components. They all employ an external speech processor that is designed for multichannel stimulation and requires individual programming for each user. They are similar in cost. Regarding children's performance after implantation, no significant difference between manufacturers has been established, and overall performance varies tremendously, even among users of the same device. Possible reasons for poor performance include later age at device fitting, poor nerve survival, inadequate device fitting, insufficient cognitive skills, poor motivation, educational and social environments emphasizing manual communication, and limited parental support (ASHA, 2003; Geers, 2002). These factors also contribute to poor performance in children who use hearing aids (Geers & Moog, 1989, 1992).

SENSORY AIDS AND SPOKEN LANGUAGE DEVELOPMENT

A variety of sensory aids (e.g., hearing aids, tactile aids, cochlear implants) have been used to provide children with hearing impairment a means of accessing auditory feedback regarding their own speech production and some degree of auditory perception of the speech of others. The best-documented effect of cochlear implantation on profoundly deaf children is a marked increase in their aided speech perception ability (Kirk, 2000). Many children who previously discriminated only among time–intensity patterns and large spectral differences in vowels using hearing aids are able to discriminate among small spectral differences including manner, place, and voicing cues for consonant identification using cochlear implants (Boothroyd & Eran, 1994). Higher levels of speech perception are associated with better language skills, resulting in children who obtain greater auditory speech perception benefit from their implant achieving more normal language levels than children who have poor speech perception after implantation (Crosson & Geers, 2001; Svirsky, Robbins, Kirk, Pisoni, &

Miyamoto, 2000; Tyler, Tomblin, Spencer, Kelsay, & Fryauf-Bertchy, 2000).

Because hearing aids and tactile aids are relatively noninvasive and inexpensive compared with the surgical insertion and cost of a cochlear implant, choosing implantation over other sensory aids requires justification. The choice of a cochlear implant is often associated with the choice of spoken language as the primary communication mode of the deaf child and family (ASHA, 2003). Therefore, the extent to which children who use implants achieve more intelligible speech and age-appropriate spoken language competence compared to children who use conventional hearing aids is an important consideration in evaluating the effectiveness of this device. However, as cochlear implants have become an increasingly common treatment for young children with profound hearing loss, fewer comparable hearing aid users are available for controlled studies. Such comparisons are important because speech and language growth may be expected to result from maturation and training as well as from implant use, and within-subject designs do not permit researchers to separate these effects.

Most device comparison studies have matched the hearing aid and cochlear implant groups for age and hearing loss but have not followed both groups of participants over a similar time period and have not controlled for other factors that could differentially affect performance in the two groups. One study that observed these controls compared language growth over time in children with different sensory aids in the same educational environment (Geers & Moog, 1994a). Three groups of 13 children were matched at the beginning of the study for age (2–12 years), unaided PTA thresholds (>100 dB HL), performance IQ (>90), language level, and phoneme production. All groups were followed over 36 months of auditory-oral instruction in the same intensive educational setting. One group continued using conventional hearing aids only (HA group), one group began using a tactile aid in addition to hearing aids (TA group), and the other group received cochlear implants and discontinued hearing aid use (CI group). Significant average improvement over time was observed for all three sensory aid groups on measures, of spoken receptive and expressive syntax and vocabulary (Geers & Moog, 1994b), and of measures of imitated and spontaneous phoneme production (Tobey, Geers, & Brenner, 1994). At the end of 36 months, test scores of implant users exceeded those of hearing aid and tactile aid users on all speech and language measures, and the differences reached statistical significance on measures of receptive syntax, expressive vocabulary, and production of intelligible vowels and consonants in spontaneous speech. In other areas, including expressive syntax and receptive vocabulary, there were no significant differences between groups, even at the end of 36 months of device use.

Figure 11.1 displays age-equivalent scores for growth in average vocabulary over 36 months of sensory aid use in relation to hearing children. Expressive vocabulary scores were based on spoken responses to the Expressive One-Word Picture Vocabulary Test (Gardner, 1979), and receptive vocabulary scores were based on comprehension of spoken words on the Peabody Picture Vocabulary Test (Dunn & Dunn, 1981). Vocabulary scores of the three sensory aid groups were indistinguishable at the beginning of the study. Children in all three sensory aid groups exhibited significant vocabulary growth over time. The fastest growth rate was observed in expressive vocabulary scores of the CI group, which was the same as that observed in hearing children (slope of 1.1). Much slower progress was observed in receptive vocabulary, where the CI group exhibited growth at just over half the rate of hearing children (0.58). At the end of the study, the CI group exhibited a significant advantage over the other sensory aid groups in expressive but not receptive vocabulary scores. Results for all three groups at the end of the study were compared to a group of age-matched children with more residual hearing (i.e., PTA thresholds of

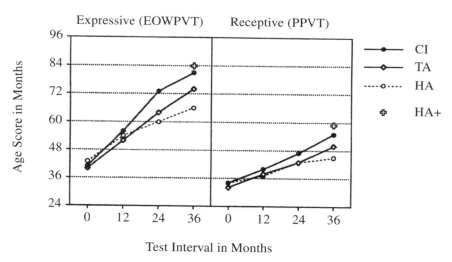

Figure 11-1. Vocabulary age scores on the Peabody Picture Vocabulary Test (PPVT; receptive) and the Expressive One-Word Picture Vocabulary Test (EOWPVT; expressive) obtained by matched groups of 13 children with cochlear implants (CI), tactile aids (TA), and hearing aids (HA) shown as a function of test interval in months. Children using hearing aids with PTA threshold between 90 and 100 dB HL (HA+) were tested only at the 36-month interval (Geers & Moog, 1994b). Figure reprinted with permission from the Alexander Graham Bell Association for the Deaf and Hard of Hearing. www.agbell.org.

90–100 dB HL) who had used hearing aids since age 3 years or younger
(HA+). These less profoundly deaf hearing aid users with slightly
lower PTA thresholds exhibited the highest average scores on all language measures, although they did not significantly exceed scores of
children with cochlear implants. It is possible that the CI group would
exhibit higher speech and language levels once they achieved a similar
duration of device use. In another study, the average language score of
children using more recent versions of the same cochlear implant device for 4 or more years was found to match that of hearing aid users
with a PTA threshold of 78 dB HL (Blamey et al., 2001).

Testing comparable groups of cochlear implant and hearing aid users
over the same time period has become increasingly difficult, because
the small number of available profoundly deaf hearing aid users who do
not elect to receive a cochlear implant may not have the same motivation for spoken language development and may not be enrolled in
programs emphasizing speech and auditory skills. One alternative has
been to compare data after implantation with data obtained from age-
matched cochlear implant candidates when they used hearing aids
(Miyamoto, Svirsky, & Robbins, 1997; Svirsky et al., 2000; Tomblin,
Spencer, Flock, Tyler, & Gantz, 1999). In these studies, the rate at which
scores on comprehensive language tests changed with age in children
with implants significantly exceeded that of age-matched, nonimplanted
children. While children without cochlear implants showed relatively
little change in language scores with increasing age, one of the best
predictors of language outcome in the cochlear implant group was length
of experience with the device.

Another approach has been to compare the language growth of cochlear implant users to the growth rate expected based on their preimplantation language quotients, a score derived by dividing a child's
language age by his or her chronological age. Language quotients provide an estimate of the size of the gap between these ages, which has
been found to widen over time in children with profound hearing loss.
In order to close the gap, the child must actually learn at a rate faster than
that of hearing children (Robbins, 2000). One study (Robbins, Kirk,
Osberger, & Ertmer, 1995) compared predicted language quotients with
language quotient scores obtained after 6 and 15 months of cochlear
implant use. Both receptive and expressive language quotients were
found to exceed the predicted quotient scores, and the advantage appeared to increase with duration of implant use. Language age scores
obtained at 15 months after implantation were 10 months higher for
receptive and 8 months higher for expressive language than would have
been predicted by preimplantation quotient scores.

Still another approach has been to compare results for implanted
children with data collected over the past few decades from profoundly
deaf children who used hearing aids before cochlear implants were

available. Using videotapes collected from good and poor hearing aid users in the 1980s, a British study compared preverbal communication strategies with a current group of age-matched cochlear implant users. Results indicated that children with implants exhibited vocal/auditory communication similar to that of proficient hearing aid users rather than the visual/gestural style that characterized poor hearing aid users (Tait & Lutman, 1994).

A literature review comparing results from a large sample of children with cochlear implants with scores on similar measures obtained over the past 30 years from groups of profoundly deaf children who used hearing aids revealed the following trends: (1) improved auditory speech perception ability, (2) a stronger relation between auditory speech perception ability and oral communication, (3) a closer approximation to the language of hearing agemates, (4) increased use of speech by children in total communication programs, and (5) accelerated acquisition of reading (Geers, 2004a).

There is a general trend across a variety of types of studies in the direction of improved auditory, speech, and language performance in children with profound hearing loss who receive cochlear implants. While results are still not clear regarding the degree of hearing loss above which children receive more benefit from a cochlear implant than a hearing aid, a conservative estimate is a PTA threshold between 90 and 100 dB HL.

ASSESSMENT OF SPOKEN LANGUAGE IN CHILDREN WITH COCHLEAR IMPLANTS

Studies that document language development in children with cochlear implants often employ measures originally developed for, and standardized on, children with normal hearing. These measures may not have the same validity when applied to deaf children. All spoken language measures require speech perception, speech production, or both. Spoken language, speech perception, and speech production are interdependent, and results must be interpreted in the light of potential interactions of these processes (Blamey, 2003). When receptive spoken language measures are applied to deaf children, the scores reflect speech perception ability in addition to the lexical and syntactic knowledge represented in the normative sample of hearing participants. Expressive spoken language measures assume that a child's speech intelligibility is commensurate with his or her language ability. To the extent that a deaf child's speech perception and production skills interfere with spoken language assessment, the scores on these tests underestimate the language age equivalent as measured in the normative sample. For example, a substantial difference is often observed between expressive and receptive spoken vocabulary test scores of children with severe to profound hearing impairment, as illustrated by the results previously reported in figure 11.1. It is not clear which of these scores most accurately represents the deaf child's vocabulary knowledge in relation to the hearing child with unimpaired speech perception and production abilities.

In order to minimize the impact of speech perception and production on language assessment after cochlear implantation, sign language has been added in the administration of tests to children from total communication educational settings (Connor, Hieber, Arts, & Zwolan, 2000; Kirk et al., 2002b; Robbins, Bollard, & Green, 1999; Svirsky et al., 2000; Tomblin et al., 1999). Adding signs results in changes in administration and scoring that deviate substantially from those procedures used in the test's standardization. Adapting the scoring procedure to accept a signed equivalent ideally should include specifying an agreed-upon sign for each item and establishing the developmental equivalence of the signed and the spoken items. Instead, accepted sign equivalents are determined by individual clinicians or test sites and may vary considerably. Assigning age-equivalent scores to children who produce signed responses as if they were identical to the spoken responses of the normative sample may be misleading if developmental equivalence has not been determined. While spoken words are nonrepresentational, some signs are quite iconic in visually depicting the word or concept they represent (e.g., patting the top of the head to represent "hat"). To the extent that including the sign along with the spoken word reduces the average age at which hearing children would receive credit for an item, the resulting score overestimates the deaf child's true language age relative to this population. On the other hand, there are also items for which no sign is available and the word must be fingerspelled. This adaptation may increase the item difficulty relative to hearing children and thus underestimate the deaf child's language age.

Additional complications are introduced when "preferred communication mode" is employed when testing groups of children who vary in their use of spoken or signed English. In this case, children who use oral communication (OC) are tested using only spoken language and children from total communication (TC) programs are tested using both speech and sign. In a study that used spoken stimuli to measure receptive vocabulary in both OC and TC children, there was no difference between scores of cochlear implant users who did or did not use sign language in their classrooms (Connor et al., 2000). However, when the same sample of children were tested on the expressive Picture Vocabulary subtest of the Woodcock Johnson Test of Cognitive Ability using their preferred communication mode, children who used sign language obtained significantly higher scores than did children who did not.

Some researchers argue that the most appropriate method to assess language skills in children who use TC is with signs in addition to speech and audition, just as the language of children who use OC is tested with both lipreading and audition. The rationale is that these are the communication modes the children are exposed to in everyday situations and therefore best reflect their overall language abilities (Robbins et al., 1999). Other researchers contend that the benefit of a cochlear implant is best reflected in the child's ability to communicate using speech with the world at large in which sign language is not generally known (Svirsky et al., 2000). Another approach has been to administer language tests to all children using simultaneous speech and signed English, regardless of the child's typical mode of communication. In this way, any advantages that may accrue to children due to the iconicity of some signs are available to all children being tested (Geers, Nicholas, & Sedey, 2003).

Regardless of the communication mode used, age-equivalent scores based on hearing norms may not have the same meaning when applied to children with hearing loss. Furthermore, tests administered in speech and sign measure something different from tests administered in a speech-only mode. Researchers need to be clear about which they are assessing and draw their conclusions accordingly.

TECHNOLOGY AND OUTCOMES AFTER IMPLANTATION

The rate of development of children's auditory skills following implantation seems to be increasing as cochlear implant technology improves and as children are implanted at younger ages (Allum, Greisiger, Straubhaar, & Carpenter, 2000; Osberger, Fisher, & Kalberer, 2000). For example, since the Nucleus 22-channel cochlear implant was first introduced, a series of stimulation strategies have evolved. The Wearable Speech Processor (WSP) encoded the fundamental frequency and the amplitude of the first two formant frequencies, the acoustic features most highly correlated with perception and discrimination of vowels. The Mini Speech Processor added the estimated amplitudes in three additional frequency bands encompassing the range from 2.0 to 6.0 kHz and was assumed to carry more consonant information than the WSP. In 1994, a processing scheme known as the SPEAK strategy was introduced. This speech processing strategy filters the incoming speech signal into a maximum of 20 channels depending on the number of available electrodes. The amplitude outputs of each channel are scanned, and the algorithm selects a subset of channels that have the highest amplitudes for stimulation during each cycle. The number of children achieving open-set speech perception increased with implementation of each new technology, and their ability to perceive speech in noise also improved (Geers, Brenner, & Davidson, 1999). Higher speech perception scores were associated with children whose processors were switched to the new technology early and implemented for a longer period of time (Geers, Brenner, & Davidson, 2003).

Programming of the speech processor of a cochlear implant typically requires establishing a threshold and a maximum stimulation level for each of the individual intracochlear electrodes. This process results in a unique program, or "map," for each cochlear implant user. Characteristics of the implant map associated with higher speech perception scores include a greater number of active electrodes in the map, a wide dynamic range between threshold and comfort level, and a large, consistent growth of perceived loudness with increasing intensity of the signal (Davidson, Brenner, & Geers, 2000). These results suggest that the skill of the audiologist in setting and adjusting the map of a cochlear implant plays an important role in the child's ability to benefit from the auditory stimulation provided.

In addition to contributing to speech perception outcome, implant characteristics also accounted for substantial variance in speech production (Tobey, Geers, Brenner, Altuna, & Gabbert, 2003) and language (Geers, Nicholas, & Sedey, 2003) outcomes. Children with even newer technology implemented on the Nucleus 24M, Clarion, or Med-El devices were reported to achieve higher speech and language scores, on average, than children using the Nucleus-22 (Connor et al., 2000). Speech perception and speech production changes have also been documented with the new Advanced Combination Encoder strategy, which uses a higher stimulation rate compared with the early SPEAK strategy (Psarros et al., 2002). This result suggests that the full impact of cochlear implants on speech and language development may only be evident in children who have continuous use of the newest generations of implant technology.

AGE AT IMPLANTATION AND OUTCOMES AFTER IMPLANTATION

Age at implantation also may play a critical role in outcome levels achieved (Cheng, Grant, & Niparko, 1999). The critical age dividing better and poorer outcomes after implantation has been variously reported at 10 years (Osberger, Maso, & Sam, 1993), at 6 years (Papsin, Gysin, Ptcton, Nedzelski, & Harrison, 2000), at 5 years (Fryauf-Bertschy, Tyler, Kelsay, Gantz, & Woodworth, 1997; Tye-Murray, Spencer, & Gilbert-Bedia, 1995), at 4 years (Bergeson, Pisoni, & Davis, 2003; Moog & Geers, 1999), at 3 years (Iler-Kirk et al., 2002; Kirk, 2000; Kirk et al., 2002a, 2002b; Miyamoto, Kirk, Svirsky, & Sehgal, 1999), at 2 years (Kirk, Miyamoto, Ying, Perdew, & Zuganelis, 2003; Osberger, Zimmerman-Phillips, & Koch, 2002; Svirsky, Teoh, & Neuburger, 2004), at 18 months (Hammes et al., 2002), and at 12 months (Houston, Ying, Pisoni, & Kirk, 2003). However, a large cross-sectional study of 8- and 9-year-olds who were implanted at 2, 3, or 4 years of age showed no effect of age at implantation on speech perception (Geers, Brenner, & Davidson, 2003), speech production (Tobey et al., 2003), language (Geers, Nicholas, & Sedey, 2003), or reading (Geers, 2003) when other contributing factors (e.g., performance IQ, family socioeconomic status, gender, implant characteristics) were held constant. While age at receiving an implant did not play a significant role in performance when the outcomes were measured after 4–6 years of cochlear implant use, possible speech and language advantages for early implantation that may have existed when these children were younger were not examined in this study.

In a further analysis of age-at-implantation effects in this sample, a subgroup of 133 children with congenital hearing losses was analyzed separately from the 48 children who lost their hearing between birth and 35 months of age (Geers, 2004b). Although correlations between age at implantation and individual outcome measures remained insignificant in the congenital hearing loss subsample, an advantage for early implantation was apparent when speech and language outcomes were considered together. Forty-three percent of the children implanted at 2 years of age achieved both speech intelligibility and language skills commensurate with their hearing agemates compared to only 16% of those implanted at 4 years of age. When combined speech and language skills were examined for the adventitiously deafened children, 80% of those implanted within a year of onset of deafness achieved normal levels on both speech and language measures, compared to only 36% of those implanted after being deaf for 2–3 years. Therefore, if the desired result after 4 years of cochlear implant use is for both speech and language levels to fall within the range of hearing agemates, the advantage appears to lie with those children who have a shorter duration of deafness, whether congenital or acquired.

THE "MOVING TARGET" PHENOMENON

Cochlear implants have generated greater interest than ever in research on the development of speech and language skills in deaf children. However, because prelingual profound hearing loss is a relatively rare occurrence, and because children receiving cochlear implants are even rarer, accumulating a sufficient number of participants to conduct generalizable research is difficult. Large-sample studies invariably assemble data collected over a number of years on patients who received implants over a wide time frame. Most studies reported to date comparing cochlear implant with hearing aid users have included participants fitted with multiple generations of cochlear implant technology and implanted at relatively late ages by current standards (i.e., 5 years or later). As cochlear implant devices continue to improve, the criteria regarding degree of hearing loss and performance with a hearing aid that warrants consideration of a cochlear implant also continue to evolve. Children implanted during the first decade of cochlear implant availability were those exhibiting no observable benefit from hearing aids. Now, children are being implanted who achieve up to 30% open-set word recognition scores with hearing aids. The impact of each of these changes is difficult to determine, because they are occurring simultaneously. However, results reported for participant populations that span several years in date of implantation must be interpreted in view of this "moving target."

Most studies have reported average language levels and communication skills after implantation that are delayed in relation to hearing agemates (Bollard, Chute, Popp, & Parisier, 1999; Dawson, Blamey, Dettman, Barker, & Clark, 1995; Geers & Moog, 1994b; Geers, Nicholas, & Sedey, 2003; Miyamoto et al., 1999; Spencer, Barker, & Tomblin, 2003; Tomblin et al., 1999; Tomblin, Spencer, & Gantz, 2000; Tye-Murray, 2003). There are at least two reasons for the observed lags in development, both of which are undergoing change. First, the auditory information provided by the implant may have been insufficient for most children to achieve normal spoken language development. Although open-set speech perception scores after implantation have averaged 50% or higher (Geers, Brenner, & Davidson, 2003), such scores still reflect substantial hearing impairment. Furthermore, even when young cochlear implant users demonstrated detection of differences in speech sounds, they exhibited less sustained attention to speech compared to hearing infants (Houston, Pisoni, Kirk, Ying, & Miyamoto, 2003). The extent to which speech perception will be affected by changes in implant technology is unknown, but so far speech perception scores have continued to improve.

Second, the period of profound deafness before a child received an implant may have made speech so inaccessible that a critical period for spoken language development was lost. Two developments may have an impact on this source of language delay: implanting younger children and implanting those children with more residual hearing. As more children with residual hearing undergo implantation, their early auditory exposure through hearing aids may serve to bridge this critical period and result in better outcomes (Osberger et al., 2002; Szagun, 2001). In addition, there is evidence that once prelingually deaf children receive cochlear implants, their characteristically slow rate of language development accelerates and they start developing language at a near-normal rate. The developmental gap between deaf and hearing agemates, which typically increases with age, remains about the same size (measured in units of language age) following cochlear implantation. If this pattern is maintained, congenitally deaf children may exhibit only a negligible delay if they receive an implant early enough in life (Svirsky et al., 2004).

It will be important to determine the independent contribution of each of these factors and alter expectations for language achievement as these factors change. The importance of changes in technology and candidacy requirements suggests that research reports to date regarding the levels achieved by children with cochlear implants may already be obsolete. As new research studies focus exclusively on children implanted in infancy, before language delays are evident, and on children who have received the newest electrode arrays and coding strategies, even higher performance may become typical. For example, a recent study examined preword learning behaviors in a group of infants who had all been implanted by 25 months of age with the newest technology available (Houston, Ying et al., 2003). The study demonstrated that children who received cochlear implants between 7 and 15 months of age demonstrated the ability to learn associations between auditory and visual stimuli in a manner similar to hearing infants, while children implanted later (16–25 months) did not. While it is not yet known whether infants' ability to learn arbitrary relations is predictive of later word-learning and language skills, this study provides evidence that very early cochlear implantation with the newest technology available may facilitate the rapid mapping of speech sounds to visual events, a precursor of vocabulary development.

EDUCATIONAL FACTORS AND OUTCOMES
AFTER IMPLANTATION

Educational choices for families of deaf and hard-of-hearing children include decisions such as (a) mainstream versus special education class placement, (b) public versus private school programs, (c) communication mode emphasis on speech, sign, or both, and (d) amount and type of individual speech and language therapy to be provided. Placement decisions are changing with increased cochlear implant experience. More children from TC programs are undergoing cochlear implantation than was the case when these devices were first available (Osberger et al., 2002). Children with cochlear implants are moving from private to public school programs and from special education to mainstream classes with hearing children (Francis, Koch, Wyatt, & Niparko, 1999; Geers & Brenner, 2003). Research describing the effects of educational placement decisions on performance after implantation is relatively rare. In a recent study of 181 8- and 9-year-old early-implanted children from across North America, the impact of educational choices on speech perception, speech production, language, and reading outcomes was examined after removing variance associated with child, family, and implant characteristics. The one educational variable that was consistently related to implant benefit was the communication mode used in the child's classroom (Moog & Geers, 2003). The extent to which the child's educational program emphasized speech and audition accounted for significant variance in outcomes achieved, even after variance due to other education variables, including amount of individual therapy, school setting (public/private), and classroom type (mainstream/ special education) was removed. While greater mainstream placement following cochlear implantation was associated with increased speech intelligibility and reading skills, regardless of communication mode used, an emphasis on speech and auditory communication was associated with better outcomes after implantation in speech perception, speech production, and language.

COMMUNICATION MODE AND OUTCOMES
AFTER IMPLANTATION

Communication mode used in English-based classrooms is most often dichotomized into OC approaches and TC approaches. Proponents of OC approaches maintain that dependence on speech and audition for communication is critical for achieving maximum auditory benefit from any sensory aid. Constant use of auditory input to monitor speech production and to comprehend spoken language provides the concentrated practice that appears to be needed for optimum benefit from a cochlear implant. Because listening and lipreading reflect common underlying articulatory events, OC children may have more experience than TC children in focusing their attention on combined auditory and visual cues even before receiving a cochlear implant, facilitating speech perception after implantation (Bergeson et al., 2003). Types of OC approaches differ in their emphasis on the auditory and visual channels for the reception of spoken language (see Beattie, chapter 6 this volume). Methods of communication range from the cued speech approach, in which manual cues are used to complement lipreading, to the auditory-verbal approach in which lipreading is discouraged and the child is taught from an early age to make use of whatever auditory information is available through his or her sensory device to understand speech.

Proponents of the TC approach maintain that the child with severe to profound deafness benefits most when some form of sign language accompanies speech. The use of sign language allows for easier assimilation of language through the unimpaired visual modality. The child is then able to associate what he or she hears through the implant with signed representations of language in order to support spoken language development. It is argued that children who are exposed to both speech and sign language have a usable communication system whether or not the cochlear implant improves their speech perception. Learning sign can allow the children to integrate more easily into the Deaf community if they choose to do this later in life. In practice, TC programs range from those that rely heavily on signed input with less emphasis on speech and English syntax to those that emphasize speech, audition, and lipreading and maintain careful adherence to English syntax and morphology.

Another approach to educating deaf children, referred to as bilingual-bicultural, emphasizes the development of American Sign Language (ASL) and emersion in Deaf culture. Children are expected to acquire fluency in ASL before learning English through literacy and/or English-based sign language. The development of an exclusively visual language system does not capitalize on the auditory speech perception skills provided by the cochlear implant. Most parents who choose a cochlear implant for their child report that the primary reason for their choice is to allow them to develop spoken language (Kluwin & Stewart, 2000). Because most bilingual-bicultural approaches do not include this objective, few children enrolled in such settings have received cochlear implants.

Several studies have examined the association between communication mode used in the child's education and outcome after implantation. Children in OC settings are reported to exhibit a marked advantage over children in TC settings in the amount of speech perception benefit they receive from a cochlear implant (Bergeson et al., 2003; Geers, Brenner, & Davidson, 2003; Kirk et al., 2003; Osberger et al., 2002). There is also ample evidence that children with cochlear implants enrolled in OC programs demonstrate better speech production skills than those from TC settings (Archbold et al., 2000; Connor et al., 2000; Miyamoto et al., 1999; Tobey et al., 2000, 2003; Tobey, Rekart, & Geers, 2004; Uchanski & Geers, 2003). Results for language improvement after implantation are less clear. Some language outcome studies of OC and TC users are case studies with too few participants to make generalizations regarding communication mode effects (Coerts & Mills, 1995; Hasenstab & Tobey, 1991). Some group comparison studies report no difference between language outcomes of children with cochlear implants enrolled in OC or TC settings (Connor et al., 2000; Kirk et al., 2003; Miyamoto et al., 1997; Robbins et al., 1999; Robbins, Svirsky, & Kirk, 1997; Svirsky et al., 2004; Tomblin et al., 1999, 2000). Other group comparison studies report better language outcomes for children enrolled in OC settings compared to those in TC classrooms (Cullington, Hodges, Butts, Dolan-Ash, & Balkany, 2000; Geers, Nicholas, & Sedey, 2003; Miyamoto et al., 1999; Svirsky et al., 2000). One possible explanation for discrepant language findings may be that while speech perception and speech production measures used identical stimulus/response demands for all children, language measures were sometimes administered in a speech-only mode and sometimes were adapted to accommodate the child's preferred modality. The speech production advantage of children in OC settings may be associated with a spoken language advantage as well.

Studies Supporting a TC Approach

Some studies suggest that use of signed English with children who use cochlear implants may result in improved spoken language competence. A case-study report examined spontaneous language samples from six children deafened at 2 or 3 years of age and implanted between 4 and 6 years of age (Coerts & Mills, 1995). Four of the children were educated in predominately OC environments, while two of them were enrolled in TC programs. All six children showed development in the morphology-syntax of their spoken language during 18 months after implantation. The two TC children who became deaf at age 2 outperformed the two OC children with similar age at onset but did not score better than the OC children deafened at age 3. The authors concluded that children who became deaf early appeared to profit most from a language environment in which signs were used. Although results based on six children cannot be considered conclusive, another study (Connor et al., 2000) used hierarchical linear modeling to analyze the trajectory of outcome growth curves of 147 children on speech and vocabulary measures. By comparing all data assembled over a number of years from children of various ages (1–10 years) and durations of implant use (6 months to 10 years), expected growth curves were constructed to compare scores of children enrolled in OC and TC classrooms. Speech production and receptive vocabulary were measured using only spoken language, while expressive vocabulary was measured using preferred communication mode. While the overall estimated growth functions did not differ between the two communication mode groups, TC children who received their implant during preschool exhibited greater expected vocabulary scores over time than did children from OC classrooms.

There is a trend toward greater acceptance of cochlear implants by families and educators who use TC (Osberger et al., 2002). The advantages of cochlear implants over hearing aids for increasing language competence in children enrolled in TC settings have been demonstrated in a number of studies (Miyamoto et al., 1997; Tomblin et al., 1999, 2000). However, because the language measures used in these studies were administered in TC and did not separate use of spoken and signed language, it is not possible to determine to what extent use of a cochlear implant affected the use of spoken language specifically. Implanted children from TC settings have been reported to use voice and sign together and to rarely use voice only or sign only during a story retell task (Tye-Murray, Spencer, & Woodworth, 1995). In a study comparing the use of inflectional endings by TC children with cochlear implants and those with hearing aids, it was found that the implant wearers not only used significantly more inflections but also tended to do so using a speech-only mode (Spencer, Tye-Murray, & Woodworth,

1998). A study of 27 children 8 and 9 years old implanted by 5 years of age and enrolled in TC settings for at least 3 years after implantation revealed a wide range of mode preference, with some children using primarily speech, some primarily sign, and some using both modes to varying extents. The TC children who used primarily speech demonstrated better comprehension and use of English syntax and were more likely to be placed in mainstream educational settings than was the case for TC children who used little or no speech (Geers, Spehar, & Sedey, 2002).

Studies Supporting an OC Approach

Research reporting spoken language results for children enrolled in auditory-oral settings following cochlear implantation demonstrates not only significant language growth over time (Geers & Moog, 1994b) but also language levels that closely approximate those of hearing agemates (Moog, 2002; Moog et al., 1999). Even when language skills were evaluated using preferred communication mode, OC children were found to exhibit a rate of English language learning that was closer to expected levels than were children enrolled in TC settings (Kirk et al., 2002b; Svirsky, 2000).

In a carefully controlled study of outcomes after implantation, language data were collected from 181 children who were similar in age (8–9 years), age at onset of deafness (<3 years), duration of implant use (4–6 years), age at implantation (<5 years), family environment (hearing English-speaking parents), and device (Nucleus-22; Geers, Nicholas, & Sedey, 2003). The participants did not represent any single educational program or method, but rather came from the full range of educational settings available across the United States and Canada (89 from TC and 92 from OC classrooms). Expressive language was measured by eliciting two spontaneous language samples from all children, regardless of their preferred communication mode. One sample was elicited in a speech-only interview where only spoken utterances were transcribed, and the other sample was elicited in a speech and sign interview where both modes were transcribed. Children enrolled primarily in OC settings after implantation produced significantly longer utterances, more different words, more bound morphemes, and more complex syntax in both interview settings. In figure 11.2, individual scores on the Index of Productive Syntax (Scarborough, 1990) obtained from the spoken language sample are plotted against scores on the spoken and signed language sample. The expressive syntax scores were quite similar in the two language samples ($r = 0.87$), and including signs did not add to the syntactic complexity of the language used by TC children. Although children from OC settings obtained significantly higher average scores on the Index of Productive Syntax than did children from TC classrooms in both language samples, there was

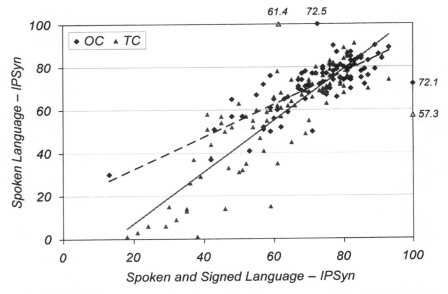

Figure 11-2. Index of Productive Syntax (IPSyn) scores are plotted for language samples collected from 180 children 8 and 9 years old who had received cochlear implants by 5 years of age. Scores obtained from transcriptions of spoken language samples are plotted against scores obtained from transcriptions of spoken and signed language samples. On the top and right axes, average scores of children from OC classrooms are plotted as diamonds, and those of children enrolled primarily in TC classrooms as triangles.

considerable overlap, particularly at the higher language levels (i.e., scores above 70). Children from TC classrooms who produced the most mature syntax did so using speech.

Conversational fluency was also affected by communication mode. Children from TC classrooms experienced communication breakdown in a spoken conversation more than twice as often (21%) as did children from OC classrooms (9%; Tye-Murray, 2003). The incidence of communication breakdown was most highly associated with speech intelligibility, which was significantly reduced in the TC sample (49%) compared to the OC sample (77%). Overall, the best educational predictor of language outcome was the amount of emphasis on speech and audition provided in the child's classroom before receiving a cochlear implant and during 4 years after cochlear implantation (Moog et al., 2003).

Possible Factors Underlying a Communication Mode Effect

Children who use TC may rely on the visual input they receive to support their language development, whereas OC children must rely more on auditory input. Studies reporting no differences in levels of language skills between TC and OC children when they are tested in their habitual modalities suggest that auditory and visual cues have been equalized for language learning purposes. That is, use of a cochlear implant has allowed the OC profoundly deaf child to acquire, through speech alone, language competence at least equivalent to that provided through the unimpaired visual modality through sign. Studies reporting better language in OC children after implantation (in either spoken or preferred communication mode) suggest that explicit instruction and concentrated practice in perceiving and producing speech actually accelerates language development. Perhaps dividing the child's attention between the talker's face, voice, and hands detracts from language acquisition (Bergeson et al., 2003).

Several studies have examined the processes thought to underlie the development of spoken language in children using different communication modalities. A subsample of the larger group of 8- and 9-year-olds (Geers, 2003) were administered a nonword repetition task to measure their phonologically based processing skills (Dillon, Burkholder, Cleary, & Pisoni, 2004). The children's ability to reproduce a novel nonword stimulus pattern was strongly correlated with communication mode, and children who used OC received significantly higher mean accuracy ratings than did children who used TC. The results were interpreted to indicate that OC methods provide children who use cochlear implants with a significant linguistic processing advantage and promote a closer coupling between speech perception and speech production (Dillon et al., 2004). Linguistic processing may also be facilitated by an increased short-term auditory memory that was documented in the OC sample (Pisoni & Cleary, 2003). The finding of shorter digit spans in children who had spent more time in TC classrooms was interpreted to suggest that less exposure to speech in the early linguistic environment after implantation may contribute to problems in both processing and rehearsing auditory information in short-term memory. This, in turn, may affect the development of automatic attention and speed with which speech signals can be rapidly identified and coded into phonological representations in short-term memory.

The Impact of Pre-existing Group Differences

The documented advantage of auditory-oral methods for spoken language development may be exaggerated if placement in OC or TC environments is not randomly determined. Children with auditory and articulation abilities that are slow to develop may be more likely to be placed in TC programs in order to learn manual methods of communication. Thus, the children who use TC may have had significantly poorer speech and language abilities even prior to implantation (Dillon et al., 2004; Svirsky, Chin, Miyamoto, Sloan, & Caldwell, 2003) and would exhibit slow spoken language development even in an OC setting. Children who exhibit good speech skill development in a TC environment may be moved into an OC class, and their classroom communication mode may be the result rather than the cause of improved speech intelligibility. Speech intelligibility scores of children who switched from TC to OC modes during the first 3 years following cochlear implantation were reported to be just as high as those who used OC exclusively throughout the period after implantation (Archbold et al., 2000). However, it is not clear from these data whether the speech skills of children who started out in TC were just as high when they switched to OC classrooms, or whether their speech skills caught up as a result of the OC instruction they received later.

Longitudinal studies may help to clarify the effect of communication mode on outcome after implantation. A longitudinal study of audiovisual speech perception in children from OC and TC environments found that there were some preimplantation differences between these groups. The OC children performed better than TC children in lipreading only and audiovisual speech perception prior to implantation. After 2 years of implant use, the TC children appeared to catch up with OC children in these areas (Bergeson et al., 2003). However, in the listening-only condition, where the groups did not differ before implantation, the OC group exhibited faster growth after implantation to significantly exceed performance of the TC group after 3 years. This result suggests that the TC children remained more visually oriented in their reception of speech, while the OC children relied more on auditory speech cues following cochlear implantation.

Differences between OC and TC groups in their spoken language proficiency may be more evident during elementary school than before, because by that age a number of years have elapsed during which a child's progress could be evaluated and poor speech users placed in TC classrooms. However, preschool placement decisions prior to cochlear implantation are more likely based on the philosophy of geographically available programs and parental preference, because a child's aptitude for speech development is not yet clear at very young ages (Geers & Moog, 1987). There is evidence that higher speech intelligibility levels achieved after 4–6 years of cochlear implant use are predicted not only by current use of OC but also by use of OC during preschool, before receiving a cochlear implant. Children enrolled in TC preschool programs prior to receiving a cochlear implant demonstrated speech intelligibility scores at 8 and 9 years of age that averaged 53%. Children enrolled in OC programs before implantation achieved substantially higher average intelligibility (70%) by 8 and 9 years of age (Tobey et al., 2004). The extent to which these children differed in their speech abilities before implantation is not known, but all of them were implanted when the candidacy requirements included no measurable benefit from hearing aids, so presumably neither group exhibited usable residual hearing before the surgery. Additional results suggest that children enrolled in OC settings from an early age were better able to use the new auditory information provided by the cochlear implant to hear and produce speech and spoken language than children who spent their preschool years in TC (Geers, 2004c).

SUMMARY AND CONCLUSIONS

The improved auditory experience provided by cochlear implants over hearing aids has facilitated the acquisition of spoken language in children with profound deafness from a wide range of educational settings, including both oral and total communication classrooms. For children who receive the implant early in their development (i.e., below 3 years of age), the average rate of language growth is very similar to that expected of hearing children (Kirk et al., 2002b). This accelerated growth of language appears to support more normal reading acquisition as well (Geers, 2003; Spencer et al., 2003; Tomblin et al., 2000; Watson, 2002). Future research is needed to confirm that reading growth continues at a normal rate through adolescence.

In general, children who receive cochlear implants by 5 years of age exhibit speech and language skills that far exceed those previously reported for profoundly deaf children. In a large nationwide sample, the majority scored 50% or better on open-set speech perception tests (Geers, Brenner, & Davidson, 2003) and had speech that was at least 75% intelligible to listeners who had no prior experience with deaf talkers (Tobey et al., 2003). Between 30% and 60% of the children achieved scores within the range of hearing agemates on various measures of receptive and expressive language (Geers, Nicholas, & Sedey, 2003), and more than half read at age level (Geers, 2003). The fact that not all children achieved these high levels of competence does not detract from the remarkable finding that such large proportions of children did so. A range of outcome levels is to be expected in any heterogeneous sample, whether or not the children use cochlear implants (Geers & Moog, 1989). The important finding here is that the proportion of children achieving high levels of speech and language competence has increased dramatically since the advent of cochlear implantation (Geers, 2004a). Spoken language acquisition appears to be facilitated by a shorter interval between onset of deafness and implantation, use of the most recent speech coding strategies and electrode designs, proper programming of the implant map, and an educational environment that focuses on the development of auditory and speech skills.

The characteristics of cochlear implants and the children who are candidates to receive them are evolving, and research studies are needed to update our knowledge of outcomes and predictors of success. New studies should document increases, if any, in the proportion of children reaching normal speech and language levels after receiving the newest speech processing strategies at very young ages, before they exhibit a spoken language delay. Better methods of assessing language skills at very young ages are needed that are appropriate for all deaf children, regardless of communication mode, but that maintain reference to development in hearing children. Cognitive underpinnings of auditory, speech, and language development should be explored and diagnostic instruments developed to quantify these factors at young ages.

Educational methods that contribute to better outcomes following cochlear implantation should be explored longitudinally. Group comparisons should control for relevant demographic differences and correct for differences in skill levels before implantation. Research in TC methodologies should seek to determine what factors lead to the successful spoken language outcomes that are evident in many children educated with both speech and sign. Some parents may continue to choose TC for their child following cochlear implantation in order to insure maximum language development if physical factors such as poor neural survival or central auditory processing problems interfere with good speech perception development. Research is needed to establish the balance of spoken and signed input (and whether they are delivered simultaneously or sequentially) that will ensure optimum development of spoken language.

The relative effectiveness of oral communication modes for speech and language development following cochlear implantation has resulted in increasing numbers of children enrolled in programs in which sign language is not provided. The lack of sign support for these children has not been associated with deficiencies in language (Geers, Nicholas, & Sedey, 2003), social adjustment (Nicholas & Geers, 2003), or reading (Geers, 2003). However, not all children develop age-appropriate spoken language. Research is needed to determine the proportion of children with implants exhibiting substantial delays in language development. Preimplantation factors that can be used for early identification of children who will have difficulty developing spoken language should be investigated, and remediation techniques developed where possible.

Regardless of communication mode used in the child's classroom, research should document when special education is needed, when the child can be most successful in the mainstream, and what support services will allow for maximum academic progress. The importance of early auditory stimulation for spoken language acquisition after cochlear implantation has been documented. Clinical research should examine methods to help parents provide this for their children. Proper fitting of cochlear implants also contributes to a child's success, and audiologists require greater experience with programming these devices for infants. New developments in cochlear implant technology and improved spoken language skills associated with early cochlear implantation may allow many individuals with prelingual profound deafness to participate more fully in a hearing society.

ACKNOWLEDGMENTS

I thank Marc Marschark, Johanna Nicholas, Allison Sedey, Pat Spencer, and Emily Tobey for reading, editing and commenting on versions of the manuscript. Figures were prepared by Christine Brenner.

REFERENCES

Allum, J. H., Greisiger, R., Straubhaar, S., & Carpenter, M. G. (2000). Auditory perception and speech identification in children with cochlear implants tested with the EARS protocol. *British Journal of Audiology, 34*, 293–303.

Archbold, S. M., Nikolopoulos, T. P., Tait, M., O'Donoghue, G. M., Lutman, M. E., & Gregory, S. (2000). Approach to communication, speech perception and intelligibility after paediatric cochlear implantation. *British Journal of Audiology, 34*, 257–264.

ASHA, (2003). Technical report: Cochlear implants. *American Speech-Language Hearing Association, 1*(Suppl. 24), 1–35.

Bergeson, T., Pisoni, D., & Davis, R. (2003). A longitudinal study of audiovisual speech perception by children with hearing loss who have cochlear implants. *Volta Review, 103*, 347–370.

Blamey, P. (2003). Development of spoken language by deaf children. In M. Marschark & P. E. Spencer (Eds.), *Deaf studies, language and education* (pp. 232–246). New York: Oxford University Press.

Blamey, P., Sarant, J. Z., Paatsch, L. E., Barry, J. G., Wales, C. P., Wright, M., et al. (2001). Relationships among speech perception, production, language, hearing loss and age in children with impaired hearing. *Journal of Speech, Language and Hearing Research, 44*, 264–285.

Bollard, P. M., Chute, P. M., Popp, A., & Parisier, S. C. (1999). Specific language growth in young children using the CLARION cochlear implant. *Annals of Otology, Rhinology, and Laryngology, 177*(Suppl.), 119–123.

Boothroyd, A., & Eran, O. (1994). Auditory speech perception capacity of child implant users expressed as equivalent hearing loss. *Volta Review, 96*, 151–169.

Boothroyd, A., Geers, A., & Moog, J. (1991). Practical implications of cochlear implants in children. *Ear and Hearing, 12*(Suppl.), 81–89.

Cheng, A. K., Grant, G. D., & Niparko, J. K. (1999). Meta-analysis of pediatric cochlear implant literature. *Annals of Otology, Rhinology, and Laryngology, 177*(Suppl.), 124–128.

Coerts, J., & Mills, A. (1995). Spontaneous language development of young deaf children with a cochlear implant. *Annals of Otology, Rhinology, and Laryngology, 166*, 385–387.

Connor, C. M., Hieber, S., Arts, H., & Zwolan, T. (2000). Speech, vocabulary, and the education of children using cochlear implants: Oral or total communication? *Journal of Speech, Language and Hearing Research, 43*, 1185–1204.

Crosson, J., & Geers, A. (2001). Analysis of narrative ability in children with cochlear implants. *Ear and Hearing, 22*, 381–394.

Cullington, H., Hodges, A. V., Butts, S. L., Dolan-Ash, S., & Balkany, T. J. (2000). Comparison of language ability in children with cochlear implants placed in oral and total communication educational settings. *Annals of Otology, Rhinology and Laryngology, 109,* 121–123.

Davidson, L., Brenner, C., & Geers, A. (2000). Predicting speech perception benefit from loudness growth measures and other map characteristics. *Annals of Otology, Rhinology, and Laryngology, 109,* 56–57.

Dawson, P. W., Blamey, P. J., Dettman, S. J., Barker, E. J., & Clark, G. M. (1995). A clinical report on receptive vocabulary skills in cochlear implant users. *Ear and Hearing, 16,* 287–294.

Dillon, C., Burkholder, R., Cleary, M., & Pisoni, D. (2004). Nonword repetition by children with cochlear implants: Accuracy ratings from normal-hearing listeners. *Journal of Speech Language Hearing Research, 47,* 1103–1116.

Dunn, L., & Dunn, L. (1981). *Peabody Picture Vocabulary Test.* (Rev. ed.). Circle Pines, MN: American Guidance.

Francis, H. W., Koch, M. E., Wyatt, J. R., & Niparko, J. K. (1999). Trends in educational placement and cost-benefit considerations in children with cochlear implants. *Archives of Otolaryngology—Head and Neck Surgery, 125,* 499–505.

Fryauf-Bertschy, H., Tyler, R. S., Kelsay, D. M., Gantz, B. J., & Woodworth, G. G. (1997). Cochlear implant use by prelingually deafened children: The influences of age at implant and length of device use. *Journal of Speech Language Hearing Research, 40,* 183–199.

Gardner, M. (1979). *Expressive One-Word Picture Vocabulary Test.* Novato, CA: Academic Therapy Publications.

Geers, A. (2002). Factors affecting the development of speech, language and literacy in children with early cochlear implantation. *Language, Speech and Hearing Services in Schools, 33,* 172–183.

Geers, A. E. (2003). Predictors of reading skill development in children with early cochlear implantation. *Ear and Hearing, 24,* 59S–68S.

Geers, A. (2004a). The ears of the deaf unstopped: Changes associated with cochlear implantation. *Seminars in Hearing, 25,* 3, 257–268.

Geers, A. (2004b). Speech, language and reading skills after early cochlear implantation. *Archives of Otolaryngology–Head and Neck Surgery, 130,* 634–638.

Geers, A. (2004c). Educational intervention and outcomes of early cochlear implantation. *International Congress Series, 1273,* 340–343.

Geers, A., & Brenner, C. (2003). Background and educational characteristics of prelingually deaf children implanted by five years of age. *Ear and Hearing, 24,* Supplement 2S–14S.

Geers, A., Brenner, C., & Davidson, L. (1999). Speech perception changes in children switching from M-Peak to SPEAK coding strategy. In S. Waltzman & N. Cohen (Eds.), *Cochlear implants* (p. 211). New York: Thieme Publications.

Geers, A., Brenner, C., & Davidson, L. (2003). Factors associated with development of speech perception skills in children implanted by age five. *Ear and Hearing, 24,* Supplement 24S–35S.

Geers, A., & Moog, J. S. (1987). Predicting spoken language acquisition in profoundly deaf children. *Journal of Speech and Hearing Disorders, 52,* 84–94.

Geers, A. E., & Moog, J. S. (1989). Factors predictive of the development of literacy in hearing-impaired adolescents. *Volta Review, 91,* 69–86.

Geers, A., & Moog, J. (1992). Speech perception and production skills of students with impaired hearing from oral and total communication education settings. *Journal of Speech and Hearing Research, 35,* 1384–1393.

Geers, A., & Moog, J. (1994a). Effectiveness of cochlear implants and tactile aids for deaf children: The sensory aids study at Central Institute for the Deaf. *Volta Review, 96*(5).

Geers, A., & Moog, J. (1994b). Spoken language results: Vocabulary, syntax and communication. *Volta Review, 96,* 131–150.

Geers, A., Moog, J., & Schick, B. (1984). Acquisition of spoken and signed English by profoundly deaf childeren. *Journal of Speech and Hearing Disorders, 49,* 378–388.

Geers, A. E., Nicholas, J. G., & Sedey, A. L. (2003). Language skills of children with early cochlear implantation. *Ear and Hearing, 24,* 46S–58S.

Geers, A., Spehar, B., & Sedey, A. (2002). Use of speech by children from total communication programs who wear cochlear implants. *American Journal of Speech-Language Pathology, 11,* 50–58.

Hammes, D. M., Novak, M. A., Rotz, L. A., Willis, M., Edmondson, D. M., & Thomas, J. F. (2002). Early identification and cochlear implantation: Critical factors for spoken language development. *Annals Otology, Rhinology, and Laryngology, 189*(Suppl.), 74–78.

Hasenstab, M., & Tobey, E. (1991). Language development in children receiving nucleus multichannel cochlear implants. *Ear and Hearing, 12,* 55S–64S.

Houston, D. M., Pisoni, D., Kirk, K., Ying, E., & Miyamoto, R. (2003). Speech perception skills of deaf infants following cochlear implantation: A first report. *International Journal of Pediatric Otorhinolaryngology, 67,* 479–495.

Houston, D. M., Ying, E., Pisoni, D., & Kirk, K. (2003). Development of pre-word learning skills in infants with cochlear implants. *Volta Review, 103,* 303–326.

Iler-Kirk, K., Miyamoto, R., Lento, C., Ying, E., O'Neill, T., & Fears, B. (2002). Effects of age at implantation in young children. *Annals of Otology, Rhinology, and Laryngology, 111,* 69–73.

Kirk, K. (2000). Challenges in the clinical investigation of cochlear implant outcomes. In J. Niparko, K. Iler-Kirk, N. Mellon, A. Robbins, D. Tucci, & B. Wilson (Eds.), *Cochlear implants: Principles and practices* (pp. 225–265). Philadelphia: Lippincott, Williams & Wilkins.

Kirk, K., Miyamoto, R., Lento, C., Ying, E., O'Neill, T., & Fears, B. (2002). Effects of age at implantation in young children. *Annals of Otology, Rhinology, and Laryngology, 111,* 69–73.

Kirk, K. I., Miyamoto, R. T., Ying, E. A., Perdew, A. E., & Zuganelis, H. (2003). Cochlear implantation in young children: Effects of age at implantation and communication mode. *Volta Review, 102,* 127–144.

Kluwin, T., & Stewart, D. (2000). Cochlear implants for younger children: A preliminary description of the parental decision and outcomes. *American Annals of the Deaf, 145,* 26–32.

Miyamoto, R. T., Kirk, K. I., Svirsky, M. A., & Sehgal, S. T. (1999). Communication skills in pediatric cochlear implant recipients. *Acta Otolaryngologia, 119,* 219–224.

Miyamoto, R. T., Svirsky, M. A., & Robbins, A. M. (1997). Enhancement of expressive language in prelingually deaf children with cochlear implants. *Acta Otolaryngologia, 117,* 154–157.

Moog, J. S. (2002). Changing expectations for children with cochlear implants. *Annals of Otology, Rhinology, and Laryngology, 111*, 138–142.

Moog, J., & Geers, A. (1999). Speech and language acquisition in young children after implantation. In K. Horn & S. McDaniel (Eds.), *Early identification and intervention of hearing-impaired infants*. The Otolaryngolic Clinics of North America, *32*, 6, 1127–1142.

Moog, J., & Geers, A. (2003). Epilogue: Major findings, conclusions and implications for deaf education. *Ear and Hearing, 24*(Suppl.), 121S–125S.

Nicholas, J., & Geers, A. (2003). Personal, social, and family adjustment in children with early cochlear implantation. *Ear and Hearing, 24*(Suppl.), 69S–81S.

Osberger, M. J., Fisher, L., & Kalberer, A. (2000). Speech perception results in children implanted with the CLARION multi-strategy cochlear implant. *Advances in Otorhinolaryngology, 57*, 417–420.

Osberger, M. J., Maso, M., & Sam, L. K. (1993). Speech intelligibility of children with cochlear implants, tactile aids, or hearing aids. *Journal of Speech and Hearing Research, 36*, 186–203.

Osberger, M. J., Zimmerman-Phillips, S., & Koch, D. B. (2002). Cochlear implant candidacy and performance trends in children. *Annals of Otology, Rhinology, and Laryngology, 111*, 62–65.

Papsin, B. C., Gysin, C., Ptcton, N., Nedzelski, J., & Harrison, R. V. (2000). Speech perception outcome measures in prelingually deaf children up to four years after cochlear implantation. *Annals of Otology, Rhinology, and Laryngology, 109*, 38–42.

Perfetti, C. A., & Sandak, R. (2000). Reading optimally builds on spoken language: Implications for deaf readers. *Journal of Deaf Studies and Deaf Education, 5*, 32–50.

Pisoni, D., & Cleary, M. (2003). Measures of working memory span and verbal rehearsal speed in deaf children after cochlear implantation. *Ear and Hearing, 24*(Suppl.) 106S–120S.

Psarros, C. E., Plant, K. L., Lee, K., Decker, J. A., Whitford, L. A., & Cowan, R. S. (2002). Conversion from the SPEAK to the ACE strategy in children using the nucleus 24 cochlear implant system: Speech perception and speech production outcomes. *Ear and Hearing, 23*(Suppl.), 18S–27S.

Robbins, A. (2000). Language development. In S. Waltzman & N. Cohen (Eds.), *Cochlear implants* (pp. 269–283). New York: Thieme.

Robbins, A. M., Bollard, P. M., & Green, J. (1999). Language development in children implanted with the CLARION cochlear implant. *Annals of Otology, Rhinology, and Laryngology, 177*(Suppl.), 113–118.

Robbins, A. M., Kirk, K. I., Osberger, M. J., & Ertmer, D. (1995). Speech intelligibility of implanted children. *Annals of Otology, Rhinology, and Laryngology, 166*(Suppl.), 399–401.

Robbins, A. M., Svirsky, M., & Kirk, K. I. (1997). Children with implants can speak, but can they communicate? *Otolaryngology–Head and Neck Surgery, 117*, 155–160.

Scarborough, H. (1990). Index of productive syntax. *Applied Psycholinguistics, 11*, 1–22.

Schick, B. (2003). The development of American Sign Language and manually coded english systems. In M. Marschark & P. E. Spencer (Eds.), *Deaf studies, language and education* (pp. 219–231). New York: Oxford University Press.

Spencer, L. J., Barker, B. A., & Tomblin, J. B. (2003). Exploring the language and literacy outcomes of pediatric cochlear implant users. *Ear and Hearing, 24,* 236–247.

Spencer, L., Tye-Murray, N., & Woodworth, G. (1998). The production of English inflectional morphology, speech production and listening performance in children with cochlear implants. *Ear and Hearing, 19,* 310–318.

Svirsky, M. A. (2000). Language development in children with profound prelingual hearing loss, without cochlear implants. *Annals of Otology, Rhinology, and Laryngology, 109,* 99–100.

Svirsky, M. A., Chin, S. B., Miyamoto, R. T., Sloan, R. B., & Caldwell, M. D. (2003). Speech intelligibility of profoundly deaf pediatric hearing aid users. *Volta Review, 102,* 175–198.

Svirsky, M. A., Robbins, A. M., Kirk, K. I., Pisoni, D. B., & Miyamoto, R. T. (2000). Language development in profoundly deaf children with cochlear implants. *Psychological Sciences, 11,* 153–158.

Svirsky, M., Teoh, S., & Neuburger, H. (2004). Development of language and speech perception in congenitally, profoundly deaf children as a function of age at cochlear implantation. *Audiology and Neuro-otology, 9,* 224–233.

Szagun, G. (2001). Language acquisition in young German-speaking children with cochlear implants: Individual differences and implications for conceptions of a "sensitive phase." *Audiology and Neuro-otology, 6,* 288–297.

Tait, M., & Lutman, M. E. (1994). Comparison of early communicative behavior in young children with cochlear implants and with hearing aids. *Ear and Hearing, 15,* 352–361.

Tobey, E., Geers, A., & Brenner, C. (1994). Speech production results: Speech feature acquisition. *Volta Review, 96,* 109–130.

Tobey, E. A., Geers, A. E., Brenner, C., Altuna, D., & Gabbert, G. (2003). Factors associated with development of speech production skills in children implanted by age five. *Ear and Hearing, 24*(Suppl.), 36S–45S.

Tobey, E., Geers, A., Douek, B. M., Perrin, J., Skellett, R., Brenner, C., et al. (2000). Factors associated with speech intelligibility in children with cochlear implants. *Annals of Otology, Rhinology, and Laryngology, 109,* 28–30.

Tobey, E., Rekart, D., & Geers, A. (2004). Communication and classroom influences on speech intelligibility. *Archives of Otolaryngology–Head and Neck Surgery, 130,* 639-643.

Tomblin, B., Spencer, L., Flock, S., Tyler, R., & Gantz, B. (1999). A comparison of language achievement in children with cochlear implants and children using hearing aids. *Journal of Speech, Language and Hearing Research, 42,* 497–511.

Tomblin, J. B., Spencer, L. J., & Gantz, B. J. (2000). Language and reading acquisition in children with and without cochlear implants. *Advances in Otorhinolaryngology, 57,* 300–304.

Tye-Murray, N. (2003). Conversational fluency of children who use cochlear implants. *Ear and Hearing, 24*(Suppl.), 82S–89S.

Tye-Murray, N., Spencer, L., & Gilbert-Bedia, E. (1995). Relationships between speech production and speech perception skills in young cochlear-implant users. *Journal of the Acoustical Society of America, 98,* 2454–2460.

Tye-Murray, N., Spencer, L., & Woodworth, G. G. (1995). Acquisition of speech by children who have prolonged cochlear implant experience. *Journal of Speech and Hearing Research, 38,* 327–337.

Tyler, R., Tomblin, B., Spencer, L., Kelsay, D., & Fryauf-Bertchy, H. (2000). How speech perception through a cochlear implant affects language and education. In S. Waltzman & N. Cohen (Eds.), *Cochlear implants* (pp. 291–292). New York: Thieme.

Uchanski, R. M., & Geers, A. E. (2003). Acoustic characteristics of the speech of young cochlear implant users: A comparison with normal-hearing age-mates. *Ear and Hearing, 24*(Suppl. 1), 90S–105S.

Watson, L. (2002). The literacy development of children with cochlear implants at age seven. *Deafness and Education International, 4*, 84–98.

12

The Process and Early Outcomes of Cochlear Implantation by Three Years of Age

Johanna G. Nicholas & Ann E. Geers

Spoken language development occurs spontaneously in the presence of normal hearing from birth, given a typical linguistic and social environment. We do not yet know how much hearing must be provided to the developing brain for the child with hearing loss to achieve speech development comparable with that of a hearing child. In addition, we do not know how soon after birth language input must be initiated for normal speech and spoken language development to occur. The primary goal of pediatric cochlear implantation is to provide critical speech information to the child's auditory system and brain to maximize the chances of developing spoken language.

Since pediatric cochlear implantation gained approval by the U.S. Food and Drug Administration (FDA) in 1990, thousands of deaf children have been given access to the sounds of spoken language via a device that is quite different from anything previously available. Although the cochlear implant does not allow for hearing of the same quality as that experienced by persons without a hearing loss, it nonetheless has revolutionized the experience of spoken language acquisition for children who otherwise might face a lifetime of struggle to communicative effectively in the everyday "hearing" world. With early cochlear implantation and educational intervention, many young deaf children are ready for mainstream school placement, exhibiting age appropriate speech and language skills, by 5 or 6 years of age (Moog, 2002).

Simultaneous with the increasing acceptance and prevalence of the cochlear implant surgery, there has been a movement in the United

States and other countries to pass legislation that requires hearing screening procedures for all newborn infants. The importance of detecting a hearing loss early and providing appropriate intervention services within the first 6 months of life was underscored in a study by Yoshinaga-Itano, Sedey, Coulter, and Mehl (1998) demonstrating that under those circumstances deaf children had significantly better outcomes than those who were identified at a later age. At the present time, a majority of states mandate such universal hearing screening and the average age for diagnosis of a significant hearing loss in the United States has been reduced substantially (Dazel et al., 2000). Such early diagnosis provides an opportunity not only for the earlier introduction of sound via hearing aids and for specialized auditory training, but also for earlier consideration of cochlear implantation should hearing aids prove unsuccessful in facilitating auditory development. This development has important implications for the acquisition of spoken language, as many have proposed that there may be a critical, or "sensitive," period of time in early childhood within which language is optimally acquired (Ruben & Schwartz, 1999). The ability to provide improved auditory input to infants and very young children provides a new opportunity to study the veracity of those claims.

Despite the exciting new opportunities for enhancing the spoken language development of young deaf children, decisions regarding the best intervention practices and their timing are still difficult for parents to make. Some questions of immediate relevance to parents who are in the decision-making process include the following: (1) What kinds of auditory input do children need to develop normal or near-normal spoken language (i.e., how closely must the coded speech signal resemble normal hearing)? (2) Which children will do better with cochlear implants than with hearing aids? (3) When making the decision to get a cochlear implant "early," how early is early enough for deaf children to achieve speech and language levels equivalent to those of hearing agemates? (4) What is the role of educational intervention in accelerating this process?

Clinicians strive to make sense of what research data are available to answer questions like these and to make recommendations to families that are based on empirical evidence. This endeavor is hampered, however, by a lack of research studies with sufficient sample sizes for reliable interpretation of results. Variables that affect speech and language development in both positive and negative directions have not been routinely controlled, either by sample selection or with statistical techniques. Existing research regarding the effect of age of implantation within the infancy/preschool period is reviewed in the present chapter, along with interpretation of their clinical significance and suggestions for further research.

ACQUIRING A COCHLEAR IMPLANT IN INFANCY: PROCESS AND PROBLEMS

The Process of Cochlear Implantation in Infancy

The outcome of cochlear implantation may be different for children who are born deaf and those who experience even a brief period of normal hearing prior to the onset of deafness. For those who have a period of normal hearing, immediate cochlear implantation (i.e., within a year of onset of deafness) may lead to very favorable outcomes, since pre-existing speech and language skills may be recovered (Geers, 2004). For the infant with congenital deafness, the duration of auditory deprivation may determine the extent of language delay the child must overcome once a sensory aid is fitted and language stimulation is initiated. Implementation of newborn hearing screening procedures, performed in the first few days of life, may reduce this period of auditory deprivation to the shortest possible interval by starting parents and clinicians on the road to early diagnosis and treatment.

The process of diagnosing permanent sensorineural hearing loss and determining cochlear implant candidacy can require several months. Suggestion of hearing loss at the time of newborn hearing screening will typically indicate a need for a more comprehensive test within 3 months, since most children who fail current screening techniques will turn out to have normal hearing. If the child fails to respond normally at the comprehensive follow-up exam and further testing reveals a loss, hearing aids will be fitted and communication intervention options discussed. Because the child's parents are typically hearing individuals with no family history or knowledge of deafness and communication options, they may need time to educate themselves about the array of choices before them. In addition, a determination must be made regarding whether the child is likely to benefit more from a cochlear implant than from a hearing aid. A period of time will be established for a hearing aid trial, during which the child's ability to hear and respond with the help of hearing aids will be evaluated. This trial period is typically 3–6 months or longer, but is sometimes shortened, as in postmeningitis cases where ossification of the cochlea may complicate surgery. Ossification is the growth of bone within the fluid chambers of the cochlea, which often makes insertion of an electrode array more difficult. It occurs often following meningitis, and surgical outcomes are much better if an implant can be placed before ossification begins.

The age and hearing loss criteria for cochlear implant candidacy have changed as clinicians gain experience with this new sensory aid. Initially, cochlear implant candidacy was confined to profoundly deaf children 2 years and older who were receiving the least amount of benefit from hearing aids. With their hearing aids, these children could not perceive spoken words without the aid of pictures or prompts. Later, the FDA made a two-part change to the candidacy criteria for the pediatric cochlear implant procedure: (a) the age limit was reduced to 12 months of age and (b) the hearing loss criterion was expanded for children 2 or more years of age to include those with severe hearing losses. The latter change allowed for implantation of children whose pure tone average (PTA) threshold was greater than 70 dB across the speech frequencies (500, 1000, 2000) or who scored less than 30% correct on a speech perception test requiring the recognition of single words without pictures or other contextual prompts. However, for children receiving an implant at age 12–23 months, the hearing loss requirement has remained at the profound range (i.e., PTA threshold >90 dB HL).

Once it has been determined that a child is not receiving adequate auditory input from hearing aids, the child is evaluated from a physical standpoint to determine whether cochlear implant surgery would be appropriate from a medical point of view. This usually involves various radiological studies of the auditory anatomy. Magnetic resonance imaging is used to identify any abnormalities in the cochlea that might affect insertion of the electrode array. An otologic examination to rule out middle ear infection is also conducted, in addition to a determination of general health and an assessment of general surgical and anesthetic risk. While the risk from general anesthesia may be slightly greater in infants (Young, 2002), the surgical procedure is the same as that used for older children.

Once a child is determined to be an appropriate candidate for the cochlear implant procedure, a cochlear implant center will require some assurance that the child will be in an appropriate rehabilitative setting that will encourage use of the implant, maintain implant function, and maximize the child's auditory input and speech development. Research indicates that better hearing sensitivity before implantation and the use of spoken communication in the child's educational setting are associated with better speech perception with the implant (Sarant, Blamey, Dowell, Clark, & Gibson, 2001; Zwolan et al., 1997).

Difficulties of Hearing Aid Trials in Infancy

Because a determination must be made that the child is likely to benefit more from a cochlear implant than from a hearing aid, trials with properly fitted hearing aids are a crucial component of the evaluation procedure. These trials typically rely on tests of aided speech perception to evaluate hearing aid benefit. Lists of words, such as the Lexical Neighborhood Test (Kirk, Pisoni, & Osberger, 1995), or sentences, such as the BKB Lists (Bamford & Wilson, 1979), are recommended for this purpose. Both of these are "open-set" tests of speech perception, meaning that the child is presented with words or sentences without contextual cues and is required to repeat the word or sentence back to the examiner. These tests are presented through audition alone. In the past, most children being evaluated for a cochlear implant were 3–5 years old or older and often had a basic vocabulary. However, the linguistic skills and word knowledge required to complete open-set speech perception tests make them inappropriate for the young deaf infants who are now being evaluated in their first and second year of life. In such cases, clinicians may compare the child's progress in developing spoken language to published data from age-matched children with hearing aids and cochlear implants (Geers & Moog, 1994; Moog & Geers, 1975; Moog, Kozak, & Geers, 1983; Svirsky & Meyer, 1999) in order to predict improvement that may be anticipated with a cochlear implant.

Parent and clinician rating scales have also been used to meet this challenge of early assessment. These include measures of parent report of everyday hearing behaviors, such as the Infant-Toddler Meaningful Auditory Integration Scale (IT-MAIS; Zimmerman-Phillips, Robbins, & Osberger, 2000); use of speech to communicate, such as Meaningful Use of Speech Scale (MUSS; Robbins & Osberger, 1991); and language acquisition using, for example, the MacArthur Communicative Development Inventory (MCDI; Fenson et al., 1993), as well as categorization schemes that seek to classify the level of auditory perception as observed by a clinician, such as Categories of Auditory Performance (CAP; Archbold, Lutman, & Marshall, 1995). Standard procedures for determining hearing aid benefit in infants and toddlers have not been established, and the process remains highly subjective.

Difficulties in Setting the Cochlear Implant Speech Processor

About a month after surgery, the family returns to the implant center for programming of the speech processor. As part of this process, the audiologist obtains thresholds and comfort levels on each electrode and adjusts parameters such as frequency allocation to electrodes to improve speech perception. A larger number of visits over a longer time period are required to adjust these parameters for infants and toddlers, and because responses may change over time, long-term audiological follow-up is required. Recently, programming techniques have been developed that are less dependent on behavioral responses from the child that may be valuable in setting these parameters for very young children. Physiological assessment using electrically evoked compound action potentials can provide information about whether the child is hearing the stimulus at a given level, thus providing a point to begin behavioral conditioning and even approximate the levels needed to program the speech processor, when necessary. These measurements are recorded from an intracochlear electrode with hardware and software provided by the cochlear implant manufacturers, and the process is referred to as neural response telemetry (NRT). While NRT-based speech processor programs are not ideal, they may provide speech perception that is adequate for language development until the child is older and can be tested with behavioral techniques. The skill of the audiologist in programming the speech processor makes a significant contribution to the child's development of auditory speech perception skills and can facilitate speech and language development (Geers, Brenner, & Davidson, 2003).

Difficulty Predicting a Child's Success in Acquiring Spoken Language as a Primary Mode of Communication

For most children who receive a cochlear implant, the primary goal is to achieve a satisfactory level of spoken language proficiency. However, the device alone will not typically lead to spontaneous spoken language acquisition. Families of children with implants are advised to enroll in a rehabilitation setting that provides an emphasis on auditory development and speech training. Many children will progress quickly after implantation, and a few will not. Predicting which children will have the best chance for success with oral communication may be an important aid at the time when decisions must be made.

In general, cochlear implants have greatly increased the proportion of profoundly deaf children who will have a good prognosis for spoken language development. Geers and Moog (1987) developed an index for predicting which profoundly deaf children would achieve spoken language proficiency with auditory/oral education. This index involves assigning weighted scores to various factors shown to be associated with success, including aided speech perception (0–30 points), nonverbal intelligence (0–25 points), English language skills compared to agemates with severe to profound deafness (0–20 points), family support (0–15 points), and speech communication attitude (0–10 points). With hearing aids alone, very few profoundly deaf children can achieve the level of speech perception necessary to receive a full-credit score for this factor (Geers & Brenner, 1994; Geers & Moog, 1989) and must exhibit compensatory skills in other areas (e.g., higher IQ and/or language proficiency) in order to be good candidates for oral instruction (>70 points total). In contrast, the vast majority of children with cochlear implants eventually achieve the full 30 points for speech perception, thus improving their prognosis for spoken language development. However, the assessments needed to assign points to the Spoken Language Predictor Index cannot be reliably administered to children younger than 3 years, and predicting spoken language success for infants and toddlers is highly intuitive. Nevertheless, in the presence of normal developmental milestones and good parental support, use of a cochlear implant may greatly increase this prognosis.

AGE OF IMPLANTATION EFFECTS
IN THE INFANCY/PRESCHOOL PERIOD

Of particular interest to parents of very young children, particularly those identified by newborn hearing screening, are studies that examine the effects of the timing of implantation surgery on speech and language acquisition. Studies of the effects of age at implantation on outcomes can be difficult to design and interpret. In the earliest studies examining the effect of age of implantation, the range of participant ages included was very wide, sometimes including both children and adults (e.g., Dowell, Blamey, & Clark, 1997). With time, and with the lowering of the ages at which implants were allowed, studies were published with a focus on children of increasingly younger and narrower age ranges. There has been interest in the concept of a "critical age" or "sensitive period" for auditory input (Ruben, 1997) and variability in the methods used to determine what a "critical age" might be. The following section reviews studies that examine age of implantation effects, focusing on outcomes achieved by children implanted at less than 3 years of age.

Age at Implantation and Auditory Speech Perception

While the most direct effect of cochlear implantation is on the auditory perception of speech, and most outcome studies focus on changes in speech perception scores, this outcome may be thought of as reflecting spoken language competence as much as auditory perception. In the case of infants and toddlers who are at the beginning stages of language acquisition, auditory perception of words and phrases is dependent upon the child's knowledge of English phonology, vocabulary, and syntax. As language skills improve, so will scores on tests of both auditory and auditory-visual speech perception, but this relation is interactive rather than unidirectionally causal (Blamey, 2003; Blamey & Sarant, 2002; Blamey et al., 2001). Furthermore, since language skills improve with age, regardless of changes in auditory skills, children who were implanted at a younger age may not exhibit better speech perception scores than children implanted later because they have less developed language skills after the same period of implant use. For example, Kirk, Miyamoto, Lento et al. (2002) compared the growth rates (the amount of improvement per year) of scores on the Mr. Potato Head task. Children were presented with a Mr. Potato Head toy and were required to manipulate various body parts and clothing accessories in response to spoken (audition alone) requests from the examiner. The children were grouped by whether they received an implant under or over 3 years of age. The growth rates were analyzed separately for those children who were using an oral approach to communication ($n = 25$ implanted younger than 3 years; $n = 17$ older than

3 years) and for those using a total communication approach ($n = 16$ younger than 3 years; $n = 16$ older than 3 years). For those children using oral-only communication, significantly faster growth rates were seen for those children implanted *after* the age of 36 months. In the total communication group, there was no significant difference in growth rates observed between the age-of-implantation groups. Kirk, Miyamoto, Ying et al. (2002) found an advantage for *later* implantation when examining speech perception scores of children in three age-of-implantation groups: <2 years ($n = 14$), 2;0–4;11 (4 years 11 months; $n = 37$), and 5;0 or older ($n = 22$) at 36 months of implant use. Both of these studies used the Mr. Potato Head test, an activity that requires a fairly well developed vocabulary and the ability to respond appropriately in a formal testing situation, factors that give older children a performance advantage. However, even on a parent report measure, the IT-MAIS, Robbins, Koch, Osberger, Zimmerman-Phillips, and Kishon-Rabin (2004) reported no difference in growth rates during the first year of cochlear implant use of children who received an implant at 12–18 months ($n = 45$), 19–23 months ($n = 32$), or 24–36 months ($n = 30$) of age.

Differences in age at test (and therefore language competence) may not be the only reason for failure to find age-of-implantation effects on speech perception scores. One study that controlled for both age at test and duration of implant use tested 181 children 8 and 9 years old who received an implant between 2 and 4 years of age (Geers, Brenner, & Davidson, 2003). No effect of age at implantation on speech perception scores was found after long-term use of a cochlear implant (i.e., 4–7 years). Geers and colleagues surmised that any initial differences in speech perception due to age of implantation that might have been evident during the first couple of years after implantation could have diminished with time. Other longitudinal studies that included children with long durations of use did not have large enough sample sizes at the follow-up test intervals (4–7 years) to refute or confirm this hypothesis. For example, Tyler et al. (2000) found that higher word recognition scores on a battery of closed- and open-speech perception tests were achieved by children implanted between 2 and 4 years of age as compared to those implanted between 4 and 5 years of age, after 6 years of implant use. However, the small numbers of children in each age of implantation group ($n = 7$ at 2;0–3;11) precluded statistical analyses to determine if these differences were significant.

The vast majority of studies have documented an advantage for children implanted earlier. Most studies demonstrating this advantage have documented greater speech perception gains during the first 1–3 years of implant use. Small sample size has prohibited statistical analysis in a number of these studies (Hehar, Nikolopoulos, Gibbin, & O'Donoghue, 2002; Muller & Wagenfeld, 2003), and some studies with larger numbers of participants did not include statistical comparisons between age-of-implantation groups in published reports (Govaerts et al., 2002; Manrique et al., 1999). These studies all report interesting trends that suggest earlier implantation may be beneficial but do not incorporate sufficient statistical analysis to provide a definitive answer.

Two studies published in the late 1990s documented that children implanted when younger than 2 years exhibited significant improvement in speech perception scores following cochlear implantation (Lenarz et al., 1999; Waltzman & Cohen, 1998). However, no control groups of similar children evaluated over the same period of time or children who received an implant at older ages were provided for comparison. More recently, four age-of-implantation groups were followed by Hammes et al. (2002). Participants were administered the Phonetically Balanced Kindergarten Word Lists (Haskins, 1949) to test open-set speech perception. This test involves the recognition and repetition of single-syllable words that are presented through audition alone. Participants had completed two years of implant use. The small number of children who met the duration-of-use criterion (2 years) and who were able to complete the testing on this measure precluded statistical analysis of results. Nevertheless, a trend toward higher scores for children implanted at earlier ages was evident. The median percentages correct were as follows: implanted at <18 months, ~80% ($n = 3$); implanted between 19 and 30 months of age, ~60% ($n = 11$), implanted between 31 and 40 months of age, ~30% ($n = 8$), and implanted between 41 and 48 months of age, ~40% ($n = 8$).

Very recent studies have examined age-of-implantation effects using substantially larger sample sizes. Svirsky, Teoh, and Neuburger (2004) reported results for three groups of children who received an implant at younger than 4 years: 14–24 months ($n = 12$), 25–36 months ($n = 34$), and 37–46 months ($n = 29$). Children in this study were evaluated with the Mr. Potato Head task. Using a longitudinal design and a novel statistical approach (Developmental Trajectory Analysis) that compared the average size of the difference between growth curves over time, significantly higher speech perception scores were documented for children implanted when younger than 2 years than for children who were implanted at 2 or 3 years of age. Similarly, a study by Baumgartner et al. (2002) reported that children who received an implant when younger than 36 months ($n = 15$) scored significantly higher in speech perception testing at 12, 18, and 24 months after surgery than did those who received the implant after the age of 36 months ($n = 18$).

Anderson, D'Haese, and Weichbold (2003) compared the scores on parent-report questionnaires of auditory and speech development of children who received an implant when younger than 2 years ($n = 37$) with those who received the implant between 2 and 4 years of age ($n = 36$). All children were assessed preoperatively and thereafter at regular intervals until 3 years after surgery. Although there were no significant differences between speech perception ratings of the two groups at any of the postimplantation test intervals, the group implanted under age 2 received significantly higher speech production ratings than the group implanted between 2 and 4 years of age, after 3 years of device use. When Robinson (1998) compared auditory skills ratings of children who were implanted in the 2–4-year-old age range with those of children who received their implant at a later age, the youngest children did not manifest an early implantation advantage until 3 years of cochlear implant use.

In summary, there appear to be conflicting results regarding the effects of age at implantation on speech perception scores. While some studies indicate no advantage for children implanted at age 2 or younger (Geers, Brenner, & Davidson, 2003; Kirk, Miyamoto, Ling et al., 2002; Robbins et al., 2004), most studies report some advantage for very early implantation, especially during the first 2 years of device use. Failure to find an advantage for early implantation may have been affected by issues that are unique to the assessment of very young deaf children. Speech perception tests, which involve the recognition of spoken words, often utilize a vocabulary level that is too high for the average preschool-age deaf child (Kirk, Diefendorf, Pisoni, & Robbins, 1997). A young child who is asked to perceive words that are unfamiliar will necessarily be at a substantial disadvantage, as compared to an older child who is more likely to have those words in his own receptive and/or productive vocabulary. Certainly this must be considered when interpreting studies that examine a change in speech perception over time in the population of children younger than 5 years. Furthermore, the speech perception advantages achieved by children who receive a cochlear implant at age 2 or younger compared to those implanted at age 3 or 4 may no longer be apparent after 4 or more years of device use.

Age at Implantation and Language Outcomes

Child development researchers have been interested in the effects of age of implantation on spoken language acquisition because this skill may be vulnerable to a "critical period" effect. They theorize that there exists a certain period of time during which language acquisition can most easily occur and that thereafter the task becomes much more difficult. For children with normal hearing and otherwise typical development, that window of time begins at birth and ends anywhere between 5 and 12 years of age. Some have reported that particular aspects of language may be differentially affected during multiple "critical" or "sensitive periods," for example, 6–12 months for optimal phonological development (Werker & Tees, 1984), syntactic development continues until about age 10, and vocabulary acquisition continues into adulthood. It has also been hypothesized that the phases of language development are fixed and highly interdependent (Locke, 1997).

Research studies examining language acquisition in children who received implants over a wide age span indicated some advantage for children with earlier age at implantation. Richter, Eissele, Laszig, and Lohle (2002) reported on 106 German-speaking children who received cochlear implants at varying ages ranging from 1 to 10 or more years and who had used their implants for a minimum of 2 years. The children were of unspecified age at time of test. The expressive and receptive language of each child was assessed pre- and postoperatively with the Scales of Early Communication Skills for Hearing Impaired Children (Moog & Geers, 1975) and the Reynell Developmental Language Scales III (RDLS-III; Edwards et al., 1997). Regression analyses performed by Richter et al. suggested that age of implantation was the most important predictor of postoperative spoken language outcome. No specific age or age range was reported as critical for maximum benefit.

As studies have narrowed the age at implant range examined in search of a critical period, various chronological turning points for language development have been identified. Some studies have concluded that 5 or 6 years represents such a point, beyond which a child appears to be less able to take advantage of incoming auditory input as compared to what was possible if the input had come earlier (Connor, Hieber, Arts, & Zwolan, 2000; Osberger, Maso & Sam, 1993; Tye-Murray, Spencer, & Woodworth, 1995). Kirk, Miyamoto, Ying et al. (2002) examined age of implantation effects in three groups of children: those implanted younger than 2;0 ($n = 14$), between 2;0 and 4;11 ($n = 37$), and older than 5;0 ($n = 22$). The authors reported on the growth rates of receptive vocabulary as measured on the third edition of the Peabody Picture Vocabulary Test (Dunn & Dunn, 1997) and receptive/expressive language as measured on the RDLS-III (Edwards et al., 1997). Significantly greater growth rates were observed for those children who received the implant when younger than under 2;0 as compared to children who received the implant later, on all measures.

With a reduction in age at implantation, research studies have begun to focus on the increased proportion of children achieving spoken language levels that are comparable to those of their hearing agemates. Instead of identifying an age at implantation that is associated with a better outcome, it has become important to ask if very early use of an implant will maximize the chances of achieving normal, or close to normal, levels of speech and spoken language development. Recent studies have shown that language growth rates of children who receive implants before 5 years of age are very close to growth rates of hearing children once the deaf child has received an implant (Robbins et al., 2004; Svirsky, Robbins, Kirk, Pisoni, & Miyamoto, 2000). The differences in language performance between children with implants and their hearing age-mates, therefore, are usually due to the existing delay in performance at the time of implantation. Ideally, therefore, implantation should occur not only early enough for normal language progress to be achieved, but also before delays are present. Exploration of language outcomes in children who are receiving implants at exceptionally young ages may allow us to find out if this is possible.

In an effort to examine learning behaviors that are presumed to contribute directly to vocabulary acquisition, Houston, Ying, Pisoni, and Kirk (2003) used the preferential looking paradigm (Hollich, Hirsh-Pasek, & Golinkoff, 2000) to assess infants' ability to learn the arbitrary associations between speech sounds and objects in their environment. They compared preferential looking times in hearing infants between 6 and 30 months of age with deaf infants implanted very early (7–15 months) and somewhat later (16–25 months). They found that those implanted very early closely resembled hearing infants in their ability to learn arbitrary pairings between speech sounds and visual events, but those implanted between 16 and 25 months did not.

Svirsky et al. (2004) evaluated children who were implanted at 16–24, 25–36, or 37–46 months of age. Language assessment was conducted preoperatively and at several intervals postoperatively on one of two language measures. Each comparison of language scores between the three age-of-implantation groups showed a statistically significant advantage for earlier cochlear implantation. Developmental Trajectory Analysis allowed for comparison of language ages achieved by each age-of-implantation group in relation to hearing children. Those children who received their implant between 12 and 24 months of age were developing language at roughly 5.5 months ahead of children implanted at 25–36 months of age. Likewise, children implanted at 25–36 months of age had language scores at about 5.5 months of age ahead of children who were in the oldest age of implantation group, at the same chronological age.

In a preliminary report of data from an ongoing study, Nicholas and Geers (2003) compared the language skills of children receiving an implant at either prior to 19 months of age (group 1; $n = 17$), at 19–24 months of age (group 2; $n = 21$), or at 28–36 months of age (group 3; $n = 17$). All children were assessed at 3.5 years of age. The study provided concurrent measures from videotaped language samples, a language rating scale completed by the child's teacher, and the MCDI (Fenson et al., 1993) completed by the parent at the same assessment point. The language samples were collected from 30-minute parent–child play sessions and transcribed to yield a measure of mean length of utterance (MLU) in words as a gross measure of syntactic development as well as the number of different words produced as a measure of productive vocabulary breadth. The MCDI (words and sentences form) allowed for measures of the breadth of productive vocabulary as well as reports of the child's longest sentences. For most outcome measures, groups 1 and 2 significantly outperformed group 3, but there was not a significant difference between the performances of the two youngest groups. These results indicate that younger than 2 years of age may indeed be a critical time for optimal benefit from an implant.

The Nicholas and Geers (2003) study also provided a point of reference for the vocabulary measure from direct observation of 3-year-old severe to profoundly deaf children with traditional hearing aids and hearing children. Hearing aid users produced, on average, only about 25 different words per 30-minute language sample, and hearing children produced roughly 200 (Nicholas, 2000). The youngest cochlear implant recipients (group 1) produced an average of 145 different words; group 2, 125 different words; and group 3, 75 different words in the same language sampling procedure. Thus, even the latest implanted group, whose duration of implant use was only 6–14 months, produced an average of three times as many different words in a 30-minute play session as their age-matched peers with traditional hearing aids at the same chronological age. Those implanted at 18 months or younger approached levels achieved by hearing 3 year olds, after only 2–2.5 years of implant use. Figures 12.1 and 12.2 depict the mean performance levels of the three groups of children with implants along with reference means

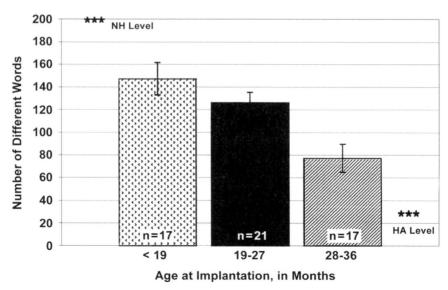

Figure 12-1. Mean number of different words produced in a 30-minute play session for each of three different ranges of age at implantation (expressed in months).

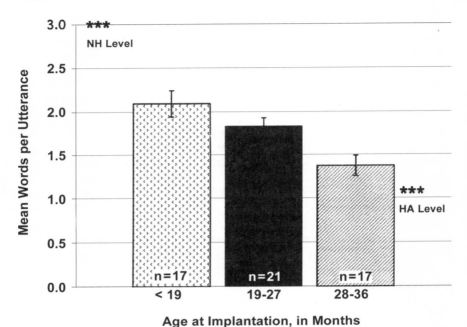

Figure 12-2. Mean number of words per utterance in a 30-minute play session for each of three different age-of-implantation age ranges (expressed in months).

for hearing children and deaf children with hearing aids. The figures indicate that when cochlear implant use is initiated early, children are able to make significant use of this input and are able to reap language learning benefits even during the first year of device use that are clearly not available to those who do not have this input.

Outcomes Beyond Early Childhood

How long-lasting is the advantage conferred by early implantation? Does the rapid language-learning progress exhibited by these children contribute to more mature language and reading skill acquisition in elementary school? Geers (2004) reported language and reading results for 133 children who were tested at 8 or 9 years of age after they had used their implant for 4–6 years (thus age at test and duration of implant use were controlled). All of the children in this sample had a nonverbal IQ of at least 80 and were reportedly deaf from birth. Three groups were considered: those implanted at 2 years, 3 years, and 4 years of age. Additionally, a comparison group of 24 hearing children were tested on all outcome measures that did not have published hearing normative data. For the deaf children, measures of speech perception, speech production, syntax, and reading were all found to have no significant correlation with age of implantation. However, a suggestive trend emerged when the percentages of children falling within a normal range for 8–9-year-old hearing children were calculated. When considering speech production alone, nearly twice the percentage of cochlear implant users who were implanted age at 2;0–2;11 were within the normal range for their age at 8–9 chronological years of age (57%), compared with those implanted at ages 4;0–4;11 (30%). When considering language alone, 52% of those implanted at age 2 achieved language within the normal range as compared with 35% implanted at age 4. Finally, when considering the percentages of children who achieved both normal speech production *and* syntactic competence, the percentages are even more disparate: 43% for those implanted at age 2;0–2;11 compared with 16% for those implanted at age 4;0–4;11 ($p < 0.05$). These trends suggest that considerable advantages accrued to children who received implants at earlier ages within the preschool period.

Degree of preimplantation residual hearing may also contribute to language outcome, because very early use of hearing aids may act as a bridge to provide auditory access to language until the child receives an implant. In a study of German-speaking pediatric cochlear implant recipients, Szagun (2001) investigated the relative importance of both preoperative hearing ability and age of implantation. Outcome measures were MLU derived from spontaneous language samples and productive vocabulary as assessed by a parent-response questionnaire. Age at implantation in this sample ranged from 14 to 46 months, and children were compared to a group of hearing children matched at the study outset for vocabulary level. Analyses revealed different results for the grammar (MLU) and the vocabulary outcome measures. Age of implantation was significantly correlated with higher MLU values but not with vocabulary scores. Preoperative hearing levels were significantly related to both grammar and vocabulary measures and explained a larger percentage of variance than did age at implant. Interestingly, the finding of a significant correlation of age of implantation with a syntax-related measure but not with a vocabulary measure was replicated by Spencer (2004), who observed 11 children who were implanted by the age of 27 months and who had used an implant for a minimum of 21 months.

General Conclusions Regarding the Effect of Age of Implantation

Because speech and language outcomes following cochlear implantation are influenced by a number of factors, not all of which can reasonably be controlled simultaneously, it is difficult to determine the independent contribution of age at implantation. However, a consensus seems to be building from a number of studies that 2 years of age represents a turning point in language development. Children who receive an implant at 2 years or younger appear to have an increased likelihood of normal spoken language development. Another critical time point may occur around 5 or 6 years of age, with decreased spoken language outcomes evident in children implanted during elementary school or later. These results should be considered only tentative at this time, however, in view of a variety of methodological difficulties discussed in the remainder of this chapter.

PROBLEMS WITH INTERPRETING RESULTS OF AGE OF IMPLANTATION COMPARISONS

Changing Sample Characteristics

Defining Age-of-Implantation Groups

Since the time of initial approval, the FDA has changed its guidelines several times to lower the age limit for approval of cochlear implant surgery. As a result, the groups of children being compared in studies of age-of-implantation effects have varied in composition. Unfortunately, there are a fair number of published studies that do not include the exact age range of implantation of all participants in all groups. This becomes problematic when comparisons are attempted across studies. At one point in time the label "younger than 3 years" meant 2–3 years of age. Shortly thereafter, the term came to mean 18 months to 3 years, and now it means 12 months or younger to 36 months of age. Combining this wide age-of-implantation range into one group helps to achieve a reasonable sample size but may obscure the contribution of those implanted at the youngest ages to the performance of the entire group. A careful reporting of ages lessens potential problems of interpretation.

Differences in Severity of Preimplantation Hearing Loss

Changes have occurred in the severity of hearing loss that is considered acceptable for cochlear implantation. At the present time, to be considered candidates for cochlear implantation, children 2 years and older with a severe to profound hearing loss may have up to 30% correct scores on an open-set speech perception test. Those children may have better speech and language outcomes (Szagun, 2001). There are more conservative criteria regarding preimplantation thresholds (i.e., >90 dB) that apply to children implanted when younger than 2 years. Therefore, if there is any advantage to providing an implant to children with more residual hearing preimplantation, this advantage will only be available to the children who receive implants at 2 years or older. Consequently, candidacy practices bias somewhat against finding better performance in the earliest implanted groups.

Advances in Technology

Further confounding the results are changes in cochlear implant technology that are co-occurring with a reduction in age at implantation. This means that the most recently implanted children, who have the newest electrode arrays and speech processors, are also, on average, younger when they received an implant than children implanted previously. When performance outcomes of groups of children who were implanted over several years' time are compared to examine age-of-implantation effects, the investigators often ignore the fact that children with the more advanced speech processing strategies may have a performance advantage over those who use the older processing strategies. Thus, performance differences that are due to technology changes may, in fact, be attributed to age at implantation.

Increasing use of upgraded speech processors with decreasing age at implantation are apparent in a nationwide study of children implanted when younger than 5 years who received Nucleus-22 implants between 1990 and 1996 (Geers, Brenner, & Davidson, 2003). During this period, the speech processor was upgraded from M-PEAK to SPEAK strategy. Most children were eventually upgraded to the new strategy or, if implanted in 1994 or later, received SPEAK at initial implant. When these children were tested at 8 or 9 years of age, the duration of use of the updated SPEAK processor was 3.72 years for children implanted at age 4, 3.93 years for those implanted at age 3, and 4.73 years for children implanted at 2 years of age. Thus, children implanted at 2 years of age averaged a year more use of the updated processor at the time of data collection. Once variance due to age at implant was removed, significant additional variance was accounted for by duration of use of the SPEAK processor (Geers, Nicholas, & Sedey, 2003). This result suggests that technology had much more to do with outcome than the age that the child received the implant.

Problems With Early Communication Assessment

Measures of auditory, speech, and language progress include rating scales, behavioral observation techniques, and formal assessment procedures. Problems with interpreting results may be associated with each set of techniques.

Criterion-Referenced Scales

One of the unique challenges of assessment of infants before and after implantation is that their developmental status may preclude formal testing. Therefore, researchers are limited to indirect methods of assessment. One method might be to use criterion-referenced rating scales, which are essentially hierarchically arranged lists of skills, for example, IT-MAIS (Zimmerman-Phillips et al., 2000), MUSS (Robbins & Osberger,

1991), and CAP (Archbold et al., 1995). These rating scales are generally completed through collaboration between parent and clinician and provide no norm-referenced scores. Performance is expressed merely as the number of skill items the child has exhibited at the criterion level. Problems include limited interrater reliability and the potential for grossly unequal intervals between levels of performance.

All of these rating scales begin with the easiest skill evaluated (e.g., awareness of environmental sound) and provide descriptions of increasing achievement (e.g., discriminates at least two speech sounds, understands common phrases without lipreading). However, increments throughout the range of items are not equated when documenting growth rates in the communicative development of young children. If the progress required to increase one level at the lower end of the rating scale is smaller than the progress required to increase one level at the higher end of the rating scale, this may lead us to conclude that faster progress in communicative development is made at the preimplantation and short-term postimplantation intervals. In a longitudinal study, this could lead to the appearance of a steep growth rate in the first year, followed by a slower growth rate in subsequent years. Alternatively, in a cross-sectional study, children who are initially assessed at a lower communicative level (1 years olds, e.g.) may show a faster growth rate than children initially assessed at 3 years of age if both groups of children are followed for 1 year.

Norm-Referenced Scales

In contrast to criterion-referenced rating scales, norm-referenced rating scales entail direct comparison to a known group of children. Use of a normative sample helps to overcome the problem of unequal intervals in the raw score distribution. For example, the Scales of Early Communication Skills for Hearing Impaired Children (Moog & Geers, 1975) is a teacher-assessment scale that provides standard scores for 2–8-year-old severely to profoundly deaf children who use hearing aids. However, the faster communicative progress typically exhibited by young cochlear implant users may result in a "topping-out" effect on norm-referenced scores in relation to agemates who use hearing aids. Scores at the top of the standard score distribution may fail to adequately reflect progress in skill development.

A norm-referenced measure that is frequently used to assess vocabulary development in infants and toddlers is the MCDI (Fenson et al., 1993), a parent report measure largely consisting of a catalog of productive vocabulary and other basic language milestones typically achieved by hearing children within the first 2.5 years of life. Originally developed as a screening measure for language development in hearing, typically developing children, the MCDI normative data was gathered from children who were between 8 and 30 months of age. These norms do not provide an appropriate reference group for children who are older than those in the normative sample, as might be the case for deaf children with similar vocabularies; however, the raw scores may be useful as an index of vocabulary growth.

Behavior Observation Techniques

An alternative to parent/teacher report is to observe children's behavior in a standard situation and count behaviors that are presumed to reflect communicative outcome. The Preferential Looking Paradigm adapted by Houston et al. (2003), for example, gives us a window into infant behaviors that may predict later language acquisition. These observations have been validated in hearing infants and are generalized to this population of young implant users. However it has not yet been determined whether preferential looking behavior is predictive of later vocabulary acquisition in deaf children.

Another, more widely used technique for observing language behavior is the collection of a language sample. Typically, a researcher will provide interesting materials within a familiar setting and have the child play with a familiar person. Great care must be taken to have the child and conversational partner feel comfortable in the setting and to try to capture a representative sample of the child's language and other communication skills. Because infants and toddlers do not yet know many words and frequently have poorer articulation skills in general, transcription is more difficult than it would be for a sample of language from an older child or an adult. Indeed, many infants are completely unaware of social conventions for the give-and-take of conversation and hence provide a challenge for a transcriber simply in knowing which communicative behaviors actually qualify as an intentionally communicative act (Nicholas, Geers, & Rollins, 1999).

Because pragmatic skills are an integral part of language competence, some researchers have opted to characterize the communicative behavior of infants, preschoolers, and older children in terms of the communicative functions that are served by various utterances (Nicholas & Geers, 1997; Nicholas & Geers, 2003a). An analysis of communicative functions allows for an examination of the various social purposes for which a child has developed communicative expression. In other words, these are the functions (greeting, protesting, giving information, calling attention, requesting information) of social interaction, facilitated by language, that the child must learn to convey by either spoken language, gesture, sign language, or other means if he or she is to operate successfully in the world. This form of assessment can be done either as a precursor to language analysis, in the case of infants, or in conjunction with a lexical or syntactic analysis in the case of slightly older children.

Formal Assessment

As children move into the preschool years, they begin to develop the attention, motivation, and cognitive skills necessary for assessment in a formal testing setting. However, the younger the child, the fewer of these skills may be brought to bear on the testing situation, potentially biasing the outcome of cross-sectional studies in favor of older children (Kirk et al., 1997). The younger child simply may not be willing to respond to the task. Older children can be motivated to put forth some effort and exhibit their optimal performance on an item. With preschool-age children, however, an examiner is much more vulnerable to the whim of the child at the moment. This situation contributes to poor reliability of the testing enterprise and causes difficulty in the interpretation of results. Specifically, poor performance at the youngest ages (potentially unrelated to language skill level) may lead to an *under-estimation* of the spoken language abilities of the youngest children. Subsequent testing, when the child has better general test-taking capabilities, might be more accurate but lead to an unintended overinflation of difference in performance at the two points in time. In longitudinal studies, this phenomenon may bias toward finding faster apparent progress in younger groups of children.

Changes in Assessment Methods Over Time

The restricted age range to which each measure applies may complicate interpretation of longitudinal data. For example, infants' beginning vocabulary development may be assessed from a parent-report instrument such as the MCDI. When a child is developing language in the preschool and early elementary school age years, the Peabody Picture Vocabulary Test may be a perfectly appropriate measure to use. Use of a different assessment instrument complicates the determination of vocabulary growth over time. Svirsky et al. (2004) devised a creative solution for extending the range of assessments for a group of deaf children with wide range of test ages. For those children whose language level allowed, the RDLS-III (Edwards et al., 1997) was administered. For those children whose language level was below that acceptable for scoring the RDLS-III, a parent rated the words produced using the MCDI. Those children who were assessed via the MCDI were then assigned a "predicted score" for the RDLS-III, based on previous work by the author and colleagues (Stallings, Svirsky, & Gao, 2000) that showed a high degree of reliability for predicting RDLS-III scores when using predictive functions based on MCDI data.

Separating Spoken and Signed Language

In many studies of language outcomes in children with cochlear implants, assessment takes place in the child's preferred mode of communication (Kirk, Miyamoto, Lento et al., 2002; Robbins, Bollard, & Green, 1999; Svirsky et al., 2000). This means that for children who use total communication, language is assessed using both speech and sign, therefore making it difficult to separate spoken language results from overall language results. If one of the major goals of cochlear implantation is to facilitate the child's use of intelligible speech and spoken English, a measure of spoken language development is needed to assess the contribution of earlier implant use to achieving this objective.

Confound of Duration of Use and Age of Implantation

A significant problem in the study of age of implantation effects is the inevitable confounding of the effect of age of implantation with the effect of the duration of implant use at any comparable test age. As the age of implantation is lowered, the duration of use is lengthened, given a particular test age. Disentangling the effects of these two variables is problematic and has been approached in a number of different ways by various researchers. Some take a statistical approach, partialing out the amount of variance due to one factor and seeing how much of the remaining variance is accounted for by the other (Geers, Nicholas, & Sedey, 2003). Others take the approach of looking at growth rates over the same period of device use, which still compares children at different test ages (Kirk, Miyamoto, Ying et al., 2002; Svirsky et al., 2000). These authors suggest that age at implantation and duration of use effects cannot be separated, but that earlier achievement of speech and language milestones is a sufficient argument for early cochlear implantation, regardless. This may not be a problem if one takes the position that any language advantage at younger ages is important. If longer duration of use is associated with better language, having longer duration of use at younger age is an advantage.

Unknown Participation Rate of Children With Other Cognitive/Language Problems

An important predictor of postimplantation language outcome is nonverbal, or performance IQ (Geers, Nicholas, & Sedey, 2003). As the age of diagnosis of deafness becomes lower and the decision regarding whether to have cochlear implant surgery occurs earlier, the task of discerning the intellectual status of the child becomes more challenging. Inevitably, as more children receive an implant in the infancy period without a formal assessment of cognitive skills, there will be a larger proportion of recipients who have below-average intelligence. Many studies do not assess the cognitive status of the children included and therefore may inadvertently bias age-of-implantation effect results in the favor of better outcomes for older implanted children simply because the youngest implanted groups may have more children with nonverbal cognitive delays or language learning disabilities that are undetected.

SUMMARY AND CONCLUSIONS

The expectations for spoken language development in young profoundly deaf children have changed dramatically in the past 20 years.
This is due, for the most part, to the widespread use of cochlear implants and the possibility of very early intervention afforded by newborn hearing screening procedures now in practice across much of the
country. As deaf children are identified and provided the opportunity
to receive audiological services at much earlier ages, the challenge for
professionals in this field is to devise new and developmentally appropriate methods for evaluating and educating a dramatically different
individual than was typical in the previous generation.

The studies reviewed in this chapter are few, because the practice of
providing cochlear implants to children younger than 3 years is still
relatively new. Because of the heterogeneity of the population of children receiving implants, it is difficult for researchers to investigate the
effect of age of implantation while simultaneously holding constant the
other important variables that might additionally influence outcomes.
Several conclusions might be drawn from the work done to date, however. First, most studies that include children who have received an
implant when younger than 2 years report growth rates over the first 1–3
years of implant use that are very similar to those of hearing children.
Second, the spoken language delays that are exhibited by children implanted when younger than 5 years appear to be largely due to the delay
that exists at the time of implantation, which is typically smallest for
children implanted at the youngest ages. Third, a substantial number
of children are approaching spoken language levels typical of hearing
children at the same chronological age when an implant is provided
within the first 2 years of life. And finally, there remains a great deal of
variability in the performance of children with implants, regardless of
the age at which they were received. However, even with that variability, it is becoming clear that mean performance levels on spoken
language measures of children with an implant exceed by a significant
margin the mean performance levels of profoundly deaf children with
hearing aids. Indeed, it is now possible and not uncommon to walk into
a mainstream nursery school classroom in many places around the
country and see profoundly deaf children listening, talking, and singing
along with their hearing peers, interacting completely and with ease
through the mode of spoken language.

We have tried to succinctly present the process of establishing implant candidacy in infants and toddlers and the studies bearing on the
issue of age implantation effects and to discuss concerns related to the
interpretation of those results. Much work remains to be done to discover the optimal setting for spoken language development. Future research must address some of the following important questions: What is

the critical age below which children with a cochlear implant achieve spoken language growth typical of hearing counterparts? What is the better ear hearing level above which infants will acquire spoken language faster with an implant than with a powerful digital hearing aid? Will auditory stimulation with a cochlear implant in infancy permit spoken language development in children with developmental delay (even though it may not reach levels typical of hearing children)? Do short-term spoken language advantages in children implanted in infancy persist, or do children implanted later (but still within the preschool period) catch up after 3 or more years of device use? These questions and others must be addressed in order to assist the decision-making process of parents of children who are deaf.

REFERENCES

Anderson, I., D'Haese, P., & Weichbold, V. (2003 April). *MAIS and MUSS results in early implanted children*. Poster presented at the 9th Symposium on Cochlear Implants in Children, Washington, DC.

Archbold, S., Lutman, M., & Marshall, D. (1995). Categories of auditory performance. *Annals of Otology, Rhinology, and Laryngology, 104*(9 Suppl. 166), 312–314.

Bamford, J., & Wilson, I. (1979). Methodological considerations and practical aspects of the BKB sentence lists. In J. Bench & J. Bamford (Eds.), *Speech-hearing tests and the spoken language of hearing impaired children* (pp. 148–187). London: Academic Press.

Baumgartner, W. D., Pok, S. M., Egelierler, B., Franz, P., Gstoettner, W., & Hamzavi, J. (2002). The role of age in pediatric cochlear implantation. *International Journal of Pediatric Otorhinolaryngology, 62*, 223–228.

Blamey, P. (2003). Development of spoken language by deaf children. In M. Marschark & P. E. Spencer (Eds.), *Deaf studies, language and education* (pp. 232–246). New York: Oxford University Press.

Blamey, P., & Sarant, J. (2002). Speech perception and language criteria for pediatric cochlear implant candidature. *Audiology and Neuro-otology, 7*, 114–121.

Blamey, P., Sarant, J., Paatsch, L., Barry, J., Wales, C., Wright, M., et al. (2001). Relationships among speech perception, production, language, hearing loss, and age in children with impaired hearing. *Journal of Speech, Language, and Hearing Research, 44*, 264–285.

Connor, C., Hieber, S., Arts, A., & Zwolan, T. (2000). Speech, vocabulary, and the education of children using cochlear implants: Oral or total communication? *Journal of Speech, Language, and Hearing Research, 43*(5), 1185–1204.

Dazel, L., Orlando, M., MacDonald, M., Berg, A., Bradley, M., Cacace, A., et al. (2000). The New York State universal newborn hearing screening demonstration project: Ages of hearing loss identification, hearing aid fitting, and enrollment in early intervention. *Ear and Hearing, 21*(2), 118–128.

Dowell, R., Blamey, P., & Clark, G. (1997). Factors affecting outcomes in children with cochlear implants. In G. M. Clark (Ed.), *Cochlear implants, XVI*

World Congress of Otorhinolaryngology Head and Neck Surgery. Bolonga, Italy: Monduzzi Editore.

Dunn, L. M., & Dunn, L. M. (1997). *The Peabody Picture Vocabulary Test* (3rd ed.). Circle Pines, MN: American Guidance Service.

Edwards, S., Fletcher, P., Garman, M., Hughes, A., Letts, C., & Sinka, I. (1997). *The Reynell Developmental Language Scales III: The University of Reading edition.* Los Angeles: Western Psychological Services.

Fenson, L., Dale, P. S., Reznick, J. S., Thal, D., Bates, E., Hartung, J. P., et al. (1993). *MacArthur Communicative Development Inventories.* San Diego, CA: Singular Publishing Group.

Geers, A. (2004). Speech, language, and reading skills after early cochlear implantation. *Archives of Otolaryngology–Head and Neck Surgery, 130,* 634–638.

Geers, A., & Brenner, C. (1994). Speech perception results: Audition and lipreading enhancement. *Volta Review, 96*(5), 97–108.

Geers, A., Brenner, C., & Davidson, L. (2003). Factors associated with the development of speech perception skills in children implanted by age 5. *Ear and Hearing, 24* (1), 24–35.

Geers, A., & Moog, J. (1987). Predicting spoken language acquisition in profoundly deaf children. *Journal of Speech and Hearing Disorders, 52*(1), 84–94.

Geers, A., & Moog, J. (1989). Factors predictive of the development of literacy in hearing-impaired adolescents. *Volta Review, 91*(2), 69–86.

Geers, A., & Moog, J. (1994). Effectiveness of cochlear implants and tactile aids for deaf children: The sensory aids study at Central Institute for the Deaf. *Volta Review, 96*(Suppl.).

Geers, A. E., Nicholas, J. G., & Sedey, A. L. (2003). Language skills of children with early cochlear implantation. *Ear and Hearing, 24,* 46S–58S.

Govaerts, P. J., De Beukelaer, C., Daemers, K., De Ceulaer, G., Yperman, M., Somers, T., et al. (2002). Outcome of cochlear implantation at different ages from 0 to 6 years. *Otology and Neuro-otology, 23,* 885–890.

Hammes, D. M., Novak, M. A., Rotz, L. A., Willis, M., Edmondson, D. M., & Thomas, J. F. (2002). Early identification and cochlear implantation: Critical factors for spoken language development. *Annals of Otology, Rhinology, and Laryngology, 111,* 74–78.

Haskins, H. (1949). A phonetically balanced test of speech discrimination for children. Unpublished master's thesis, Northwestern University, Evanston, IL, USA.

Hehar, S. S., Nikolopoulos, T., Gibbin, K., & O'Donoghue, G. M. (2002). Surgery and functional outcomes in deaf children receiving cochlear implants before age 2 years. *Archives of Otolaryngology–Head and Neck Surgery, 128,* 11–14.

Hollich, G., Hirsh-Pasek, K., & Golinkoff, R. (2000). *Breaking the language barrier: An emergentist coalition model of word learning* (Monographs of the Society for Research in Child Development, 65[3, Serial No. 262]).: Blackwell Publishing.

Houston, D. M., Ying, E., Pisoni, D. B., & Kirk, K. I. (2003). Development of pre-word learning skills in infants with cochlear implants. *Volta Review, 103*(4), 303–326.

Kirk, K. I., Diefendorf, A. O., Pisoni, D. B., & Robbins, A. M. (1997). Assessing speech perception in children. In L. Mendel & J. Danhauer (Eds.), *Audiologic evaluation and management and speech perception assessment.* 101–132. San Diego: Singular Publishing Group.

Kirk, K. I., Miyamoto, R. T., Lento, C. L., Ying, E., O'Neill, T., & Fears, B. (2002). Effects of age at implantation in young children. *Annals of Otology, Rhinology, and Laryngology, 111*, 69–73.

Kirk, K. I., Miyamoto, R. T., Ying, E., Perdew, A. E., & Zuganelis, H. (2002). Cochlear implantation in young children: Effects of age at implantation and communication mode. *Volta Review, 102*(4), 127–144.

Kirk, K. I., Pisoni, D., & Osberger, M. (1995). Lexical effects of spoken word recognition by pediatric cochlear implant users. *Ear and Hearing, 16*, 225–259.

Lenarz, T., Lesinski-Schiedat, A., von der Haar-Heise, S., Illg, A., Bertram, B., & Battmer, R. (1999). Cochlear implantation in children under the age of two: The MHH experience with the Clarion cochlear implant. *Annals of Otology, Rhinology, and Laryngology, 108*(4, Pt. 2, Suppl. 177), 4–49.

Locke, J. L. (1997). A theory of neurolinguistic development. *Brain and Language, 58*, 26–326.

Manrique, M., Cervera-Paz, F. J., Huarate, A., Perez, N., Molina, M., & Garcia-Tapia, R. (1999). Cerebral auditory plasticity and cochlear implants. *International Journal of Pediatric Otorhinolaryngology, 49*(Suppl. 1), S193–S197.

Moog, J. (2002). Changing expectations for children with cochlear implants. *Annals of Otology, Rhinology, and Laryngology, 111*, 138–142.

Moog, J., & Geers, A. (1975). *Scales of early communication skills for hearing-impaired children.* St. Louis, MO: Central Institute for the Deaf.

Moog, J., Kozak, V., & Geers, A. (1983). *Grammatical analysis of elicited language: Pre-sentence level.* St. Louis. MO: Central Institute for the Deaf.

Muller, A., & Wagenfeld, D. (2003 April). *Cochlear implantation in children under 2 years and between 2 and 3 years: A comparative study.* Paper presented at the 9th Symposium on Cochlear Implants in Children, Washington, DC.

Nicholas, J. G. (2000). Age differences in the use of informative/heuristic communicative functions in young children with and without hearing loss who are learning spoken language. *Journal of Speech, Language, and Hearing Research, 43*, 380–394.

Nicholas, J. G., & Geers, A. E. (1997). Communication of oral deaf and normally hearing children at 36 months. *Journal of Speech, Language, and Hearing Research, 40*, 1314–1327.

Nicholas, J. G., & Geers, A. E. (2003a). Hearing status, language modality, and young children's communicative and linguistic behavior. *Journal of Deaf Studies and Deaf Education, 8*(4), 422–437.

Nicholas, J. G., & Geers, A. E. (2003b April). *Effect of very early cochlear implantation on language: An interim report.* Paper presented at the 9th Symposium on Cochlear Implants in Children, Washington, DC.

Nicholas, J. G., Geers, A. E., & Rollins, P. (1999). Inter-rater reliability as a reflection of ambiguity in the communication of deaf and normally hearing children. *Journal of Communication Disorders, 32*, 121–134.

Osberger, M. J., Maso, M., & Sam, L. (1993). Speech intelligibility of children with cochlear implants, tactile aids, or hearing aids. *Journal of Speech and Hearing Research, 36*(1), 186–203.

Richter, B., Eissele, S., Laszig, R., & Lohle, E. (2002). Receptive and expressive language skills of 106 children with a minimum of 2 years' experience in hearing with a cochlear implant. *International Journal of Pediatric Otorhinolaryngology, 64*, 111–125.

Robbins, A. M., Bollard, P. M., & Green, J. (1999). Language development in children implanted with the Clarion cochlear implant. *Annals of Otology, Rhinology, and Laryngology, 177*(Suppl.), 113–118.

Robbins, A. M., Koch, D. B., Osberger, M. J., Zimmerman-Phillips, S., & Kishon-Rabin, L. (2004). Effect of age at implantation on auditory-skill development in infants and toddlers. *Archives of Otolaryngology–Head and Neck Surgery, 130,* 570–574.

Robbins, A. M., & Osberger, M. J. (1991). *Meaningful Use of Speech Scale.* Indianapolis, Indiana University School of Medicine.

Robinson, K. (1998). Implications of developmental plasticity for the language acquisition of deaf children with cochlear implants. *International Journal of Pediatric Otorhinolaryngology, 46,* 71–80.

Ruben, R. J. (1997). A time frame of critical/sensitive periods of language development. *Acta Otolaryngologica, 117,* 202–205.

Ruben, R. J., & Schwartz, R. (1999). Necessity versus sufficiency: The role of input in language acquisition. *International Journal of Pediatric Otorhinolaryngology, 47,* 137–140.

Sarant, J. Z., Blamey, P. J., Dowell, R. C., Clark, G. M., & Gibson, W. P. (2001). Variation in speech perception scores among children with cochlear implants. *Ear and Hearing, 22,* 18–28.

Spencer, P. E. (2004). Individual differences in language performance after cochlear implantation at one to three years of age: Child, family and linguistic factors. *Journal of Deaf Studies and Deaf Education, 9,* 395–412.

Stallings, L. M., Svirsky, M., & Gao, S. (2000). Assessing the language abilities of pediatric cochlear implant users across a broad range of ages and performance abilities. *Volta Review, 102*(4), 215–235.

Svirsky, M. A., & Meyer, T. A. (1999). Comparison of speech perception in pediatric CLARION cochlear implant and hearing aid users. *Annals of Otolaryngology, Rhinology, and Laryngology, 177*(Suppl.), 104–109.

Svirsky, M. A., Robbins, A. M., Kirk, K. I., Pisoni, D. B., & Miyamoto, R. T. (2000). Language development in profoundly deaf children with cochlear implants. *Psychological Science, 11*(2), 153–158.

Svirsky, M. A., Teoh, S. W., & Neuburger, H. (2004). Development of language and speech perception in congenitally, profoundly deaf children as a function of age at cochlear implantation. *Audiology and Neuro-otology, 9,* 224–233.

Szagun, G. (2001). Language acquisition in young German-speaking children cochlear implants: Individual differences and implications for conceptions of a "sensitive phase." *Audiology and Neuro-otology, 6*(5), 288–297.

Tye-Murray, N., Spencer, L., & Woodworth, G. (1995). Acquisition of speech by children who have prolonged cochlear implant experience. *Journal of Speech and Hearing Research, 38,* 327–337.

Tyler, R., Teagle, H. F., Kelsay, D. M. R., Gantz, B. J., Woodworth, G. G., & Parkinson, A. J. (2000). Speech perception by prelingually deaf children after six years of cochlear implant use: Effects of age at implantation. *Annals of Otology, Rhinology, and Laryngology, 109* (Suppl. 185), 82–84.

Waltzman, S. B., & Cohen, N. L. (1998). Cochlear implantation in children younger than 2 years old. *American Journal of Otology, 19,* 158–162.

Werker, J. F., & Tees, R. C. (1984). Cross-language speech perception: Evidence for perceptual reorganization during the first year of life. *Infant Behavior and Development, 7,* 49–63.

Yoshinaga-Itano, C., Sedey, A., Coulter, D., & Mehl, A. (1998). Language of early- and later-identified children with hearing loss. *Pediatrics, 102,* 1161–1171.

Young, N. M. (2002). Infant cochlear implantation and anesthetic risk. *Annals of Otology, Rhinology, and Laryngology, 111,* 49–51.

Zimmerman-Phillips, S., Robbins, A. M., & Osberger, M. J. (2000). Assessing cochlear implant benefit in very young children. *Annals of Otology, Rhinology, and Laryngology, 109*(Suppl. 185), 42–43.

Zwolan, T. A., Zimmerman-Phillips, S., Ashbaugh, C. J., Hieber, S. J., Kileny, P. R., & Telian, S. A. (1997). Cochlear implantation of children with minimal open-set speech recognition skills. *Ear and Hearing, 18,* 240–251.

13

Early Identification, Communication Modality, and the Development of Speech and Spoken Language Skills: Patterns and Considerations

Christine Yoshinaga-Itano

Despite the volume of research on speech development of children with significant hearing loss, there are many unanswered questions about how speech and spoken language develop, what methods of intervention are the most effective, and what variables predict optimal spoken language outcomes. One variable of special interest has been that of age of identification of hearing loss: Will children whose hearing loss is identified during the neonatal period achieve better speech and spoken language skills than those who are identified at later ages? The increasing adoption of universal newborn hearing screening, that is, hearing testing of all infants at or near birth, is providing a first opportunity to be able to investigate these issues in a large population of children.

This chapter focuses on information that has been gained about the speech and spoken language development of children whose hearing loss has been identified through universal newborn hearing screening programs in Colorado. Ninety percent of the children in Colorado whose hearing loss was identified between 1994 and 2004 have participated in the statewide early intervention program (Colorado Home Intervention Program [CHIP]). This chapter begins with a description of this program. Data are then presented that demonstrate rates of development of speech skills by this population, with reference to influential variables and patterns that differ from those of earlier cohorts of deaf and hard of hearing children. Finally, case studies are presented for three children who were identified in Colorado's newborn hearing screening program, who participated in the state's early intervention program, and whose speech and language development has been supported in part by the use of cochlear implants. These case studies were chosen because they were the first three children with early-identified hearing loss through universal newborn hearing screening with age-appropriate language levels preimplantation to receive cochlear implants.

THE EARLY INTERVENTION PROGRAM—CHIP

Universal newborn hearing screening programs began in 1992 in Colorado, and by 1996 60% of the births in the state of Colorado were being screened each year during the neonatal period. In 1998, legislation was passed mandating universal newborn hearing screening programs throughout the state. By the year 2000, all 60 of the birthing hospitals in Colorado were screening hearing of all newborns. As a result, the number of later-identified children has decreased substantially within the state. Today, the average age of identification of hearing loss in Colorado is 2 months.

Intervention referrals are made within 48 hours after the diagnosis of the hearing loss. Contact with the family occurs within days of the diagnosis of hearing loss. The system of care is a statewide provision of service with professionals specially trained in providing parent–infant intervention to families of children with hearing loss. Children receive intervention services within 2 months of the diagnosis of their hearing loss.

Fitting and Managing Amplification

Hearing aids are fit by an average of 4 months of age in Colorado. The vast proportion of children are fitted with state-of-the-art technology, analog programmable or digital hearing aids. The recommended protocol for fitting hearing aids follows the amplification protocol approved by the Colorado Newborn Hearing Advisory Board (2000) and uses standardized prescriptive techniques for fitting hearing aids on young infants and children. These techniques use the physiological thresholds obtained from auditory brainstem response testing and mathematical calculations that are developmental age dependent to determine the appropriate amount of amplification at each frequency that will allow the child to hear conversational speech across the frequency range (see Ackley & Decker, chapter 4 this volume).

Because hearing aids of newborns must be fitted before infants are old enough to be able to respond reliably to behavioral testing, initial amplification decisions are made on the basis of physiological thresholds. Physiological thresholds can differ from behavioral thresholds by ±15–20 dB HL. Thus, without verification of behavioral responses with amplification, hearing aids may underamplify or overamplify. Additionally, there are no reliable measures of tolerance to loudness. Therefore, children must return to diagnostic audiologists at 3-month intervals to be rechecked and provide complete audiological diagnostic information. At these visits, parents learn how to provide the fitting audiologist with information to ensure the best possible fitting and programming of amplification.

The best time to detect differential responses to auditory stimuli is when the child's hearing aids are first being turned on each day. Awareness to sounds is typically strongest when a child is going from no-sound conditions (without amplification) to amplified sounds. Therefore, when amplification is first turned on in the morning, parents are asked to stimulate the child without visual cues, using the six Ling sounds: /a/, /i/, /u/, /s/, /sh/, and /m/ (Ling, 1978). This procedure surveys sounds that demonstrate ability to hear conversational speech, from 500 to 2000 Hz. Parents are advised that newborn infants may have very subtle responses to sounds or may have overt observable changes in their behavior. These responses can include eye widening, eye localization, smile, vocalization, and motor responses.

Parents are asked to prepare an auditory profile of sounds that the child responds to within the home environment and to note the type of response observed. Additionally, parents are taught how to socially reinforce the child's responses to sounds through smiles, clapping, drawing attention to the sounds, touches and hugs, or imitation. After determining whether the child can respond to the Ling sounds (Ling, 1978), parents can focus on stimulation using one of the vowel sounds of spoken English, using a different vowel each day. The vowels are good vocal stimuli and are developmentally appropriate to the speech development of infants in the first 6 months of life. Each day, the parents can stimulate the child auditorally with a new speech sound, in order to develop an auditory profile that is a description of the child's awareness to different speech sounds and responses observed. Awareness should be then determined for consonants, beginning with those consonants that can be sustained, such as /m/, /n/, /z/, and /zh/ (see Oller, chapter 2 this volume).

Assessment of Speech and Language Progress

Children and families are assessed at 6-month intervals. The assessment protocol consists of parent questionnaires and a videotaped parent–child interaction that provide information about vocabulary, syntax, pragmatic, speech, auditory skills, fine motor, gross motor, self-help, nonverbal cognitive skills, symbolic play, and social-emotional development. Families use results of the assessment to make decisions about the appropriateness of the intervention goals and procedures.

Speech skills are assessed by analyzing a spontaneous speech sample of parent–child interaction in the home. Analysis is done using the Logical International Phonetics Program (LIPP; Oller & Delgado, 1999). Language skills are also assessed using a spontaneous language sample analysis. Analysis is done using the spontaneous analysis of language transcriptions (SALT) for parts of speech, syntax, and pragmatic language analysis. Other measures include but are not limited to the Minnesota Child Development Inventory (Ireton & Thwing, 1974), the MacArthur Communicative Development Inventory (Fenson et al., 1993; words and gestures, words and sentences, or MacArthur III versions, depending upon child age), and the Expressive One-Word Picture Vocabulary Test (Gardner, 1990).

Choices of Mode of Communication

Parents choose from a menu of offerings that focus on developmental skills rather than mode of communication. Thus, they decide upon vocabulary development, speech development, syntax development, auditory development, cognitive development, and social-emotional development goals. Although some families choose to focus on a single method or primary modality for language training, others choose to combine services that give them access to different models of language modality. For example, it has become relatively common for families to choose combinations such as visits from an expert in auditory/speech development and spoken language as well as a deaf sign language instructor. The CHIP program, therefore, allows families considerable flexibility in their choice of services and language modalities.

Special Supports for Families

There is a statewide parent-to-parent organization, Families for Hands and Voices, which provides resources to all families with newly identified children with hearing loss. They update the *Colorado Resource Manual*, which is provided to all families at the time of diagnosis of hearing loss, and they maintain a website (www.Handsandvoices.org). The organization also provides advocacy services to families and interacts with the Deaf and hard-of-hearing community.

There are parent–infant care providers who are themselves deaf or hard-of-hearing who have been trained to provide families with intervention services in language, cognitive, social-emotional, and sometimes speech and auditory skill development. Some deaf or hard-of-hearing professionals work in conjunction with a hearing care providers who focus on speech and audition. In addition, there are deaf/hard-of-hearing professionals who provide sign language instruction to families following a curriculum developed for work with hearing families of deaf and hard-of-hearing infants, toddlers, and preschool-age children. Some deaf and hard-of-hearing professionals have also been trained to be "shared reading" instructors, who teach the families to sign stories in American Sign Language (Delk & Weidekamp, 2001). Others have been trained as "integrated reading" instructors, who teach families to sign stories in a manually coded English program. The CHIP program adapted the shared reading program in American Sign Language and developed the integrated reading program, which shares similar characteristics but can be used with English-based sign systems.

Deaf/hard-of-hearing individuals are also available to families statewide through the Deaf/Hard-of-Hearing Role Model program. About 60 individuals participate statewide in this program. Unlike the other roles of deaf/hard-of-hearing individuals in the CHIP, their contacts with families do not occur on a regular weekly basis but can be a single instance or only occasionally. Role models are available to families to answer questions about growing up deaf or hard-of-hearing, their experiences, or any other questions that a parent might ask. Parents often ask to meet deaf/hard-of-hearing individuals who identify themselves as part of Deaf culture, have cochlear implants, have been raised orally or with sign language, have grown up in deaf families or in hearing families, or went to residential schools, center-based schools, or mainstream schools.

EARLY IDENTIFICATION AND DEVELOPMENT
OF SPEECH PRODUCTION SKILLS

Most available reports providing speech production information on children who have significant hearing loss between the ages of birth and 3 years consist of case study descriptions (e.g., Ertmer et al., 2002; Ertmer, 2000; Ertmer & Mellon, 2004; Kent, Osberger, Netsell, & Hustedde, 1987). In contrast, Yoshinaga-Itano and Stredler-Brown (1992) reported vocal production of more than 100 children between the ages of birth and 36 months who were participating in the CHIP. These children were all identified with hearing loss prior to the establishment of universal newborn hearing screening programs in the state of Colorado. Prior to 1992, the average age of identification of hearing loss both in the United States and worldwide was about 2–2.5 years of age. As a result, there had been established protocols for assessment of speech or spoken language production of children from birth through 3 years of age.

Existing speech production protocols for children with hearing loss assumed some vocabulary knowledge and other language skills. Clearly, such protocols could not be used with children at prelinguistic stages of communication development. With the advent of universal newborn hearing screening programs in the United States, and the resulting significant numbers of children entering intervention programs in the first few months of life, there has been a recognized need to identify assessment procedures that can be used with children younger than 3 years. Clinic-administered assessments for children below the age of 3 can be difficult to obtain, and the reliability and validity of these measures have not been demonstrated for children at these young ages. In the Colorado early identification and intervention project, we have therefore relied on observations of communication performance and parent report data in building a protocol for use with these young children.

The speech data are derived from the half-hour videotapes of parent–child interactions that are part of the assessment process and are obtained at 6-month intervals. Parents are asked to interact with their child and play in a natural manner that would represent typical interaction. The speech data are transcribed by a graduate student in linguistics with expertise in phonetic and phonologic transcription. Although there can be differences of opinion on precise identification of vowel production of infants, particularly in the first year of life, there is greater consistency in the coding about the quantity of number of different phones for both vowels and consonants. These discriminations are most accurate from 9 months and older. Intensive speech production analysis of inflection, type of phoneme, and voice quality have not provided as powerful information for prediction of future speech intelligibility as the developmental frequency of number of different consonant types in the spontaneous speech production of the infant, toddler, or preschool child. Fortunately, determining the number of different consonant types has strong reliability among intervention providers and can be done quickly and easily.

We have found that phonetic inventories displayed in spontaneous speech and language samples of videotaped interactions between parents and child provide valuable data for intervention planning. Information can be provided to parents about a child's speech development as compared to other children with similar developmental characteristics, such as age of identification of hearing loss, expressive language development, and degree of hearing loss. Thus, parents are able to determine whether their child's speech production is at, below, or above the 25th, 50th, or 75th percentile for children with similar hearing losses and similar language levels. This objective information assists the parents in making intervention decisions. Distributions for children's speech are also provided by mode of communication used. Thus, parents can determine how their child's speech development compares with other children who are being educated in either aural-oral communication only or communication strategies that include the use of sign language. Parents may decide that the chosen mode of communication is working well for their child (at or above the 50th percentile) when considering both language and speech development. Or, for example, they may discover that their child is functioning below the 10th percentile both when compared to children communicating in a similar mode of communication or when compared to children whose families have combined both auditory and visual modes of communication. These discoveries typically open up dialogue between the family and the interventionist about possible changes in intervention plans, particularly when the child's potential for optimal development is higher than the development observed.

When considering children with mild through severe hearing losses, even when later identified or multiply disabled, 75% of the Colorado children achieve intelligible speech by 60–72 months of age. (All of these children, even those later identified, first received early intervention services between the ages of birth and 36 months.) In contrast, only 25% of the children with profound hearing loss who have received early intervention services between birth and 36 months of age approach intelligible speech between 5 and 6 years of age. Thus, the level of residual hearing has strong impact on the probability of early speech development. Children with profound hearing loss are disadvantaged even when early identified and receiving early conventional amplification (hearing aids) with appropriate intervention (see Geers, chapter 11 this volume). In addition, we have found that children with significant hearing loss whose spontaneous phonetic inventories include fewer than eight consonant phones by 36 months of age have a very low probability of developing intelligible speech by 6 years of age.

VARIABLES THAT AFFECT SPEECH PRODUCTION

Children who are early identified have significantly better speech production than do children who are later identified (Apuzzo & Yoshinaga-Itano, 1995, 1998; Yoshinaga-Itano & Apuzzo, 1998a,b; Yoshinaga-Itano, Coulter, & Thomson, 2000, 2001). Although early-identified children have better speech production, we have proposed that this improved speech production is not directly due to the age of identification, but rather to the impact that age of identification has upon language development in general. That is, the ability to produce the lexical and grammatical units of language, regardless of the modalities in which those productions occur, seems to provide a framework in which deaf and hard-of-hearing children can hone their articulation of speech sounds.

Children with higher nonverbal cognitive development have better speech production than do children with lower nonverbal cognitive skills in the first 6 years of life. But the route through which cognition influences speech production may not be direct. Instead, nonverbal cognition probably influences a child's acquisition of language itself, which in turn allows the child to improve the clarity of speech production.

In fact, expressive language development as measured by the Minnesota Child Development Inventory, whether assessed through spoken language or sign language, predicted a significant amount of variance in speech production in the Colorado population. Children with the best expressive language development were those with the best vocal development.

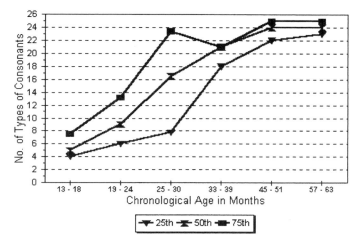

Figure 13-1. Number of types of simple consonants produced by children with expressive language quotients of at least 80.

Figure 13.1 shows speech production data for children with hearing loss whose language development is at least 80% of that expected for hearing children of the same age—that is, within the normal range of development. From 13 through 39 months, there was a range of 33–62 children at each age level. At 40–45 months, there were 17 children, and between 46 and 63 months there were 12 children. Table 13.1 provides the number of children at each age level by expressive language quotient group.

Figure 13.1 depicts the number of consonants produced by children at the 75th percentile (the top line), at the 50th percentile (the middle line), and at the 25th percentile (the bottom line) at each age level from 13 to 63 months of age. A child with eight consonants when 13–18 months of age is at the 75th percentile of all children with data at this age group, while a child with four consonants is at the 25th percentile compared to all children at this age. The developmental trend is similar for children at the 25th, 50th, and 75th percentiles. These children rapidly increase the number of consonants they produce correctly between 13 and 30 months of age. By 33–39 months of age, even the children whose speech production is at the 25th percentile spontaneously produce the vast majority of the consonant phones in spoken English.

Figure 13.2 shows that children with expressive language development between 60% and 79% of their chronological age have slow but steady increases in consonant production from 13 to 63 months of age. For the first 30 months of life the children begin to use an average of two more phones each assessment period, with a development spurt

Table 13-1: Speech Development as Coded From a Spontaneous Language
Sample of 25 Minutes: Number of Types of Simple Consonants
by Age and Expressive Language Quotient on the Minnesota
Child Development Inventory.

Chronological Age (months)	Expressive Language Quotient	n	Number of Types of Simple Consonants (percentile rank)		
			25	50	75
13–18	<60	19	2	3	4
	60–79	21	3	5	7
	≥80	41	4	5	7.5
19–24	<60	30	3	4.5	6
	60–79	28	3	6	10.5
	≥80	62	6	9	13.2
25–30	<60	47	2	3	5
	60–79	34	5	7.5	12.2
	≥80	42	7.8	16.5	23.4
33–39	<60	54	2	5	10.2
	60–79	54	7	12.5	18
	≥80	33	18	21	21
45–51	<60	53	5	10	16
	60–79	25	19	21	23
	≥80	17	22	24	25
57–63	<60	39	8	15	21
	60–79	17	18	21	25
	≥80	12	23	24	25

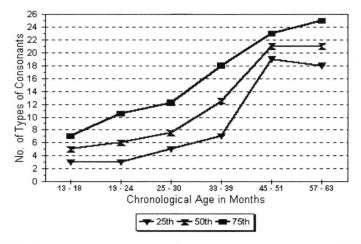

Figure 13-2. Number of types of simple consonants produced by children with
expressive language quotients between 60 and 79.

from 8 to 12 phones from the 25–30-month age group to the 33–39-month age group.

Figure 13.3 shows that children with expressive language skills below a quotient of 60% (i.e., a child 36 months old who has a language age of 21.6 months) show a delay in their pattern of increased consonant production. A rapid rise in number of consonants (again produced in a 20–minute spontaneous language sample) does not occur until about 30–51 months of age.

Low expressive language quotients can occur because of late identification of hearing loss, cognitive disability, extenuating family characteristics such as poverty or other hardship, or intervention strategies that are not meeting the individual needs of the child and family. There is a relatively flat development through the first 30 months of life followed by a steep rise from the 25–30-month period through the 57–63-month period.

Hearing Levels and Speech Production

Although degree of hearing loss is believed to be the most important variable in the prediction of speech production skills, expressive language quotients accounted for slightly more variance than did degree of hearing loss in the Colorado population from birth to 6 years of age. However, the relationship between degree of hearing loss and spoken language development changes with age during the first 5 years of life.

In the first 12 months of life, children identified with hearing loss of any degree, from mild to profound, have highly similar vocal productions (Wallace, Menn, & Yoshinaga-Itano, 2000). The quantity of

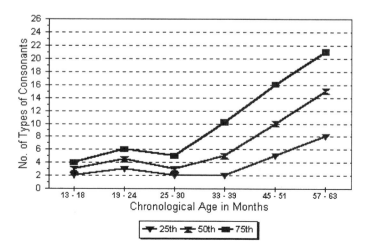

Figure 13-3. Number of types of simple consonants in children with expressive language quotients less than 60.

productions, the vowel inventory, consonant inventory, and babble index were all similar in the first year of life. Despite the fact that these
children's hearing losses have been identified and amplified within the
first few months of life, they can be expected to have vocal productions
that are significantly different from those of age-matched hearing peers.
All children with hearing loss regardless of degree (mild through profound) produce fewer consonant–vowel productions in the first year of
life than do children with normal hearing.

At the end of the first year of life, the impact of degree of hearing loss
begins to differentiate among children with early-identified hearing loss
by their degree of loss. During the second year, the vocal productions of
children with profound hearing losses significantly differ from those of
children with mild through severe hearing losses. Children with the
highest likelihood of the largest phonetic inventories are those children
who have less severe hearing loss and who also exhibit rising inflections
in their vocal productions. (Obenchain, Menn, & Yoshinaga-Itano, 2000).

From 24 through 72 months of age, children with profound hearing
loss continue to have significantly different developmental trajectories
for speech production development than children with mild through
severe hearing loss.

Number of Consonant Types

As shown in figure 13.4, children functioning at the 50th percentile of
the children with mild to severe hearing losses control approximately
15 consonant types in their spontaneous speech production by 33–38

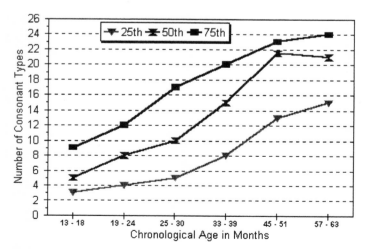

Figure 13-4. **Number of consonant types: mild to severe hearing loss at 13–18,
19–24, 25–30, 33–39, 45–51, and 57–63 months of age.**

months of age. This compares with a median of 21 consonants produced by children who have relatively normal expressive language
quotients (i.e., at 75th percentile). Speech production for the average
child with mild through severe hearing loss does not include all of the
English consonant phonemes in spoken English until about 48 months
of age. The average child with mild hearing loss still has significant
delays in speech production at 3 years of age.

In contrast, children with normal hearing perform at or above the
top 75th percentile of the distributions for children with hearing loss.
Hearing children have rapid development of both vowel and consonant production between 2 and 3 years of age. Only the top 25% of the
deaf and hard-of-hearing population have speech production development comparable to children with normal hearing. This is the case
despite the fact that the hearing losses of most children in this group
were identified by 2 months of age, amplification was used by 4 months
of age, and intervention was provided in the third month of life. However, the picture is even more problematic for children with profound
hearing loss, for whom only minimal speech production development is
typical. As can be seen in figure 13.5, the median consonant repertoire of
children with profound hearing loss at 57–63 months is 10 consonant
phones. At the 75th percentile, some children with profound hearing
loss have mastered 18 consonant phones by 5 years of age.

Communication Modalities and Speech Production

Mode of communication accounted for a small amount of the variance
in speech production between the ages of birth and 60 months of age.

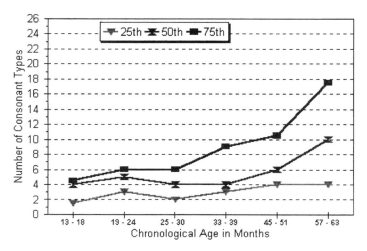

Figure 13-5. Number of consonant types: profound hearing loss at 13–18,
19–24, 25–30, 33–39, 45–51, and 57–63 months of age.

However, children with hearing losses from mild through profound were included in this study. Families whose children had milder hearing losses tended to choose aural-oral methods of communication and also had children with more intelligible speech (Yoshinaga-Itano & Sedey, 2000). At the severe to profound levels of hearing loss, equal numbers of children educated orally or with some form of sign language achieved intelligible speech. Parents make decisions related to their children's language modalities by comparing their assessed progress with the results shown in the above figures of the Colorado population. It is not unusual for parents in CHIP to change methods of communication during the infant/toddler period or to add additional strategies. In addition, cochlear implantation is increasing as a choice of parents with children who have profound hearing loss, as only the top 25th percentile of the distribution has been found to achieve intelligible speech using conventional amplification.

In summary, several variables at the infant/toddler/preschool stages predict intelligible speech by 6 years of age. Children with language levels that are within the normal range, based on vocabulary and syntax knowledge and regardless of language modalities, are the most likely to develop intelligible speech. Children with milder hearing loss, if language levels are equal, have a higher probability of developing intelligible speech than do children with greater degrees of hearing loss and achieve intelligible speech at an earlier average age.

Recommendations for Supporting Children's Development of Intelligible Spoken English

The information presented above, and more than a decade of observing the provision of intervention services to families whose children have an early identified hearing loss, leads to the following recommendations for interventionists working with families of children with early identified hearing loss who want to maximize the potential for spoken language skills:

- Provide frequent assessments to determine that the intervention strategies chosen are promoting expressive language skills that are within the normal range of development, regardless of whether that language is through spoken English or sign language.
- Audiologist(s), interventionist(s), and family members should work together to ensure that amplification is fitted at the earliest possible age and that the fitting is adjusted to the specific characteristics of the child's hearing loss.
- Provide families with instruction about how they can incorporate auditory skill development into their daily routines and teach them to identify and create "auditory moments" that can

be used as natural opportunities to teach listening skills. This may include creating opportunities to use sound in meaningful but natural ways. The parents can learn to identify sounds that have particular meaning in the life of the child and can use this knowledge to intentionally signal that meaning. Thus, naturally occurring events can provide optimal opportunities for learning to listen and identify sounds such as a door knock, a door bell, a telephone ring, the refrigerator door opening or closing, a parent or sibling's call, or footsteps. In addition, parents can use speech sound signals to signify important events—"uh oh" for unusual or surprise events, "whee" for action or moving events, "up up up" for lifting and tossing, "oooo" or "vrrrm" for noises that vehicles make.

- Parents should be taught to observe their child's behavior so that they can recognize when the child is responding to sounds in the environment. They should be taught techniques to socially condition their children to respond to sounds in the environment and to use natural reinforcers for behaviors that let the parent know that the child heard something.
- Parents can be encouraged to make auditory and speech "practice" playful and enjoyable. For example, animal sound play can be used to practice vowel sounds. Music, musical toys, dancing, and singing can make auditory experiences more fun. Motion play such as sliding, bouncing, or jumping may help the child vocalize in the most relaxed physical state that will prevent abnormal quality of speech production.

COCHLEAR IMPLANTATION, SPEECH PRODUCTION, AND SPOKEN LANGUAGE DEVELOPMENT

The majority of existing literature on developmental outcomes of children with cochlear implants has focused on their speech perception and speech production skills (see Geers, chapter 11 this volume). Most of the children reported in older studies were late identified and (compared with current guidelines) older at age of implantation. Most of those studies found that children in oral programs acquired language perception and production skills faster than did those in total communication or signing programs. For example, Osberger, Robbins, Todd, and Riley (1994) in a study of 18 children implanted before 5 years of age found that the average speech intelligibility of children using oral methods of communication was 46%, whereas the children using simultaneous communication had speech intelligibility of 21%. Miyamoto et al. (1994), in a study of speech perception of 61 children with cochlear implants, found that older age at onset of hearing loss, shorter duration of hearing loss, processor type, and an oral mode of communication predicted better speech perception.

More recently, Chin and Kaiser (2002), in a study of 20 children 4–9 years of age with cochlear implant use of 2–6 years' duration, found that children educated through oral communication had better articulation than did those educated through total communication. Chin and Finnegan (2002), in a study of consonant cluster production of 12 children whose age at implantation ranged from 1.4 to 6.1 years and who had used the implant from 5.0 to 6.7 years, found that children educated orally had 75% correct production as compared to 21% correct production for those children educated through total communication. Miyamoto, Kirk, Svirsky, and Sehgal (1999) reported that children educated through oral communication had significantly better speech perception than did those educated through total communication. Geers et al. (2002) reported that oral communication was a significant predictor of better speech perception, speech production, spoken English, and reading but not of total language production. She also concluded that English syntax was significantly better for children with cochlear implants educated orally than those who were educated through total communication.

In contrast with the above studies, other research findings indicate that children with cochlear implants educated with some form of sign language communication have significantly higher vocabulary levels than do those educated orally (e.g., Connor, Hieber, Arts, & Zwolan, 2000; Robbins, Bollard, & Green, 1999). It is probably significant that the children on whom these reports are based (Connor et al., 2000) first used cochlear implants at relatively early ages. Therefore, effects of communication mode may interact with effects of age of implantation. For example, Hammes, Novak, Rotz, Willis, and Edmondson (2002) and Novak et al. (2000) reported that a transition from sign to spoken communication was dependent upon the age of implantation. Children implanted before 18 months of age were able to make the transition. Fifty percent of children implanted between 18 and 30 months of age were able to make the transition. If implantation occurred after 30 months of age, the probability of transition from sign to speech was significantly reduced.

Speech and Language Acquisition With a Cochlear Implant: Case Studies From the Colorado Database

An increasing number of families whose children have bilateral profound hearing loss are choosing to pursue the option of cochlear implantation. When children are identified within the first few months of life and receive immediate and appropriate intervention, the nature and characteristics of the hearing loss as well as the benefit from conventional amplification, hearing aids, can be determined. Families are often comfortable with the decisions about cochlear implantation by the end of the first year of life. Some families have invited their deaf sign language instructor to the cochlear implant candidacy meeting.

Some members of our first cohort of children in Colorado with profound hearing loss identified through universal newborn hearing screening programs have now received cochlear implants and worn them for more than 1 year. Examination of the language development of the first three children in this group has revealed an interesting development sequence. These three children had signed lexicons at the time of their implantation that showed them to have a vocabulary size within the low average level compared to hearing children's lexicon. The evidence presented below regarding these children's development suggests that they used their symbolic knowledge and sign lexicon for rapid mapping of phonetic (speech vocalizations that were nonwords) to phonemic (speech vocalization that were words or word approximations) knowledge and, subsequently, spoken language. Within approximately 14 months after implantation they demonstrated not only intelligible speech but also spoken vocabularies beyond 500 words. These children's rapid development of spoken language suggests that having access to language during the first or second year of life, regardless of modality, can provide a base on which skills in a different language modality can be built.

Case 1. Ivan

Ivan was born in a Colorado Hospital with a universal newborn hearing screening program, and his hearing was screened in the first 24 hours after birth. He was then referred for an outpatient follow-up screening, after which his family was referred for a complete diagnostic audiological evaluation. A profound bilateral hearing loss was diagnosed at 2 weeks of age. Home intervention services were initiated at 6 weeks of age, and amplification was fitted at 6 weeks of age. Ivan's family received family centered home intervention for 1.5 hours a week that focused on language, social-emotional, speech, and auditory development. In addition, the family received sign language instruction from a deaf sign language instructor 1 hour per week in the home. Despite auditory skill development intervention since 6 weeks of age and regular use of amplification, no benefit from conventional amplification was noted. Ivan received a cochlear implant at 21 months of age, and the implant was stimulated at 22 months of age.

Language and Speech Development Ivan's language development prior to the cochlear implant, expressed through signs, was within the normal range of development. As table 13.2 illustrates, his parents reported that Ivan demonstrated his first 4 signs at 10 months of age and 14 signs at 15 months of age, before the implant was received. After implantation, his

Table 13-2: Ivan: Summary of Available Speech and Language Development Measures

Age (mo.)	Parent Report			Language Sample			
	MAC Expressive Vocabulary	MCDI LQ – Expressive	MCDI LQ – Receptive	Number of Utterances	Number Words/ Number Different Words	Number Phones	Speech Intelligibility
10	4 SL	105 LA = 10.5	130 LA = 13	NA	NA	8V 4C	NA
15	14 SL	93 LA = 14	86.5 LA = 13	NA	NA	10V 8C	NA
22 CI							
23	232 SL 1 SP	91 LA = 21	130 LA = 30	37 100% sign 8% speech	37/2	10V 7C	Unintelligible
28	92 SL 8 SP 218 SLSP	91 LA = 25.5	101 LA = 28.5	162 71% sign 80% speech	120/42	Prewords 12V 12C Words 15V 12C	Intelligible 50% of utterances
36	56 SP 522 SLSP	91 LA = 33	115 LA = 42	288 24% sign 95% speech	424/92	Words 15V 20C	Fully intelligible with careful listening
42	EOWPVT 44 months-55%ile SP	109 LA = 48 mo.	123 LA = 54 mo.	303 6% sign 99% speech	668/174	15V 21C	Intelligible

Diagnosis of hearing loss: 2 weeks. First intervention/amplification: 6 weeks. Language modalities: oral (speech) and sign.
SL = sign; SP = speech; SLSP = sign + speech; LA = language age; NA = not applicable (insufficient language to analyze); V = vowels; C = consonants; MAC = MacArthur Communicative Development Inventories (parent questionnaire for vocabulary from birth–36 months); EOWPVT = Expressive One-Word Picture Vocabulary Test, clinician/teacher administered expressive test; LQ = language quotient (language age/chronological age × 100), based on Minnesota Child Development Inventory (MCDI).
Number of words produced in 25-minute spontaneous sample typically includes small percentage of words in child's lexicon. Speech sample phonetic production analysis included nonword (babbling, jargon) and true word productions.

scores on both the MacArthur Communicative Development Inventory, a parent-questionnaire vocabulary inventory, and the Minnesota Child Development Inventory, a parent questionnaire on general receptive and expressive language, remained within the normal range of development.

As table 13.2 also illustrates, Ivan's expressive vocabulary (as assessed by the MacArthur Communicative Development Inventory) was still produced primarily through signs at 1 month after the first implant stimulation. However, at 28 months of age, just 5 months after implant stimulation, Ivan's expressive lexicon had grown to 318 items. Of these, 8 were produced through speech alone, 92 through sign alone, and 218 bimodally (speech and sign). Clearly, Ivan was making a transition from sign only to bimodal speech and sign production, vocabulary in two different modalities. This trend toward increasing the number of items in his lexicon while also increasing the proportion of those lexical items that were expressed with speech (either speech alone or speech plus signs) continued. By 36 months of age, all of his lexicon was reported to be produced either by speech alone or by speech plus signs.

Ivan's language growth was also assessed using the Expressive and Receptive scales of the Minnesota Child Development Inventory (Ireton & Thwing, 1974). His expressive score at 10 months of age was well within the normal range, with a language quotient (LQ) of 105. (LQ is determined by dividing "language age" score obtained on the test by chronological age, then multiplying by 100.) Ivan's performance remained within the normal range, with quotients between 91 and 93, at all ages at which he was assessed.

Ivan's receptive language developmental quotients were in the above-average range as early as 10 months of age, when his LQ was 130. His scores varied somewhat with age, and he obtained LQs of 86.5 at 15 months, 130 at 23 months, 101 at 28 months, and 115 at 36 months.

Observations of Ivan's speech and language skills were also made during 25-minute sessions of parent–child interaction. Fairly brief language sampling cannot capture the full range of a child's lexical knowledge and usage; therefore, it cannot be expected that the observations of parent–child interaction will provide a complete census of the lexicon. However, language samples have the advantage of providing directly observed information about a child's actual language performance in a reasonably typical situation. Despite the differences in data collection methods, observations of Ivan's language skills during parent–infant interaction sessions were consistent with the results of the parent-report standardized instruments discussed above.

As table 13.2 illustrates, the quantity of utterances Ivan produced at the data collection sessions from 23 to 42 months of age (all post-implantation) increased steadily. In addition, there is a clear progression toward increasing production of speech and decreasing production of signed language. Although his communication at 23 months (just 1 month after the cochlear implant was first turned on) was primarily through use of signs, almost all (99%) of his utterances at 42 months of age were speech based. This progression is also evident when considering the number of spoken words (and the number of different spoken words) Ivan produced after beginning to use the cochlear implant. Only 14 months after first cochlear implant stimulation, Ivan produced more than 92 different spoken words during the language sample; 6 months later, this increased to production of 174 different spoken words.

Ivan had been observed to vocalize prior to obtaining the cochlear implant, and his repertoire of phones grew over time, but the development was slow and appeared to plateau between 15 and 23 months of age. In the 10-month language sample, he produced eight vowel sounds and four consonants. One month after cochlear implant activation, he produced 10 different vowel types and 7 consonants. Importantly, this included the production of two identifiable spoken words. (In addition, three signs were accompanied by vocalization.) This soon after cochlear implantation, Ivan had begun a transition from nonverbal vocalizations to true word or verbal vocalizations. Both his production of vowels and consonants and his transition to production of intelligible words in the language sample increased dramatically. At 23 months of age, his speech-like vocalizations were not intelligible to adult listeners. However, by 36 months of age (14 months after cochlear implant stimulation) Ivan showed control of 15 vowels and 21 consonants, and his vocalizations were always judged to be intelligible. By 42 months of age, his productions were considered to be "intelligible" by the phonetic transcriber, the parents, and the parent–infant care provider.

At 2.5 years of age, Ivan enrolled in a public school center-based program. The program had 10 other children with significant hearing loss, and a simultaneous communication mode was used by the teacher. Ivan had a half-day of toddler-preschool group interaction each day. Ivan's family continued sign language instruction. By 36 months of age, Ivan chose to communicate predominantly in oral speech with hearing conversational partners. He code-switched and occasionally used sign language communication only or simultaneous communication. His auditory processing development appeared sufficient to receptively understand speech both in quiet and noisy environments. He showed evidence of sound/symbol relationships, phonics skills, and letter correspondence.

Case 2. Ellen

The experiences of Ellen and her family differed in several important ways from those of Ivan and his family. Ellen was born in a hospital that had universal newborn hearing screening and was screened prior to hospital discharge. However, there was a system failure, and Ellen's

Table 13-4: Hillary: Summary of Available Speech and Language Development Measures

Age (mo.)	Parent Report			Language Sample			Intelligibility
	MAC Vocabulary	MCDI Expressive	MCDI – Receptive	Number of Utterances	Number Words/Number Different Words	Number Phones	
8	0	<6 MO	<6 MO	0	0	8V 4C	NA
14	41 SL	LQ = 125 LA = 17.5	LQ = 101 LA = 14.5	26	SP 0/0 SL 29/10	3V 2C	Unintelligible
20	183 SL (99%ile)	LQ = 120 LA = 24	LQ = 112.5 LA = 22.5	110	SL 127/41 (10 signs with voc)	9V 5C	
21 CI							
27	251 SL 2 SP 1 SLSP	LQ = 89 LA = 24	LQ = 100 LA = 27	68 94% SL 8% SP	SP 6/2 SL 74/36	13V 9C	
35	311 SL 4 SP 31 SLSP	LQ = 79 LA = 27.5	LQ = 80 LA = 28	116 84% SL 78% SP	SP 104/46 SL 112/51	11V 16C	
51	EOWPVT 37% ile SP	LQ = 65 LA = 33	LQ = 110 LA = 56	226 6% SL 99% SP	SP 439/104 SL 14/12	15V 20C	Intelligible

Age diagnosis hearing loss, 6 weeks (progressive vision loss diagnosed at 20 months); age at first intervention/amplification, 6 weeks; languages and modalities, American Sign Language and conceptual signed english.
SL = sign; SP = speech; SLSP = sign + speech; SL = sign; SP = speech; V = vowels; C = consonants; CI = Cochlear Implant; LA = Language age; LQ = language quotient (language age/chronological age × 100); EOWPTV = Expressive One-Word Picture Vocabulary Test.

scored at the 39th percentile in receptive language, the 25th percentile in expressive language, and the 32nd percentile in total language with a language age score of 51 months.

By 73 months of age, Ellen's performance on the Expressive One-Word Picture Vocabulary Test in speech was at the 47th percentile, with an age equivalency of 70 months. She had acquired sufficient auditory skills to learn spoken English at the rate of the typical development of hearing children.

Case 3: Hillary

Hillary was identified with a bilaterally symmetrical profound hearing loss shortly after birth. She received amplification at 6 weeks and began intervention at 6 weeks. The etiology was determined to be genetic because of family history, but the gene has not yet been identified. She was diagnosed with a progressive degenerative visual disorder prior to implantation at 20 months. The family chose American Sign Language with some pidgin signed English as the primary mode of communication.

Table 13.4 presents a summary of Hillary's speech and language development. Hillary had excellent vocabulary development by 20 months of age, when the first assessment was performed. She scored at the 99th percentile on the MacArthur Communicative Development Inventory Words and Sentences form compared to the hearing norms. The 183 lexical items she was reported to produce were produced as signs. She did not produce any spoken words or any speech approximations.

By 6 months after the activation of her cochlear implant, Hillary was reported to have used 254 of the words on the MacArthur inventory. One of those was produced in sign and speech and two others were produced in speech only. She continued to rely primarily on signs at 35 months but was beginning to accompany more of her signs with vocalizations. Although her vocabulary size continued to increase, it was felt that her visual disorder was increasingly impacting the rate of her vocabulary development. This made it more significant that she was beginning to transition from sign only to sign and speech.

At 30 months after cochlear implant stimulation (51 months of age), Hillary achieved an age equivalent of 3 years 11 months on the Expressive One-Word Vocabulary test, which indicates functioning at the 37th percentile for her age compared to hearing peers.

Table 13.4 shows an increase with age in the number of different vowels and consonants that Hillary produced during the 25-minute language samples, increasing from 9 vowels and 5 consonants at 20 months (prior to cochlear implantation) to 15 vowels and 20 consonants at 51 months of age. Not surprisingly, at this age she was rated as an intelligible speaker by the coder, her parents, and the parent–infant care provider.

Hillary's performance in the language samples reflected both the increasing lexical size shown in her MacArthur scores and her increasing use of speech as shown in the number of phones that she produced. At 20 months, the 127 signs produced (41 different signs) were produced either without vocalization or with "random" vocal accompaniment. By 27 months of age (6 months after activation of the cochlear implant), she was beginning to produce a few spoken words as her production of signs increased. The increase in spoken words was dramatic from that point. At 35 months, she produced a total of 104 words (46 different words) during the language sample, and the number of spoken word productions was almost equal to her signs. At 51 months of age, Hillary produced a total of 226 utterances, 99% of which included the use of spoken language and 6% included the use of sign language. Hillary had transitioned to a spoken language communicator.

In summary, Hillary's transition from sign language to spoken English was somewhat slower than Ivan's and Ellen's. The progression of her visual disorder complicated this transition. Twenty-six months after cochlear implant stimulation, Hillary had mastered all but a few of the phonemes of spoken English and was an intelligible speaker. Her rate of vocabulary development had increased through the use of both audition and sign language. She had developed bilingually. She was observed to use speech only, sign only, and occasional sign plus speech communication. The modality of her communication was largely dependent upon her communicative partner.

SUMMARY AND CONCLUSIONS: SPOKEN LANGUAGE GETS A PIGGYBACK RIDE ON LANGUAGE IN ANY MODALITY

Expressive language ability in any modality plays a major role in the development of spoken language development. The first part of this chapter presented information about speech and spoken language development of both early- and later-identified children between the ages of birth and 6 years of age. Expressive language development (even if expressed through signs) and degree of hearing loss play a major role in predicting spoken language outcome for children with hearing loss. In the first 3 years of life, all children with hearing loss, even those with mild early-identified losses, are more like other children with hearing loss than they are like hearing children. When considering speech development, two categories of hearing loss are pertinent, those with mild through severe hearing loss and those with profound hearing loss. Profound hearing loss with conventional amplification results in greatly decreased potential for spoken language development in the first 5 years of life, even with early identification and intervention. However, early-identified profound hearing loss with early cochlear implantation and a high-quality auditory stimulation program results in expectations that are similar to those for early-identified mild-to-severe hearing loss and the use of conventional amplification.

All three of the profoundly deaf children described here in case studies had substantial sign vocabulary before implantation, that is, at or above the average vocabulary range for hearing children on the Mac-Arthur inventory (about 50th percentile). None of the three appeared to have any spoken language at implantation, according to their Mac-Arthur reports. All three wore amplification but had no documented speech perception or speech discrimination skills prior to cochlear implantation. However, they had some awareness of sound and some ability to produce vocalizations before implantation. All three received a high-quality auditory and speech stimulation program provided in a parent-centered home intervention program prior to implantation. It should be noted that this combination of different modalities is an unusual characteristic of the CHIP program. In addition to establishing universal newborn hearing screening programs, intervention follow-through programs also changed. Intervention providers agreed to allow parents to make choices and to request options that were not typically within the mode of communication options. As a result, some parents began to ask for American Sign Language instruction and to combine this with an auditory and speech stimulation program. Thus, there is an unusual combination from early infancy of American Sign Language and auditory/speech stimulation in the case of Hillary.

After cochlear implantation, all three children appeared to fast map their speech production onto their sign vocabulary; chronological-age-appropriate or near-age-appropriate spoken vocabulary was acquired within 12–14 months after implantation. Hillary's development was slightly slower than that of the other two children, probably due to the impact of the severe progressive visual disorder. However, there are strong similarities in the rapid increase from nonverbal to intelligible speech. This development appears to be evidence of an oral phonology piggybacking onto the lexical sign language foundation. That is, these three children discovered that the sounds they were hearing with the cochlear implant were just another code for the sign vocabulary that they used to communicate. Following this discovery, a rapid mapping of the sounds of English onto the sign vocabulary appears to have happened.

These case histories represent an unusual first-language to second-language transition, which is transition from language in a visual/manual modality to language in an oral/auditory modality. The "first language" in the first two cases was incomplete with respect to syntax and morphology, pragmatics and phonology. In the first two cases, there was a simultaneous mapping of sign language to oral speech, whereas for Hillary, the family used American Sign Language with no speech and began to transition to a pidgin signed English (combined with speech) after the cochlear implantation.

One of the unique aspects of the use of spoken English with manually coded English is that the child receives two language symbols simultaneously. This simultaneous presentation may account for the unusually rapid development of the spoken English system. In other bilingual models, presentation of the vocabulary in the two languages is at best sequential, so that the cognitive demands must be much greater. Yoshinaga-Itano and Menn (2003) suggested that this simultaneous presentation is the reason that these children were able to transition from no spoken words to more than 500 English words in the space of about 6–8 months, even faster than what is found in typical first-language development. The first 6 months involved the development of listening and the acquisition of vowel/diphthong and consonant phones, and the second 6–8 months after cochlear implant stimulation involved a rapid mapping of these newly learned sounds onto hundreds of signed words.

REFERENCES

Apuzzo, M. & Yoshinaga-Itano, C. (1995). Early identification of infants with significant hearing loss and the Minnesota Child Development Inventory, *Seminars in Hearing, 16*(2), 124–139.

Chin, S. B., & Finnegan, K. R. (2002). Consonant cluster production by pediatric users of cochlear implants. *Volta Review, 102*(4), 157–174.

Chin, S. B., & Kaiser, C. L. (2002). Measurement of articulation in pediatric users of cochlear implants. *Volta Review, 102*(4), 145–156.

Colorado Infant Hearing Advisory Committee Guidelines for Infant Hearing Screening, Audiologic Assessment, and Intervention. Colorado Department of Public Health and Environment, Dec. 14, 2000 pp. 17–21.

Colorado Resource Guide for Families of Children Who Are Deaf/Hard of Hearing (2003 Revised Edition) Jan. 24, 2004 www.handsandvoices.org Colorado Families for Hands and Voices and the Colorado Department of Education.

Connor, C. M., Hieber, S., Arts, H. A., & Zwolan, T. A. (2000). Speech, vocabulary and the education of children using cochlear implants: Oral or total communication? *Journal of Speech/Language and Hearing Research, 43*(5), 1185–204.

Delk, L., & Weidekamp, L (2001). *Shared reading project: Evaluating implementation processes and family outcomes.* Washington, DC: Laurent Clerc National Deaf Education Center.

Ertmer, D. J. (2001). Emergence of a vowel system in a young cochlear implant recipient. *Journal of Speech, Language and Hearing Research, 44*, 803–813.

Ertmer, D. J., & Mellon, J. A. (2001). Beginning to talk at 20 months: Early vocal development in a young cochlear implant recipient. *Journal of Speech, Language and Hearing Research, 44*, 192–206.

Ertmer, D. J., Young, N., Grohne, K., Mellon, J. A., Johnson, C., Corbett, K., et al. (2002). Vocal development in young children with cochlear implants:

Profiles and implications for intervention. *Language, Speech, and Hearing Services in Schools, 33*(3), 184–195.

Fenson, L., Dale, P., Reznick, J. S., Thal, D., Bates, E., Hartung, J., et al. (1993). *MacArthur Communicative Development Inventories: User's guide and technical manual.* San Diego: Singular Publications.

Gardner, M. F. (1990). *Expressive One Word Picture Vocabulary Test–Revised.* Novato, CA: Academic Therapy Publication.

Geers, A., Brenner, C., Nicholas, J., Uchanski, R., Tye-Murray, N., & Tobey, E. (2002). Rehabilitation factors contributing to benefits in children. *Annals of Otology, Rhinology, and Laryngology, 189*(Suppl.), 127–130.

Hammes, D. M., Novak, M. A., Rotz, L. A., Willis, M., & Edmondson, D. M. (2002). Early identification and cochlear implantation: Critical factors for spoken language development. *Annals of Otology, Rhinology and Laryngology, 189*(Suppl.), 74–78.

Ireton, H., & Thwing, E. (1974). *The Minnesota Child Development Inventory.* Minneapolis: University of Minnesota.

Kent, R. D., Osberger, M. J., Netsell, R., & Hustedde C. G. (1987). Phonetic development in identical twins differing in auditory function. *Journal of Speech and Hearing Disorders, 52,* 64–75.

Ling, D. (1978). *Speech and the hearing impaired child. Theory and practice.* Washington, DC: A G Bell.

Miyamoto, R. T., Kirk, K. I., Svirsky, M. A., & Sehgal, S. T. (1999). Communication skills of pediatric cochlear implant recipients. *Acta Otolaryngologica, 119*(2), 219–224.

Miyamoto, R., Osberger, M. J., Todd, S. L., Robbins, A. M., Stoer, B. S., Zimmerman-Phillips, S., et al. (1994). Variables affecting implant performance in children. *Laryngoscope, 104*(9), 1120–1124.

Novak, M. A., Firszt, J. B., Rotz, L. A., Hammes, D., Reeder, R., & Willis, M. (2000). Cochlear implants in infants and toddlers. *Annals of Otology, Rhinology and Laryngology, 185*(Suppl.), 46–49.

Obenchain, P., Menn, L., & Yoshinaga-Itano, C. (2000) Can speech development at thirty-six months in children with hearing loss be predicted from information available in the second year of life? *Volta Review, 100*(5), 149–180.

Oller, D. K., & Delgado, R. E. (1999). *Logical International Phonetics Program.* Miami, FL: Intelligent Hearing Systems Corporation.

Osberger, M. P., Robbins, A. M., Todd, S. L., & Riley, A. I. (1994). Speech intelligibility of children with cochlear implants. *Volta Review, 96,* 169–180.

Robbins, A. M., Bollard, P. M., & Green, J. (1999). Language development in children implanted with the Clarion cochlear implant. *American Journal of Otology, Rhinology, and Laryngology, 108,* 113–118.

Semel, E., Wiig, E. H., & Secord, W. A. (1995). *Clinical Evaluation of Language Fundamentals 3 (CELF-3).* San Antonio, TX: Psychological Corporation.

Spencer, P. (2004). Individual differences in language performance after cochlear implantation at one to three years of age: child, family, and linguistic factors. *Journal of Deaf Studies and Deaf Education, 9*(4), 395–412.

Wallace, V., Menn, L., & Yoshinaga-Itano, C. (2000). Is babble the gateway to speech for all children? A longitudinal study of deaf and hard-of-hearing infants. *Volta Review, 100*(5), 121–148.

Yoshinaga-Itano, C. & Apuzzo, M. (1998a). Identification of hearing loss after 18 months is not early enough. *American Annals of the Deaf, 143*, 380–387.

Yoshinaga-Itano, C. & Apuzzo, M. (1998b). The development of deaf and hard-of-hearing children identified through the high risk registry. *American Annals of the Deaf, 143*, 416–424.

Yoshinaga-Itano, C., Coulter, D., & Thomson, V. (2000). The Colorado Newborn Hearing Screening Project: Effects on speech and language development for children with hearing loss. *Journal of Perinatology, 20*(8:2), S132–S137.

Yoshinaga-Itano, C., Coulter, D., & Thomson, V. (2001). Developmental outcomes of children born in Colorado hospitals with universal newborn hearing screening programs. *Seminars in Neonatology, 6*, 521–529.

Yoshinaga-Itano, C., & Menn, L. (2003 June). *Lexical sign language bootstrap to spoken English phonology: Qualitative study.* Paper Presented at the International Child Phonology Conference, Vancouver, BC.

Yoshinaga-Itano, C., & Sedey, A. (2000b). Speech development of deaf and hard-of-hearing children in early childhood: Interrelationships with language and hearing. *Volta Review, 100*(5), 181–212.

Yoshinaga-Itano, C., Stredler-Brown, A., & Jancosek, E. (1992). From phone to phoneme: Can we find meaning in babble? *Volta Review, 94*(3), 283–314.

14

Working Memory Capacity, Verbal Rehearsal Speed, and Scanning in Deaf Children With Cochlear Implants

Rose A. Burkholder & David B. Pisoni

The development of spoken language and other fundamental cognitive skills is strongly influenced by a variety of early social and sensory experiences. Although both vision and audition contribute to the early sensory experience of typical infants, audition may play a more important role in the earliest stages of perceptual and cognitive development. For instance, even before birth, in the third trimester, sounds and voices that penetrate the womb are easily detectable to most fetuses (Aslin, Jusczyk, & Pisoni, 1998). This auditory prenatal experience has been shown to have an impact on infants' subsequent abilities to recognize speech after birth (DeCasper & Spence, 1986). Thus, early vocal input is highly salient to infants and important for the development of communicative abilities.

In addition, at birth, although inner ear structures are still developing, the hearing of infants is nearly as acute as that of adults (Aslin et al., 1998). However, visual acuity is extremely poor at birth and is typically not fully mature until several months later (Morrone & Burr, 1986). The precocious development of audition in infants suggests that hearing is likely to be the dominant sensory modality that contributes to early language and communication development and may also facilitate the development of cognitive abilities in other domains, including multimodal processing, attention, learning, and memory.

Based on these findings from hearing, typically developing populations, it is important from both a theoretical and clinical perspective to begin investigating the cognitive development of infants who have been deprived of early sensory experience with sound. The lack of sufficient auditory input in humans has been found to have detrimental effects on the development of speech and language in a handful of well-known cases of abused and abandoned children such as Genie (Curtis, 1977) and Victor the "Wild Boy of Aveyron" (Lane, 1979). Unfortunately, in examinations of such feral children, any experimental outcomes and interpretations are confounded by the social and emotional isolation and abuse that these children may have experienced. However, unlike these rare cases, profoundly deaf children are likely to be unscathed by such severe and tragic circumstances, making them a unique and potentially important clinical population in which to examine the impact of early spoken language deprivation on cognitive and linguistic development. In addition, in recent years, a smaller subset of profoundly deaf children has provided an unusual opportunity to answer what is perhaps an even more provocative question: What happens to the cognitive development of deaf children deprived of early auditory and linguistic experience who later gain exposure to sound and spoken language through a cochlear implant? In this chapter, some preliminary answers to this question are provided.

Due to prior inadequacies in diagnosing hearing problems in newborns and current constraints by the U.S. Food and Drug Administration on implanting deaf children very soon after birth, most profoundly deaf children who receive a cochlear implant have been deprived of auditory input for one or more years (Kirk, 2002). In addition, for many congenitally and prelingually deaf children, cochlear implants provide the first exposure to both environmental sounds and spoken language and, in some cases, may provide the first opportunity for these children to learn any language, spoken or signed. Because of this delayed onset of exposure to spoken language, deaf children using cochlear implants are a unique clinical population in which researchers can examine the ramifications of extended periods of auditory deprivation on the development of speech, language, and other cognitive abilities. In addition to the effects that early auditory deprivation can have on the eventual development of deaf children who have received cochlear implants, the children's behavioral and physiological responses to their new sensory input are important to study as well. Another paramount question to address in these deaf children is whether the sensory input from a cochlear implant can adequately facilitate normal spoken language development and other cognitive abilities that typically rely heavily on auditory and verbal coding skills.

However, some of these questions are not easy to answer because cochlear implants do not simply restore hearing completely. Rather, they provide listeners with direct electrical stimulation of the auditory nerve and its afferents that must be translated into identifiable auditory percepts and used appropriately for whatever cognitive task is currently required (Rauschecker & Shannon, 2002). Therefore, a child with a cochlear implant must determine what sounds represent and mean and must learn to link these sounds to the visual and auditory events occurring around him or her. This complex perceptual learning task is also important to understand in order to successfully assess the speech, language, attention, learning, and memory skills of profoundly deaf children who have received cochlear implants.

Profoundly deaf children with cochlear implants are also an ideal population in which to study the effects of different *types* of early linguistic experience on language development. The amount and nature of aural-oral experience received after cochlear implantation differ substantially from child to child (Connor, Hieber, Arts, & Zwolan, 2000). The auditory-oral training and educational placement that a deaf child receives after cochlear implantation are typically referred to as his or her communication mode. Communication modes for these children fall along a continuum between exclusively oral communication, which uses only speech, and total communication, which uses a form of signing such as signed exact English or cued speech in addition to spoken language. Although American Sign Language (ASL) falls on this continuum, it is rarely used by deaf children who have received cochlear implants.

Differences in each child's communication mode after cochlear implantation allow for comparisons between groups of children based on the richness and robustness of their exposure to spoken language and their experience using primarily oral-aural communication. Such comparisons are informative because they can provide solid behavioral evidence of the degree to which the amount and quality of spoken language exposure received by deaf children with cochlear implants have an effect on the development of their speech, language, and other cognitive abilities. However, one caveat in examining effects of communication mode on speech and language development in deaf children with cochlear implants is that placement into a communication mode or educational program is not random, and children who fail to thrive in oral communication programs are often put into total communication programs.

Although the development of the speech and language skills of deaf children after cochlear implantation has been the primary area of interest to most clinicians who are interested in measuring benefit and outcome in this population, several recent studies have begun to study other cognitive skills of these children such as attention, learning, and memory. However, this new interest in cognitive processes should not be viewed as a divergence from research focused on speech and language in deaf children using cochlear implants. Rather, recent investigations of learning and memory processes in deaf children using cochlear implants may provide new insights into speech and language development and provide principled explanations for the enormous individual differences in outcome and benefit that have been observed in this clinical population (Pisoni, Cleary, Geers, & Tobey, 2000).

An extensive body of literature examining hearing populations has shown that attention, learning, and memory processes are all intertwined and closely related to vocabulary development and language learning. Attention, learning, and memory account for a large amount of variability that is observed in the language skills of hearing adults and children (Baddeley, Gathercole, & Papagno, 1998; Cowan, 1996; Cowan, Nugent, Elliott, Ponomarev, & Sults, 1999; Gupta, 2003). For example, differences in working memory have been found to be closely related to vocabulary knowledge and the development of spoken and written language abilities in hearing adults and children (Cowan, 1996; Gathercole & Baddeley, 1989; Gathercole, Willis, Emslie, & Baddeley, 1992; Gupta, 2003). In addition, working memory processes have also been linked to language proficiency in deaf children who do not use cochlear implants (Bebko, Bell, Metcalfe-Haggert, & McKinnon, 1998). Thus, in addition to providing vital knowledge about the role of early auditory and linguistic experience in learning and memory, the study of memory processes in deaf children with cochlear implants may also yield new fundamental knowledge about speech and language development.

Direct links between working memory performance and the development of speech and language skills have recently been documented in deaf children using cochlear implants. Pisoni and Cleary (2003) found that immediate memory capacity, measured by forward digit span, was strongly correlated with deaf children's scores on several different word recognition tasks. In addition, serial recall has also been found to be related to the receptive vocabulary of deaf children using cochlear implants (Dawson, Busby, McKay, & Clark, 2002). However, only recently have some of the more intricate aspects of memory processing abilities in deaf children with cochlear implants been explored to uncover how they may influence speech and language development.

The following sections present recent findings examining several memory processes that may be intimately connected to speech and language development. Specifically, we summarize research on working memory capacity, verbal rehearsal, and serial scanning processes in profoundly deaf children using cochlear implants and discuss how they are related to the basic cognitive skills that have been shown to be important to traditional speech and language outcome measures used to assess benefit with a cochlear implant. The importance of measuring temporal characteristics of speech, such as speaking rate and interword pause durations, to index the speed of subvocal verbal rehearsal and serial scanning in deaf children using cochlear implants is also discussed. We present the results of these speech-timing studies, consider their implications for the development and the use of subvocal verbal rehearsal and serial scanning in deaf children with cochlear implants, and discuss why these two fundamental memory processes contribute to the shorter immediate memory spans observed in these children. Overall, the findings presented here indicate that, in addition to perceptual difficulties related to their hearing impairment and the encoding of degraded auditory signals, atypical development of subvocal verbal rehearsal and serial scanning also contributes to the decreased memory spans of deaf children using cochlear implants. Interestingly, these results are similar to what has been found in deaf children who do not use cochlear implants (see Marschark & Mayer, 1998, for a review).

In addition to research on immediate memory and scanning, several recent findings on the nonword repetition skills of deaf children with cochlear implants are described. These new results suggest that some deaf children with cochlear implants have substantial difficulties in rapidly encoding, rehearsing, and repeating novel phonological patterns. Such difficulties indicate that deaf children with cochlear implants have developed atypical phonological processing skills. Finally, we discuss the influence of communication mode and early oral-aural experience on memory and nonword repetition performance. These differences in communication mode suggest that early linguistic experiences and activities after cochlear implantation play a substantial role in perceptual and cognitive development. Taken together, the findings presented here suggest that fundamental linguistic and phonological processing skills used in memory and nonword repetition tasks may play a foundational role in the development of speech and language skills following cochlear implantation. In addition, these findings reveal that basic memory processes such as encoding, subvocal verbal rehearsal, and serial scanning of short-term memory are atypical in deaf children using cochlear implants and appear to be closely related to the nature and amount of early auditory and linguistic exposure received by these children after cochlear implantation.

MEMORY ABILITIES IN DEAF CHILDREN
WITHOUT COCHLEAR IMPLANTS

Prior to the recent interest in deaf children with cochlear implants and their aural and oral rehabilitation, a great deal of research focused on deaf children who used manually signed visual-spatial language such as ASL or one of the signing systems created to accompany spoken language. Research concerning the acquisition of signed language and its influence on cognitive and social development encouraged a series of investigations of memory development in this population (e.g., Bebko, 1984; Campbell & Wright, 1990; Liben & Drury, 1977; Marschark & Mayer, 1998). The early work on the memory processes of deaf children who used manual signs and lack a fully developed native spoken language was an important precursor to the current investigations of the memory of deaf children with cochlear implants (Marschark & Mayer, 1998). Several studies have shown that when confronted with a specific language processing task that relies on memory, many deaf children, like their hearing peers, use covert verbal rehearsal as a strategy to maintain items in short-tem memory (Bebko, 1984; Liben & Drury, 1977). Covert verbal rehearsal is assumed to involve the repeated cycling of verbally coded memory representations within the phonological loop of working memory in order to prevent memory decay (Baddeley, Thompson, & Buchanan, 1975).

One of the strongest pieces of evidence that deaf children use covert verbal rehearsal strategies came from a study by Campbell and Wright (1990). They found that deaf children, like hearing children and adults, are susceptible to the word length effect. Word length effects are observed when the number of lexical items that can be recalled from immediate memory is determined by the length of the words in the list. Word length effects occur because longer words take more time to articulate and subvocally rehearse and cannot be refreshed as quickly and efficiently within the phonological loop. As a result of the decreased rate of subvocal verbal rehearsal, memory spans for lists of longer words will be shorter. Evidence of the word length effect and covert verbal rehearsal strategies in deaf children suggests that they are capable of processing and repeatedly recycling linguistic input within the short-term memory store (Baddeley et al., 1975).

Despite utilizing memory strategies that are similar to their hearing peers, deaf children behave atypically on a wide variety of memory tasks. In particular, phonological memory tasks appear to be the most difficult for deaf children to carry out, especially when they involve encoding and retrieval of sequential information (Banks, Gray, & Fyfe, 1990; Waters & Doehring, 1990). Early-onset deafness can also produce substantial differences in performance on memory tasks that require the management and manipulation of phonological or linguistic information. However, what has previously remained unknown is whether, after a prolonged period of auditory and spoken language deprivation, cochlear implantation can ameliorate or even prevent some of these disadvantages and allow deaf children who receive a sensory aid to perform more like their hearing peers on a wide range of language and memory tasks.

WORKING MEMORY CAPACITY IN DEAF CHILDREN WITH COCHLEAR IMPLANTS

Several recent studies have shown that deaf children with cochlear implants have shorter immediate memory spans than do their hearing, age-matched peers. The first evidence of shorter memory spans in deaf children using cochlear implants was obtained using the Wechsler

Intelligence Scale for Children (Wechsler, 1991) auditory digit span task, which provided a measure of immediate memory capacity (Pisoni et al., 2000; Pisoni & Geers, 2000). The WISC-III auditory digit span task is administered to children with live voice, with lip reading cues available, and involves two different recall conditions. In forward digit span recall, children are simply asked to repeat back a sequence of digits in their exact order of presentation. In the backward digit span task, children are required to repeat the digits in the reverse order of their original presentation.

In both the forward and backward digit span tasks, deaf children with cochlear implants performed worse than their hearing peers. Figure 14.1, adapted from Pisoni and Cleary (2003), displays the forward and backward digit spans obtained from 176 deaf children using cochlear implants obtained over a 4-year period along with a comparison group of 44 age-matched, hearing children. All children were between 8 and 9 years old, and the deaf children had around 4–7 years of experience with their implant (Geers et al., 1999). Subsets of this group of children were used for all of the subsequent studies discussed in this chapter that were conducted by our lab. Figure 14.1A shows that the digit spans of all four groups of deaf children using cochlear implants were significantly shorter than the digit spans of the hearing children who are shown on the right. Figure 14.1B shows that, in addition to memory span differences found between hearing children and deaf children using cochlear implants, deaf children with cochlear implants who used oral communication methods had longer forward digit spans than did children who used total communication. These results provided the first evidence that the quality and quantity of aural and oral exposure can have a systematic effect on immediate memory span capacity for sequential patterns in deaf children using cochlear implants. Specifically, as reported in earlier studies of deaf children without cochlear implants, the quality and quantity of oral and aural experience of deaf children with the devices may mediate or influence memory processing strategies such as perceptual and phonological encoding, subvocal verbal rehearsal, and serial scanning (Bebko & Metcalfe-Haggert, 1997).

Given that digit span recall requires the verbal repetition of auditory stimuli, it is reasonable to ask whether perceptual encoding or articulatory difficulties may have substantially contributed to the shorter digit spans observed in the deaf children using cochlear implants, particularly those who used total communication. If a deaf child who has a cochlear implant cannot detect and accurately perceive what digit was spoken or has such unintelligible speech that even when the correct response is known, it cannot be articulated in any identifiable form, memory capacity may be significantly underestimated. It is also important to consider the role of perceptual or articulatory difficulties in

A

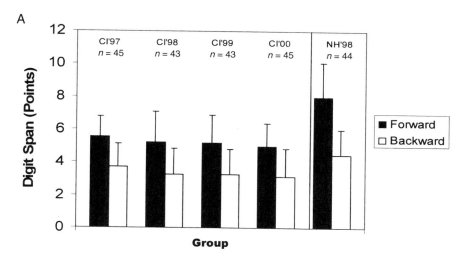

B

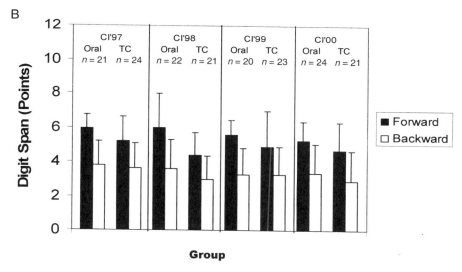

Figure 14-1. Mean WISC-III digit spans from four groups of 8- and 9-year-old deaf children with cochlear implants and hearing children. A, Digit spans of all deaf and hearing children. B, The group of deaf children with cochlear implants, split according to communication mode. Error bars represent standard error of the mean. Adapted from Pisoni and Cleary (2003).

memory performance, because in some memory tasks using only visual stimuli and nonverbal responses, deaf children with cochlear implants perform as well as their hearing peers. For instance, in memory tasks requiring recognition memory for faces or the reproduction of a pattern of visually and spatially arranged dots, deaf children with cochlear implants fall within the normative range of scores obtained for hearing children (Cleary & Pisoni, 2004). Not surprisingly, this result is similar to the findings that have been reported in deaf children who do not use cochlear implants (Campbell & Wright, 1990; McDaniel, 1980; Olsson & Furth, 1966).

However, deaf children with cochlear implants have been found to have shorter memory spans than their hearing peers in visual memory tasks in which the stimuli are presented sequentially. Using a customized version of Milton Bradley's popular memory game Simon, Cleary, Pisoni, and Geers (2001) reported that deaf children with cochlear implants had shorter reproductive visual memory spans than did their hearing peers. Figure 14.2 shows a version of the Simon apparatus that was used to measure memory span in the deaf and hearing children.

Cleary et al.'s findings suggest that problems with memory processes other than the early auditory encoding of linguistic input may

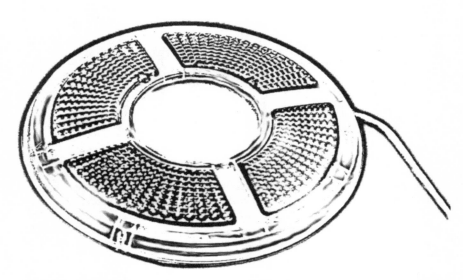

Figure 14-2. Simon memory span game adapted for experimental use with deaf and hearing children. Randomly generated sequences of colored lights (blue, green, yellow, red) are presented and children respond by pushing colored buttons on the game to reproduce the sequences.

also contribute to the shorter digit spans of deaf children who use cochlear implants. They reasoned that deaf children using cochlear implants performed poorly even on a visual memory span task because they had difficulty in coding visual sequences verbally and were slower at subvocally rehearsing the verbally coded sequential information in working memory (Cleary et al., 2001). Thus, although the Simon memory task is ostensively based on visual information (the colors of buttons), the most successful strategy to complete the task is to use some form of verbal coding and subvocal verbal rehearsal of color names rather than relying exclusively on visual cues.

Although the deaf children with cochlear implants were able to use subvocal verbal rehearsal, they were at a disadvantage relative to their hearing peers because of their lack of early linguistic experience and aural-oral activities that would ordinarily facilitate rapid execution of this rehearsal strategy. However, the effects of deafness and lack of sensory input on memory performance appear to dissipate when stimuli in memory tasks are not as likely to be verbally encoded (Cleary & Pisoni, 2004; Dawson et al., 2002). For instance, in several serial short-term memory tasks using either tones or hand gestures as stimuli, Dawson and her colleagues found that deaf children with cochlear implants performed just as well as their hearing peers.

Taken together, these recent results indicate that verbal encoding problems most likely prevent deaf children with cochlear implants from performing as well as their hearing peers on both auditory and visual memory tasks. However, verbal encoding is not the only underlying memory process required to perform a digit span recall or serial short-term memory task. As mentioned above, subvocal verbal rehearsal is also an important component of working memory. To gain a better understanding of how working memory functions in this clinical population, we explored the verbal rehearsal process in much greater detail using several different measures of speech timing.

SPEECH TIMING AND MEMORY PROCESSES IN DEAF CHILDREN WITH COCHLEAR IMPLANTS

In hearing children, several fundamental memory components have been successfully delineated by examining temporal aspects of speech production using speech timing measures. Measures of speech timing during memory tasks completed by hearing children have been used to index both subvocal or covert verbal rehearsal as well as serial scanning of items in short-term memory (Cowan, 1992; Cowan et al., 1998). One basic form of speech timing that Cowan and colleagues have measured is overt speaking rate. Measures of overt speaking rate can be used to estimate the rate of subvocal verbal rehearsal in immediate memory. The idea that overt speaking rate is an appropriate measure of subvocal verbal rehearsal is based on a large body of memory research that has found a consistent and strong linear relationship between speaking rate and memory span in both hearing children and adults (Baddeley et al., 1975; Hitch, Halliday, & Littler, 1989; Hulme & Tordoff, 1989; Kail & Park, 1994; Schweickert, Guentert, & Hersberger, 1990). In general, these studies have found that speakers who articulated faster also had longer digit spans. According to Baddeley et al. (1975), the relationship between speaking rate and immediate memory span occurs because the faster an individual speaks and thus rehearses subvocally, the more frequently items can be refreshed within the phonological loop. A faster rate of rehearsal through this loop will facilitate the recall of more items and ultimately result in a longer memory span.

The finding that speech-timing measures may reflect basic memory processes was explored further by Cowan and his colleagues (Cowan, 1992; Cowan et al., 1994) using measures of serial scanning. Scanning is the process by which each item in a list is individually located in short-term memory. This process is carried out by retrieving the items within a list serially during each interword pause taken during the period of recall (Sternberg, 1966). In contrast to measures of overt speaking rate that are frequently derived from sentence repetition or speeded artic-ulation tasks, measures used to estimate serial scanning speed are made during the actual recall process of immediate serial recall tasks. Memory scanning activities can be conveniently indexed by measuring the durations of the interword or interitem pause durations that occur during digit span recall. Figure 14.3, adapted from Burkholder and Pisoni (2003b), shows a schematic representation of how interword pauses are measured from speech production samples made during digit span recall.

The serial scanning process begins with the onset of the first pause taken during recall and continues until the next item on the list is determined. Thus, during the first pause in serial recall, between the

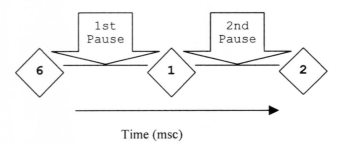

Time (msc)

Figure 14-3. Schematic representation of interword pause duration measures made on WISC-III forward digit span responses: example of a three-digit list (6, 1, 2). Adapted from Burkholder and Pisoni (2003b).

first and second item on the list, scanning occurs until the second item in the list is located and articulated. Similarly, during the pause between the second to last and last item, nearly the entire list has to be scanned until the final item to be recalled is located. Cowan (1992) observed that the pause durations during immediate recall increase as later digits are recalled. This increase in duration occurs because more items from the list must be scanned through in serial order as the ending items of the list are recalled.

Cowan et al. (1994) also examined maturational effects on speech timing in hearing children. They found that 8-year-olds spoke significantly faster and had shorter interword pause durations in immediate recall than did 4-year-olds. These findings suggested developmental increases in speed of subvocal verbal rehearsal and serial scanning. Increases in subvocal verbal rehearsal speed and serial scanning rates appeared to facilitate immediate memory span recall in the children Cowan examined. In addition to having faster speaking rates and shorter pause times in recall, the 8-year-old children also displayed significantly longer memory spans than did the 4-year-old children.

Based on Cowan's findings that speech-timing measures in recall can be used as an index of covert memory processes that influence the immediate memory spans in hearing children, Burkholder and Pisoni (2003b) conducted a speech-timing analysis on the digit span responses of 37 profoundly deaf children using cochlear implants. The children were between 8 and 9 years old and had 4.5–7 years of experience with their cochlear implant. In our study, both the overt speaking rates and pause durations of profoundly deaf children with cochlear implants were compared to a set of measures obtained from a group of 36 age-matched, hearing controls. Speaking rate was obtained from the two groups by measuring the durations of short sentences taken from the McGarr Sentence Intelligibility task (McGarr, 1981).

The McGarr stimulus materials consisted of 36 sentences of three, five, and seven syllables, with 12 sentences at each syllable length. The sentences were elicited by simply asking the children to listen to each sentence as it was read by the clinician or experimenter and then providing them with the written text of the sentence. With the text of the sentence placed in front of them, the children were asked to repeat the sentence at their usual speaking rate. Providing the written text of the sentences reduces the memory load involved in the task and also guards against errors in repetition due to misperception of the spoken sentence. Further assurance that the deaf children with cochlear implants repeated the sentences correctly was achieved by allowing them up to three chances to repeat each sentence. All sentences spoken by both groups of children were digitally recorded and measured using waveform editing software.

Figure 14.4, redrawn from Burkholder and Pisoni (2003b), displays the McGarr sentence durations obtained from the 8- and 9-year-old

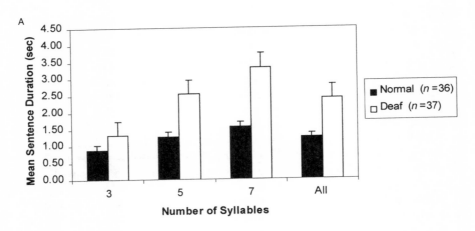

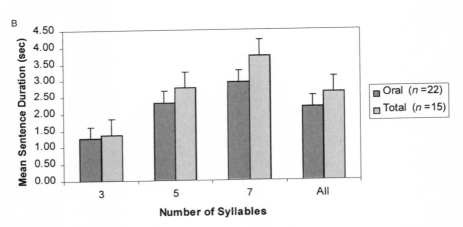

Figure 14-4. Mean sentence durations of hearing children and deaf children using cochlear implants. *A*, Sentence durations of hearing children and deaf children using cochlear implants. *B*, Sentence durations of the deaf children with cochlear implants, split according to communication mode. Error bars represent standard error of the mean. Redrawn from Burkholder and Pisoni (2003b).

deaf children with cochlear implants and their age-matched hearing peers. The mean durations of the three-, five-, and seven-syllable sentences are each shown separately on the abscissa. In addition, the mean duration of all sentences combined together is shown in figure 14.4. Figure 14.4A clearly illustrates that deaf children using cochlear implants had significantly slower speaking rates than did their hearing peers on these sentences. In addition, figure 14.4B shows that children who used total communication spoke significantly slower than did children who used oral communication methods.

Slower speaking rates have been documented in deaf individuals previously and are attributed in part to the lack of auditory feedback while speaking (Bochner, Barefoot, & Johnson, 1987). However, even with the newly provided auditory feedback from a cochlear implant, deaf children still appear to be unable to produce speaking rates within normal ranges. Based on the findings obtained in previous research examining speaking rate and memory, the pediatric cochlear implant users' inability to overtly articulate at rapid paces may underlie differences in covert verbal rehearsal and result in these children having shorter digit spans than their hearing peers.

The proposal that slower speaking rates and subvocal rehearsal speeds may contribute to the shorter memory spans of the deaf children with cochlear implants was further confirmed through analyses showing a robust correlation between their speaking rates and digit spans (Burkholder & Pisoni, 2003b; Pisoni & Cleary, 2003). Figure 14.5, adapted from Pisoni and Cleary (2003), displays the correlation between sentence durations and forward digit spans of 176 deaf children using

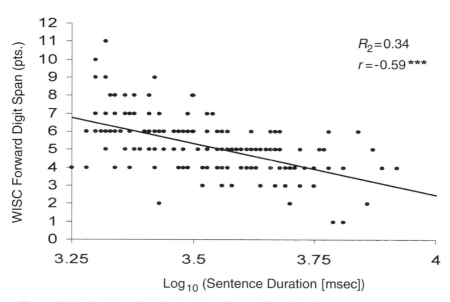

Figure 14-5. Scatter plot illustrating the relationship between average sentence durations for the seven-syllable McGarr sentences and WISC-III forward digit span scored by points. The sentence durations were log-transformed. R^2 values indicate percentage of variance accounted for by the linear relation. Adapted from Pisoni and Cleary (2003).

cochlear implants. The log-based transformation of McGarr sentence durations appears on the abscissa, and WISC-III digit span points appear on the ordinate.

Based on the strong correlation between sentence durations and memory span, it appears that deaf children with cochlear implants perform worse than their hearing peers on serial recall tasks such as digit span recall because they are not able to subvocally rehearse the digits fast enough. This interpretation is consistent with what has been found previously in deaf children that do not use cochlear implants (see Marschark & Mayer, 1998, for a review). In addition, the correlations between forward digit spans and speaking rate obtained within both the hearing children and deaf children using cochlear implants were of a similar magnitude. These results indicate that basic subvocal verbal rehearsal processes operate similarly in these two different populations and may contribute in comparable ways to immediate memory span for spoken digits.

Although both the pediatric cochlear implant users' shorter forward digit spans and their strong correlation with speaking rate were expected, one other result from this study was unexpected and interesting. Correlations carried out on backward digit span and speaking rate revealed a strong relationship for the group of deaf children with cochlear implants. However, the group of hearing children did not display a correlation between backward digit span and speaking rate (Burkholder & Pisoni, 2003b). This result suggests that the deaf children with cochlear implants may be using the same subvocal verbal rehearsal strategy to complete the backward digit span task that they used in the forward digit span task. This strategy may not be as efficient as the executive planning and organizational strategies that hearing children use to perform the same memory task. Thus, not only may some of the pediatric cochlear implant users' subvocal verbal processing strategies suffer because they are carried out more slowly than are hearing children's, but the subvocal verbal rehearsal strategies could also be inappropriately engaged during certain tasks, such as backward digit span recall, in which other planning, rehearsal, and recall strategies would be more useful (Thomas, Milner, & Haberlandt, 2003).

In addition, it is also possible that the shorter digit spans observed in the deaf children with cochlear implants may be due to their inability to scan test items in memory as fast as hearing children. Following the same procedures that Cowan et al. (1994) used, scanning rates during the digit span task were obtained by measuring the interword pause durations taken from digital audio recordings of pediatric cochlear implant users and hearing children completing the actual recall portion of the task. Figure 14.6, redrawn from Burkholder and Pisoni (2003b), displays mean interword pause durations produced by deaf children

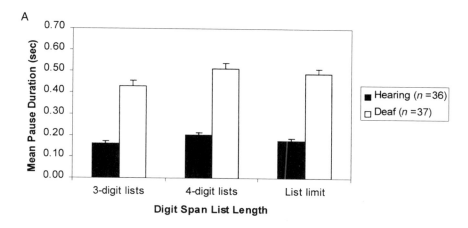

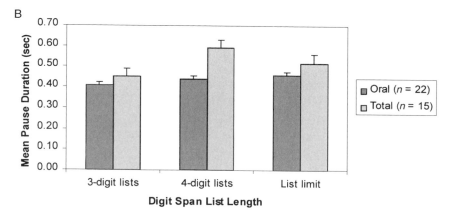

Figure 14-6. Mean interword pause durations taken during WISC-III forward digit span recall for list lengths of three and four digits and the span limiting list or longest list correctly recalled. *A*, Pause durations of both hearing and deaf children using cochlear implants. *B*, Pause durations of deaf children using cochlear implants split according to communication mode. Error bars represent standard error of the mean. Redrawn from Burkholder and Pisoni (2003b).

with cochlear implants and hearing children during WISC-III forward digit span recall. Mean interword pause durations are shown for digit span lists of three and four digits and the longest list recalled by each child, which is denoted as the list limit.

Figure 14.6A illustrates that the deaf children who used cochlear implants were significantly slower than their hearing peers while scanning items during digit span recall. In fact, the pediatric cochlear implant users' interword pause durations taken during digit span recall were nearly twice as long as the hearing children's interword pause durations when recalling lists of three and four digits and at the longest list they were able to correctly recall. These slower serial scanning rates may also be responsible for the shorter memory spans of deaf children using cochlear implants.

Subvocal verbal rehearsal and serial scanning processes both rely on phonological encoding. Thus, the lack of early auditory input and linguistic stimulation in the deaf children is likely to be another important factor affecting subvocal verbal rehearsal speed and serial scanning rates, resulting in shorter digit spans. When considered together with Cowan et al.'s (1994, 1999) findings on speech timing and memory, the speech-timing study in deaf children using cochlear implants suggests that maturation of subvocal verbal rehearsal and serial scanning depend not only on chronological age but also on the amount and type of early linguistic exposure that children receive. The role that linguistic information plays in these memory processes also explains why the children who used communication methods that stress auditory-oral training performed better than the children who used total communication. The richer auditory-oral exposure and experience that the children using oral communication receive likely facilitates their performance on a wide range of linguistic tasks that use subvocal verbal rehearsal and serial scanning of short-term memory because they are able to rapidly decompose and linguistically represent auditory-verbal sensory information. In addition, children using oral communication methods may have an advantage on auditory memory tasks because they have less difficulty retrieving the phonological representation of these items and reassembling them into an intelligible spoken response.

MEMORY RECALL ERRORS IN DEAF CHILDREN USING COCHLEAR IMPLANTS

Recently, additional evidence has been collected suggesting that the pediatric cochlear implant users' shorter auditory digit spans are primarily related to memory processing problems such as subvocal verbal rehearsal and serial scanning. Burkholder and Pisoni (2004) examined and categorized the errors made during digit span recall by deaf children using cochlear implants to determine whether their errors were primarily due to encoding item or order information incorrectly. Each individual error made during spoken recall was classified as one of four types of errors. Errors caused by the recall of digits in an incorrect order were considered to be order errors. Errors caused by the recall of a digit or digits that were not present in the original list were considered to be item errors. Errors in digit span recall caused by the failure to repeat one or more digits were considered to be omissions. Finally, errors that represented both item and order errors were considered to be combination errors.

The two types of errors with the most relevance in this analysis were item and order errors (Conrad, 1965). Order errors result from the loss of temporal order information during encoding or spoken recall. In a serial recall task, encoding sequential order and maintaining this information until recall is a complex process. Therefore, errors in order are most likely related to mistakes in processing due to increased cognitive load. In contrast, item errors result in the replacement of an individual digit in the list with a digit that was not presented in the original list. In a group of deaf children using cochlear implants, item errors are likely indicative of encoding problems rather than slowed or inefficient rehearsal or scanning. Therefore, it is important to dissociate these two types of errors from one another in memory recall.

Figure 14.7, adapted from Burkholder and Pisoni (2004), shows the proportion of each type of error made in the forward (A) and backward (B) digit span task for both the deaf children using cochlear implants and the group of age-matched, hearing peers. Using this categorization process, Burkholder and Pisoni (2004) found that the proportion of order errors exceeded all other types of errors made by deaf children with cochlear implants during auditory digit span recall. Although this was an auditory memory task, the performance of the deaf children with cochlear implants appeared to be more influenced by order errors rather than by item errors.

The pattern of errors made by the deaf children using cochlear implants was similar to the results found for hearing children. Both the deaf and hearing children committed significantly more order errors than item errors during digit span recall. In addition, order errors were more numerous in backward digit span recall than in forward digit span recall. This result is not surprising because backward digit span is considered to be a more complex and demanding task requiring planning and recall strategies and executive function that may lead to an increased processing load (Li & Lewandowsky, 1995).

Taken together, three converging sets of findings suggest that deaf children with cochlear implants perform more poorly on memory span tasks because they covertly rehearse and scan items in short-term memory more slowly than do hearing children. First, deaf children with cochlear implants do poorly even on memory span tasks that do not require encoding of auditory stimuli and spoken responses (see Cleary et al., 2001). This result provides support for the proposal that deaf children with cochlear implants not only have difficulty perceiving and encoding auditory stimuli but also may have other memory processing problems that are not tied exclusively to input modalities used in the memory assessments.

A
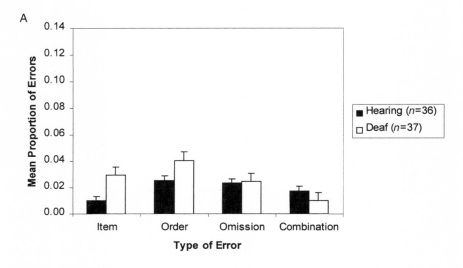

B
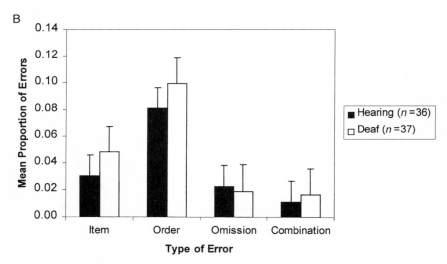

Figure 14-7. Mean proportion of error types made by hearing children and deaf children using cochlear implants during digit span recall in forward (A) and backward (B) recall conditions. Error bars represent standard error of the mean. Adapted from Burkholder and Pisoni (2004).

Second, Burkholder and Pisoni's (2003b) speech-timing analysis revealed that the pediatric cochlear implant users' sentence and interword pause durations were significantly longer than the sentence and interword pause durations of their hearing peers. These results suggest that the memory processes reflected in these measures, subvocal verbal rehearsal and serial scanning of short-term memory, also operate more slowly in the deaf children with cochlear implants. Finally, by directly examining the nature of the errors in digit span recall, Burkholder and Pisoni (2004) found a greater proportion of order errors than item errors made in immediate serial recall by deaf children using cochlear implants. This pattern of results suggests that deaf children with cochlear implants not only have difficulty in perceiving spoken digits but also frequently fail to encode and maintain the correct serial order of the digits in a test sequence (Gupta, 2003). Therefore, a solid body of evidence suggests that encoding order information may be more difficult for deaf children with cochlear implants than is correctly perceiving the degraded stimuli received through their cochlear implant.

NONWORD REPETITION IN DEAF CHILDREN WITH COCHLEAR IMPLANTS

In addition to measures of immediate memory capacity using digit span tasks, nonword repetition has also been a useful methodology to examine phonological working memory skills in hearing children. Differences in nonword repetition performance have been found to be related to novel word learning in both adults and children (Gathercole & Baddeley, 1989; Gathercole et al., 1992; Gupta, 2003). The relationship between novel word learning and nonword repetition should come as no surprise. In any word learning task, whether in an experimental or real-world setting, words originally begin as nonword sound patterns for those trying to learn them. Therefore, measures of nonword repetition may be useful in assessing the fundamental operation of word-learning ability in deaf children using cochlear implants. Unlike spoken word recognition or sentence repetition tasks, nonword repetition is one method that can be used to measure both speech perception and production skills in the absence of higher level contextual and lexical influences.

Several information processing skills play a role in successfully completing a nonword repetition task. Although the task of repeating a nonword may intuitively sound as if it is fairly easy, successful nonword repetition requires the completion of a complex sequence of sensory, perceptual, and linguistic processes that are executed very rapidly in a short period of time. To complete nonword repetition, a listener must encode a novel sound pattern in an auditory-only mode, retain and rehearse the pattern within the phonological loop, and then reassemble the sound pattern into an articulatory motor program for speech. This complex sequence of tasks may be particularly difficult for deaf children who use cochlear implants. Therefore, by examining pediatric cochlear implant users' nonword repetition skills, valuable information can be gathered on several important processes of speech, language, and memory to provide new insights into how these children apply phonological processing skills to novel nonword patterns.

The nonword repetition task utilized in our research was adapted from the stimulus materials developed by Gathercole, Willis, Baddeley, and Emslie (1994). The original nonword list included 40 nonwords that sound like plausible English words. From the original set of 40 nonwords, 20 were selected for use as stimuli for the nonword repetition task conducted with the deaf children who used cochlear implants. These 20 nonwords were selected because of the high degree of variability that was observed when they were used with hearing children (Carlson, Cleary, & Pisoni, 1998).

Unlike the McGarr Sentence Intelligibility task used to elicit small samples of connected speech to measure speaking rate, the nonword repetition task is not administered via live voice and does not involve providing the deaf children with the written text of each nonword. Instead, the prerecorded nonwords are played back at a comfortable listening level over a loudspeaker placed directly in front of the child. The auditory-only administration method used in the nonword repetition paradigm is significant because no visual cues from the speaker's face are available to the children during the task.

To evaluate the nonword repetition skills of deaf children with cochlear implants, we employed several analysis methods. Detailed and time-consuming methods for evaluating the accuracy of the deaf children's nonword repetitions involved the use of both segmental and suprasegmental scoring procedures carried out by several trained transcribers (Carter, Dillon, & Pisoni, 2002; Dillon, Cleary, Pisoni, & Carter, 2004). In these initial analyses, children were scored on their ability to correctly reproduce a number of aspects in each nonword, such as the number of syllables, stress pattern, and segmental phonemes. When scored using traditional segmental and suprasegmental methods, the deaf children correctly produced nonwords only 5% of the time, which indicates a floor performance. Such strict scoring criteria make it difficult to examine any variation in the nonword repetition skills of these deaf children. However, an alternative nonword repetition scoring method using perceptual ratings made by naive listeners has been developed to quantify the nonword repetition skills of deaf children with cochlear implants.

In the perceptual rating paradigm that we developed, hearing adult listeners were first presented with one of the same target nonwords, spoken by an adult female, originally presented to the deaf children with cochlear implants. After hearing the nonword target, the listeners were presented with the repetition of that same nonword by one of the deaf children using a cochlear implant. The listeners were told to rate the utterances produced by the children using a scale from 1 to 7 according to how accurate they believe the child's response was, ignoring differences in pitch, when compared to the target pattern that preceded it.

cortex by visual pathways have consequences for the later development of auditory-based language.

Associations between preoperative PET scans in deaf children and their subsequent performance on speech and language tasks after cochlear implantation have also been reported recently by Lee, Oh, Sun, Joo, and Soo (2004). They found that children who go on to be more successful users of cochlear implants had more metabolic activity in cortical areas that are suspected to be active in working memory tasks. This is a theoretically significant finding because it suggests that memory processes not only affect the abilities and mechanisms of language acquisition directly but also may affect them indirectly by playing a more general neurocognitive role in how a deaf child using a cochlear implant learns to encode and derive meaning from the degraded auditory signals provided by the device.

A major problem facing researchers interested in how deaf children using cochlear implants develop speech and language is to determine how these children learn to use the auditory signals provided to them through an implant in the first place. In addition to relying on working memory processes, the task of encoding and interpreting the new sounds processed by a cochlear implant may also make use of specific perceptual learning abilities, attention, and multimodal audiovisual integration skills. Therefore, in addition to further considering the relationship between memory and language in deaf children using cochlear implants, new research efforts should focus on other important cognitive processes such as perceptual learning, long-term memory, selective attention, and executive function if we are to gain a more detailed picture on both neural and behavioral levels of how profoundly deaf children develop speech and language skills with a cochlear implant.

ACKNOWLEDGMENTS

Research presented in this chapter was supported by National Institutes of Health (NIH)–National Institute on Deafness and Other Communication Disorders (NIDCD) research grant DC00111 and NIH T32 training grant DC00012 from the NIDCD to Indiana University, Bloomington; NIH research grant DC00064 to the Indiana University School of Medicine; and NIH research grant DC03100 to the Central Institute for the Deaf. We thank Dr. Ann Geers and the staff at Central Institute for the Deaf in St. Louis, Missouri, for testing the deaf children with cochlear implants and making data available for our use. We also thank Dr. Emily Tobey and the staff at the Callier Advanced Hearing Institute at the University of Texas–Dallas for providing McGarr sentence duration measures, and Brianna Conrey and Caitlin Dillon for comments on an earlier version of the manuscript.

REFERENCES

Aslin, J., Jusczyk, P., & Pisoni, D. (1998). Speech and auditory processing during infancy: Constraints on and precursors to language. *Handbook of Child Psychology, 2*, 147–198.

Baddeley, A., Gathercole, S., & Papagno, C. (1998). The phonological loop as a language learning device. *Psychological Review, 105*, 158–173.

Baddeley, A. D., Thompson, N., & Buchanan, M. (1975). Word length and the structure of short-term memory. *Journal of Verbal Learning and Behavior, 14*(6), 575–589.

Banks, J., Gray, D., & Fyfe, R. (1990). The written recall of primed stories by severely deaf children. *British Journal of Educational Psychology, 60*, 192–206.

Bebko, J. (1984). Memory and rehearsal characteristics of profoundly deaf children. *Journal of Experimental Child Psychology, 38*, 415–428.

Bebko, J. M., Bell, M. A., Metcalfe-Haggert, A., & McKinnon, E. (1998). Language proficiency and the prediction of spontaneous rehearsal in children who are deaf. *Journal of Experimental Child Psychology, 68*, 51–69.

Bebko, J. M., & Metcalfe-Haggert, A. (1997). Deafness, language skills, and rehearsal: A model for the development of a memory strategy. *Journal of Deaf Studies and Deaf Education, 2*(3), 131–139.

Bergeson, T. R., & Pisoni, D. B. (2004). Audiovisual speech perception in deaf adults and children following cochlear implantation. In G. Calvert, C. Spence, & B. E. Stein (Eds.), *Handbook of Multisensory Processes*. (pp. 749–772). MIT Press Boston, MA.

Bergeson, T. R., Pisoni, D. B., & Davis, R. A. O. (2003). A longitudinal study of audiovisual speech perception by children with hearing loss who have cochlear implants. *Volta Review, 103*(4), 347–370.

Bochner, J. H., Barefoot, S. M., & Johnson, B. A. (1987). Pausing in the speech of deaf young adults. *Journal of Phonetics, 15*(4), 323–333.

Burkholder, R. A., & Pisoni, D. B. (2003a, March). *Nonword repetition in children using cochlear implants: Latencies and durations*. Poster presented at the American Auditory Society Science and Technical Meeting, Scottsdale, AZ.

Burkholder, R. A., & Pisoni, D. B. (2003b). Speech timing and working memory in profoundly deaf children after cochlear implantation. *Journal of Experimental Child Psychology, 85*, 63–88.

Burkholder, R. A., & Pisoni, D. B. (2004, May). *Analysis of digit span recall errors in paediatric cochlear implant users*. Poster presented at the European Symposium of Paediatric Cochlear Implantation, Geneva, Switzerland.

Campbell, R., & Wright, H. (1990). Deafness and immediate memory for pictures: Dissociations between "inner speech" and "inner ear." *Journal of Experimental Child Psychology, 50*, 259–286.

Carlson, J. L., Cleary, M., & Pisoni, D. B. (1998). Performance of normal-hearing children on a new working memory span task. In *Research on spoken language processing* (Progress Report No. 22, pp. 251–275). Bloomington: Speech Research Laboratory, Indiana University.

Carter, A., Dillon, C., & Pisoni, D. B. (2002). Imitation of nonwords by hearing impaired children with cochlear implants: Suprasegmental analysis. *Clinical Linguistics and Phonetics, 16*(8), 619–638.

Cleary, M., & Pisoni, D. B. (2004, May). *Visual and visual-spatial memory measures in children with cochlear implants*. Poster presented at the International Cochlear Implant Conference, Indianapolis, IN.

Cleary, M., Pisoni, D. B., & Geers, A. (2001). Some measures of verbal and spatial working memory in eight- and nine-year-old hearing-impaired children with cochlear implants. *Ear and Hearing, 22*(5), 395–411.

Connor, C., Hieber, S., Arts, H., & Zwolan, T. A. (2000). Speech, vocabulary, and the education of children using cochlear implants: Oral or total communication. *Journal of Speech, Language, and Hearing Research, 43*, 1185–1204.

Conrad, R. (1965). Order error in immediate recall of sequences. *Journal of Verbal Learning and Verbal Behavior, 4*(3), 161–169.

Cowan, N. (1992). Verbal memory span and the timing of spoken recall. *Journal of Memory and Language, 31*, 668–684.

Cowan, N. (1996). Short-term memory, working memory, and their importance in language processing. *Topics in Language Disorders, 17*, 1–18.

Cowan, N., Keller, T., Hulme, C., Roodenrys, S., McDougall, S., & Rack, J. (1994). Verbal memory span in children: Speech timing clues to the mechanisms underlying age and word length effects. *Journal of Memory and Language, 33*, 234–250.

Cowan, N., Nugent, L. D., Elliott, E. M., Ponomarev, I., & Sults, J. S. (1999). The role of attention in the development of short-term memory: Age differences in the verbal span of apprehension. *Child Development, 70*(5), 1082–1097.

Cowan, N., Wood, N., Wood, P., Keller, T., Nugent, L., & Keller, C. (1998). Two separate verbal processing rates contributing to short-term memory span. *Journal of Experimental Psychology, 127*(2), 141–160.

Curtis, S. (1977). *Genie: A psycholinguistic study of a modern day "wild child."* New York: Academic Press.

Dawson, P., Busby, P., McKay, C., & Clark, G. (2002). Short-term auditory memory in children using cochlear implants and its relevance to receptive language. *Journal of Speech, Language, and Hearing Research, 45*, 789–801.

DeCasper, A. J., & Spence, M. J. (1986). Prenatal maternal speech influences newborns' perception of speech sounds. *Infant Behavior and Development, 9*(2), 133–150.

Dillon, C. M., Burkholder, R. A., Cleary, M., & Pisoni, D. B. (2004). Perceptual ratings of nonword repetition responses by deaf children after cochlear implantation: Correlations with measures of speech, language, and working memory. *Journal of Speech, Language, and Hearing Research, 47*(5), 1103–1116.

Dillon, C. M., Cleary, M., Pisoni, D. B., & Carter, A. K. (2004). Imitation of nonwords hearing-impaired children with cochlear implants: Segmental analyses. *Clinical Linguistics and Phonetics, 86*(1), 39–55.

Gathercole, S. E., & Baddeley, A. D. (1989). Evaluation of the role of phonological STM in the development of vocabulary in children: A longitudinal study. *Journal of Memory and Language, 28*, 200–213.

Gathercole, S., Willis, C., Baddeley, A., & Emslie, H. (1994). The children's test of nonword repetition: A test of phonological working memory. *Memory, 2*(2), 103-127.

Gathercole, S., Willis, C., Emslie, H., & Baddeley, A. (1992). Phonological memory and vocabulary development during the early school years: A longitudinal study. *Developmental Psychology, 28*, 887–898.

Geers, A. E., Nicholas, J., Tye-Murray, N. Uchanski, R., Brenner, C., Crosson, J. et al. (1999). Center for Childhood Deafness and Adult Aural Rehabilitation. Current research projects: Cochlear implants and education of the deaf child, second-year results. In: *Central Institute for the Deaf research* (Periodic Progress Report No. 35, pp. 5–20). St. Louis, MO: Central Institute for the Deaf.

Gupta, P. (2003). Examining the relationship between word learning, non-word repetition, and immediate serial recall in adults. *Quarterly Journal of Experimental Psychology, 56A*(7), 1213–1236.

Hitch, G., Halliday, M., & Littler, J. (1989). Item identification and rehearsal rate as predictors of memory span in children. *Quarterly Journal of Experimental Psychology, 41*, 321–337.

Hulme, C., & Tordoff, V. (1989). Working memory development: The effects of speech rate, word length, and acoustic similarity on serial recall. *Journal of Experimental Child Psychology, 47*, 72–87.

Kail, R., & Park, Y. (1994). Processing time, articulation time, and memory span. *Journal of Experimental Child Psychology, 57*, 281–291.

Kirk, K. (2002 March). *Cochlear implants.* Paper presented at the Cochlear Implant Conference: Practices and Research for Audiologists and Speech Language Pathologists, Bloomington, IN.

Lachs, L., Pisoni, D., & Kirk, K. (2001). Use of audiovisual information in speech perception by prelingually deaf children with cochlear implants: A first report. *Ear and Hearing, 22*, 236–251.

Lane, H. (1979). *The wild boy of Aveyron.* Boston, MA: Harvard University Press.

Lee, D. S., Lee, J. S., Oh, S. H., Kim, S., Kim, J., Chung, J., et al. (2001). Cross-modal plasticity and cochlear implants. *Nature, 409*, 149–150.

Lee, H. J., Oh, S., Sun, K. C., Joo, K. E., & Soo, L. D. (2004, February). *Predicting cochlear implant outcome in a highly variable group of congenitally deaf children: Importance of central processing.* Poster presented at the midwinter meeting of the Association for Research in Otolaryngology, Daytona Beach, FL.

Leybaert, J., & Lechat, J. (2001). Phonological similarity effects in memory for serial order of cued speech. *Journal of Speech, Language, and Hearing Research, 44*, 949–963.

Li, S. C., & Lewandowsky, S. (1995). Forward and backward recall: Different retrieval processes. *Journal of Experimental Psychology: Learning, Memory, and Cognition, 21*, 837–847.

Liben, L., & Drury, A. (1977). Short-term memory in deaf and hearing children in relation to stimulus characteristics. *Journal of Experimental Child Psychology, 24*, 60–73.

Lichtenstein, E. (1998). The relationships between reading processes and English skills of deaf college students. *Journal of Deaf Studies and Deaf Education, 1*, 249–262.

MacLeod, A., & Summerfield, Q. (1987). Quantifying the contribution of vision to speech perception in noise. *British Journal of Audiology, 21*, 131–141.

Marschark, M., & Mayer, T. S. (1998). Mental representation and memory in deaf adults and children. In M. Marschark &. M. D. Clark (Eds.), *Psychological perspectives on deafness* (Vol. 2, pp. 53–77). Mahwah, NJ: Lawrence Erlbaum.

McDaniel, E. D. (1980). Visual memory in the deaf. *American Annals of the Deaf, 125*(1), 17–20.

McGarr, N. (1981). The effect of context on the intelligibility of hearing and deaf children's speech. *Language and Speech, 24,* 255–263.

Morrone, M. C., & Burr, D. C. (1986) Evidence for the existence and development of visual inhibition in humans. *Nature, 321,* 235–237.

Oh, S., Kim, C., Kang, E. J., Lee, D. S., Lee, H. J., Chang, S. O., et al. (2003). Speech perception after cochlear implantation over a 4-year time period. *Acta Otolaryngologia, 123,* 148–153.

Olsson, J. E., & Furth, H. G. (1966). Visual memory span in the deaf. *American Journal of Psychology, 79*(3), 480–484.

Pisoni, D. B. (2000). Cognitive factors and cochlear implants: Some thoughts on perception, learning, and memory in speech perception. *Ear and Hearing, 21,* 70–78.

Pisoni, D. B., & Cleary, M. (2003). Measures of working memory span and verbal rehearsal speed in deaf children after cochlear implantation. *Ear and Hearing, 24,* 106S–120S.

Pisoni, D., Cleary, M., Geers, A., & Tobey, E. (2000). Individual differences in effectiveness of cochlear implants in children who are prelingually deaf: New process measures of performance. *Volta Review, 101,* 111–164.

Pisoni, D., & Geers, A. (2000). Working memory in deaf children with cochlear implants: Correlations between digit span and measures of spoken language processing. *Annals of Otology, Rhinology, and Laryngology, 185,* 92–93.

Rauschecker, J., & Shannon, R. (2002). Sending sound to the brain. *Science, 295,* 1025–1029.

Schweickert, R., Guentert, L., & Hersberger, L. (1990). Phonological similarity, pronunciation rate, and memory span. *Psychological Science, 1*(1), 74–77.

Shepherd, R. K., & Hardie, N. (2001). Deafness-induced changes in the auditory pathway: Implications for cochlear implants. *Audiology and Neuro-otology, 6,* 305–318.

Sternberg, S. (1966). High-speed scanning in human memory. *Science, 153,* 652–654.

Sumby, W. H., & Pollack, I. (1954). Visual contribution to speech intelligibility in noise. *Journal of the Acoustical Society of America, 26*(2), 212–215.

Thomas, J., Milner, H., & Haberlandt, K. (2003). Forward and backward recall: Different response time patterns, same retrieval order. *Psychological Science, 14*(2), 169–174.

Tyler, R. F., Fryauf-Bertschy, H., Kelsay, D. M., Gantz, B., Woodworth, G., & Parkinson, A. (1997). Speech perception by prelingually deaf children using cochlear implants. *Otolaryngology Head and Neck Surgery, 117,* 180–187.

Tyler, R. F., Parkinson, A. J., Woodworth, G. G., Lowder, M. W., & Gantz, B. J. (1997). Performance over time of adult patients using the Ineraid or nucleus cochlear implant. *Journal of the Acoustical Society of America, 102,* 508–522.

Waters, G., & Doehring, D. (1990). Reading acquisition in congenitally deaf children who communicate orally: Insights from an analysis of component reading, language, and memory skills. In C. B. A. Levy (Ed.), *Reading and its development* (pp. 323–373). New York: Academic Press.

Wechsler, D. (1991). Wechsler intelligence scale for children (WISC-III) (3rd ed.). San Antonio, TX: The Psychological Corporation.

Author Index

effect on consonant types
produced, 308–309
effect on language development,
127, 323
effect on speech production,
179, 307–309
preimplantation, 286
speech modality and, 216–217
as study confounder, 141
hearing screening, newborn, 65–66,
81, 127, 153, 272, 298
behavioral responses, 70
electrophysiological standards,
71–72
failure of, 317
Heinicke, Samuel, 7
home visits, 157

imitation, 9
development of, 48–51
immersion, 153
Index of Productive Syntax,
185, 259
Individuals with Disabilities
Act, 137
Infant-Toddler Meaningful Auditory
Integration Scale, 275
inflections, 308
sign input for, 183
use of, 184, 185, 258
information processing, 223
phonological, 261
time, 350
information sources, 216–217
multiple, 227, 237
innate ability, 127
inner ear fluid, 77
integration. *See* sensory integration
intelligence, 125, 168
performance, 291
relation to spoken language skills,
13, 181
intelligibility. *See* speech
intelligibility
intention, communicative, 36, 289
intercellular ion channels, 76
International Congress of
Educators of the Deaf, 9
interrater reliability, 288

interword pauses, 338, 339,
342–344, 346
intonation, 13
intrusiveness, verbal, 148
isolation, effects of, 329
Israel, identification of hearing
loss, 65

Joint Committee on Infant
Hearing, 70

Kind und Welt, 6

labeling, 57–58
language
context, 172
errors, 99
exposure to, 196
maximizing experience of, 153
models, 175, 183, 198, 302
samples, 289, 315
language development, 6–8, 90.
See also language outcomes;
spoken language, development
assessing, 86, 142–143, 250–251,
275, 288, 300–301
auditory experience and, 263
characteristics of babbling
and, 55
cochlear implantation and,
120–121, 208, 312–323
critical period, 80, 277, 280,
281, 285–286
delays in, 73, 213
disruption of, 317
effect of Cued Speech on, 195–203,
206–208, 209
effect of hearing aids on,
78, 121
effect of joint attention on, 147
rate of, 254, 261
recovery of skills, 273
relation to attention and memory,
331
role of motherese, 117
role of vocabulary, 228
theories of, 137
language disabilities, as a study
confounder, 291

imitation of patterns, 50
play, 311
 developmentally appropriate, 156
 effect on language learning, 150
pointing, 57–58, 147
pragmatic skills, 289
preferential looking, 282, 289
prepositions, 199
preschool programs, 262
progressive degenerative visual
 disorder, 322, 323
psychologists
 on cochlear implantation
 team, 80
 role in diagnosing hearing
 loss, 65
psychology, use in deaf education, 7
Public Law 99-957, 137

quality of life
 effect of cochlear implants on, 80
 as outcome measure, 140
quasivowels, 29, 38

reading
 aloud, 231
 cochlear implantation and, 249,
 253, 285
 comprehension, 186, 228
 enhancement by Cued Speech, 209
 interactive approach, 124
 mainstreaming and, 256
 as means to acquire spoken
 language, 8
 oral methods and, 115, 167–168
 parent to child, 147
 program in American Sign
 Language, 302
 speech perception and, 121
recall, 225, 338
 errors, 344–347
 serial, 331
receptive language, 142–143, 186,
 246, 317, 331
 effect of cochlear implantation on,
 121, 263
 of total communication users, 258
redirection, 147
repetition

nonword, 347–350
 of speech, 53
requests, 58
research, 120
 comparison studies, 10, 246,
 248, 286–291
 interpretation of, 141
 on oral methods, 119
 single-subject, 141
 study samples, 253, 286–287
residual hearing, 78, 103–104
 impact on speech production, 304
 preimplantation, 285, 286
 understanding of, 104–105
 use in maternal reflective
 method, 115
 use in oral methods, 14, 111, 113
 word perception and, 93
respiratory control, 46
responsiveness
 parental, 148–149, 156
 social, 151
retention, language, 233
Reynell Developmental Language
 Scales II, 281, 290
Rhode Island Test of Language
 Structure, 185
Rosetti Infant-Toddler Language
 Scale, 157
routines, effect on language
 learning, 150

saccule, 77
samples, study
 characteristics of, 286–287
 sizes, 253
scanning, serial, 332, 338–339, 344,
 345, 347, 351
 rates, 342
Schleicher, August, 7
sedation, during hearing
 screening, 72
self-esteem, total communication
 and, 12
semantic errors, 230
semicircular canals, 77
sensitivity
 of tutors, 137
 verbal, 148